Approaches to Teaching Shorter Elizabethan Poetry

Approaches to Teaching
World Literature

Joseph Gibaldi, series editor

For a complete listing of titles,
see the last pages of this book.

Approaches to Teaching Shorter Elizabethan Poetry

Edited by

Patrick Cheney

and

Anne Lake Prescott

The Modern Language Association of America
New York   2000

© 2000 by The Modern Language Association of America
All rights reserved
Printed in the United States of America

For information about obtaining permission to reprint material from
MLA book publications, send your request by mail (see address below),
e-mail (permissions@mla.org), or fax (212 477-9863).

Library of Congress Cataloging-in-Publication Data

Approaches to teaching shorter Elizabethan poetry / edited by
Patrick Cheney and Anne Lake Prescott.
p. cm. — (Approaches to teaching world literature, ISSN 1059-1133 ; 65)
Includes bibliographical references (p.) and index.
ISBN 0-87352-753-4 (cloth) — ISBN 0-87352-754-2 (paper)
1. English poetry—Early modern, 1500–1700—History and criticism. 2. English
poetry—Early modern, 1500–1700—Study and teaching. I. Cheney, Patrick Gerard, 1949–
II. Prescott, Anne Lake, 1936– III. Series.
PR533.A73 2000
821'.30907—dc21   00-025804

Cover illustration for the paperback edition: Portrait of Henry Percy,
9th earl of Northumberland, by Nicholas Hilliard (1547–1619).
Reproduction by permission of
the Syndics of the Fitzwilliam Museum, Cambridge.

Set in Caledonia and Bodoni. Printed on recycled paper

Published by The Modern Language Association of America
10 Astor Place, New York, New York 10003-6981

To Robert B. Johnstone and to the memory of Walter N. King
—Patrick Cheney

To the memory of William Nelson and Hugh Maclean
—Anne Lake Prescott

CONTENTS

Preface to the Series	xi
Preface to the Volume	xiii

PART ONE: MATERIALS *Patrick Cheney*

Introduction	3
Classroom Texts	3
Individual Poets	4
Anthologies	8
Additional Student Readings	13
The Instructor's Library	14
Editions	15
Reference Works	16
Background Studies and Critical Works	22
Cheney's Choice	54
Note on Texts	57

PART TWO: APPROACHES

Introduction *Anne Lake Prescott*	61

Teaching Backgrounds

Elizabethan Poetry in the Postmodern Classroom *Clark Hulse*	66
The Origins and Art of Versification in Early Modern English *Susanne Woods*	75
From Medieval to Tudor Lyric: Familiarizing Rhetoric *Judith H. Anderson*	81

Framing the Authentic Petrarch: From the *Rime sparse* to
   Astrophil and Stella
   William J. Kennedy
	85

Religious Backgrounds of Elizabethan Shorter Poetry *Debora Shuger*	89

"Tradition and the Individual Talent": Teaching Ovid and the
   Epyllion in the Context of the 1590s
   Georgia E. Brown
	93

"The Mushroom Conception of Idle Brains": Antipoetic Sentiment
   in the Classroom
   Peter C. Herman
	98

viii   CONTENTS

Selected Pedagogical Strategies, Courses, Units, Assignments

Sex and the Shorter Poem   103
Julia Reinhard Lupton

Giving Voice to Renaissance Lyric   109
Theresa M. Krier

Philomela and the Gender of Nightingales   115
Mary Ellen Lamb

The Multiple Readerships of Elizabethan Poetry   119
Caroline McManus

Placing Elizabethan Poetry: Some Classroom Ideas   123
Louise Schleiner

Infinite Riches and Very Little Room: Speeding through
   Some Sonnets in the Introductory Historical Survey   128
Clare R. Kinney

Incorporating Women Writers into the Survey Course:
   The Countess of Pembroke's Psalm 73 and
   Astrophil and Stella, Sonnet 5   133
Margaret P. Hannay

Teaching Renaissance Manuscript Poetry   139
Steven W. May

Editing an Elizabethan Poem: A Course Assignment   141
Sheila T. Cavanagh

The Elizabethan Age Portfolio: Using Writing to Teach
   Shorter Elizabethan Poetry   145
John Webster

Critical and Theoretical Approaches

Teaching Genre   150
Heather Dubrow

Impressions of Poetry: The Publication of Elizabethan Lyric Verse   156
David Scott Kastan

New Historicism and the Cultural Aesthetics of the High
   Elizabethan Lyric   161
Patricia Fumerton

Poststructuralism: Teaching the *Amoretti*   167
Roger Kuin

"Love Is Not (Heterosexual) Love": Historicizing Sexuality
   in Elizabethan Poetry   173
Mario DiGangi

CONTENTS ix

What's Race Got to Do with It? Teaching Shorter
    Elizabethan Poetry   179
  Margo Hendricks

Teaching Specific Poems and Poets

Motives for Metaphor in Gascoigne's and Ralegh's Poems   184
  Jane Hedley

A Week with the *Calender*   190
  John W. Moore, Jr.

Learning to Love the Star Lover: Teaching *Astrophil and Stella*   196
  Diana E. Henderson

Elizabeth I: Poet of Danger   202
  Janel Mueller

Teaching Noncanonical Poetry to Undergraduates:
    The Sonnets of Anne Vaughan Lock   210
  Susan M. Felch

Words and Music: Campion and the Song Tradition   216
  Stephen Ratcliffe

Reading Marlowe's Lyric   220
  Arthur F. Kinney

Teaching Spenser's Marriage Poetry: *Amoretti, Epithalamion,*
    Prothalamion   226
  Patrick Cheney and Anne Lake Prescott

Making Shakespeare's *Sonnets* Matter in the Classroom   239
  Michael Schoenfeldt

Teaching Critical Narratives of the Elizabethan Age

A Story of Generations   245
  Richard Helgerson

Chaucer and the Elizabethan Invention of the "Selfe"   249
  Elizabeth Fowler

Wolves in Shepherds' Folds: Elizabethan Shorter Poetry
    and Reformation Culture   256
  John N. King

The Experimental and the Local   258
  Roland Greene

Elizabethan Lyric Poetry and Early Modern Print Culture   263
  Arthur F. Marotti

x   CONTENTS

Notes on Contributors   269

Survey Participants   275

Works Cited   277

Index of Selected Works   321

Index of Names   323

PREFACE TO THE SERIES

In *The Art of Teaching* Gilbert Highet wrote, "Bad teaching wastes a great deal of effort, and spoils many lives which might have been full of energy and happiness." All too many teachers have failed in their work, Highet argued, simply "because they have not thought about it." We hope that the Approaches to Teaching World Literature series, sponsored by the Modern Language Association's Publications Committee, will not only improve the craft—as well as the art—of teaching but also encourage serious and continuing discussion of the aims and methods of teaching literature.

The principal objective of the series is to collect within each volume different points of view on teaching a specific literary work, a literary tradition, or a writer widely taught at the undergraduate level. The preparation of each volume begins with a wide-ranging survey of instructors, thus enabling us to include in the volume the philosophies and approaches, thoughts and methods of scores of experienced teachers. The result is a sourcebook of material, information, and ideas on teaching the subject of the volume to undergraduates.

The series is intended to serve nonspecialists as well as specialists, inexperienced as well as experienced teachers, graduate students who wish to learn effective ways of teaching as well as senior professors who wish to compare their own approaches with the approaches of colleagues in other schools. Of course, no volume in the series can ever substitute for erudition, intelligence, creativity, and sensitivity in teaching. We hope merely that each book will point readers in useful directions; at most each will offer only a first step in the long journey to successful teaching.

Joseph Gibaldi
Series Editor

PREFACE TO THE VOLUME

As many teachers realize, not without gratitude on busy days, many lovely and compelling Elizabethan poems are short. Indeed, Donne might have said, had "The Canonization" been about the classroom and not the bedchamber, one can build good pedagogy in pretty rooms as well as in half-acre epics and romances. Exploring these pretty rooms can provide pleasure and insight, but it can also be a challenge: modern students, and even modern teachers, sometimes find shorter Elizabethan poems aesthetically or emotionally engaging but culturally remote and intellectually difficult. There have been, moreover, profound changes over the past several decades in how scholars and critics approach these texts and even in their thinking about which texts repay attention. For all these reasons, it seems valuable to have advice and suggestion from experienced teachers of English Renaissance literature. We are enormously grateful to the many fine teachers who here contribute their thoughts and share their experiences, and we also thank the many who took the time to fill out our survey. The mansion of Elizabethan poetry has many, many rooms in which to teach. We hope you will join us in visiting them.

We would like to thank the many anonymous readers of the various documents we submitted to the MLA, especially the two anonymous readers of the final manuscript. In particular, we would like to thank Rebeca Helfer, of Columbia University, for checking quotations and citations in the first complete version of the manuscript; Amy Barber, of Penn State, for presiding over the processing of the intermediary version; Todd Preston, also of Penn State, for helping with the final version; and Colin Fewer, of Penn State as well, for preparing the index. We would like also to thank several friends and colleagues who read versions of either the "Materials" section or the essay "Spenser's Marriage Poetry" or otherwise contributed information, support, or sometimes articles and books: Andrea Brady, John Buck, Colin Burrow, Don Bialostosky, Robert R. Edwards, Arthur F. Kinney, Laura Knoppers, Richard McCabe, David Lee Miller, John W. Moore, Jr., James Schiffer, Michael C. Schoenfeldt, Lauren Silberman, Garrett Sullivan, and Linda Woodbridge.

Finally, we would like to express our sincerest gratitude to our editor at the MLA, Joseph Gibaldi, who provided encouragement and expertise over a very long time for a very complex project, and to Michael Kandel, who expertly presided over the copyediting phase of the book.

PC and ALP

Part One

MATERIALS

Introduction

This part of the volume presents an introduction to, an update of, or simply a review of pedagogic materials that might otherwise appear in dizzying array: those works that instructors can find useful when teaching shorter Elizabethan poetry. Much of the material comes from colleagues who generously responded to our questionnaire (see "Survey Participants"). The material divides into three primary sections—"Classroom Texts," "Additional Student Readings," "The Instructor's Library"—and one secondary section, "Cheney's Choice."

The editions suggested as classroom texts are relatively inexpensive and generally represent the most recent, authoritative scholarship. The list of student readings suggests works both in the very broad topic of shorter Elizabethan poetry and in those even broader topics outside it, such as comparative literature, which many instructors find useful for reference and context. The detailed "Instructor's Library," which forms the bulk and center of part 1, categorizes and briefly describes as many influential and recent scholarly works as space permits. The final section, "Cheney's Choice," offers a "survival kit" for instructors caught alone at night on the haunted platform.

Classroom Texts

In the field of shorter Elizabethan poetry, instructors confront an immediate challenge—and probably an insoluble problem—simply when they set about to select texts for classroom use: the topic is so naturally rich that no single text can mine it. For instance, in an anthology assembled in 1925, *Elizabethan Lyrics from the Original Texts*, Norman Ault reports that he surveyed "the whole field of Elizabethan verse, entailing [. . .] upwards of two thousand printed books, and nearly three hundred manuscripts of the sixteenth and seventeenth centuries," including "2300 lyrics" (x). The field, however, has more virtue than sheer mass. In a mid-century anthology, *The Portable Elizabethan Reader*, Hiram Haydn remains firm and convincing: "There has never before or since been so glorious an out-pouring of song in all the rest of the ages of man. Anyone who reads poetry, reads the Elizabethans" (32). In yet another anthology, assembled in the United States in 1990, *English Renaissance Poetry: A Collection of Shorter Poems from Skelton to Jonson*, John Williams is succinct for the present volume: "Excepting only the drama written by Shakespeare, the short poem is the most important literary form of the age" (xxxiii). Shorter Elizabethan poetry breathtakingly exceeds the limits of any single binding, from its groundbreaking documents *Tottel's Miscellany* and *The Mirror for Magistrates* to its benchmarks for artistic achievement *The Shepheardes Calender* and *Astrophil and Stella* to its final

4 CLASSROOM TEXTS

high-water marks *Hero and Leander* and the *Sonnets*. Nearly all respondents to the questionnaire expressed dismay at this predicament (as well as dissatisfaction with the available options), and it is not clear whether an imaginable text could be a Tamburlainian concretion or simply the grand illusion of Sir Epicure Mammon. In any event, would-be instructors, like Seneca's heroes and heroines, need to steel themselves to this, the first obstacle in the classroom of shorter Elizabethan poetry.

Having steeled themselves, instructors will discover that the available texts divide between individual editions of single poets or poems and anthologies for wider circulation. They may also find that the present volume's focus on shorter Elizabethan poetry does not match the scope of the course they are teaching and the texts they wish to select. As the questionnaires reveal, most instructors teach shorter Elizabethan poetry within a larger rubric: 46% in an English literature survey, 30% in either a sixteenth-century British literature course or a course in the Renaissance. In the end, instructors may choose to rely on either a single text (most likely an anthology) or an assembly of texts (an anthology and one individual edition or more or even a group of editions). Even so, in such a rich, diverse, and constantly changing field the available texts can only continue to fluctuate, as old favored texts inexplicably evaporate (*Shakespeare's Songs and Poems*, edited by Edward Hubler) and new ones unexpectedly appear (Richard A. McCabe's Penguin edition of Spenser's shorter poems). For some poets or poems, a dismaying number of options might be available (as for William Shakespeare's *Sonnets*), while for others, few or no options exist (as for Mary Sidney). Even for major canonical poets (such as Marlowe), the options can be confusing or troubling. While no single text or group of texts is likely to satisfy everyone—perhaps anyone—enough texts do exist to make the selection, if made in a pioneering frame of mind, a pleasant challenge.

Individual Poets

Because "shorter Elizabethan poetry" covers so much material, the following suggestions concentrate on classroom texts for the four poets that instructors teach most often in undergraduate courses: Spenser, Philip Sidney, Marlowe, and Shakespeare. The "Anthologies" section covers other poets.

Spenser

Even for so significant an Elizabethan as Spenser, no single classroom text prints the whole of his poetry (there is no *Riverside Spenser*). The Clarendon paperback *The Poetical Works of Edmund Spenser*, which reprints the J. C. Smith and Ernest de Selincourt texts of 1909–10, is still used by some instructors, although it hardly qualifies as a primary classroom text; its only pedagogical virtues are its compact completeness and its authoritative text; its primary vices are very small print and an even smaller, long outdated editorial apparatus. Nonetheless, with the exception of Shakespeare among poets covered here, the situation for Spenser is still the best.

Six primary classroom texts now exist. The most widely used remains *The Yale Edition of the Shorter Poems of Edmund Spenser*, edited by William A. Oram et al. This edition prints all of Spenser's shorter poetry and has a full editorial apparatus: a word list, a chronology, textual notes, suggestions for further reading, a list of works cited, introductions to each poem (and to each *Calender* eclogue), as well as detailed notes and glosses. Available in paperback, the Oram edition remains an attractive choice, especially for those wishing to have access to all of Spenser's shorter poems in a scholarly edition friendly to students.

The text most resembling the Oram edition is Douglas Brooks-Davies's Longman volume, *Edmund Spenser: Selected Shorter Poems* (the advertised companion to A. C. Hamilton's Longman *Faerie Queene*). At the time of writing, this text is not widely known in the United States, but it is already a controversial editing venture. Not merely has Brooks-Davies omitted such poems as *The Complaints* and *Colin Clouts Come Home Againe* (under marketing pressure), but he has "modernised" the poetry he prints: *The Shepheardes Calender*, *Amoretti*, *Epithalamion*, *Fowre Hymnes*, and *Prothalamion*. When Brooks-Davies says "modernise," he means it. He has changed not only spelling and punctuation but also diction, producing what are arguably new versions of old poems. Still, instructors will benefit from his learned, up-to-date editorial apparatus, which includes detailed headnotes, factual and interpretive notes, and spectacular bibliographies.

Better known is the Oram edition's chief competitor, Hugh Maclean and Anne Lake Prescott's third edition of the Norton *Edmund Spenser's Poetry: Authoritative Texts and Criticism*. For instructors who want good selections of both the shorter poetry and *The Faerie Queene*, including a useful editorial apparatus in a text friendly to students and scholars alike, the Norton Spenser is hard to beat. The first part of the volume includes all of *Faerie Queene* 1 and 3, selections from the other four books, selections from *The Shepheardes Calender* (*Januarye*, *Februarie*, *Aprill*, *October*, *November*, and *December*), as well as complete versions of *The Mutabilitie Cantos*, *Muiopotmos*, *Colin Clouts*, *Amoretti*, *Epithalamion*, and *Prothalamion*. Each poem is followed with an informed editor's note. The second part includes a useful selection of criticism, ranging from William Camden, John Hughes, and Samuel Taylor Coleridge to A. C. Hamilton, William Nelson, and A. Bartlett Giamatti to Louis Montrose, Richard Helgerson, and David Lee Miller. The volume concludes with a chronology and one of the most useful selected bibliographies in print.

Similar in its goal of excerpting both *The Faerie Queene* and the shorter poetry is the much older edition by Robert Kellogg and Oliver Steele, which modernizes books 1 and 2 of *The Faerie Queene*, *The Mutabilitie Cantos*, *November*, *Epithalamion*, *Fowre Hymnes*, *Muiopotmos*, and selections from *Amoretti* (without substantively changing the text) and which provides an outline of Spenser's life, an introduction to each poem, detailed notes and glosses,

6 CLASSROOM TEXTS

and a now-dated works-cited list. The primary motivations for choosing Kellogg and Steele over Maclean and Prescott would be their modernized spelling and their inclusion of *Faerie Queene 2*.

Like both the Kellogg and Steele and the Maclean and Prescott volumes, Elizabeth Porges Watson's Routledge edition, *Spenser: Selected Writings*, includes a full editorial apparatus, plus book 1 of *The Faerie Queene* and some of the shorter poetry: *June, October, Muiopotmos, Visions of the Worlds Vanitie, Colin Clouts, Epithalamion, Prothalamion*, and *The Mutabilitie Cantos* (no *Amoretti*).

Penguin has recently published what will surely be a challenger to all these editions: McCabe's *Edmund Spenser: The Shorter Poems* contains all of Spenser's poetry except *The Faerie Queene*, including the Latin poetry from the Spenser-Harvey letters, complete with a new translation. McCabe's paperback also reproduces the illustrations to *A Theatre for Worldlings* and *The Shepheardes Calender*, and McCabe supplies a remarkably full editorial apparatus: a critical introduction, a chronology for Spenser's life, a headnote to each work, a full commentary for each work, a glossary, a textual apparatus, and a bibliography.

(The Everyman Library tells me that John Lee has a new edition called *Edmund Spenser, Shorter Poems: A Selection*. It prints *The Shepheardes Calender, Amoretti, Epithalamion, Muiopotmos, Colin Clouts*, and *Prothalamion*. It includes maps, a scholarly introduction, a chronology, and extensive notes.)

Philip Sidney

The situation in Philip Sidney studies parallels that in Spenser studies on a reduced scale. Instructors can choose among three excellent editions excerpting representative portions of the Sidney canon (poetry and prose, shorter and longer poetry) or one edition printing only the poetry. Robert Kimbrough's second edition of *Sir Philip Sidney: Selected Prose and Poetry* is useful for the kinds of courses in which Sidney typically appears. In addition to all of *The Lady of May, The Defence of Poesy* (also published under the title *Apology for Poetry*), and *Astrophil and Stella*, Kimbrough excerpts *Certain Sonnets, The Psalms of David* and the letters, and he includes teachable selections of the *Old Arcadia* (all of book 1) and the *New Arcadia* (all of book 1 and selections from books 2 and 3). The volume contains an excellent editorial apparatus, despite its now being a bit dated, especially the otherwise helpful bibliography.

Katherine Duncan-Jones's *Sir Philip Sidney* is also excellent and has the virtue of being more recent. It contains more of Sidney's letters; includes five excerpts from Sidney's contemporaries; and prints the whole of *Astrophil and Stella, The Defence of Poesy*, and (a real plus) *Certain Sonnets*. Its notes are more substantial. Its only drawback—limited selections of the *Arcadias*—is not pertinent here.

Catherine Bates's *Sir Philip Sidney: Selected Poems* is more recent than the other two but not as inclusive, and it lacks all prose. For courses covering just Sidney's poetry, including poetry from the *Arcadias*, this is an inexpensive and authoritative option with useful notes and recent bibliographies.

Finally, Watson's Defence of Poesie, Astrophil and Stella, *and Other Writings* is out in paperback from Everyman Library. In addition to the two works identified in the title, it includes *The Lady of May*, *Two Pastoralls*, and selections from *Certain Sonnets* and the *Psalms*. The text comes complete with a nicely orienting introduction, notes on the works, a glossary, and a chronology of Sidney's life and times.

Marlowe

Compared with the situation for Sidney and Spenser, the one for Marlowe is simple. Instructors can choose between two principal editions. The favorite remains Stephen Orgel's 1971 Penguin edition, *Christopher Marlowe: The Complete Poems and Translations*, which usefully reprints all of Marlowe's extant poetry: *Hero and Leander*, *Ovid's Elegies*, *Lucan's First Book*, "The Passionate Shepherd to His Love," and even "On the Death of Sir Roger Manwood," together with three continuations of *Hero and Leander*: George Chapman's, Henry Petowe's, and the anonymous *Containing Their Further Fortunes*. With a useful editorial apparatus, this remains an attractive student text, despite its 1971 publication date. An update would be welcome.

The alternative is E. D. Pendry and J. C. Maxwell's Everyman edition, *Christopher Marlowe: Complete Plays and Poems*. Its chief virtue is its inexpensive completeness; it prints even the rarely seen Latin *Dedicatory Epistle* to Mary Sidney (together with an English translation) and the "Baines Note." Unfortunately, the editorial apparatus is slender and unfriendly to undergraduates, and the bibliography is dated. (Mark Thornton Burnett has just edited an Everyman paperback edition of the complete plays, and he is now editing the poetry for Everyman.)

If Clarendon ever puts out a paperback edition of Roma Gill's 1987 volume of Marlowe's translations, which includes all the poetry, instructors would likely discover a standard classroom text.

Shakespeare

In the area of classroom texts, Marlowe and Shakespeare are mighty opposites. A recent *Paperbound Books in Print* lists over twenty texts that would work in the undergraduate classroom—nearly half on the *Sonnets*. The questionnaires mentioned half a dozen of these. The favorites were Stephen Booth's still authoritative *Shakespeare's Sonnets* and John Kerrigan's more recent *The Sonnets and* A Lover's Complaint. Both paperback editions present attractively readable texts and detailed, learned commentary, but Kerrigan's edition would probably be more appropriate for undergraduates, even though its scholarly introduction does not address the needs of most North American undergraduates. While

8   CLASSROOM TEXTS

Kerrigan prints two sonnets per page, Booth prints parallel texts (a facsimile of the 1609 quarto and a modernized version). A less ambitious, yet perhaps more useful (and inexpensive), edition is the curious Signet amalgam *The Sonnets / The Narrative Poems: The Complete Non-dramatic Poetry*, edited by William Burto, which glues together and updates two older Signet editions, including two sets of the usual Signet commentaries. Yet another alternative remains the two inexpensive, friendly, but now dated texts of nondramatic poetry in the Pelican series, *The Narrative Poems and Poems of Doubtful Authenticity*, coedited by Alfred Harbage and Richard Wilbur, and *The Sonnets*, coedited by Douglas Bush and Harbage. Another option is to assemble a package from the mostly recent paperback editions printed by two distinguished series: the Arden Shakespeare (third series) and the New Cambridge Shakespeare. For the Arden series, instructors will need to rely on *The Poems*, edited by F. T. Prince in 1969, until an update appears, but they will now be able to rely on *Shakespeare's* Sonnets edited in 1997 by Duncan-Jones, who matches Kerrigan by printing *A Lover's Complaint*, complete with full editorial apparatus. For the New Cambridge series, instructors may turn to *The Poems* edited in 1992 by John Roe and *The Sonnets* edited by G. Blakemore Evans in 1996 (which does not print *A Lover's Complaint*); both contain superb and full editoral apparatuses. One final edition is important to mention: Helen Vendler's magisterial 1997 *The Art of Shakespeare's* Sonnets. Vendler matches Booth in two valuable ways: she prints both a facsimile of the 1609 edition and a modern edition, except that for each sonnet she usefully prints representations of both editions on a single page; and she supplies detailed, learned, and sensitive commentary that indeed delivers the promise of the title by "our most accomplished interpreter of poetry" (jacket cover). Finally, instructors teaching the nondramatic works in the context of the plays can rely on any number of complete editions of Shakespeare, such as David Bevington's *Complete Works of Shakespeare*, Evans's new *Riverside Shakespeare*, or Stephen Greenblatt's equally new *Norton Shakespeare*, all of which provide useful headnotes and bibliographies.

Anthologies

As an alternative to single-author or single-poem editions, instructors can choose from a wide array of anthologies; the questionnaires turned up nearly fifteen. Despite this wealth, no anthology devotes itself to shorter Elizabethan poetry. Several that include "Elizabethan" in the title do not limit the period to the queen's reign (1558–1603), starting usually with Thomas Wyatt and Henry Howard, earl of Surrey (or even John Skelton) and running as late as 1626. Ault is still helpful on including Wyatt and Surrey under the rubric "Elizabethan": *Tottel's Miscellany* "leapt into instant and enduring popularity, so that [Wyatt] and [. . .] Surrey, its chief contributors, may be said to have become Elizabethan by adoption" (xii). In fact, most anthologies cover either "the sixteenth century" or "the English Renaissance." Similarly, many anthologies do not limit themselves to poetry, and some do not limit themselves to shorter poetry. Consequently, instructors will need to consider at least two major criteria: the excellence of the volume in itself and the pertinence of the volume's coverage to the course at hand.

As the questionnaires reveal, in this wide and competitive field most instructors rely on one of six anthologies. Nearly 50% report using *The Norton Anthology of English Literature*, volume 1; 27%, Richard S. Sylvester's *Anchor Anthology of English Sixteenth-Century Verse*; 22%, H. E. Rollins and Herschel Baker's *The Renaissance in England: Non-dramatic Prose and Verse of the Sixteenth Century*; 15%, Emrys Jones's *The New Oxford Book of Sixteenth Century Verse*; 15%, Roy Lamson and Hallett Smith's *The Golden Hind: An Anthology of Elizabethan Prose and Poetry*; and 12%, David G. Norbrook and H. R. Woudhuysen's *Penguin Book of Renaissance Verse, 1509–1659*. This last text—the most recent—will likely become more widely used as time passes.

Volume 1 of *The Norton Anthology* was the most popular among the respondents. Hallett Smith and Barbara Lewalski edit the section "The Sixteenth Century." Now in its sixth edition, this 1993 volume is in tune with current Renaissance studies, printing, for instance, poems by three women writers: Elizabeth I, Mary Sidney, and Aemilia Lanyer. Not surprisingly, however, the selections of shorter Elizabethan poetry cannot compete with those in the other five anthologies, which devote themselves to the Renaissance or the sixteenth century. Instructors will nonetheless discover useful selections from Wyatt and Surrey to John Donne and Ben Jonson (the last two printed under "The Early Seventeenth Century"). Instructors will also likely feel the pinch where the poetry is at its richest: in Spenser, Sidney, and Shakespeare. The selection of Spenser's shorter poems consists of "To His Booke," *Aprill*, *October*, eleven sonnets from *Amoretti*, and *Epithalamion*; the selection of Sidney, thirty-three poems from *Astrophil and Stella* and four other poems; and the selection of Shakespeare, eleven songs from the plays and thirty-four of the *Sonnets*. Marlowe is represented adequately by *Hero and Leander* and "The Passionate Shepherd to His Love," but one regrets the absence of his most revolutionary poem, *Ovid's Elegies*. George Gascoigne, Thomas Nashe, Walter Ralegh, Robert Southwell, Thomas Campion, John Davies, Samuel Daniel, Michael Drayton, and Fulke Greville get into print, as do some anonymous lyrics. The editorial apparatus is useful: headnotes for each poet or poem and brief glosses or explanatory notes. Smith and Lewalski supply an excellent introduction for students, divided into such sections as "Humanism," "The Reformation," "Nationalism—Elizabeth I," "Patrons, Writers, and Publishers," and "Poetic Conventions, Modes, and Genres." They offer a succinct cultural history of the sixteenth century, including a literary history; a definition of such key cultural events and movements as Renaissance, humanism, and Reformation; and a shrewd sense of the differences between current beliefs and those widely held in the sixteenth century.

10 CLASSROOM TEXTS

Sylvester's *Anchor Anthology* was the next most popular text—despite its 1974 publication date. The volume has a good selection of verse from Skelton to Marlowe. It ends with a unit of nearly 150 pages on the sonneteers, with excerpts from Thomas Watson, Thomas Lodge, Giles Fletcher, Barnabe Barnes, Henry Constable, William Percy, Bartholomew Griffin, the anonymous *Zepheria*, Richard Lynche, William Smith, Richard Barnfield, Daniel, Drayton, and Greville. It excludes Shakespeare's *Sonnets* but includes several other important poems in their entirety: *Amoretti, Epithalamion, Prothalamion, Astrophil and Stella*, and *Hero and Leander*. The other "Elizabethan" poets represented are Wyatt and Surrey, Thomas Sackville and Gascoigne, Ralegh and Campion, with Gascoigne gleefully receiving close to a century of pages. As we might expect from a 1974 text, it includes no women poets and very few "minor" ones (at the level, say, of Chidiock Tichborne) and nothing from longer poems such as *The Faerie Queene* (not pertinent here). The glosses are brief and pertain largely to diction, occasionally giving short explanations, while the bibliography and commentary are both short and dated, the latter being confined to a page or less on each poet. Sylvester's fifteen-page introduction focuses on a standard narrative about the maturation of English verse from Chaucer to Marlowe: poets tried "to reconcile word accent with metrical accent" (xxiv).

Like Sylvester's anthology, Rollins and Baker's *The Renaissance in England* continues to be a solid old standby. By far the most ambitious anthology (weighing in at 1,014 pages), this text remains intriguing, in part because it has so many parcels, in part because Rollins and Baker really know what they are doing. Even though published in 1954, this text is dated primarily by its bibliographies, although it includes only one poem by a woman, Mary Sidney's "A Dialogue between Two Shepherds." Rollins and Baker divide the selections into ten parts, including "The Historical Setting," "The Reformation in England," "Poetical Miscellanies, Ballads, and Song Books," "Early Elizabethan Poetry," "Later Elizabethan Poetry," "Translations," and "Critical Theory." Under the heading "Later Elizabethan Poetry," they print a subpart, "Sonnet Sequences," with Greville, Fletcher, Constable, Percy, Griffin, Robert Tofte, and Shakespeare represented. Unfortunately, both *Amoretti* and *Astrophil and Stella* show up in less than full dress. Counterbalancing this deficiency are ample excerpts from the miscellanies and the ballad and songbooks. The text may prove a challenge for undergraduates to use (or even carry), but some will find this part of the fun; for instance, a "minor" writer like Robert Greene shows up in seven different places. If the volume is rich in its selections, it remains less than wealthy in its editorial commentary. Alone among the anthologies, it does not contain an introduction; the glosses lie buried at the back of the volume; and the brief introductions to individual writers and texts are long on printing history and short on useful explanatory or background information. Nonetheless, Rollins and Baker will likely continue to make us marvel as they head off to the millennium with a second half-century of publication under way. For some instructors, an update would be a textbook dream.

Jones's *New Oxford Book of Sixteenth Century Verse* does not have the wide selection of Rollins and Baker's anthology, but it is wider than Sylvester's. Unlike both those older volumes, Jones's is a recent publication (1991), and thus it is a timely practitioner of trends with which many teachers will now sympathize. For instance, Jones does not privilege the sonneteers or present full versions of the more widely read poems of Spenser, Sidney, and Shakespeare. Conversely, he amply includes women poets (from Anne Askew and Queen Elizabeth to Isabella Whitney and Mary Sidney), as well as a good deal of both anonymous and lesser-known male poets (have you heard of Bewe, "first name unknown"?). Altogether, this is a much more modern—postmodern?—edition, and it feels right for the (present) time. Some instructors may be saddened that Jones has skimped on well-known longer poems (such as *Astrophil and Stella*), and they may find themselves succumbing to despair when they cannot find *The Shepheardes Calender*. Nonetheless, they can take cheer in discovering full versions of *Hero and Leander*, *Epithalamion*, and *Prothalamion*. Jones's glosses and notes are brief, but his introduction contains much useful information. Whereas Sylvester concentrates on the issue of verse, Jones opens with the "age" as an age of "transition," with all its revolutions, and he includes helpful information on the political history and on the history of poetry (xxix–xxx). He constructs a narrative for the century, even as he warns us of the dangers of his or any narrative: "Viewed as a whole, what we witness in the course of the sixteenth century is the recession, the cessation indeed, of one great literary system or order (the medieval) and the initiation of a new one (Renaissance [. . .])" (xxx). The anthology nicely reconstructs the flavor of the century, relying on "diversity" to represent a diverse period (xxxiv).

Unlike Jones's relatively recent anthology, Lamson and Smith's *The Golden Hind* is nearly as old as Francis Drake's ship, but it joins Sylvester's and Rollins and Baker's editions in proving a paradox through sheer merit: like Eros, it keeps young through longevity. The volume contains both poetry and prose. Although it favors male writers, it includes two poems by Elizabeth. Poets represented are largely the expected, with "Tichborne's Elegy" functioning as a benchmark. Also expected is a favoring of the sonnet cycle, from Sidney, Spenser, and Shakespeare (represented amply but not fully) to Lynche, Smith, and *Zepheria* (represented by one poem each). Three eclogues from *The Shepheardes Calender* show up, as do a selection of songs from Shakespeare's plays and full versions of those three staples of the modern anthology: *Hero and Leander*, *Epithalamion*, and *Prothalamion*. The editorial apparatus is standard—that is to say, not full. The introduction is one of the better ones, because Lamson and Smith know the Elizabethan era from the inside. Throughout, they distinguish carefully between the sixteenth-century mind and that of the twentieth century, allowing *us* to see *them*. By concentrating on three sources or sites of literary production—court, city, university—they take us back to what feels like the concretions of the period.

Despite the virtues of the other anthologies, Norbrook and Woudhuysen's *Penguin Book of Renaissance Verse* will likely become the preferred text within

12   CLASSROOM TEXTS

the next few years. Like Jones's Oxford, Norbrook and Woudhuysen's Penguin seeks to revise the idea of a Renaissance anthology. Like Jones, too, Norbrook transmits a fresh breath of pedagogical air. His text is intriguing and fun—a toy with which to work. Unlike Jones's text (or any of the other four), Norbrook's is "arranged thematically," advertising itself as "the first anthology fully to bring out the relationship between the period's poetry and politics, and to explore the growth of humanist ideas and forms" (back cover). In its 920 pocket-size pages, the paperback divides among eight themes, although at least a few look generically inclined: "The Public World," "Images of Love," "Topographies," "Friends, Patrons and the Good Life," "Church, State and Belief," "Elegy and Epitaph," "Translation," and "Writer, Language and Public." As the title designates, the volume covers verse wider in time span than the Elizabethan era. Similarly, the volume draws from longer as well as shorter poetry, but even so the selections for shorter Elizabethan poetry are rich. Norbrook includes a lot of anonymous verse, and he prints the widest array of women poets in any of the six anthologies, from Askew and Anne Dowriche to Whitney and Lanyer. Perhaps necessarily, whole poems get the axe, especially canonical ones. For instance, Spenser's shorter poetry consists of five sonnets of *Amoretti*, all of *Epithalamion*, *Maye* from *The Shepheardes Calender* (be bold, be bold, be very bold), and one sonnet from *The Ruines of Rome*. To help readers orient themselves in a complex volume, Norbrook and Woudhuysen include a considerable editorial apparatus, including notes on the text and some useful appendixes, especially the glossary of classical names and biographical notes on authors. Unlike many anthologies, this one presents an introduction (at sixty-seven pages) and notes (nearly one hundred pages) that are sustained and substantive. In fact, Norbrook's introduction is among the best overviews of the period in print. The commentary manages to be fresh even as it engages poststructuralist criticism.

The Everyman Library has three paperback 1994 anthologies that are extremely useful to the instructor. The most comprehensive is Brooks-Davies's splendid and timely revision of Gerald Bullett's *Silver Poets of the Sixteenth Century*, which features "new texts with considerable completeness" of the "expected major figures" of Wyatt, Surrey, Ralegh, and Sidney (liii), as well as new sets of texts for Davies (*Hymns of Astraea* replaces *Nosce Teipsum* but *Orchestra* remains), Mary Sidney (*Triumph of Death*, selections from *The Psalms of David*, and "A Dialogue between Two Shepherds"), and Drayton (*Endymion and Phoebe*). Maurice Evans's *Elizabethan Sonnets* (revised by Roy J. Booth) prints useful selections from seventeen sonnet writers: K. Soowthern, Philip Sidney, Daniel, Drayton, Spenser, Constable, Barnes, Giles Fletcher the Elder, Lodge, the anonymous author of *Zepheria*, Barnfield, Robert Sidney, Griffin, Smith, Davies, Mary Wroth, and Mark Alexander Boyd. Sandra Clark's *Amorous Rites: Elizabethan Erotic Verse* prints five Ovidian narrative poems: Lodge's *Scylla's Metamorphosis*, Shakespeare's *Venus and Adonis*, Marlowe's *Hero and Leander*, Francis Beaumont's *Salmacis and Hermaphroditus*, and John Marston's *The Metamorphosis of Pygmalion's Image*.

Other anthologies, used by a small percentage of instructors, include Ault's *Elizabethan Lyrics*, Bullett's reissued *Silver Poets of the Sixteenth Century*, Haydn's *Portable Elizabethan Reader*, Geoffrey G. Hiller's *Poems of the Elizabethan Age*, Nigel Alexander's *Elizabethan Narrative Verse*, John Williams's *English Renaissance Poetry* (which contains a fine introduction), and John Hollander and Frank Kermode's *The Literature of Renaissance England*. More specialized volumes exist, including *The Penguin Book of Homosexual Verse*, edited by Stephen Coote; *Poetry of the Stewart Court* (Scottish verse), edited by Joan Hughes and W. S. Ramson; *Paradise of Women*, edited by Betty S. Travitsky; and the 1997 *Women Writers in Renaissance England* from Longman, edited by Randall Martin.

In a special category by itself is a hybrid work to be discussed more later: Steven W. May's *The Elizabethan Courtier Poets: The Poems and Their Contexts*, half critical study (part 1), half "representative anthology" (part 2 [5]); part 2 includes "full editions of the poems of the earls of Cumberland, Derby, Essex, and Oxford," Edward Dyer, Mary Cheke, Francis Drake, Thomas Heneage, and Henry Noel, as well as "new or newly edited texts" by Roger Ascham, William Cecil, Elizabeth I, John Harington, Edward Hoby, the earl of Arundel, Henry Lee, Ralegh, Elizabeth Russell, Dr. Thomas Wilson, and John Wolley (5).

Before selecting an anthology, instructors might wish to consult at least some of these texts.

Additional Student Readings

As for which poets and poems respondents teach, a list may prove useful, including numbers for the percentage of instructors who teach a given poet (where available):

Anonymous	Barnabe Googe	Shakespeare (76%)
Barnfield	Greville	Skelton (15%)
William Byrd	Jonson (15%)	Southwell
Campion (15%)	Lanyer (7%)	Spenser (78%)
Chapman	Anne Lock	Mary Stuart
Constable	Lodge	Surrey (27%)
Daniel	Marlowe (58%)	Tichborne
Davies	*Mirror for Magistrates*	*Tottel's Miscellany*
Donne (44%)	Thomas Morley	George Turbervile
John Dowland	Nashe	Thomas Tusser
Drayton (17%)	*Paradise of Pleasures*	Whitney
Elizabeth I (15%)	Ralegh (32%)	Wroth (15%)
England's Helicon	Mary Sidney (22%)	Wyatt (41%)
Gascoigne (37%)	Philip Sidney (78%)	
Arthur Golding	Robert Sidney	

14   THE INSTRUCTOR'S LIBRARY

Anonymous poems mentioned include "Back and Side Go Bare"; "In Praise of a Contented Mind"; "Though Amaryllis Dance in Green"; "Come Away, Come Sweet Love!"; "Thule, Period of Cosmography"; "Silver Swain"; and "Constant Penelope."

Instructors continue to spend much time on the main sonnet cycles, while Wyatt's "They Flee from Me" and Donne's *Songs and Sonets* remain popular, and *Hero and Leander* continues to receive a good deal of pedagogical press. Respondents complained that while they would like to teach women poets, anthologies do not allow them to do so. With the appearance of such anthologies as Jones's Oxford and Norbrook's Penguin, however, this complaint is likely to decrease, and the overall list of poets taught is likely to grow considerably. Let's hear it for Bewe (first name unknown) and Dowriche!

In addition to citing the anthologies, respondents to the questionnaire reported relying on supplemental or background readings, the precise nature of which depends on the type of course offered and the instructor's inclinations. Such readings divide into the following groups:

> Classical: Theocritus, *Idylls*; Moschus, *Lament for Bion*; Vergil, *Eclogues*, *Georgics*, *Aeneid*; Ovid, *Amores*, *Ars Amatoria*, *Metamorphoses*
> Biblical: *Geneva Bible*
> Early Christian and Medieval: Augustine, *Confessions*, *City of God*; Dante, *La Vita Nuova*, *Divine Comedy*; Chaucer, *House of Fame*, *Parliament of Fowls*, *Canterbury Tales*
> Continental Renaissance: Petrarch, *Rime sparse*; Sannazaro, *Arcadia*; Pico, *Oration on the Dignity of Man*; Scaliger, *Poetics*; Machiavelli, *Prince*; Castiglione, *Courtier* (trans. Hoby); Ronsard, "Quand tu seras"
> English Renaissance: John Foxe, *Acts and Monuments*; John Stubbs, *Anatomy of Abuses*; Raphael Holinshed, *Chronicles of England*; John Stow, *A Survey of London*; Thomas Elyot, *Governor*; Ascham, *Scholemaster*; Wilson, *Art of Rhetoric*; George Puttenham, *Art of English Poesie*; Philip Sidney, *Defence of Poesie*

For undergraduate classes in North America today, this rather slender list may not appear surprising. Evidently, instructors find it too difficult logistically to devote much time to background works. By far, the most cited was Petrarch's *Rime sparse*, although Vergil, Ovid, and the Bible luckily remain important.

The Instructor's Library

As is to be expected for one of the richest fields in the profession, the instructor's library for shorter Elizabethan poetry is expansive, but it is not so vast as to be unsurveyable. A quick glance at the following discussion may belie this claim, but the goal of the information is to be sturdily helpful in a wide-ranging way. The works described are necessarily controlled by the describer's limitations, including library access to relevant materials. At one point, these materials looked the way the ocean presumably appeared to Columbus, but through a narrow circumnavigation of the globe, the current ship was at least able to reach port.

Editions

The idea of a standard edition for shorter Elizabethan poetry seems today (or any day) a pleasurably hapless dream. Not simply is there no single text for the topic (nor can there be), but for nearly all individual poets or poems the standard is—up in the air. Consider, for instance, the challenge mounted by Greenblatt's new Norton edition of Shakespeare, which, like *Tamburlaine* with respect to the 1590 *Faerie Queene*, appeared within months of the new *Riverside Shakespeare*. Two truths are told. Or is it three? Who does not admire Bevington's Shakespeare? If this seems an embarrassment of New World riches, consider the specifics relevant here: there is no standard edition of Shakespeare's nondramatic poetry in print (some continue to mourn the loss of Hubler's *Songs and Poems*). Booth's edition of the *Sonnets* has the scholarly reputation of a standard edition, even though it prints only the 154 sonnets. Even Kerrigan's fine edition prints only the *Sonnets* and *A Lover's Complaint*. Lovers have a right to complain.

Still, one has to push on, despite winds. Until the waters clear, the following volumes will serve to buoy the enterprising instructor.

Spenser   Volume 1 of *The Poetical Works of Edmund Spenser*, edited by Smith and de Selincourt, titled *Spenser's Minor Poems*. This 1909–10 text has been the standard since the early twentieth century; unfortunately, it still lacks much of an editorial apparatus. Its primary competitor is Oram's *Yale Edition of the Shorter Poems*. And now we will see what McCabe and Penguin can do. Fierce wars and faithful loves shall moralize their song.

Philip Sidney   *The Poems of Sir Philip Sidney*, edited by William A. Ringler, Jr. This 1962 Oxford hardback is a splendid edition, printing all of Sidney's verse, including that from the *Old Arcadia* and the *New Arcadia*. Its notes are detailed and scrupulous, but it could benefit from an update. For those wishing for an alternative (both less expensive and more recent), one can do no better than Oxford's Sidney text (also available in hardback): Duncan-Jones's *Sir Philip Sidney*. Look in thine heart and read.

Marlowe   That's hard. Gill's hardback, multivolume Clarendon edition may become the standard edition, as its fifth and final volume has just appeared.

16   THE INSTRUCTOR'S LIBRARY

Many instructors, however, consider Fredson Bowers's two-volume 1981 *Complete Works of Christopher Marlowe* the standard; volume 2 includes some of the plays and all the poetry. But what happens if Penguin updates its Orgel edition, or the Revels Plays series finishes its updating of the Marlowe canon by revising Millar MacLure's *The Poems: Christopher Marlowe*? And what will Burnett add? Infinite riches . . .

Shakespeare   The *Riverside* or the *Norton*: "Nothing neither way." Booth and Kerrigan are "palpable hits."

Anthology   Norbrook and Woudhuysen's Penguin or Jones's Oxford: Hell strives with grace for conquest in our breasts.

Reference Works

No comprehensive, relatively up-to-date bibliography of critical and scholarly works exists for sixteenth-century poetry, Elizabethan poetry, or shorter Elizabethan poetry. This is a sobering reminder of at least one difference between the present topic and that of, say, metaphysical poetry, where ongoing bibliographies have long existed (see Gottlieb). The 1968 Goldentree bibliography, *The Sixteenth Century: Skelton through Hooker*, edited by John Leon Lievsay, is now behind the times, but it is still useful for older studies, as is the bibliography for C. S. Lewis's *English Literature in the Sixteenth Century, Excluding Drama*. A more recent alternative is Gary Waller's general bibliographies for his *English Poetry of the Sixteenth Century*, which should get instructors started. They might also consult Jones's "Notes and References" in his Oxford anthology or Norbrook and Woudhuysen's "Notes on the Text" and "Biographical Notes on Authors" in their Penguin anthology. To stay up-to-date, instructors can look at the journal *Studies in English Literature, 1500–1900*, which annually prints a review essay on the year's books, one number of which is devoted to Renaissance nondramatic literature. The reading lists under each poet in the four-volume *Dictionary of Literary Biography* are also excellent and up-to-date.

Instructors may also complement general bibliographies with more detailed ones for individual poets. Three of the four central poets here have superb bibliographic support.

Spenser Bibliographies   The most current Spenser bibliography is "Spenser Bibliography Update," by John W. Moore, Jr., appearing annually in the *Spenser Newsletter*. Moore's scrupulous unannotated bibliography continues Waldo F. McNeir and Foster Provost's *Annotated Bibliography of Edmund Spenser: 1937–1960* and remains indispensable. For an acute and comprehensive overview, especially of more recent scholarship, Alexander Dunlop's "Materials" section of his and David Lee Miller's *Approaches to Teaching Spenser's* Faerie Queene is a blessing. *The Spenser Encyclopedia*, under the general editorship of A. C. Hamilton, remains the most heroic New Poet enterprise of the century, including an extensive works-cited list and selected readings for each entry, even though this material was published in 1990.

Philip Sidney Bibliographies   Sidneians are even luckier than Spenserians, for they possess a recent, authoritative, annotated bibliography, compiled by Donald V. Stump, Jerome S. Dees, and C. Stuart Hunter: *Sir Philip Sidney: An Annotated Bibliography of Texts and Criticism (1554–1984)*. This indispensable resource complements the three-bibliography sequence in the Recent Studies series of *English Literary Renaissance*: from 1940 to 1969 by William L. Godshalk ("Recent Studies in Sidney"), from 1970 to 1977 by A. J. Colaianne and Godshalk, and from 1978 to 1986 by Derek B. Alwes and Godshalk. Like the Stump, Dees, and Hunter volume, Arthur F. Kinney's bibliography in his *Essential Articles for the Study of Sir Philip Sidney* is dated, but it is still valuable for its judicious selection. For more recent information, either the *Sidney Journal and Newsletter* (formerly called the *Sidney Newsletter*) or *The MLA Bibliography* will have to suffice.

Marlowe Bibliographies   For Marlowe, we have no up-to-date comprehensive bibliography, but useful resources are within reach. *English Literary Renaissance's* Recent Studies prints a two-sequence annotated bibliography: Jonathan F. S. Post's (1968–76) and Ronald Levao's (1977–86). I will be supplying a third bibliography (1987–98). Bruce E. Brandt's *Christopher Marlowe in the Eighties: An Annotated Bibliography of Marlowe Criticism from 1978 through 1989* is indispensable, although in need of an update. Older still are two volumes that both cover through 1977: Lois Mai Chan and Sarah A. Pedersen's Hall volume, *Marlowe Criticism: A Bibliography*, and Kenneth Friedenreich's *Christopher Marlowe: An Annotated Bibliography of Criticism since 1950*. Again, for more recent information, either the *Marlowe Newsletter* or *The MLA Bibliography* will have to suffice.

Shakespeare Bibliographies   The standard resource remains the *World Shakespeare Bibliography*, formerly edited by Harrison T. Meserole and now edited by James L. Harner. Printed annually in volume 5 of *Shakespeare Quarterly*, this bibliography is detailed and intermittently annotated. Alternatively, shortcuts remain open. For many instructors, two of the handiest may be the selective but still extensive bibliographies in the new *Riverside Shakespeare* and the equally new *Norton Shakespeare*. In the Norton edition, under each poem, Greenblatt's team prints ten or so carefully selected items. Other shortcuts include Larry S. Champion's 1986 *The Essential Shakespeare: An Annotated Bibliography of Major Modern Studies*, which provides "a convenient and annotated checklist of the most important criticism on Shakespeare in the twentieth century" (xi); David M. Bergeron and Geraldo U. de Sousa's 1995 *Shakespeare: A Study and Research Guide*, which supplies discursive commentary;

18   THE INSTRUCTOR'S LIBRARY

Linda Woodbridge's unannotated but excellent 1988 *Shakespeare: A Selective Bibliography of Modern Criticism*, which covers "roughly" between 1900 and 1985 (vii); and Stanley Wells's new edition of *Shakespeare: A Bibliographical Guide*, which includes a bibliographic essay on the nondramatic poems by Duncan-Jones followed by a listing of useful works. To keep up, instructors can consult *Shakespeare Survey* for a review of the year's publications.

Bibliographies for Other Poets   In addition to bibliographies for these poets, bibliographies for the following appear in *English Literary Renaissance*'s Recent Studies series: Daniel (Godshalk), Davies (James L. Sanderson), Elizabeth I (May), Gascoigne (Jerry Leath Mills), Mary Sidney (Josephine A. Roberts), Robert Greene (Kevin Donovan), Greville (Paula Bennett), Surrey (Ellen C. Caldwell), Lodge (Donovan), George Peele (Donovan), Nashe (Robert J. Fehrenbach), Ralegh (Mills), Southwell (John N. King), and Wyatt (Caldwell). Also pertinent from this series are the bibliographies "*A Mirror for Magistrates*" (Mills), "Poetry and Music in the English Renaissance" (Louise Schleiner), "Protestant Poetics" (King and Smith), "Renaissance Pastoral" (John Bernard), and "Women Writers of Tudor England" (Georgianna M. Ziegler).

Other Resources   To complement these bibliographies, instructors may rely on a number of useful general reference works specific to the period. One of the most visible and useful is *The Spenser Encyclopedia*, which contains entries on nearly every topic imaginable, including Sidney, Shakespeare, and Marlowe, as well as on other Elizabethan poets and all the pertinent genres, and such essays helpful in the classroom as "Renaissance" (Thomas M. Greene), "Reformation" (King), and "Humanism" (O. B. Hardison, Jr.). For information on the period's language or culture, respondents report using such guides as Marjorie Donker and George M. Muldrow's 1982 *Dictionary of Literary-Rhetorical Conventions of the English Renaissance* (especially useful for short articles on genres and on such topics as blank verse, conceit, and imitation), Richard A. Lanham's timeless *Handlist of Rhetorical Terms: A Guide for Students of English Literature* (indispensable for the rhetorical dimension of the literature), Jeffrey L. Singman's 1995 *Daily Life in Elizabethan England* (which includes chapters like "A Brief History of Tudor England," "Clothing and Accoutrements," and "Food and Drink," as well as nearly one hundred illustrations), and Ronald H. Fritze's 1991 *Historical Dictionary of Tudor England, 1485–1603* (which includes articles like "The Elizabethan Settlement" and "*The Book of Common Prayer*"). Several respondents report that they use Isabel Rivers's *Classical and Christian Ideas in English Renaissance Poetry: A Students' Guide* as a supplementary text. Now in its second edition (1994), this book describes such topics as the pagan gods, Platonism and Neoplatonism, and Cosmology; includes excerpts of primary texts under these headings; and provides a useful editorial apparatus, including suggestions for further reading.
    In addition to Rivers, several texts reprint or excerpt Elizabethan documents

useful to the classroom. Chief among them are G. Gregory Smith's *Elizabethan Critical Essays* and Arthur F. Kinney's *Elizabethan Backgrounds: Historical Documents of the Age of Elizabeth I*. Smith's 1904 two-volume hardback is more a standard reference work, excerpting most of the important commentaries produced by the Elizabethans on the art of poetry and literature, ranging from Elyot and Ascham to Sidney and Spenser. Kinney's background book is a more practical classroom text; in paperback, it includes nineteen documents, complete with introductions, ranging from the "Homily on Obedience" to "Queen Elizabeth's Speech to Her Last Parliament." Just out in Longman's Crosscurrents series is *Writing and the English Renaissance*, edited by William Zunder and Suzanne Trill; part 1 prints new essays on individual writers (including Spenser, Marlowe, and Mary Sidney), and part 2 excerpts selected documents contextualizing the literature examined (including selections from the *Homilies* and *The Book of Common Prayer*). Instructors continue to rely on John Nichols's three-volume 1823 *Progresses and Public Processions of Queen Elizabeth*. Ringler has provided an ancillary resource tool in *Bibliography and Index of English Verse Printed 1476–1558*, but May is now completing a *Bibliography and First-Line Index of English Verse, 1559–1603*.

The Oxford English Dictionary, by virtue of its wide use by respondents, is in a category by itself. It supplies an "endlesse worke" for concrete classroom use through its detailed definitions and chronological examples of individual words in the language, as several essays in the present volume testify.

In addition to these general reference tools, specific ones exist for each of the four poets.

Other Spenser Reference Works   In addition to *The Spenser Encyclopedia* and the bibliographies already identified, instructors can rely on Charles Grosvenor Osgood's *Concordance to the Poems of Edmund Spenser*, Henry Gibbons Lotspeich's *Classical Mythology in the Poetry of Edmund Spenser*, Naseeb Shaheen's *Biblical References in* The Faerie Queene (not on the shorter poetry), Charles G. Smith's *Spenser's Proverb Lore*, and Charles Huntington Whitman's *Subject-Index to the Poems of Edmund Spenser*. Several works excerpt early modern (and sometimes later) references to and accounts of Spenser, the two fullest being R. M. Cummings's *Spenser: The Critical Heritage* and William Wells's *Spenser Allusions in the Sixteenth and Seventeenth Centuries* (see also *The Prince of Poets: Essays on Edmund Spenser*, by John R. Elliott, Jr., and Paul J. Alpers's *Edmund Spenser: A Critical Anthology*). Two other reference works have just emerged: Willy Maley's indispensable *Spenser Chronology* and David Hill Radcliffe's *Edmund Spenser: A Reception History*, which includes chronological chapters and works-cited lists entitled "Ancients and Moderns," "British Literature," "English Studies," and "Groves of Academe." For some readers, the standard biography remains Alexander C. Judson's 1945 variorum edition, *The Life of Edmund Spenser*, but Gary Waller's 1994 *Edmund Spenser: A Literary Life* has the virtue of being more recent. A

20   THE INSTRUCTOR'S LIBRARY

short cut is Ruth Mohl's essay "Spenser, Edmund" in *The Spenser Encyclopedia*. Instructors should also consult the newly published *Spenser's Life and the Subject of Biography*, a collection of essays edited by Judith H. Anderson, Donald Cheney, and David A. Richardson. Spenser studies boasts two publications: *Spenser Studies: A Renaissance Poetry Annual*, edited by Patrick Cullen, Anne Lake Prescott, and Thomas P. Roche, Jr., and the *Spenser Newsletter*, currently edited by Jerome S. Dees.

Other Philip Sidney Reference Works   Complementing the bibliographies are Herbert S. Donow's *Concordance to the Poems of Sir Philip Sidney*. The standard biography is Duncan-Jones's *Sir Philip Sidney: Courtier Poet*, although instructors may also consult an old favorite, Malcolm William Wallace's 1915 *Life of Sir Philip Sidney*, as well as James M. Osborn's *Young Philip Sidney, 1572–1577*. Another favorite is John Buxton's *Sir Philip Sidney and the English Renaissance*, now in its third edition. Finally, the *Sidney Journal and Newsletter* is edited by Gerald Rubio.

Other Marlowe Reference Works   In addition to the bibliographies, instructors may rely on two concordances, Fehrenbach, Lea Ann Boone, and Mario A. Di Cesare's *Concordance to the Plays, Poems, and Translations of Christopher Marlowe* and Louis Ule's *Concordance to the Works of Christopher Marlowe*. At present we have no standard biography, but at least two are being completed. Old favorites still valuable are Frederick S. Boas's *Christopher Marlowe: A Biographical and Critical Study* and John Bakeless's *The Tragicall History of Christopher Marlowe*. A. D. Wraight and Virginia F. Stern have printed a 1993 version of *In Search of Christopher Marlowe: A Pictorial Biography*, which is delightful for the photos alone, while William Urry has written the most authoritative account, *Christopher Marlowe and Canterbury*, and Charles Nicholl has written the most recent and intriguing narrative theorizing an assassination plot against Marlowe at Deptford, *The Reckoning: The Murder of Christopher Marlowe*. MacLure's *Marlowe: The Critical Heritage, 1588–1896* remains an indispensable tool excerpting three hundred years of commentary, while the *Marlowe Newsletter*, edited by Brandt, continues to supply up-to-date information.

Other Shakespeare Reference Works   For Shakespeare, resources are practically countless. Greenblatt's *Norton Shakespeare*, for instance, lists twenty-three items in its select bibliography under the heading "Shakespeare's Life"; among these, the series by Samuel Schoenbaum still reigns sovereign, including his groundbreaking 1975 *William Shakespeare: A Documentary Life*, his revised *William Shakespeare: A Compact Documentary Life*, and his new edition of *Shakespeare's Lives*. Recently published is Jonathan Bate's *The Genius of Shakespeare*, which advertises itself as "a new kind of biography: a biography of Shakespeare's talent and reputation, beyond the limits of his actual life" (jacket cover). A pure delight, the book should be high on everyone's reading list. Instructors may also wish to consult Stanley Wells's *Shakespeare: A Life in Drama*, Russell Fraser's *Young Shakespeare* and *Shakespeare: The Later Years*, Dennis Kay's Twayne *William Shakespeare: His Life and Times*, and Eric Sams's *The Real Shakespeare: Retrieving the Early Years, 1564–1594*. Concordances include John Bartlett's 1894 *New and Complete Concordance to Shakespeare* and Marvin Spevack's nine-volume *Complete and Systematic Concordance to the Works of Shakespeare* or Spevack's one-volume *Harvard Concordance to Shakespeare*. Reference works exist on practically every topic, among them Geoffrey Bullough's eight-volume *Narrative and Dramatic Sources of Shakespeare*, Oscar James Campbell and Edward G. Quinn's *The Reader's Encyclopedia of Shakespeare*, R. W. Dent's *Shakespeare's Proverbial Language: An Index*, Brian Vickers's six-volume *Shakespeare: The Critical Heritage*, and Stanley Wells's *Shakespeare: An Illustrated Dictionary*. Especially important to teachers is the new *Bedford Companion to Shakespeare: An Introduction with Documents*, ably edited by Russ McDonald. An excellent companion text in any Shakespeare course, this volume includes nine chapters, each with two parts, the first providing introductory information and the second excerpting illustrations and documents. Almost all the information addresses Shakespeare's career as a dramatist, but a number of chapters are useful for the poetry, including "Shakespeare, 'Shakespeare,' and the Problem of Authorship," "'I Loved My Books': Shakespeare's Reading," and "Town and Country: Life in Shakespeare's England." Journals are plentiful, and some of the more important are *Shakespeare Quarterly*, *Shakespeare Jahrbuch* (Germany), *Shakespeare Newsletter*, *Shakespeare Studies*, and *Shakespeare Survey* (England).

Reference Works for Other Poets   For other poets, instructors may first want to consult the appropriate entries in the *Dictionary of Literary Biography*—one of the best guides to individual poets in print. As of 1996, the *Dictionary of Literary Biography* has printed four volumes in its Sixteenth-Century British Nondramatic Writers series, edited by David A. Richardson. Authoritative and useful overview essays, complete with lists of texts, illustrations, and bibliographies, are now available for many poets, including, in volume 132, Wyatt (Caldwell); in volume 136, Elizabeth I (Mary Thomas Crane) and Gascoigne (Susan C. Staub); in volume 167, Greene (Clark), John Lyly (Alwes), *A Mirror for Magistrates* (Frederick Kiefer), Nashe (Reid Barbour), Peele (Charles Whitworth), and Mary Sidney (Margaret P. Hannay); and in volume 172, Barnfield (Kenneth Borris), Campion (Elise Bickford Jorgens), Davies (Robert Wiltenburg), Greville (John Gouws), Lodge (Whitworth), and Ralegh (Mills). Essays exist for Philip Sidney, Spenser, and Shakespeare, but not for Marlowe, Chapman, Daniel, or Drayton. To supplement the *Dictionary of Literary Biography*, instructors may consult relevant essays in the present volume, including Stephen Ratcliffe on Campion, Hannay on Mary Sidney, Janel Mueller on Queen Elizabeth, Jane Hedley on Gascoigne and Ralegh, and Susan Felch on Anne Vaughan Lock. *The MLA*

22 THE INSTRUCTOR'S LIBRARY

Bibliography is now fully online and will prove expeditious in turning up reading lists for all poets.

Background Studies and Critical Works

Studies devoted to background and criticism are so numerous as to defy categorization. One way to limit the scope is to take the cue of the preceding paragraph and exclude those topics covered by essays in this volume: Clark Hulse on computer resources; Susanne Woods on versification; Anderson and Elizabeth Fowler on the Middle Ages; Debora Shuger and King on the Bible and Reformation; Ratcliffe and Theresa M. Krier on music; David Scott Kastan, May, and Arthur F. Marotti on manuscript and print culture; Mario DiGangi on homoeroticism; Margo Hendricks on race; and Mueller, Felch, and Hannay on women writers.

Even so, the materials remain formidable, and so the following listing concentrates on recent, well-known, or standard works useful to the teacher. The boundaries separating the categories are not always distinct, and so inclusion of a particular work under one category may appear arbitrary, while some works could well have shown up under more than one category.

The books of two critics stand out as warranting mention up front, for they underlie much of the conversation on shorter Elizabethan poetry during the last twenty years. Greenblatt's *Renaissance Self-Fashioning: From More to Shakespeare* is the inaugural text of the new historicism and includes deeply influential chapters on Spenser, Marlowe, and Shakespeare; his *Shakespearean Negotiations: The Circulation of Social Energy in Renaissance England* is more specific, although it concentrates on drama. Richard Helgerson's *Self-Crowned Laureates: Spenser, Jonson, Milton, and the Literary System* applies Greenblatt's famous principle of "self-fashioning" to the idea of a literary career, while *The Elizabethan Prodigals* anticipates this approach in excellent chapters on Gascoigne, Lyly, Greene, Lodge, and Sidney. Helgerson's *Forms of Nationhood: The Elizabethan Writing of England* includes much on Spenser, Daniel, Drayton, and Shakespeare.

Overviews of Renaissance Studies

Instructors wishing to observe distinguished English Renaissance critics reflecting on the state of their discipline at the close of the millennium can do no better than turn to the twenty-fifth anniversary issue of Arthur F. Kinney's periodical *English Literary Renaissance* (1995), titled *The State of Renaissance Studies*. The volume includes essays by Lisa Jardine, Bevington, Lynda Boose, Jonathan Crewe, Stanley Fish, Hamilton, Leah S. Marcus, Katharine Eisaman Maus, Kathleen E. McLuskie, Annabel Patterson, Prescott, and Raymond B. Waddington. For a single-essay review, Marcus's "Renaissance/Early Modern Studies" in *Redrawing the Boundaries: The Transformation of English and*

American Literary Studies, edited by Greenblatt and Giles Gunn, is also heroic. Recent books reflecting on the discipline in terms of specific literary texts include Jonathan Goldberg's 1986 *Voice Terminal Echo: Postmodernism and English Renaissance Texts* (including a chapter on *The Shepheardes Calender*), Crewe's 1986 *Hidden Designs: The Critical Profession and Renaissance Literature* (including a chapter on Spenser generally), Howard Felperin's 1990 *The Uses of the Canon: Elizabethan Literature and Contemporary Theory* (including chapters on Shakespeare's *Sonnets*, Marlowe, and Donne), and Thomas Healy's 1992 *New Latitudes: Theory and English Renaissance Literature* (including chapters discussing the sonnets of Sidney and Shakespeare, as well as Spenser, principally *The Faerie Queene* and *A View of the Present State of Ireland*).

Overviews of the Renaissance

Instructors searching for a period overview can do no better than consult some among the following: William Kerrigan and Gordon Braden's *The Idea of the Renaissance* (esp. ch. 1, "Burckhardt's Renaissance"), the most important recent work on the period concept; Thomas M. Greene's entry "Renaissance" in *The Spenser Encyclopedia* (a good student handout); and Norbrook's comprehensive introduction to his Penguin anthology. Even more recently, Margreta de Grazia has concerned herself with "periodization," in such excellent essays as "Fin de Siècle Renaissance England" and "The Ideology of Superfluous Things: *King Lear* as a Period Piece."

Collections of Essays

Instructors have access to a wide array of essay collections, and each year several new ones appear. Some, like Alpers's superb 1967 *Elizabethan Poetry: Modern Essays in Criticism*, are close to being specific to shorter works. In fact, Alpers prints what some regard as the most influential essay ever written on this topic, Yvor Winters's "The Sixteenth Century Lyric in England: A Critical and Historical Reinterpretation," as well as several other classics, including Hallett Smith on *The Shepheardes Calender*; David Kalstone and Neil Rudenstine on *Astrophil and Stella* and *Certain Sonnets*; C. S. Lewis on *Hero and Leander*; W. B. C. Watkins, L. C. Knights, and C. L. Barber on Shakespeare's nondramatic poetry; and T. S. Eliot on John Davies. Most of the collections mentioned here do not target shorter Elizabethan poetry, but each is filled with major essays important to the field of Renaissance studies.

The most recent may be the most important; de Grazia, Maureen Quilligan, and Peter Stallybrass's 1996 *Subject and Object in Renaissance Culture* is likely to enter the millennium as the best register and summation of one generation's critical wisdom and practice. The editors' introduction is the volume in miniature and stands as one of the best short overviews of the Renaissance and our critical writing of it in print. Essays that lie within the scope of the present

24   THE INSTRUCTOR'S LIBRARY

volume are Louis Adrian Montrose's "Spenser's Domestic Domain: Poetry, Property, and the Early Modern Subject"; Orgel's "Gendering the Crown" (on Elizabeth), Ann Rosalind Jones's "Dematerializations: Textile and Textual Properties in Ovid, Sandys, and Spenser," Goldberg's "The Countess of Pembroke's Literal Translation," Greenblatt's "Remnants of the Sacred in Early Modern England," and Jonathan Dollimore's "Desire Is Death" (on Shakespeare's *Sonnets*). In fact, Montrose's essay is arguably the most important written on Spenser this generation, opening as it does with a thrilling indictment of the great Foucault ("my intellectual response is that his argument is unconvincing, and my visceral response is that it is intolerable" [92]) and closing with criticism of current new historicist actualities: "I am concerned that in their eagerness to present their political credentials or merely to make an academic fashion statement, some contemporary workers in the field have lost interest in trying to hear the ideologically alien voices that are intrinsic to the historicist dialogue" (122). Montrose may claim that he has "no investment in rehabilitating Spenser's character" from recent "condemnations of [. . .] his racist/misogynistic/elitist/imperialist biases" (122), but, for all this noble brushing aside of magnificence, in the domain of rehabilitation few can compete with Montrose.

Other relevant collections of slightly older vintage include Heather Dubrow and Richard Strier's 1988 *The Historical Renaissance: New Essays on Tudor and Stuart Literature and Culture*, which prints "Sidney and His Queen," by Quilligan, and "Barbarous Tongues: The Ideology of Poetic Form in Renaissance England," by Helgerson. Margaret W. Ferguson, Quilligan, and Nancy J. Vickers's oft-cited 1986 *Rewriting the Renaissance: The Discourses of Sexual Difference in Early Modern Europe* includes Elizabeth Cropper's essay "The Beauty of Woman: Problems in the Rhetoric of Renaissance Portraiture" and Hulse's "Stella's Wit: Penelope Rich as Reader of Sidney's Sonnets." Patricia Parker and David Quint's 1986 *Literary Theory / Renaissance Texts* is also frequently cited and includes Montrose's "The Elizabethan Subject and the Spenserian Text," John Freccero's "The Fig Tree and the Laurel: Petrarch's Poetics," and Greenblatt's controversial "Psychoanalytic and Renaissance Culture." This last title serves as the topic of Valerie Finucci and Regina Schwartz's *Desire in the Renaissance: Psychoanalysis and Literature*, which includes Lynn Enterline's "Embodied Voices: Petrarch Reading (Himself Reading) Ovid." A decade earlier, Gerald Hammond published in the Casebook series a fine volume, *Elizabethan Poetry: Lyrical and Narrative*, which excerpts statements between the sixteenth and nineteenth centuries and reprints essays up to 1979, from Eliot, William Empson, and Winters to Barbara Herrnstein Smith, Alastair Fowler, and John Hollander. Instructors may also rely on Chaviva Hošek and Patricia Parker's *Lyric Poetry: Beyond New Criticism*, which includes Northrop Frye's "Approaching the Lyric," Sheldon Zitner's "Surrey's 'Epitaph on Thomas Clere': Lyric and History," and Joel Fineman's influential "Shakespeare's *Sonnets*' Perjured Eye." More recent collections include *Enclosure*

Patrick Cheney 25

Acts: Sexuality, Property, and Culture in Early Modern England, edited by Richard Burt and John Michael Archer; and *Sexuality and Gender in Early Modern Europe: Institutions, Texts, Images*, edited by James Grantham Turner.

Forthcoming is *The Cambridge Companion to English Literature, 1500–1600*, edited by Kinney, which will include several essays pertinent to shorter Elizabethan poetry, including one on satire by Prescott and one on lyric by Dubrow.

Literary Histories

A number of histories of literature covering the Elizabethan period or the sixteenth century are available. As the questionnaires revealed, the standard work remains Lewis's 1954 *English Literature in the Sixteenth Century*, with its famous distinction between "drab" and "golden" poetry (and its equally famous eccentricity). Douglas Bush's *Prefaces to Renaissance Literature* is also still useful, not to mention a good deal shorter. Recently, in *The Idea of the Renaissance* Kerrigan and Braden pitted Bush's thesis about the Renaissance as an age of Christian humanism against Jacob Burckhardt's thesis about an age of secular individualism (in his foundational text for Renaissance studies, *The Civilization of the Renaissance in Italy*). Kerrigan and Braden resurrect "Burckhardt's Renaissance" (3–35) because they find the story Burckhardt tells more accurate than Bush's (another useful chapter is "Petrarch Refracted: The Evolution of the English Love Lyric" [157–89]). For any course in the Renaissance, a dialogue among all three "period" works makes a useful starting point, although we may now wish to add the introduction to *Subject and Object*, because it so superbly emphasizes the role of the object in the story of Renaissance subjectivity.

Instructors may wish to rely heavily on two other, brand-new literary histories—one an essay, one a book. The essay is Colin Burrow's very handy overview "The Sixteenth Century: An Introduction," which begins Kinney's *Cambridge Companion to English Literature, 1500–1600*. Suspicious of "grand unified narratives about the sixteenth century," Burrow draws attention to the way in which "English monarchs sought consciously to fashion an image and a posthumous reputation for themselves, and to construct a version of history for popular consumption." Relying on the work of "revisionist historians over the past twenty years," he seeks to "take a closer look at some of the attempts made in this period to fashion a Tudor mythology through art." Specifically telling "a story of a kind" that "began in or around 1485," he argues that the "shifts towards print, and from a literature of the court towards a literature which has a dominantly urban focus and feel are the central changes in the nature of literary activity in the sixteenth century." Burrow concludes with this fine and compelling thought: "The development of a form of authorship which was located in London life and articulated through the medium of print was by no means the sole source of riches in the sixteenth century; but after the death of Elizabeth in 1603 it was perhaps the chief legacy left by the dying century."

26   THE INSTRUCTOR'S LIBRARY

The book-length literary history is Julia Briggs's 1997 edition of *This Stage-Play World: Texts and Contexts, 1580–1625*. Substantially revised in the light of recent historicism, this useful study provides nine chapters on the social conditions producing such writers as Shakespeare, Sidney, Spenser, Marlowe, Donne, Jonson, Nashe, and Francis Bacon. Representative chapters include "Women and the Family," "Other Peoples, Other Lands," "Religion," "Education," and "The Court and Its Arts." Briggs's

> approach has focused on two key aspects: first, the conditions of living and thought that shaped literature and determined the particular forms it took; and second, the ways in which individual texts articulate society's concerns in direct and often highly imaginative ways; if the first suggests the need for the student of literature to know something of history, the second suggests the rewards that Renaissance literature can offer the student of history. (xiii)

Instructors may also wish to consult the relevant chapter in a recent history of English literature: Peter Conrad's *The Everyman History of English Literature*, Coote's more recent *The Penguin Short History of English Literature*, Andrew Sanders's brand-new *The Short Oxford History of English Literature*, and Alastair Fowler's authoritative *A History of English Literature: Forms and Kinds from the Middle Ages to the Present*. Respondents also mentioned Howard C. Cole's *A Quest of Inquirie: Some Contexts of Tudor Literature* and Lawrence Manley's *Convention, 1500–1750*. Five older studies by authoritative scholars are also worth examining for the differing stories they tell. Hardin Craig's *The Literature of the English Renaissance (1485–1600)* remains a solid overview (especially its opening chapter, "Humanism and Reformation"), but it is the least original. Haydn's *The Counter-Renaissance* sees the Counter-Reformation as the crucial transitional stage between humanism and the scientific revolution. Paul Oskar Kristeller's widely influential *Renaissance Thought and Its Sources* emphasizes the classical origins of the period as a distinguishing feature from the Middle Ages. And Murray Roston's *Sixteenth-Century English Literature* speaks of the "dual vision" of the Renaissance, "the idealistic and the pragmatic," represented by Pico and Machiavelli (6, 7).

Finally, Annabel Patterson's *Censorship and Interpretation: The Conditions of Writing and Reading in Early Modern England* argues that censorship laws were paradoxically productive: "what we can find [. . .] is a system of communication ('literature') in which ambiguity becomes a creative and necessary instrument, while at the same time the art (and the theory) of interpretation was reinvented, expanded, and honed. I call this phenomenon 'the hermeneutics of censorship'" (18). More recently, Kevin Pask's *The Emergence of the English Author: Scripting the Life of the Poet in Early Modern England* focuses on "the development of the genre of the 'life of the poet' in England" (1) and has chapters on Sidney, Spenser, and Donne (as well as Chaucer and Milton).

Histories

The questionnaires identified Lawrence Stone's *The Crisis of the Aristocracy, 1558–1641* as the most widely cited general history of the period, while also highly regarded is his *The Family, Sex, and Marriage in England, 1500–1800* (both contain biases that have been vigorously challenged). Other historical studies mentioned include A. B. Ferguson's *Clio Unbound: Perception of the Social and Cultural Past in Renaissance England*, A. L. Rowse's *The Elizabethan Renaissance: The Cultural Achievement*, and Perez Zagorin's *The Court and the Country: The Beginnings of the English Revolution*. Instructors might also wish to look at the long, magisterial, and recent study by John Guy, *Tudor England*. Among the work of current historians in the United States, that by the prolific Anthony Grafton is proving especially compatible with literary studies: *From Humanism to the Humanities: Education and the Liberal Arts in Fifteenth- and Sixteenth-Century Europe* (1986, coauthored by Lisa Jardine), *Forgers and Critics: Creativity and Duplicity in Western Scholarship* (1990), *The Transmission of Culture in Early Modern Europe* (1990), *Defenders of the Text: The Traditions of Scholarship in an Age of Science, 1450–1800* (1991), and *New Worlds, Ancient Texts: The Power of Tradition and the Shock of Discovery* (1992, with April Shelford and Nancy Siraisi).

More recent is Jardine's beautifully produced *Worldly Goods: A New History of the Renaissance*, complete with a wealth of illustrations and plates and advertising itself as "a radical new interpretation, arguing that the creation of culture during the Renaissance was inextricably tied to the creation of wealth —that the expansion of commerce spurred the expansion of thought" (jacket cover). Jardine pursues the age's "entrepreneurial spirit" to "sustain [. . . her] claim that the seeds of our own exuberant multiculturalism and bravura consumerism were planted in the European Renaissance" (34).

Poetry Histories

The most widely used history of poetry is Waller's *English Poetry of the Sixteenth Century*, with its poststructuralist emphasis: "From our perspective in the late twentieth century [. . .] our picture of the sixteenth century [. . .] shows not a world of beauty, order, and natural (let alone supernatural) harmony, but a world of danger, intrigue, [and] devious self-serving politicians" (30). In addition to Norbrook and Woudhuysen's poetic history (already mentioned), Maurice Evans's *English Poetry in the Sixteenth Century* is still useful, as is Hallett Smith's genre-based *Elizabethan Poetry: A Study in Conventions, Meaning, and Expression*, with its excellent chapters "Pastoral Poetry," "Ovidian Poetry," "The Sonnets," "Satire," and "Poetry for Music." A. C. Spearing specializes in the relation between the Middle Ages and the Renaissance, and his 1985 *Medieval to Renaissance in English Poetry* remains a primary text. A broader work that has become a classic is Ernst Robert Curtius's *European Literature and the Latin Middle Ages*, which supplies a virtual compendium of Renaissance background material.

28   THE INSTRUCTOR'S LIBRARY

Intellectual Models

No longer much in fashion, intellectual models of the age nonetheless sport a
number of influential books that instructors will find useful, for themselves and
in the classroom. Among these, the most infamous is the whipping text of the
new historicism, *The Elizabethan World Picture*, by E. M. W. Tillyard (to
whom Waller above responds). While few instructors are now comfortable with
the "order" displayed by such a "world picture," readers may wish to know that
teachers are still using Tillyard in the classroom, and with very good reason: he
passes along much introductory material that is still pertinent—such deep-
seated ideas as the four humors, the microcosm and macrocosm, the corre-
spondences, and the great dance of the cosmos. Putting Tillyard in dialogue
with a more recent critic such as Waller can only prove fruitful to students, in
part because it allows for a more honest appraisal of each. Several respondents
mentioned Lewis's brilliant *Discarded Image: An Introduction to Medieval and
Renaissance Literature*, and here one has to feel especially saddened by the
passing of time, so superb a read this book remains. Like Tillyard, Lewis makes
it difficult to speak about the period without him. Three other older scholars
warrant mentioning: Rosalie L. Colie's *Paradoxica Epidemica: The Renaissance
Tradition of Paradox*, Craig's *The Enchanted Glass: The Elizabethan Mind in
Literature*, and Arthur O. Lovejoy's *The Great Chain of Being: A Study of the
History of an Idea*. More recent is Shuger's *Habits of Thought in the English
Renaissance: Religion, Politics, and the Dominant Culture*, which critiques new
historicist reviews of Tillyard in Greenblatt's series by attempting to fill "an aca-
demic *aporeia*, to reconstruct not a monologic yet nonexistent 'world picture'
shared by all literate persons but the dominant culture of the period between
the Elizabethan Settlement and the Civil War" (4).

Classical Matrices

Histories of the Renaissance acknowledge the important contribution the pe-
riod's scholars made through their discovery, translation, and printing of—not to
mention commentary on—classical texts. Indeed, as the example of Kristeller
intimates, twentieth-century scholars have made the classical origins of Renais-
sance thought one of its most fertile areas. The most recent, sustained publica-
tion pertinent here is Robin Sowerby's 1994 Longman volume *The Classical
Legacy in Renaissance Poetry*, which includes such useful chapters as "Pastoral
and Georgic," "Ovidian Genres: The Epyllion, the Love Elegy, and the Heroic
Epistle," and "Satire," as well as an instructor's gem: "Brief Outline of the
Graeco-Roman World." The short bibliography will prove indispensable to the
new teacher. Much shorter, but quite long on utility, is Charles Martindale's *Re-
deeming the Text: Latin Poetry and the Hermeneutics of Reception*, which fo-
cuses on Vergil, Ovid, Lucan, and "translation as rereading," including in the
Renaissance. Perhaps the most influential book is Thomas Greene's *The Light
in Troy: Imitation and Discovery in Renaissance Poetry*, which remains a re-

markable text, constructing a model by which humanist writers, from Petrarch on, "imitated" classical texts. His four-part model of imitation—"reproductive," "eclectic," "heuristic," and "dialectical" (38–45)—remains pedagogically useful.

Vying in fame is the inimitable Leonard Barkan, whose *The Gods Made Flesh: Metamorphosis and the Pursuit of Paganism* remains the central Ovidian work, as Greene's remains the central Petrarchan one. Barkan traces the influence of Ovid's *Metamorphoses* on Renaissance writers and artists, including Spenser and Shakespeare. More recently, Bate narrows the field in *Shakespeare and Ovid*, which emphasizes the plays but also discusses some of the poetry. Even more recent is the specialized study by M. L. Stapleton, *Harmful Eloquence: Ovid's* Amores *from Antiquity to Shakespeare*, which recognizes the historical significance of that other Ovid poem, focusing on the Ovidian persona of the *desultor amoris*.

Several older studies remain useful, prodigious as they are in their scholarship: Don Cameron Allen's *Mysteriously Meant: The Rediscovery of Pagan Symbolism and Allegorical Interpretation in the Renaissance*, Jean Seznec's *The Survival of the Pagan Gods: The Mythological Tradition and Its Place in Renaissance Humanism and Art*, Edgar Wind's *Pagan Mysteries in the Renaissance*, Harry Levin's *The Myth of the Golden Age in the Renaissance*, and Bush's *Mythology and the Renaissance Tradition in English Poetry*.

Continental Matrices

Related are studies on the Continental Renaissance. Prescott has written the standard book, *French Poets and the English Renaissance: Studies in Fame and Transformation*; it has chapters on Clément Marot, Joachim du Bellay, Ronsard, Philippe Desportes, and Bartas. She has also written several recent essays, including "Du Bellay in Renaissance England: Recent Work on Translation and Response," "Spenser (Re)Reading du Bellay: Chronology and Literary Response," and "*Translatio Lupae*: Du Bellay's Roman Whore Goes North." Quint is probably the most influential critic writing on England and Italy. His *Origin and Originality in Renaissance Literature* focuses on the theme of the source as it originated in antiquity and flowed into the period through a global system of rivers for divinity and truth that found its locus in the Bible. Especially pertinent is chapter 5, "The Jordan Comes to England" (133–66), which centers on Spenser. Related but quite different in scope and intent is Robin Kirkpatrick's 1995 Longman publication, *English and Italian Literature from Dante to Shakespeare: A Study of Source, Analogue and Divergence*, which includes one chapter especially pertinent here, "Humanism and Poetry," treating Wyatt, Petrarch, Sidney, and others. Kinney's *Humanist Poetics: Thought, Rhetoric, and Fiction in Sixteenth-Century England* does not concern poetry but is still worth mentioning, as is his *Continental Humanistic Poetics: Studies in Erasmus, Castiglione, Marguerite de Navarre, Rabelais, and Cervantes*. Similarly, a number of books concentrate on the epic but are too important to neglect: Thomas

30 THE INSTRUCTOR'S LIBRARY

Greene's *The Descent from Heaven: A Study in Epic Continuity*, Robert M. Durling's *The Figure of the Poet in Renaissance Epic*, A. Bartlett Giamatti's *The Earthly Paradise and the Renaissance Epic*, Michael Murrin's *The Allegorical Epic: Essays in Its Rise and Decline* and his new *History and Warfare in Renaissance Epic*, Andrew Fichter's *Poets Historical: Dynastic Epic in the Renaissance*, Mihoko Suzuki's *Metamorphoses of Helen: Authority and Difference in Homer, Virgil, Spenser, and Shakespeare*, Elizabeth J. Bellamy's *Translations of Power: Narcissus and the Unconscious in Epic History*, Quint's *Epic and Empire: Politics and Generic Form from Virgil to Milton*, Burrow's *Epic Romance: Homer to Milton*, and Linda Gregerson's *The Reformation of the Subject: Spenser, Milton, and the English Protestant Epic*.

Genre (General)

Scholars agree that Renaissance writers tend to think about poetics in terms of genre, and not surprisingly studies of genre and of individual genres have received a great deal of attention. Tellingly, three of the best general books have been written by Renaissance critics. Colie's *The Resources of Kind: Genre-Theory in the Renaissance* remains an excellent and still influential study of genre in the Renaissance. Alastair Fowler's wide-ranging *Kinds of Literature: An Introduction to the Theory of Genres and Modes* has perhaps become the standard book; it includes useful units on many individual genres. And Dubrow's *Genre* in the Critical Idiom series remains the handiest study available. Instructors might also consult individual pieces in *Renaissance Genres: Essays on Theory, History, and Interpretation*, edited by Lewalski, while her *Paradise Lost and the Rhetoric of Literary Forms*, although nominally beyond the scope here, reads like a register of the topic at hand, so generically eclectic does Milton's epic prove.

Individual Genres

For overviews of individual genres and bibliographies through 1979, instructors might consult Donker and Muldrow's *Dictionary of Literary-Rhetorical Conventions of the English Renaissance*.

Lyric   A good place to begin is Roland Greene's forthcoming overview essay "The Lyric," which speaks of "the most fugitive of genres when it comes to a theory of its identity." Three other authors in the present volume have written recent books. In *Power in Verse: Metaphor and Metonymy in the Renaissance Lyric*, Hedley takes as her "double purpose" to "map the history of the English lyric from Wyatt and Donne into consecutive stylistic phases, and to put Roman Jakobson's theory of language to work in a systematic way" (ix). In *Passion Made Public: Elizabethan Lyric, Gender, and Performance*, Diana E. Henderson "explains how lyric poetry in plays by Peele, Marlowe, and Shakespeare reflected a range of attitudes toward female power and created an alternative landscape

Patrick Cheney 31

in which to reconsider political and sexual ideologies" (cover). Finally, in *The Elizabethan Courtier-Poets*, May provides the authoritative "Critical History of Elizabethan Courtier Verse" (9–229). Older studies include Hardison's influential *The Enduring Monument: A Study of the Idea of Praise in Renaissance Literary Theory and Practice*, Fred Inglis's *The Elizabethan Poets: The Making of English Poetry from Wyatt to Ben Jonson*, Jerome Mazzaro's *Transformations in the Renaissance English Lyric*, and Douglas L. Peterson's widely used *The English Lyric from Wyatt to Donne: A History of the Plain and Eloquent Styles*. More recent are Anthony Easthope's *Poetry as Discourse*; Harold Tolliver's *Lyric Provinces in the English Renaissance* (mostly on the seventeenth century); and Christopher Martin's *Policy in Love: Lyric and Public in Ovid, Petrarch, and Shakespeare*, which usefully bridges classical, Continental humanist, and English Renaissance lyrics. Still more recent is James Biester's *Lyric Wonder: Rhetoric and Wit in Renaissance English Poetry*, which concentrates on Donne and the seventeenth century.

Books also range over periods other than the Renaissance. Timothy Bahti's 1996 *Ends of the Lyric: Direction and Consequence in Western Poetry* is the most recent, emphasizing the "formal, structural, and semantic domains of how poems end" (2) in European lyrics from Shakespeare's *Sonnets* (ch. 1) to the poems of Wallace Stevens. W. R. Johnson's *The Idea of Lyric: Lyric Modes in Ancient and Modern Poetry* ranges from Archilochus and Anacreon to Whitman and Pound, however quickly and intermittently it moves through the Renaissance. Andrew Welsh's *The Roots of Lyric: Primitive Poetry and Modern Poetics* similarly pursues origins, while David Lindley's handy Critical Idiom *Lyric* identifies "three qualities that have fairly consistently been attached to the idea of lyric as a universal category": "a first-person speaker"; "the present tense, with the immediacy of felt experience"; and "brevity" (2–3).

Pastoral   Criticism on pastoral is vast and intimidating, so intriguing has the past century found whatever pastoral is—a genre, a mode, a form of story, a way of life. Luckily, we possess Alpers's 1996 *What Is Pastoral?* As a quick introduction to the topic, Alpers's 429-page "formalist account" (x) may seem part of the intimidation, but his two-part structure proves friendly. In part 1, Alpers answers his title question: "pastoral is a literary *mode* based on what Kenneth Burke calls a *representative anecdote*" (ix). Alpers "argues that the central fiction of pastoral [. . .] is not the Golden Age or idyllic landscapes, but herdsmen and their lives" (x). Readers should start with this "synchronic" (ix) analysis, but they might also consult the "diachronic" part 2, which discusses pastoral poetry and prose narrative "from ancient writers through works of the nineteenth and twentieth centuries" (ix–x).

Commentary on pastoral is among the most sophisticated of the genres or modes. The evolution of this commentary is itself intriguing, and instructors may want to know something of its history (simplified here). Until the advent of the new historicism, the prevailing version of pastoral was famously articulated

32 THE INSTRUCTOR'S LIBRARY

by Renato Poggioli in *The Oaten Flute: Essays on Pastoral Poetry and the Pastoral Ideal*: "The psychological root of the pastoral is a double longing after innocence and happiness, to be recovered not through conversion or regeneration but merely through a retreat" (1). This version is eloquently rearticulated by Peter V. Marinelli in his 1971 Critical Idiom *Pastoral*. In an influential series of essays, however, Montrose counters the otiose version by emphasizing "negotiation." Taking his cues from Puttenham in *The Arte of English Poesie* and William Empson in *Some Versions of Pastoral*, Montrose argues that "the symbolic mediation of social relationship was a central function of Elizabethan pastoral forms; and that social relationships are, intrinsically, relationships of power" ("Eliza" 153).

If Alpers responds to both versions (especially Poggioli's; for Alpers's response to Montrose's version, see "Pastoral and the Domain of Lyric"), Judith Haber's 1994 *Pastoral and the Poetics of Self-Contradiction: Theocritus to Marvell* responds especially to Montrose, providing a useful historical context for the self-consciousness ordering the pastoral of Andrew Marvell.

Five books written in the 1980s can be plotted along the axes of the two primary versions of pastoral, the idyllic and the ideological. David M. Halperin's *Before Pastoral: Theocritus and the Ancient Tradition of Bucolic Poetry* argues that "pastoral is the name commonly given to literature about or pertaining to herdsmen and their activities in a country setting [. . .]: caring for the animals under their charge, singing or playing musical instruments, and making love" (61). Andrew V. Ettin's *Literature and the Pastoral* argues that "pastoral is an ironic form, based on a perceivable distance between the alleged and the implied" (12). Annabel Patterson's *Pastoral and Ideology: Virgil to Valéry* sees the "attempt to define the nature of pastoral" as "a cause lost as early as the sixteenth century" (7), alternatively pursuing the influence of Vergil's eclogues into the modern period. *Revisionary Play: Studies in the Spenserian Dynamics*, by Harry Berger, Jr., excerpts influential essays on *The Shepheardes Calender*, offers revisions, and adds new essays, arguing that the "fundamental object of Spenser's criticism is the longing for paradise as the psychological basis of the pastoral retreat from life" (277). Finally, Sukanta Chaudhuri's *Renaissance Pastoral and Its English Developments* examines the English Renaissance tradition, including Alexander Barclay, Spenser, and Drayton.

Recently published is Susan Snyder's *Pastoral Process: Spenser, Marvell, Milton*, which usefully "balance[s the] outlawed [. . .] orientation" of current pastoral criticism with "an inward orientation to the writer's own past, now lost but still feeling like home" (18).

Petrarchan Sonnet   Competing with pastoral in critical sophistication and intimidation is the Petrarchan sonnet. This field has also been marked by a refreshing critical rift. Excellent earlier studies, such as Hallett Smith's *Elizabethan Poetry* (ch. 3), J. W. Lever's *The Elizabethan Love Sonnet*, Leonard Forster's *The Icy Fire: Five Studies in European Petrarchism*, and John Fuller's

Critical Idiom *The Sonnet*, reach a pinnacle in David Kalstone's 1965 *Sidney's Poetry: Contexts and Interpretations*, which includes "The Petrarchan Vision" (105–32). In 1982, however, Marotti's "'Love Is Not Love': Elizabethan Sonnet Sequences and the Social Order" presented a new historicist analogue to Montrose on pastoral, arguing that Sidney "crafted a sonnet sequence as a form of mediation between socioeconomic or sociopolitical desires and the constraints of established order" (400). As the questionnaires reveal, Marotti's essay is among the most widely cited discussions of this topic.

In the 1980s, several studies concentrated less on formal elements than on inwardness and subjectivity, including Thomas Greene's *Light in Troy* and Anne Ferry's *The "Inward" Language: Sonnets of Wyatt, Sidney, Shakespeare, Donne. Petrarch and the English Sonnet Sequences*, by Thomas P. Roche, Jr., provides a much-needed survey.

The 1990s also produced several significant books. Roland Greene's *Post-Petrarchism: Origins and Innovations of the Western Lyric Sequence* ranges widely, from Petrarch and Sidney to Pablo Neruda and Martín Adán, proposing an eclectic and synthesizing theory in which formal, generic, and cultural matrices converge. Ann Rosalind Jones's *The Currency of Eros: Women's Love Lyric in Europe, 1540–1620* is also comparative but concentrates on eight women poets, including Whitney and Wroth, arguing that these "poets were able to write and to publish because they drew upon certain potentially productive contradictions in early modern culture" (1). Michael R. G. Spiller's *The Development of the Sonnet* is an introduction—an excellent one—to the English Renaissance sonnet. Dubrow's *Echoes of Desire: English Petrarchism and Its Counterdiscourses* is interested not merely in English Petrarchism but also in two forms of "interrogation": those that are "anti-Petrarchan" and those that "call into question [. . .] academic discourses that examine Petrarchism," including "the connections between gender and power" (2–3). Like Dubrow, Barbara L. Estrin is interested in gender and genre, but in *Laura: Uncovering Gender and Genre in Wyatt, Donne, and Marvell* these become twin topics. Finally, unlike Estrin or Dubrow, William J. Kennedy in *Authorizing Petrarch* "examines the authorizing of Petrarch's *Rime Sparse* as a canonical lyric text for a broad fifteenth- and sixteenth-century European readership and for an equally broad assemblage of lyric poets in Italy, France, and England" (ix–x); the book includes a chapter on *Amoretti*. Roger Kuin's *Chamber Music: Elizabethan Sonnet-Sequences and the Pleasure of Criticism* appeared recently, and so has Paul Innes's *Shakespeare and the English Renaissance Sonnet*, both of which engage the genre in current critical theory.

Respondents also mentioned Charles Altieri's "Rhetoric, Rhetoricity, and the Sonnet as Performance," Bruce R. Smith's *Homosexual Desire in Shakespeare's England: A Cultural Poetics* (ch. 7), Eugene Vance's "Love's Concordance: The Poetics of Desire and the Joy of the Text," and Germaine Warkentin's "Sonnet, Sonnet Sequence" in *The Spenser Encyclopedia* (see also Warkentin's "Robert Sidney's 'Darcke Offerings'").

34   THE INSTRUCTOR'S LIBRARY

Epyllion   For better or for worse, studies of the Ovidian-based epyllion are not as crowded as those for the pastoral or sonnet. The forthcoming book from Cambridge University Press by Georgia Brown, *The Generation of Shame: Defining Literature in the 1590s*, will include a chapter on the epyllion, in which she argues that the genre is one of several marginal forms by which Elizabethan writers explore threshold states and points of coming into being. Specifically, she argues, the epyllion challenges the possibility and even the nature of literary morality. Even after this book appears, instructors can rely on two excellent works. William Keach's 1977 *Elizabethan Erotic Narratives: Irony and Pathos in the Ovidian Poetry of Shakespeare, Marlowe, and Their Contemporaries* is the first study of the genre. With chapters on Ovid, Lodge's *Glaucus and Scilla*, *Venus and Adonis*, and *Hero and Leander*, Keach attends to "ambivalence" (xi) to show how young poets used Ovid to contest the allegorized or moralized Ovid. Like Keach, Hulse in his 1981 *Metamorphic Verse: The Elizabethan Minor Epic* underscores the importance of the genre, but he remains critically more up-to-date, locating genre within the culture that produced it. Hulse focuses on "metamorphosis" as a force shaping "the subject matter of the genre, its narrative principles, its mode of symbolism, its ability to combine and to remake other genres, and its power to transform the poet" (4). His chapter "Minor Epic as Genre" (16–34) may be the best introduction available.

Shorter, older introductions include Elizabeth Story Donno's introduction to *Elizabethan Minor Epics* and her essay "The Epyllion," as well as chapter 2 in Hallett Smith's *Elizabethan Poetry*.

Elegy   For this genre, a manageable group of excellent, recent book-length studies exists. G. W. Pigman III's *Grief and English Renaissance Elegy* focuses on the shift in attitudes toward mourning and consolation from the sixteenth to the seventeenth centuries within a Christian context that pits grief against faith; chapter 5 is on Surrey and Spenser. Like Pigman's study, Peter M. Sacks's *The English Elegy: Studies in the Genre from Spenser to Yeats* appeared in 1985, but it focuses on the role of language in tempering grief with the pleasures of symbolization. Chapter 1, "Interpreting the Genre: The Elegy and the Work of Mourning" (1–37), supplies a fine introduction, while chapter 2 is on Spenser's *Shepheardes Calender* and *Astrophel* (38–63). Arnold Stein's *The House of Death: Messages from the English Renaissance* focuses on representations of death and literary responses to it, including chapters on "Tichborne's Elegy," Ralegh, and Donne. Unlike Stein's book, but like Sacks's, Celeste Marguerite Schenck's 1988 *Mourning and Panegyric: The Poetics of Pastoral Ceremony* goes well beyond the Renaissance, but it goes back to classical culture, making it the most wide-ranging of the books. Chapters 1 and 2 treat Spenser: "The Funeral Elegy and Careerism: Theocritus, Virgil, and Spenser" (33–53) and "Sacred Ceremonies: Spenser's *Epithalamion* and *Prothalamion*" (55–71). Finally, Kay's *Melodious Tears: The English Funeral Elegy from Spenser to Milton* covers familiar ground in a fresh way by charting "the movement of the elegy [. . .] from the time when it was the province of professional writers, the balladeers and chroniclers, to the time of *Lycidas*" (8); chapters include "The English Tradition of Elegy," "The Elegies of Spenser and Sidney," and "Elegies on Sidney (1568 [sic]) and on Queen Elizabeth (1603)."

Also useful are Morton W. Bloomfield's "The Elegy and the Elegiac Mode: Praise and Alienation" and Matthew Greenfield's forthcoming "The Cultural Functions of English Renaissance Elegy."

Complaint   Related to the elegy (and pastoral) is the genre of the complaint, although here much less work is available. The standard work is now John Kerrigan's 1991 *Motives of Woe: Shakespeare and "Female Complaint": A Critical Anthology*, which supplies both a useful collection of complaints from the medieval period through the eighteenth century and an excellent eighty-three-page introduction to the genre, including its history and its special features. Two articles by Hugh Maclean are also valuable introductions, although more specific: "Complaints" in *The Spenser Encyclopedia* and "'Restlesse Anguish and Unquiet Paine': Spenser and the Complaint, 1579–90." Also useful are interspersed comments in Hallett Smith's *Elizabethan Poetry* and Hulse's *Metamorphic Verse* (see indexes to these works).

Epithalamium   Related to both the Petrarchan and the Ovidian genres is the epithalamium, which has nonetheless produced a good deal less commentary. The standard work is Dubrow's 1990 *A Happier Eden: The Politics of Marriage in the Stuart Epithalamium*, which includes useful information on Spenser's *Epithalamion* (35–39). Dubrow examines the genre of marriage in the context of court politics, linking formal and cultural matrices, by focusing on "the attitudes to marriage which so deeply affect that institution and the genre commemorating it" (ix). Her introduction remains one of the best descriptions of marriage theory in the Renaissance. More formalist in approach but still a favorite is Thomas Greene's 1957 "Spenser and the Epithalamic Convention," while Virginia J. Tufte's 1970 *The Poetry of Marriage: The Epithalamium in Europe and Its Development in England* supplies a comparative view.

Hymn   What Hardison says about Renaissance theorists holds true for modern critics: "Because the hymn is a very specialized form of poetry, Renaissance critics generally paid lip-service to its merits and then devoted major attention to [. . .] epic and tragedy" (*Enduring Monument* 70). In addition to Hardison (95–102) and the long section in Lily B. Campbell's *Divine Poetry and Drama in Sixteenth-Century England* (9–138), three influential studies are by Philip B. Rollinson, all formalist in approach: "The Renaissance of the Literary Hymn," "A Generic View of Spenser's *Four Hymns*," and "Hymn" in *The Spenser Encyclopedia*. Lewalski's *Protestant Poetics and the Seventeenth-Century Religious Lyric* and her *Paradise Lost and the Rhetoric of Literary Forms* (160–72) will also prove useful, as will Francis C. Blessington's "'That Undisturbed Song

36 THE INSTRUCTOR'S LIBRARY

of Pure Concent': *Paradise Lost* and the Epic-Hymn" and my chapter "Hymn; or, Flying Back to Heaven Apace: Returning to the Vatic Source in *Fowre Hymnes*" (195–224), in *Spenser's Famous Flight: A Renaissance Idea of a Literary Career*. Of all the "major" Renaissance genres, the hymn remains the most undertheorized.

Satire Thanks to Prescott, instructors have an up-to-date, authoritative introduction to a much discussed genre. In her "Evolution of Tudor Satire," she overviews the Renaissance understanding of satire as it grows from classical roots, especially the Horatian (with its "sophisticated jesting and [. . .] irony") and the Juvenalian (with its "complaint [, . . .] vitriol [, . . .] or the less festive modes of saturnalian subversion"): even though "Renaissance writers could [. . .] mistake the nature of what they imitated," their "blurring of distinctions [. . .] gave Renaissance wit its freedom and vitality, its continuing power to disturb and amuse."

A wide range of general accounts exist. In his 1960 *The Power of Satire: Magic, Ritual, Art*, Robert C. Elliot examines the "origins of satire in primitive magic and incantation and also [. . .] some of satire's towering achievements" (vii), while Dustin Griffin's 1994 *Satire: A Critical Reintroduction* offers an excellent overview of criticism during the last half century, builds "on the insights in the best contemporary practical criticism of satire," and responds to "the challenges of recent literary theory," in the process offering "a set of critical perspectives, organized not around individual authors or periods but around critical problems" (3–4). Of older vintage, Ronald Paulson's *Satire: Modern Essays in Criticism* collects a wide selection of essays, including Alvin B. Kernan's "A Theory of Satire" from *The Cankered Muse: Satire of the English Renaissance*, a standard reference work. Of similar vintage and utility, though shorter, is Hallett Smith's chapter 4 in *Elizabethan Poetry*, "Satire: The English Tradition, the Poet, and the Age." Frye's section in the third essay of *Anatomy of Criticism*, "The Mythos of Winter: Irony and Satire" (223–39), remains indispensable. More recent studies of satire in the Renaissance include Raman Selden's *English Verse Satire, 1590–1765*, which includes the chapter "The Elizabethan Satyr-Satirist," and W. Scott Blanchard's *Scholar's Bedlam: Menippean Satire in the Renaissance*. Instructors might also consult Allen G. Wood's *Literary Satire and Theory: A Study of Horace, Boileau, and Pope*, while those interested in satire and recent critical theory will find a good deal in Brian A. Connery and Kirk Combe's 1995 *Theorizing Satire: Essays in Literary Criticism*, which opens with an orienting "Retrospective and Introduction" (1–15) laying out a "history of satire criticism" (7).

Special Topics

Respondents to the questionnaires recommended critical works that spread over a number of special topics. Several essays in the present volume cover some of them (Mueller on Queen Elizabeth; Kastan, May, and Marotti on manuscript and print culture; or Hannay, Mary Ellen Lamb, and Dubrow on gender), but some topics warrant brief treatment here.

Chivalry and Courtship Since Daniel Javitch's *Poetry and Courtliness in Renaissance England* was published in 1978, critics, especially new historicists, have been turning to the allied topics of chivalry and courtship. Javitch's pioneering work explains that the court of Queen Elizabeth "acted virtually as a nursery of English Renaissance poetry" because of the "affinities between proper court conduct and the stylistic procedures of poetry" (3, 6). Frank Whigham's *Ambition and Privilege: The Social Tropes of Elizabethan Courtesy Theory* treats "Elizabethan courtesy literature as a repertoire of actions invoked by, and meant to order, the surge of social mobility that occurred at the boundaries between ruling and subject classes in late sixteenth-century England" (xi). Richard C. McCoy's *Rites of Knighthood: The Literature and Politics of Elizabethan Chivalry* has been influential as well, focusing on "the cultural practices and literary texts of Elizabethan chivalry" by "analyzing the more contentious aspects," especially in the careers of Robert Devereux, earl of Essex; Philip Sidney; and Robert Dudley, earl of Leicester (1, 2). Recently, Bates's *The Rhetoric of Courtship in Elizabethan Language and Literature* takes as its starting point the semantic shift of *courtship* from "being at court" to "wooing someone" in an analysis of Elizabeth's court; chapter 5 is on Spenser.

Language: Rhetoric, Imagery, and Metaphor This multifaceted topic is enormous, but between Rosemond Tuve's pioneering and influential 1947 *Elizabethan and Metaphysical Imagery: Renaissance Poetic and Twentieth-Century Critics* and Judith Anderson's 1996 *Words That Matter: Linguistic Perception in Renaissance English*, instructors will find a good deal that does matter, including Lanham's *The Motives of Eloquence: Literary Rhetoric in the Renaissance*, James V. Mirollo's *Mannerism and Renaissance Poetry: Concept, Mode, Inner Design*, Thomas O. Sloane's *Donne, Milton, and the End of Humanist Rhetoric* (largely on the seventeenth century), Ferry's *The Art of Naming* (centering on Spenser), Shuger's *Sacred Rhetoric: The Christian Grand Style in the English Renaissance*, Martin Elsky's *Authorizing Words: Speech, Writing, and Print in the English Renaissance*, and Crane's *Framing Authority: Sayings, Self, and Society in Sixteenth-Century England*. Judith Anderson, for instance, pursues the idea that Renaissance grammarians and rhetoricians emphasized the word over the sentence, while Crane shares Anderson's commitment to rhetoric but shifts focus from "print and lexicography" (Anderson 4) to "the commonplace book in its intellectual, social, and ideological milieus," arguing that "the notebook method was far more than just a mnemo-technical aid involving the cataloging and rote memorization of aphorisms" (Crane 3).

Platonism and Neoplatonism No longer as fashionable as it once was, Platonism or Neoplatonism remains a topic to which instructors will nonetheless

38 THE INSTRUCTOR'S LIBRARY

wish to have access. Michael J. B. Allen has written a series of translations and critical works, much of it centering on Ficino, including *Marsilio Ficino: The Philebus Commentary*, *Marsilio Ficino and the Phaedran Charioteer*, *The Platonism of Marsilio Ficino: A Study of His Phaedrus Commentary, Its Sources and Genesis*, *Icastes: Marsilio Ficino's Interpretation of Plato's Sophist*, and *Plato's Third Eye: Studies in Marsilio Ficino's Metaphysics and Its Sources*. An overview appears in Sears Reynolds Jayne's introduction to *Marsilio Ficino's Commentary on Plato's Symposium*, while more recently in *Plato in Renaissance England* Jayne offers "a history of allusions to Plato in England during the 180 years between 1423 and 1603" (xvi). More specific are Robert Ellrodt's *Neoplatonism in the Poetry of Spenser*, Elizabeth Bieman's *Plato Baptized: Towards the Interpretation of Spenser's Mimetic Fictions*, and Jon A. Quitslund's "Platonism" in *The Spenser Encyclopedia*. The 1948 anthology edited by Ernst Cassirer, Kristeller, and John Herman Randall, Jr., *The Renaissance Philosophy of Man*, includes excerpts from Ficino and Pico. For a breathtaking entry into and critique of Pico, see Berger's "Pico and Neoplatonist Idealism: Philosophy as Escape" in *Second World and Green World*.

Occult, Magic, and Numerology   The unholy topics of the occult, magic, and numerology are undergoing a revival, although much of the work is on witchcraft in Renaissance drama. Instructors may wish to begin with Frances A. Yates's *Giordano Bruno and the Hermetic Tradition* or, more pertinent here, her *Occult Philosophy in the Elizabethan Age*, which includes chapters on John Dee and Spenser, as well as on Marlowe, Chapman, and Shakespeare. Peter French's *John Dee: The World of an Elizabethan Magus* remains a readable text with plenty of reference to Spenser and other Elizabethan poets, but instructors will also want to look at both Nicholas H. Clulee's *John Dee's Natural Philosophy: Between Science and Religion* and William H. Sherman's *John Dee: The Politics of Reading and Writing in the English Renaissance*. (See also Gerald Suster's *John Dee: Essential Readings* and Wayne Shumaker's *John Dee on Astronomy: Propaedeumata Aphoristica [1558–1568].*) Other important texts include Keith Thomas's magisterial *Religion and the Decline of Magic*, Brian Vickers's *Occult and Scientific Mentalities in the Renaissance*, and D. P. Walker's *Spiritual and Demonic Magic: From Ficino to Campanella*. The work of S. K. Heninger, Jr., includes *The Cosmographical Glass: Renaissance Diagrams of the Universe*, *Touches of Sweet Harmony: Pythagorean Cosmology and Renaissance Poetics*, and recently *The Subtext of Form in the English Renaissance: Proportion Poetical*, which has a chapter on the origin of the sonnet. Nicholl's *The Chemical Theatre*, Brooks-Davies's *The Mercurian Monarch: Magical Politics from Spenser to Pope*, and John S. Mebane's *Renaissance Magic and the Return of the Golden Age: The Occult Tradition and Marlowe, Jonson, and Shakespeare* are also valuable. More recent are Gareth Roberts's *The Mirror of Alchemy: Alchemical Ideas and Images in Manuscripts and Books from Antiquity to the Seventeenth Century* and Stanton J. Linden's

Darke Hierogliphicks: Alchemy in English Literature from Chaucer to the Restoration (esp. ch. 3, "Posers and Imposters: Sixteenth-Century Alchemical Satire" [62–103]). Of older vintage but still important are A. Kent Hieatt's *Short Time's Endless Monument: The Symbolism of the Numbers in Edmund Spenser's* Epithalamion and Alastair Fowler's *Spenser and the Numbers of Time* (on *The Faerie Queene*). Fowler's 1996 *Time's Purpled Masquers: Stars and the Afterlife in Renaissance English Literature* focuses on "the extraordinary prominence of astronomical imagery" (vii). Robert M. Schuler's *Alchemical Poetry, 1575–1700: From Previously Unpublished Manuscripts* prints works by two "Elizabethan versifying alchemists," Edward Cradock (3–48) and Simon Forman (49–70).

Nationhood   In this increasingly discussed topic, the premier work is Helgerson's *Forms of Nationhood*, which emphasizes Spenser and his generation's "larger project of English self-representation": "To remake it ["the whole cultural system"], and presumably themselves as well, according to some ideal pattern" (3). "In most of that writing [about nationhood]," Helgerson continues, "some other interest or cultural formation—the nobility, the law, the land, the economy, the common people, the church—rivals the monarch as the fundamental source of national identity" (10). For Helgerson, the six "cultural formations" he introduces (including much on Drayton) are oppositional to a seventh, royal absolutism, represented by Shakespeare (244).

On the Elizabethan literary nation, instructors will also wish to consult Philip Edwards's *Threshold of a Nation: A Study in English and Irish Drama*; Walter Cohen's *Drama of a Nation*; Claire McEachern's *The Poetics of English Nationhood, 1590–1612*; Heather James's *Shakespeare's Troy: Drama, Politics, and the Translation of Empire*; and especially Andrew Hadfield's *Literature, Politics and National Identity: Reformation to Renaissance*, which observes that "the problem of national identity required urgent attention in the sixteenth century" (9). My *Marlowe's Counterfeit Profession: Ovid, Spenser, Counter-nationhood* theorizes the nonpatriotic idea of a "counter-nationhood." Related is a recent series of fine books on England and Ireland, usually foregrounding Spenser: David J. Baker's *Between Nations: Shakespeare, Spenser, Marvell, and the Question of Britain*, Hadfield's *Edmund Spenser's Irish Experience: Wilde Fruit and Salvage Soyl*, Christopher Highley's *Shakespeare, Spenser, and the Elizabethan Crisis in Ireland*, and Maley's *Salvaging Spenser: Colonialism, Culture and Identity*. For historical studies, instructors have a wide selection of important books to choose from, including Joel Hurstfield's compact *The Elizabethan Nation*, Jürgen Habermas's seminal essay "The Public Sphere: An Encyclopedia Article (1964)," Perry Anderson's superb *Lineages of the Absolutist State*, Benedict Anderson's widely influential *Imagined Communities: Reflections on the Origins and Spread of Nationalism*, Anthony D. Smith's *Theories of Nationalism*, Anthony Giddens's *The Nation-State and Violence* (vol. 2 of *A Contemporary Critique of Historical Materialism*), E. J. Hobsbawm's *Nations and*

40 THE INSTRUCTOR'S LIBRARY

Nationalism since 1780: Programme, Myth, Reality, and Elie Kedouri's recent revision of *Nationalism*. For theoretical and practical criticism on "nation and narration," instructors can examine the collection edited by Homi K. Bhabha.

Patronage   Like nationhood, patronage has become an important topic. Guy Fitch Lytle and Orgel's ground-breaking 1981 collection of essays, *Patronage in the Renaissance*, remains a standard work, while a more recent version is the collection edited by Cedric C. Brown, *Patronage, Politics, and Literary Traditions in England, 1558–1658*, which includes Marotti's "Patronage, Poetry, and Print," Mark Thornton Burnett's "Apprentice Literature and the 'Crisis' of the 1590s," and Lewalski's "Re-writing Patriarchy and Patronage: Margaret Clifford, Anne Clifford, and Aemylia Lanyer." Michael Brennan's *Literary Patronage in the English Renaissance: The Pembroke Family* focuses on a single family circle, but this family is the very hub of the wheel.

Teaching

Instructors have at least one useful forum of information on pedagogy in the period: the column "Teaching the Renaissance" in the Renaissance Society of America's *Renaissance News and Notes*, in which each column is written by a society member.

Studies of Individual Poets and Poems

Because the present volume covers what many of its readers will regard as the greatest single concentration of poetry in history and because the volume focuses on four of the most significant poets in any age, country, or language, discussion of individual poets and poems faces an awesome challenge. Luckily, the canons of Spenser, Sidney, Marlowe, and Shakespeare share a narrowing stricture: generic bifurcation. For Spenser, the bifurcation is between longer poem and shorter poetry; for Sidney, between the longer prose work(s) and shorter poetry; and for both Marlowe and Shakespeare, between drama and shorter poetry. Even so, each of the four fields remains an industry, with Shakespeare one indeed! Because earlier sections have directed instructors to bibliographies and other reference works, the following discussion restricts items to a few of the most useful, comprehensive, or influential critical studies.

Spenser Studies   Overwhelmingly, books on Spenser concentrate on *The Faerie Queene*, but probably the best single work to consult for the shorter poetry is the most recent: Oram's 1997 *Edmund Spenser*, from Kinney's Twayne's English Author Series. In addition to a chronology, a selected reading list, and the opening and concluding chapters, "Spenser's Career" and "Refashioning Spenser," Oram includes chapters on *The Shepheardes Calender*, the *Complaints*, *Amoretti* and *Epithalamion*, and the "last poems" (*Fowre Hymnes, Prothalamion*, and *The Mutabilitie Cantos*), but he also discusses all the other poems. A shorter variation on Oram's comprehensive, up-to-date theme is Burrow's excellent 1996 *Edmund Spenser*, which includes two opening chapters on Spenser's life and most of his shorter works and a final chapter discussing *Fowre Hymnes* and *Amoretti*; in the process Burrow presents Spenser as "a poet who is—generously, magnificently, and creatively—not quite in complete control of his poem" (100). An even shorter variation is Stump's fine "Edmund Spenser" in the *Dictionary of Literary Biography*, which offers a judicious overview of Spenser's career. Even shorter is McCabe's superb and influential Chatterton Lecture on Poetry, "Edmund Spenser, Poet of Exile," which emphasizes Spenser as an Englishman writing in Ireland: *The Mutabilitie Cantos*

> confirm [. . .] the sense of alienation and estrangement evident in *The Shepheardes Calender*, the *Amoretti*, *Colin Clouts Come Home Againe*, and throughout *The Faerie Queene*. The final stanzas of the *Mutabilitie Cantos* repose no trust in earthly goddesses but seek instead an escape from history itself into the "stedfast rest" of eternity. It is perhaps indicative of Spenser's final state of mind that [. . .] he invokes the deity as Lord of Hosts (Sabbaoth God) as though heaven itself were a well-garrisoned civil plantation in an otherwise "salvage" universe.   (103)

A much earlier variation is William Nelson's *The Poetry of Edmund Spenser*, which remains learned, useful, and friendly to the general reader. Also older is Helena Shire's short volume *A Preface to Spenser*, which offers useful overviews on Spenser's life and much background material, as well as critical analyses of *Amoretti* 78, Colin's Song of Eliza in *Aprill*, and *Prothalamion*. A recent study approaching comprehensiveness is my *Spenser's Famous Flight*, which includes chapters on *The Shepheardes Calender*, the *Amoretti* and *Epithalamion* volume, *Fowre Hymnes*, and *Prothalamion*—all in the context of Spenser's career as England's Christianized Vergil—and has full works-cited lists up through the early 1990s for each poem. Still authoritative is A. Leigh DeNeef's *Spenser and the Motives of Metaphor*, which emphasizes Spenserian poetics and includes chapters on the *Shepheardes Calender*, *The Ruines of Time*, *Daphnaida* and *Colin Clouts*, *Amoretti*, and *Fowre Hymnes*. Heninger's *Sidney and Spenser: The Poet as Maker* discusses some of the shorter poetry in detail, especially *Amoretti*, *Epithalamion*, *Fowre Hymnes*, *Muiopotmos*, and *The Shepheardes Calender*. Simon Shepherd's *Spenser* is an "old-fashioned Marxist" reading (2) and includes a chapter on *The Shepheardes Calender*. Two essays by David Lee Miller discussing the shorter poetry have been influential, "Spenser's Vocation, Spenser's Career" and "Authorship, Anonymity, and *The Shepheardes Calender*," while his recently published "The Earl of Cork's Lute" offers a breathtaking rejoinder to the now fashionable "biographical portrait of Spenser as colonial oppressor" (162) and even to the apologists of this portrait. Camille Paglia's "Spenser and Apollo: *The Faerie Queene*," although not on the shorter poetry, may be the most provocative piece—and one of the most suggestive—

42   THE INSTRUCTOR'S LIBRARY

in print, sharply demarcating, as it does, Spenser's originary role in the founding of English poetry. Individual articles on each shorter poem in *The Spenser Encyclopedia* should aid the instructor greatly.

Recent books devoted to *The Shepheardes Calender* include Lynn Staley Johnson's The Shepheardes Calender: *An Introduction*, which offers just what it promises; Robert Craig Lane's *Shepherds Devises: Edmund Spenser's* Sheapheardes Calender *and the Institutions of Elizabethan Society*, which capitalizes on the new historicist political and ideological versions of Renaissance pastoral; and Schleiner's *Cultural Semiotics, Spenser, and the Captive Woman*, which uses "a Greimassian discourse analysis" to identify "a Renaissance ideologeme" (14). Several books examine Spenser's pastorals more widely. The most recent is Bernard's *Ceremonies of Innocence: Pastoralism in the Poetry of Edmund Spenser*, which is especially useful on the classical heritage, but Patrick Cullen's *Spenser, Marvell, and Renaissance Pastoral*, Richard Mallette's *Spenser, Milton, and Renaissance Pastoral*, and David R. Shore's *Spenser and the Poetics of Pastoral: A Study of the World of Colin Clout* are also important, as is Snyder's *Pastoral Process*, which includes a chapter on *The Shepheardes Calender*, Marvell's *Mower Poems*, and *Lycidas*. Perhaps the two most influential studies are sets of essays by two of Renaissance studies' most important critics: Berger's seven-essay sequence on the *Calender* in his *Revisionary Play* and Montrose's "'The Perfecte Paterne of a Poete': The Poetics of Courtship in *The Shepheardes Calender*," "'Eliza, Queene of Shepheardes,'" "Of Gentlemen and Shepherds: The Politics of Elizabethan Pastoral Form," and "The Elizabethan Subject." Of related importance is the work of Alpers, especially the essay "Pastoral and the Domain of Lyric in Spenser's *Shepheardes Calender*" and the discussion retained in *What Is Pastoral?* (174–84). Finally, Richard Rambuss's *Spenser's Secret Career*, which examines the "secretarial" role of secrecy in *The Shepheardes Calender*, has been widely cited (see his more recent "Spenser's Lives, Spenser's Careers"), while recent, useful chapters on the theological matrix exist in King's *Spenser's Poetry and the Reformation Tradition* and Anthea Hume's *Edmund Spenser: Protestant Poet*. Finally, two important essays by United Kingdom colleagues have appeared. McCabe's "'Little Booke: Thy Selfe Present': The Politics of Presentation in *The Shepheardes Calender*" is an invaluable contribution, emphasizing "the mood of alienation pervading the sequence as a whole and so accurately reflecting the mood of Elisa's England in December 1579. [. . .] Perhaps it is the private dimension of public grief that is characterised in Colin's melancholy. [. . .] The personal, subjective realm of the poem subsumes all others and remains the most resonant and enduring" (4). And Maley's "'Who Knowes Not Colin Clout': *The Shepheardes Calender* as Colonial Text" (*Salvaging Spenser* 11–33) is the first attempt to "establish [. . .] an intimate association" between Spenser's pastoral and "contemporary Irish politics" (8).

No book-length study of the *Complaints* now exists, but Mark Rasmussen is writing one. Rambuss's *Spenser's Secret Career* contains an excellent discussion of the volume in the context of Spenser's career, while Hulse in *Metamorphic*

Verse offers a generic study. J. R. Brink in "Who Fashioned Edmund Spenser? The Textual History of *Complaints*" writes a challenging essay, while Maclean and Prescott excerpt several studies of *Muiopotmos*. On official censorship of *Complaints*, see R. S. Peterson's "Laurel Crown and Ape's Tail."

Two main books exist on *Amoretti*, both published in 1990: Donna Gibbs's *Spenser's* Amoretti: *A Critical Study* and William C. Johnson's *Spenser's* Amoretti: *Analogies of Love*, which is more widely known and emphasizes the Christian structure of the sequence in the context of the liturgical calendar. Four recent essays warrant mention: Reed Way Dasenbrock's "The Petrarchan Context of Spenser's *Amoretti*"; Prescott's "The Thirsty Deer and the Lord of Life: Some Contexts for *Amoretti* 67–70"; Bates's "The Politics of Spenser's *Amoretti*"; and Lisa A. Klein's "'Let Us Love, Dear Love, Lyke As We Ought': Protestant Marriage and the Revision of Petrarchan Loving in Spenser's *Amoretti*."

Only a single book exists on *Epithalamion*: Hieatt's *Short Time's Endless Monument*. In addition to Hieatt's and two other studies, Thomas Greene's "Spenser and the Epithalamic Convention" and Dubrow's *Happier Eden*, useful essays include Richard Neuse's older "The Triumph over Hasty Accidents: A Note on the Symbolic Mode of the *Epithalamion*" and revisionist attempts by Douglas Anderson in "'Unto My Selfe Alone': Spenser's Plenary *Epithalamion*," Joseph Loewenstein in "Echo's Ring: Orpheus and Spenser's Career," and Elizabeth Mazzola in "Marrying Medusa: Spenser's *Epithalamion* and Renaissance Reconstructions of Female Privacy."

Carol V. Kaske's 1978 "Spenser's *Amoretti* and *Epithalamion* of 1595: Structure, Genre, and Numerology" remains the best single analysis of the complete 1595 volume (which includes the *Anacreontics*), while Charlotte Thompson's "Love in an Orderly Universe: A Unification of Spenser's *Amoretti*, 'Anacreontics,' and *Epithalamion*" goes into considerably more detail.

Similarly, only one book exists on *Colin Clouts*, Sam Meyer's 1969 *An Interpretation of Edmund Spenser's* Colin Clout, but useful discussions appear in the studies of Oram, Shore, Mallette, DeNeef, Bernard, and Rambuss, while David W. Burchmore's 1977 "The Image of the Centre in *Colin Clouts Come Home Againe*" is excellent. More recently, a number of essays and book chapters examine Spenser's late pastoral, often in the context of his larger career: Alpers's "Spenser's Late Pastorals," Hadfield's "The Context of the 1590s" (*Edmund Spenser's Irish Experience* 13–50, esp. 13–16, 24, 35, 49), Oram's "1591–1595: Return to Pastoral" (*Edmund Spenser* 155–76, esp. 160–71), Montrose's "Spenser's Domestic Domain," Burrow's "A Renaissance Poet" (*Edmund Spenser* 11–26, esp. 22–23), and J. Christopher Warner's "Poetry and Praise in *Colin Clouts Come Home Againe*."

Although no book devotes itself exclusively to *Fowre Hymnes*, Ellrodt's *Neoplatonism in the Poetry of Spenser* has much to offer on this currently neglected poem. Recently, the most important essay is probably Mary I. Oates's 1984 "*Fowre Hymnes*: Spenser's Retractations of Paradise," while Einar Bjorvand's

44   THE INSTRUCTOR'S LIBRARY

"Spenser's Defence of Poetry: Some Structural Aspects of *Fowre Hymnes*" is also valuable, as is Quitslund's "Spenser and the Patronesses of the *Fowre Hymnes*: 'Ornaments of All True Love and Beautie.'" Critics continue to be troubled by the structure and program of the volume, which includes two "earthly" hymns, two "heavenly" hymns, and a *Dedicatory Epistle* that appears to contradict them (see D. L. Miller, *The Poem's Two Bodies* 76–80).

Finally, no book exists on *Prothalamion*, but several essays remain useful. Berger's "Spenser's *Prothalamion*: An Interpretation" and Alastair Fowler's "Spenser's *Prothalamion*" are foundational essays, while Manley's "Spenser and the City: The Minor Poems," Wyman H. Herendeen's "Spenserian Specifics: Spenser's Appropriation of a River Topos," and my "The Old Poet Presents Himself: *Prothalamion* as a Defense of Spenser's Career" are among the more widely cited. As with *Fowre Hymnes*, critics continue to be troubled by Spenser's puzzling structure, which opens and closes a celebration of a double marriage of important courtiers with representations of private woes and joys.

Several recent collections of essays complement such standard collections as Berger's Twentieth Century Views volume, *Spenser: A Collection of Critical Essays* or Hamilton's *Essential Articles for the Study of Edmund Spenser*. Both Hadfield's Longman collection, *Edmund Spenser*, and Mihoko Suzuki's Prentice-Hall volume, *Critical Essays on Edmund Spenser*, reprint essays written in the last twenty years of the twentieth century, although both limit the shorter poetry to *The Shepheardes Calender*. Nonetheless, their timely conjunction should arm the instructor with much of the best criticism written since the advent of the new historicism. Recently published is a specialized collection of new essays, *Spenser's Life and the Subject of Biography*, edited by Judith Anderson, Donald Cheney, and David Richardson. And forthcoming is *The Cambridge Companion to Spenser*, edited by Hadfield, which will contain two essays especially pertinent here: my essay entitled "Spenser's Pastorals: *The Shepheardes Calender* and *Colin Clouts Come Home Againe*" and Prescott's essay entitled "The Shorter Poems."

Philip Sidney Studies   Unlike Spenser studies, Sidney studies devotes a few books to the (shorter) poetry, although much of the work is devoted to Sidney's two (largely) prose *Arcadia*s and *The Defence of Poesy*. Three older studies on the poetry are especially illuminating: Kalstone's *Sidney's Poetry* and both Rudenstine's *Sidney's Poetic Development* and J. G. Nichols's *The Poetry of Sir Philip Sidney*. The best general book remains Hamilton's 1977 *Sir Philip Sidney: A Study of His Life and Works*, which includes a chapter on Sidney's poetics. Marvin Hunt's more recent essay in the *Dictionary of Literary Biography* marks an excellent point of departure. Other general studies include Dorothy Connell's *Sir Philip Sidney: The Maker's Mind* and Robert Kimbrough's Twayne volume, *Sir Philip Sidney*. McCoy's *Sir Philip Sidney: Rebellion in Arcadia* studies the "major works of literature," including *Astrophil and Stella*, and their relation to Elizabethan politics (ix). Robert E. Stillman's *Sidney's Poetic Justice:*

The Old Arcadia, *Its Eclogues, and Renaissance Pastoral Traditions* has a good deal on Sidney's poetry within his prose romance. More recently, Woudhuysen's massive *Sir Philip Sidney and the Circulation of Manuscripts, 1558–1640* includes much on the print culture of the shorter poetry, while William Craft's even-handed *Labyrinth of Desire: Invention and Culture in the Work of Sir Philip Sidney* argues that "Sidney's work imitates his experience in a culture—Protestant, humanist, Tudor—that was at once constraining and liberating" (ix); it includes useful chapters on the poems. M. J. Doherty's *The Mistress-Knowledge: Sir Philip Sidney's* Defence of Poesie *and Literary Architectonics in the English Renaissance* has much on Sidney's poetics. Alan Hager's *Dazzling Images: The Masks of Sir Philip Sidney* "maps the fictive impersonation of a Renaissance artist who made only brief forays into the world of dramatic writing [. . .] but whose major theme in essay, poem, and romance was that of roles and how we play them, from transvestite to savage" (7), while Anthony Low's "Sir Philip Sidney: 'Huge Desyre'" from *The Reinvention of Love: Poetry, Politics and Culture from Sidney to Milton* is a recent, incisive contextualization of Sidney's erotic project in terms of "changing cultural, political, and economic circumstances" (1). Finally, Raphael Falco's *Conceived Presences: Literary Genealogy in Renaissance England* responds importantly to Helgerson (*Self-Crowned Laureates*) by concentrating on Sidney's poetic career as a model for Spenser, Milton, and others (see especially the introduction; chapter 1, "Vernacular Elegies for Sir Philip Sidney"; and chapter 2 on Spenser's *Astrophel*).

Much of the more influential criticism, however, exists in articles and tends to be on *Astrophil and Stella*. Respondents singled out Marotti's "'Love Is Not Love,'" Ann Rosalind Jones and Stallybrass's "The Politics of *Astrophil and Stella*," Nona Feinberg's "The Emergence of Stella in *Astrophil and Stella*," Hulse's "Stella's Wit," and Quilligan's "Sidney and His Queen."

On *Astrophil and Stella*, the essays mentioned above could be complemented by a vast storehouse, including Jack Stillinger's "The Biographical Problem of *Astrophil and Stella*." More recent are Andrew D. Weiner's "Structure and 'Fore Conceit' in *Astrophil and Stella*," Alan Sinfield's "Double Meanings: II: Sexual Puns in *Astrophil and Stella*" and "Sidney and Astrophil," Jacqueline T. Miller's "'Love Doth Hold My Hand': Writing and Wooing in the Sonnets of Sidney and Spenser," de Grazia's "Lost Potential in Grammar and Nature: Sidney's *Astrophil and Stella*," Roche's "*Astrophil and Stella*: A Radical Reading," and Kim F. Hall's "*Astrophil and Stella*: 'New Found Tropes with Problemes Old'" in *Things of Darkness: Economies of Race and Gender in Early Modern England*.

On *The Lady of May*, one of the best essays remains Orgel's "Sidney's Experiment in Pastoral: *The Lady of May*." Other recent essays include Stillman's "Justice and the 'Good Word' in Sidney's *The Lady in May*" and Montrose's "Celebration and Insinuation: Sir Philip Sidney and the Motives of Elizabethan Courtship."

On *Certain Sonnets*, two essays by Warkentin stand out: "The Meeting of the Muses: Sidney and the Mid-Tudor Poets" and "Sidney's *Certain Sonnets*:

46   THE INSTRUCTOR'S LIBRARY

Speculations on the Evolution of the Text." Instructors may also wish to consult Mary Ellen Lamb's "'Nett Which Paultrye Prayes Disdaines': Sidney's Influence on Two Unattributed Poems in the Bright Manuscript."

On the *Psalms*, recent essays include Coburn Freer's "The Style of Sidney's *Psalms*," Roland Greene's wide-ranging "Sir Philip Sidney's *Psalms*, the Sixteenth-Century Psalter, and the Nature of Lyric," Theodore L. Steinberg's "The Sidneys and the Psalms," and Prescott's "King David as a 'Right Poet': Sidney and the Psalmist." Finally, instructors will want to examine relevant portions of Rivkah Zim's *English Metrical Psalms: Poetry as Praise and Prayer, 1535–1601*.

The best of both older and newer criticism is reprinted in Kinney's 1986 *Essential Articles*. Appearing in the same year was *Sir Philip Sidney: 1586 and the Creation of a Legend*, edited by Jan van Dorsten, Dominic Baker-Smith, and Kinney. The year after that, Dennis Kay edited *Sir Philip Sidney: An Anthology of Modern Criticism*, reprinting a number of seminal essays, including three essays on *Astrophil and Stella*: Warkentin's "Sidney and the Supple Muse: Compositional Procedures in Some Sonnets of *Astrophil and Stella*," Roche's "*Astrophil and Stella*: A Radical Reading," and Colin Williamson's "Structure and Syntax in *Astrophil and Stella*." Waller and Michael D. Moore's 1984 *Sir Philip Sidney and the Interpretation of Renaissance Culture: The Poet in His Time and Ours* also includes important essays, among them four on *Astrophil and Stella*. In 1988, Kinney edited *Sidney in Retrospect*, collecting essays from *English Literary Renaissance*, including the three "Recent Studies in Sidney." The same year William A. Sessions edited *New Readings of Sidney: Experiment and Tradition*, a special issue of *Studies in the Literary Imagination*, which includes oft-cited essays on *Astrophil and Stella* by Waller ("Acts of Reading: The Production of Meaning in *Astrophil and Stella*") and Warkentin ("Sidney and the Supple Muse").

Marlowe Studies   Unlike Sidney and Spenser studies, Marlowe studies affords instructors no substantial body of commentary to draw on. Disproportionate to the percentage of nondramatic verse in his canon (30%), criticism on the plays shows a Tamburlainian domination. This lack of criticism is a paradox, for three of the five poems have acquired the status of masterpieces—even *Lucan's First Book*, which Martindale calls "arguably one of the underrated masterpieces of Elizabethan literature" (*Redeeming* 71). In 1925, R. S. Forsythe observed that "The Passionate Shepherd" has "exercised [. . .] upon English poetry an influence [. . .] equalled by that of few poems" (742), while nearly as old is the commonplace that in the genre of the epyllion, where the "comparison between Marlowe's *Hero and Leander* and Shakespeare's *Venus and Adonis* is a critic's set piece," the youth from Stratford could not compete with the youth from Canterbury (H. D. Smith, *Elizabethan Poetry* 84). As Lewis put it, as if in whisper and in private, "I must frankly confess that [. . .] Marlowe seems to me far superior to Shakespeare in this kind" ("*Hero*" 236).

In fact, critics assessing Marlowe's overall achievement have largely ignored the poetry, at least as a single body; most general studies ignore the poetry altogether, and a few discuss *Hero and Leander* (examples from excellent books include Malcolm Kelsall's *Christopher Marlowe* and Zunder's *Elizabethan Marlowe: Writing and Culture in the English Renaissance*). My book *Marlowe's Counterfeit Profession* seeks remuneration against this tradition, which anachronistically views Marlowe through the lens of Shakespearean drama. Given that this book is a recent comprehensive study, with chapters on four of the five poems, instructors can do worse than start here (neglected is the epitaph on Manwood). Briefly, it contextualizes Marlowe's "Ovidian" poetry, drama, and translation in terms of his rivalry with the "Vergilian" Spenser in the writing of Elizabethan nationhood.

Two earlier comprehensive studies remain valuable: J. B. Steane's 1964 *Christopher Marlowe: A Critical Study* and Clifford Leech's 1986 *Christopher Marlowe: Poet for the Stage*. Both include either chapters or sections on the major poems, though Steane ignores "The Passionate Shepherd." A recent study approaching comprehensiveness is Fred B. Tromly's *Playing with Desire: Christopher Marlowe and the Art of Tantalization*, which examines everything except *Lucan* in the context of the Tantalus myth. T. S. Eliot's "Christopher Marlowe" is the starting place for twentieth-century criticism. As with Eliot, Healy's 1994 *Christopher Marlowe*—perhaps the best recent, short introduction—focuses on Marlowe's drama (vii), but it contains brief, illuminating discussions of Marlowe's poetry.

Even though widely neglected, *Ovid's Elegies* is the only Marlowe poem to boast of an individual book—if not exactly devoted to it, at least devoted to its shadow. M. L. Stapleton's *Harmful Eloquence* includes a chapter on Marlowe's translation. Working from R. R. Bolgar's *The Classical Heritage and Its Beneficiaries* (530–33), Eric Jacobsen in *Translation: A Traditional Craft* first articulated the historical significance of Marlowe's achievement (see 156), but Brian Jay Striar in "Theories and Practices of Renaissance Verse Translation" competes well: "what is particularly remarkable about Marlowe's translation of Ovid's *Amores* is that it is the very first translation of this work into any vernacular" (187). Most earlier work emphasized the accuracy of Marlowe's translation: from Una M. Ellis-Fermor's *Christopher Marlowe* (10–14) and Gill's "Snakes Leape by Verse" to Leech's *Christopher Marlowe* (26–32) and Gill's "Marlowe and the Art of Translation." A few essays concentrate on philological matters: Gill and Robert Krueger's "The Early Editions of Marlowe's Elegies and Davies's Epigrams: Sequence and Authority" and J. M. Nosworthy's "Marlowe's Ovid and Davies's Epigrams: A Postscript" and "The Publication of Marlowe's Elegies and Davies's Epigrams." Among critics, Lee T. Pearcy in *The Mediated Muse: English Translations of Ovid, 1560–1700* best clarifies Marlowe's appropriation of Ovid: "The paradoxical effect of Marlowe's special kind of literalness is to deny the original the importance it usually has in literal translation and to place the imprint of his choice of words on every line" (6).

48 THE INSTRUCTOR'S LIBRARY

For "The Passionate Shepherd to His Love," the two best studies are among the most recent: Douglas Bruster's "'Come to the Tent Again': 'The Passionate Shepherd,' Dramatic Rape, and Lyric Time," which relies on Bakhtin to theorize Marlowe's lyric in terms of the "political aspects" of the invitation mode (50), and Henderson's *Passion Made Public*, which discusses the lyric in the context of Marlowe's plays (120–66). Instructors may also wish to consult my essay in *ELH*, "Career Rivalry and the Writing of Counter-nationhood: Ovid, Spenser, and Philomela in Marlowe's "The Passionate Shepherd to His Love.'" An earlier, excellent essay is Heninger's "The Passionate Shepherd and the Philosophical Nymph," which focuses on the relation between Marlowe's lyric and Ralegh's rejoinder and which sees Marlowe's poem as a "cosmopolitan sort of pastoral" (69). Critics discussing the two poems with Donne's "The Bait" include Mirollo, "Postlude: Three Versions of the Pastoral Invitation to Love" in *Mannerism and Renaissance Poetry*; Low, "The Compleat Angler's 'Baite'; or, The Subverter Subverted"; and Eugene R. Cunnar, "Donne's Witty Theory of Atonement in 'The Baite.'" Finally, Louis H. Leiter, in "Deification through Love: Marlowe's 'The Passionate Shepherd to His Love,'" identifies the shepherd's nymph as "Flora-Venus" and sees this archetypal figure enacting an "adornment ritual" (447) derived from "the festival of Flora in Rome" (446).

Among Marlowe's poems, *Lucan's First Book* has proved the most impermeable to criticism. We possess only three article-length studies, one note, and several short overviews in books. The three studies are by Steane (249–79); Gill, "Marlowe, Lucan, and Sulpitius"; and James Shapiro, "'Metre Meete to Furnish Lucans Style': Reconsidering Marlowe's *Lucan*" (a good place to begin). The one note is by Clifford J. Ronan, "*Pharsalia* 1.373–378: Roman Parricide and Marlowe's Editors." The short overviews are by Ellis-Fermor, *Christopher Marlowe* (14-17); Boas, *Christopher Marlowe* (42–48); Bakeless, *Tragicall History* (2: 163–66); William Blissett, "Lucan's Caesar and the Elizabethan Villain" (562–66); Robert E. Knoll, *Christopher Marlowe* (29–32); and Leech, *Christopher Marlowe* (32–35). To this list instructors may add the remarks by Harry Levin in *The Overreacher: A Study of Christopher Marlowe* (10, 17, 21, 32, 48, 53, 100, 165). Such criticism emphasizes an array of topics: the dating of the translation, its textual history, Marlowe's kinship with Lucan, the accuracy of Marlowe's translation, and attempts to formulate the literary significance of his document.

Unlike the other three important poems, *Hero and Leander* has produced a sustained body of important criticism, and thus it is not so easily canvassed. Narrowing the field to recent criticism helps. Along this path, instructors will want to turn quickly to David Miller's "The Death of the Modern: Gender and Desire in Marlowe's *Hero and Leander*," which argues for the value of psychoanalytical criticism in the context of the new historicism and sees *Hero and Leander* as an example of "the symbolically masculine character of the specular quest for an authentic language of death" (761). Also valuable is Hulse's chapter in *Metamorphic Verse*, entitled "Marlowe: The Primeval Poet," which attends to poetic inspiration and places Marlowe in the Orphic tradition of Musaeus. Gordon Braden's chapter in *The Classics and English Renaissance Poetry* (55–153) examines the style of Mousaios's *Hero and Leander* and its imitations, including that of Marlowe, who presents "a work of much the same kind as Mousaios's: a simple love story dramatically overwritten. [. . .] Marlowe is closer to Mousaios than any of the other Renaissance adapters are, and he is also in many ways closer to Mousaios than he is to any of them" (124). Keach's chapter 4 in *Elizabethan Erotic Narratives* concentrates on Marlowe's ironic narrator as a unifying force (85–116). Robert A. Logan in "Perspective in Marlowe's *Hero and Leander*: Engaging Our Detachment" extends "perspective" to Marlowe himself, who remains detached from Hero and Leander. Conversely, Pamela Royston in "*Hero and Leander* and the Eavesdropping Reader" focuses on the perspective of the reader.

Finally, Marion Campbell follows up on hints by Muriel C. Bradbrook (*Shakespeare and Elizabethan Poetry*) and Neuse ("Atheism and Some Functions of Myth in Marlowe's *Hero and Leander*") to side with Louis L. Martz, who in 1972 published a facsimile edition of the first or earlier edition, free of Marlowe's famous continuer, Chapman. Campbell argues that "what we read as 'Marlowe's *Hero and Leander*' is in fact a construct designed by Chapman to validate his own poem, and that to read the two pieces as parts of a single whole is to obscure the shape and significance of Marlowe's poem" (241). Gill virtually institutionalizes this line of criticism by eliminating Chapman's continuation in her 1987 Oxford edition: "I can see no justification for including Chapman's work in a modern edition of Marlowe's poem" (*Complete Works* 1: 185). Related to this crux is the status of the text: Is it complete or incomplete? The most recent essay on this topic, Godshalk's "*Hero and Leander*: The Sense of an Ending," argues for completeness.

The tenor of *Hero and Leander* has also created debate: Is the poem a tragedy or a comedy? Critics such as Martz, Gill, and Godshalk represent the comedic faction, as do Brian Morris in "Comic Method in Marlowe's *Hero and Leander*" and Bieman in "Comic Rhyme in Marlowe's *Hero and Leander*." Critics such as David Miller ("Death of the Modern") represent the tragedic faction, as do Myron Turner in "Pastoral and Hermaphrodite: A Study in the Naturalism of Marlowe's *Hero and Leander*" and William P. Walsh in "Sexual Discovery and Renaissance Morality in Marlowe's *Hero and Leander*."

While many critics attend to the problem of fate in the poem (see, e.g., Boas 230; and Neuse, "Atheism" 427), A. R. Braunmuller in "Marlowe's Amorous Fates in *Hero and Leander*" focuses on the Mercury digression to see Marlowe fusing two traditions: in the first, the fates derive from Chaos and order, while in the second, which is Neoplatonic, the fates derive from Love, who creates order out of chaos. Finally, Joanne Altieri in "*Hero and Leander*: Sensible Myth and Lyric Subjectivity" relates Marlowe's use of myth to the topic of early modern subjectivity.

Two collections of new essays have just appeared, both the product of the

50   THE INSTRUCTOR'S LIBRARY

four-hundredth anniversary of Marlowe's death. *Christopher Marlowe and English Renaissance Culture*, edited by Darryll Grantley and Peter Roberts, contains fourteen essays, but only one of them discusses the poetry—and from a biographical perspective: Nicholl's "'At Middleborough': Some Reflections on Marlowe's Visit to the Low Countries in 1592." Michael Hattaway's "Christopher Marlowe: Ideology and Subversion" is authoritative as an up-to-date gauging of Marlowe today. *Marlowe, History, and Sexuality: New Critical Essays on Christopher Marlowe*, edited by Paul Whitfield White for the Marlowe Society of America, is more wide-ranging, devoting two essays to the poetry, one by Georgia Brown on *Hero and Leander*, "Breaking the Canon: Marlowe's Challenge to the Literary Status Quo in *Hero and Leander*," and one by Ian Frederick Moulton on *Ovid's Elegies*, "'Printed Abroad and Uncastrated': Marlowe's *Elegies* with Davies' *Epigrams*." Recently published, too, is Emily C. Bartels's collection of previously published essays, *Critical Essays on Christopher Marlowe*, in the Prentice-Hall series, which reprints David Miller's "Death of the Modern." Previous to these three collections, the two best volumes have been another Marlowe Society publication, *"A Poet and a Filthy Play-maker": New Essays on Christopher Marlowe*, edited by Friedenreich, Gill, and Constance B. Kuriyama, which includes Shapiro on *Lucan*, Godshalk on *Hero and Leander*, and Gill on the art of translation, and Harold Bloom's *Modern Critical Views: Christopher Marlowe*, which concentrates on the plays but does reproduce Keach on *Hero and Leander*.

Shakespeare Studies   Even more than with *Hero and Leander*, with Shakespeare's nondramatic works we need to limit the scope by attending primarily to recent works, so overwhelming is the criticism even on this lesser part of his canon. We do possess two other volumes on Shakespeare in the MLA's Approaches to Teaching series, although both address the author as a playwright: Robert H. Ray's *Approaches to Teaching Shakespeare's* King Lear; and Maurice Hunt's *Approaches to Teaching Shakespeare's* Tempest *and Other Late Romances*. Probably the best place to begin is with Kay's fine essay in the *Dictionary of Literary Biography*, which offers an up-to-date overview of the nondramatic poetry. Kay rightly begins by observing that "William Shakespeare's reputation is based primarily on his plays. [. . .] [T]he non-dramatic writings have traditionally been pushed to the margins of the Shakespeare industry. Yet Shakespeare first achieved celebrity as a writer through his narrative poems, and the study of his non-dramatic poetry can illuminate Shakespeare's activity as a poet emphatically of his own age" (221). Kay's specific thesis is that when the theaters closed, "Shakespeare turned from the business of scripting to the pursuit of art and patronage; unable to pursue his career in the theatrical market place, he adopted a more conventional course" (222). The primary problem here is that Shakespeare's turn to poetry is understood to be a deficit career: "unable to pursue his career in the theatrical market place." The next best place to go to is Kay's brand-new *William Shakespeare:* Sonnets *and* Poems, which is the best—

Patrick Cheney 51

perhaps the first—comprehensive study of all of Shakespeare's poetry, with excellent individual chapters on *Venus and Adonis*, *The Rape of Lucrece*, the *Sonnets* and *A Lover's Complaint*, and even miscellaneous poems.

To complement Kay, readers will want to turn quickly to Burrow's equally new Chatterton Lecture on Poetry, "Life and Work in Shakespeare's Poems." Burrow's "chief aim" is "to think about the Sonnets and narrative poems as a group, and to relate them to some of the material realities from which they grew" (16–17). Boldly, Burrow finds "strong grounds for putting the poems at the front of our thinking about Shakespeare, and perhaps even at the front of collected editions of his works" (17). He is also prompted "to ask why we do not think of Shakespeare as primarily a non-dramatic poet" (17), and in superb close analyses of each of the three poems he discovers, contrary to recent "materialist" criticism (especially de Grazia, Quilligan, and Stallybrass's), that "minds and material entities do not marry in Shakespeare's verse" (33). Thus he argues that "Shakespeare's poems [. . .] are poems of material non-disclosures" (33). For instance, "The Sonnets [. . .] offer clues to lives and mental experiences which remain nonetheless irretrievable" (44).

Another recent overview study, Gary Schmidgall's 1990 *Shakespeare and the Poet's Life*, follows this conventional line, devoting a whole book to an explanation of why Shakespeare stopped writing poetry and turned to plays. The recent discovery and canonization of *A Funeral Elegy for Master William Peter* (1612), printed in the new *Riverside Shakespeare*, *The Norton Shakespeare*, and the Longman Shakespeare, invalidates Schmidgall's major premise: "Barring either the unlikely discovery of other poems in manuscript or the appearance of hither-to-lost editions, we can say that Shakespeare devoted himself solely to writing for the stage during his last two London decades" (1). The publication dates of Shakespeare's known poetry also invalidate this formulation: *Venus and Adonis* (1593), *The Rape of Lucrece* (1594), *The Phoenix and the Turtle* (1601), the *Sonnets* and *A Lover's Complaint* (1609), and *A Funeral Elegy* (1612). Even though scholars tend to date the composition of the *Sonnets* in the mid 1590s, they usually believe that Shakespeare revised some of the poems into the seventeenth century (G. B. Evans 110–15). In *The Norton Shakespeare*, for instance, Walter Cohen remarks that the "occasional pieces" that form Shakespeare's "Various Poems" were "composed from the early 1590s until shortly before Shakespeare's death" (Greenblatt et al. 1991).

Critics still rely on two older studies: Bradbrook's 1961 *Shakespeare and Elizabethan Poetry* and G. Wilson Knight's 1955 *The Mutual Flame: On Shakespeare's* Sonnets *and* The Phoenix and the Turtle. Hamilton's 1967 *The Early Shakespeare* contains two useful chapters on the poems: one on *Venus and Adonis* (143–66) and one on *The Rape of Lucrece* (167–85). Hamilton contextualizes both epyllia in terms of the development of Shakespeare's early career, but he neglects the *Sonnets* in particular.

Not surprisingly, the bulk of commentary exists on the three most famous poems: the *Sonnets*, *Venus and Adonis*, and *The Rape of Lucrece*. Probably the

52   THE INSTRUCTOR'S LIBRARY

next best place to begin, then, is with Dubrow's *Captive Victors: Shakespeare's Narrative Poems and* Sonnets, the most recent and comprehensive study of all three. Reacting to the tradition that "regret[s]" the two narrative poems (15), Dubrow devotes a chapter to each, arguing that they "deserve more attention" in part because they are "deeply involved with the uses and abuses of power and of language": "Shakespeare adopts the most conventional generic and rhetorical motifs to elucidate the most idiosyncratic psychological patterns" (19). Dubrow extends this assertion to the *Sonnets*, suggesting that "all three poems form a type of triptych, raising as they do strikingly similar questions about human behavior and human experience" (19–20). A shorter recent work bringing all three poems together is Ted Hughes's chapter in *Shakespeare and the Goddess of Complete Being*, "Conception and Gestation of the Equation's Tragic Myth: The *Sonnets, Venus and Adonis, Lucrece*," which traces "connections between the *Sonnets* and *Venus and Adonis*, and between *Venus and Adonis* and *Lucrece*, suggesting how this group of works came to be the foundation of the mythic form of the Tragic Equation as it appears in the mature plays" (50).

Forthcoming is a book on skepticism in Shakespeare's poems by A. D. Cousins, titled *The* Sonnets *and the Narrative Poems*. Cousins writes that his "book focuses in particular on their [the narrative poems' and the *Sonnets*] variously manifested scepticism, their concern both with what wisdom might be in human conduct and with the extent to which human conduct might be directed by wisdom, their preoccupation with knowing, inventing, or reinventing the past, their exploration of the relations among self-knowledge, sexuality, and death, and their ambiguous figuring of gender." The book will feature one chapter on *Venus and Adonis*, one on *The Rape of Lucrece*, and three on the *Sonnets*. Until the book appears, instructors will want to consult a series of recent essays by Cousins: "Venus Reconsidered: The Goddess of Love in *Venus and Adonis*"; "Towards a Reconsideration of Shakespeare's Adonis: Rhetoric, Narcissus, and the Male Gaze"; and "Subjectivity, Exemplarity, and the Interplay of Discourse: The Establishing of Characterization in *Lucrece*."

Finally, de Grazia's *Shakespeare Verbatim: The Reproduction of Authenticity and the 1790 Apparatus* has some important discussions of the role of the poetry, especially the *Sonnets* and the two narrative poems, in the history of publishing Shakespeare's works (152–76). De Grazia usefully recalls that Edmund Malone's 1790 edition is the first to be titled *The Plays and Poems of William Shakespeare* (154).

On *Venus and Adonis* in particular, the relevant chapters in Keach's *Elizabethan Erotic Narratives* (52–84) and Hulse's *Metamorphic Verse* (143–75) are especially illuminating on Shakespeare's reworking of the Ovidian subtext, while Gordon Williams in "The Coming of Age of Shakespeare's Adonis" focuses on the iconographic dimension of both studies, especially the analogy between Shakespeare's and Titian's handling of the Adonis myth. Coppélia Kahn in "Self as Eros in *Venus and Adonis*," from *Man's Estate*, highlights feminist issues of gender and sexuality (21–46), while Catherine Belsey examines "Love

Patrick Cheney   53

as Trompe-l'Oeil: Taxonomies of Desire in *Venus and Adonis.*" Out in 1997, however, is the instructor's dream come true: volume 16 in Garland's Shakespeare Criticism series, Philip C. Kolin's Venus and Adonis: *Critical Essays*, which prints "the most essential criticism and reviews of Shakespeare's work from the seventeenth century to the present" (xi), including Kolin's orienting essay "*Venus and Adonis* among the Critics" (3–65) and his "Chronological Bibliography of Scholarship and Commentary on *Venus and Adonis*, Including Editions and Reviews of Performances" (407–29). Kolin prints twenty-nine essays, seven of them new.

On *The Rape of Lucrece*, Garland has not yet produced a companion volume, but instructors can rely on relevant chapters in Keach and Hulse. As Duncan-Jones observes in her bibliographic essay "The Non-dramatic Poems," much of the debate is "concerned with the question of whether [. . .] Lucrece is to be seen as unequivocally admirable, or whether [. . .] Shakespeare shows awareness of the debate about her moral status initiated by St. Augustine" (72). The most important critic here is Ian Donaldson in *The Rapes of Lucretia: A Myth and Its Transformations*, whose chapter 3 examines Shakespeare's use of the myth. Stephanie H. Jed's *Chaste Thinking: The Rape of Lucretia and the Birth of Humanism* supplies additional historical background. Richard Levin addresses "The Ironic Reading of *The Rape of Lucrece* and the Problem of External Evidence," while Jerome A. Kramer and Judith Kaminsky offer a useful formalist reading in "'These Contraries Such Unity Do Hold': Structure in *The Rape of Lucrece*." Nancy Vickers's "'The Blazon of Sweet Beauty's Best': Shakespeare's *Lucrece*" is often cited, but so are Catharine R. Stimpson's "Shakespeare and the Soil of Rape," Laura G. Bromley's "Lucrece's Re-Creation," Kahn's "The Rape in Shakespeare's *Lucrece*," and Katharine Eisaman Maus's "Taking Tropes Seriously: Language and Violence in Shakespeare's *Rape of Lucrece*." Lastly, Fineman approaches issues of will in the context of early modern subjectivity in "Shakespeare's Will: The Temporality of Rape."

A useful but older overview of both *Venus and Adonis* and *The Rape of Lucrece* is J. W. Lever's "Shakespeare's Narrative Poems" in that wonderful 1971 instructor's helpmeet, *A New Companion to Shakespeare Studies*, edited by Kenneth Muir and S. Schoenbaum. The updated volume, *The Cambridge Companion to Shakespeare Studies*, edited by Stanley Wells, contains a very general overview essay, "Shakespeare the Non-dramatic Poet," by Ellrodt, which concentrates on the *Sonnets*. A more recent analysis of the two epyllia appears in Bate's *Shakespeare and Ovid* (esp. 48–67 on *Venus and Adonis* and 65–83 on *The Rape of Lucrece*).

Among the three major nondramatic poems, the *Sonnets* has attracted the greatest interest. Perhaps the most influential book remains Fineman's *Shakespeare's Perjured Eye: The Invention of Poetic Subjectivity in the* Sonnets, although instructors should be warned about the difficulty of the material. De Grazia's articles, which emphasize the fusion of subjectivity and textual materiality, constitute another important contribution: "The Motive for Interiority:

54   CHENEY'S CHOICE

Shakespeare's *Sonnets* and *Hamlet*" and "The Scandal of Shakespeare's *Sonnets*."
Allied is Stallybrass's "Editing as Cultural Formation: The Sexing of Shake-
speare's *Sonnets*." As in Sidney studies, Marotti's "'Love is Not Love'" has had
an effect here. Older books include Booth's *An Essay on Shakespeare's* Sonnets
and Hallett Smith's *The Tension of the Lyre: Poetry in Shakespeare's* Sonnets.
Older collections on the *Sonnets* remain useful: Barbara Herrnstein Smith's
Discussions of Shakespeare's Sonnets and Gerald Willen and Victor B. Reed's
A Casebook on Shakespeare's Sonnets. Several recent studies provide a homo-
erotic lens: Joseph Pequigney's *Such Is My Love: A Study of Shakespeare's*
Sonnets and Bruce R. Smith's *Homosexual Desire in Shakespeare's England*
(228–70). James Schiffer's recent Garland collection, *Shakespeare's Sonnets:
Critical Essays* is a companion to Kolin's collection on *Venus and Adonis*. In
addition to Schiffer's survey of criticism, the volume reprints four essays, in-
cluding Stallybrass's "Editing as Cultural Formation" and de Grazia's "The
Scandal of Shakespeare's *Sonnets*"; the volume also prints fifteen new essays,
including "Shakespeare's Petrarchism" (Braden); "The Matter of Inwardness:
Shakespeare's *Sonnets*" (Schoenfeldt); and "I, You, He, She, and We: On the
Sexual Politics of Shakespeare's *Sonnets*" (Bruce Smith). Finally, as Duncan-
Jones reminds us, instructors will not want to forget Lewis's discussion in *En-
glish Literature of the Sixteenth Century* (498–509).

A large number even of recent collections of Shakespeare criticism await the
intrepid instructor, although many seminal ones, such as Murray M. Schwartz
and Kahn's *Representing Shakespeare: New Psychoanalytic Essays* and Jean
Howard and Marion F. O'Connor's *Shakespeare Reproduced: The Text in His-
tory and Ideology*, do not address the nondramatic poetry. Among those that
do are *Shakespeare and the Question of Theory*, edited by Parker and Geoffrey
Hartman, and *Shakespeare Reread: The Texts in New Contexts*, edited by Mc-
Donald. Important older collections are Leonard F. Dean's *Shakespeare: Mod-
ern Essays in Criticism* and Alvin B. Kernan's *Modern Shakespearean
Criticism: Essays on Style, Dramaturgy, and the Major Plays*.

Cheney's Choice

Let us say that you are teaching a course in shorter Elizabethan poetry for the
first time, that you have not had adequate time to prepare for it, and that you
are anxiously searching for concrete advice. In other words, you are alone at
night on the platform. The ghostly course you have inherited is to function as
a survey but is to emphasize Spenser, Sidney, Marlowe, and Shakespeare. The
night is bitter cold, you are sick at heart, and you feel harrowed with fear and
wonder. What follows aims to help you pass the minutes of this night: a shorter
Elizabethan poetry survival kit. This personalized platform kit should help you
begin to answer the question, "Who's there?"

Classroom Texts

Anthology: Norbrook and Woudhuysen, eds., *Penguin Book of Renaissance Verse*

Spenser: Oram et al., eds., *Shorter Poems of Edmund Spenser*

Sidney: Duncan-Jones, ed., *Sir Philip Sidney*

Marlowe: Orgel, ed., *Complete Poems and Translations*

Shakespeare: G. B. Evans, ed., *The Sonnets*; Roe, ed., *The Poems*

Optional: A. Kinney, ed., *Elizabethan Backgrounds*; I. Rivers, ed., *Classical and Christian Ideas in English Renaissance Poetry*

Reference Works

Major tools

Donker and Muldrow, *Dictionary of Literary-Rhetorical Conventions of the English Renaissance*

Fritze, ed., *Historical Dictionary of Tudor England*

W. Kerrigan and Braden, *The Idea of the Renaissance*

Singman, *Daily Life in Elizabethan England*

Sixteenth-Century British Nondramatic Writers, *Dictionary of Literary Biography*, ed. Richardson, vols. 132, 136, 167, 172

The Spenser Encyclopedia, ed. Hamilton

Waller, *English Poetry of the Sixteenth-Century*

Biographies

Bakeless, *The Tragicall History of Christopher Marlowe*

Duncan-Jones, *Sir Philip Sidney: Courtier Poet*

Schoenbaum, *William Shakespeare: A Compact Documentary Life*

Waller, *Edmund Spenser*

Histories and Background

J. Briggs, *The Stage-Play World*

Burrow, "The Sixteenth Century"

A. Fowler, *Kinds of Literature*

T. M. Greene, *The Light in Troy*

Hadfield, *Literature, Politics, and National Identity*

Lewis, *English Literature of the Sixteenth Century*

Prescott, *French Poets and the English Renaissance*

Sanders, "Renaissance and Reformation: Literature 1510–1620," *The Short Oxford History of English Literature*

Shuger, *Habits of Thought in the English Renaissance*

H. Smith, *Elizabethan Poetry*

Sowerby, *The Classical Legacy in Renaissance Poetry*

Critical Studies

General

de Grazia, Quilligan, and Stallybrass, eds., *Subject and Object in Renaissance Culture* (editors' introduction)

Greenblatt, *Renaissance Self-Fashioning* (chs. on Marlowe, Spenser, Shakespeare); *Shakespearean Negotiations*

56 CHENEY'S CHOICE

Helgerson, *The Elizabethan Prodigals* (chs. on Gascoigne, Lyly,
Greene, Lodge, Sidney); *Forms of Nationhood* (much on
Spenser, Daniel, Drayton, Shakespeare); *Self-Crowned
Laureates* (ch. on Spenser)

Spenser

Berger, *Revisionary Play*
Burrow, *Edmund Spenser*
Cheney, *Spenser's Famous Flight*
DeNeef, *Spenser and the Motives of Metaphor*
Hadfield, ed., *Cambridge Companion to Spenser*; *Edmund
Spenser*
McCabe, "Edmund Spenser, Poet of Exile"; "'Little Booke: Thy
Selfe Present'"
D. L. Miller, "Authorship, Anonymity, and *The Shepheardes
Calender*"; "The Earl of Cork's Lute"; *The Poem's Two Bodies;*
"Spenser's Vocation, Spenser's Career"
Montrose, "The Elizabethan Subject"; "'Eliza, Queene of
Shepheardes'"; "Of Gentlemen and Shepherds"; "'The Perfecte
Paterne of a Poete'"
Oram, *Edmund Spenser*
Paglia, "Spenser and Apollo"
Stump, "Edmund Spenser"
Suzuki, ed., *Critical Essays on Edmund Spenser*

Sidney

Craft, *Labyrinth of Desire*
Hamilton, *Sir Philip Sidney*
Hulse, "Stella's Wit"
Marvin Hunt, "Sir Philip Sidney"
A. R. Jones and Stallybrass, "The Politics of *Astrophil and Stella*"
Kay, ed., *Sir Philip Sidney*
A. Kinney, ed., *Essential Articles*
Marotti, "'Love Is Not Love'"
McCoy, *Sir Philip Sidney: Rebellion in Arcadia*
Quilligan, "Sidney and His Queen"
Woudhuysen, *Sir Philip Sidney and the Circulation of
Manuscripts*

Marlowe

Bartels, ed., *Critical Essays on Christopher Marlowe*
Bruster, "'Come to the Tent Again': 'The Passionate Shepherd,'
Dramatic Rape, and Lyric Time"
Cheney, *Marlowe's Counterfeit Profession*
Eliot, "Christopher Marlowe"
Hattaway, "Christopher Marlowe: Ideology and Subversion"

Healy, *Christopher Marlowe*
Leech, *Christopher Marlowe: Poet for the Stage*
H. Levin, *The Overreacher*
D. L. Miller, "The Death of the Modern"
Nicholl, *The Reckoning*
White, ed., *Marlowe, History, and Sexuality*

Shakespeare
Bate, *Genius of Shakespeare*; *Shakespeare and Ovid*
Burrow, "Life and Work in Shakespeare's Poems"
de Grazia, "The Motive for Interiority"; "The Scandal of
Shakespeare's *Sonnets*"; *Shakespeare Verbatim*
Donaldson, *The Rapes of Lucretia*
Dubrow, *Captive Victors*
Fineman, *Shakespeare's Perjured Eye*; "Shakespeare's *Sonnets'*
Perjured Eye"; "Shakespeare's Will"
T. Hughes, "Conception and Gestation of the Equation's Tragic
Myth"
Kay, "William Shakespeare"; *William Shakespeare:* Sonnets *and
Poems*
Kolin, ed., Venus and Adonis: *Critical Essays*
McDonald, ed., *Shakespeare Reread*
Schiffer, ed., *Shakespeare's* Sonnets
N. Vickers, "'The Blazon of Sweet Beauty's Best': Shakespeare's
Lucrece"

If this platform survival kit does not help defend you from spirit of health
or goblin damned, the rest is silence.

Note on Texts

The essays in this volume cite and quote from the following editions, unless
otherwise specified:

Chaucer
Riverside Chaucer. Larry D. Benson et al. 3rd ed. Boston: Houghton, 1987.
Based on *The Works of Geoffrey Chaucer*. Ed. F. N. Robinson. 2nd ed.
Boston: Houghton, 1957.
Daniel
Poems and a Defence of Ryme. Ed. Arthur C. Sprague. Cambridge: Har-
vard UP, 1930.

58 NOTE ON TEXTS

Marlowe
Poems and Translations and Dido, Queen of Carthage. Ed. Roma Gill. Oxford: Clarendon, 1987. Vol. 1 of *The Complete Works of Christopher Marlowe*. 5 vols. 1987–98.

Ralegh
The Poems of Sir Walter Ralegh. Ed. Agnes M. C. Latham. Boston: Houghton, 1929.

Shakespeare
Riverside Shakespeare. Ed. G. Blakemore Evans et al. 2nd ed. Boston: Houghton, 1997.

Sidney, Mary
The Psalms *of Sir Philip Sidney and the Countess of Pembroke*. Ed. J. C. A. Rathmell. New York: New York UP, 1963.

Sidney, Philip
The Poems of Sir Philip Sidney. Ed. William A. Ringler, Jr. Oxford: Clarendon, 1962.

Spenser
The Yale Edition of the Shorter Poems of Edmund Spenser. Ed. William A. Oram et al. New Haven: Yale UP, 1989.
The Faerie Queene. Ed. A. C. Hamilton. Longman Annotated English Poets. London: Longman, 1977.

Surrey
Howard, Henry. *Poems*. Ed. Emrys Jones. Oxford: Clarendon, 1964.

Wyatt
The Complete Poems. Ed. R. A. Rebholz. New Haven: Yale UP, 1978.

Bible
The Geneva Bible: A Facsimile Edition. Ed. Lloyd E. Berry. Madison: U of Wisconsin P, 1969.

Classical authors
Loeb Classical Library.

Part Two

APPROACHES

Introduction

Anne Lake Prescott

Toward the start of a recent term, a worried undergraduate in my Tudor literature course came to me after class and said, "Professor, I just can't seem to identify with these writers." Postponing for the moment my usual advice on diachronic anthropology (think of Elizabethans as an extinct tribe) and relativism (it's good for modern Americans, whose own society is hardly perfect, to exercise their imaginative empathy on truly different cultures, ones that never even heard of Burger King, bacteria, and the big bang, let alone individual human rights), I heard myself saying, "Right. I wouldn't want students who identify with patriarchal royalists in a country that tortured people, believed the sun goes around the earth, and kept women out of law school." She looked startled but also amused and relieved, which was of course the point. Time enough later, I thought, to learn that Campion's lyrics are lovely, that Spenser's sonnet sequence is wisely witty, that Marlowe's *Hero and Leander* is refreshingly wayward, that Mary Sidney's psalms are something of which any religious poet would be proud, and that Elizabethans were, for all their peculiarities by our standards, able to write verse that embeds itself in even a postmodern imagination. For the moment, my student's uneasiness seemed to require acknowledgment.

In the best of current circumstances, teaching poetry can be difficult. Even good students can arrive at college afraid of it, some because they think it a mystery into which they are not initiated and some because they take poems to be cryptic messages with nuggets of advice or belief—like a fortune cookie processed by a smart cryptographer who hoped that a reader's inner intelligence agency might decode it. Students can also be regrettably, and regretfully, ignorant of myth ("Oh, isn't Venus goddess of chastity?" one asked me with genuine surprise) and history ("You can tell Marlowe was an atheist because he laughed at the pope, the most famous symbol of religion," explained a young woman who must have dozed off during our class on the Reformation). Terms can puzzle them: "Spenser believed in a new morology," wrote one to whom I had outlined, but only orally, A. Kent Hieatt's discovery about the numerological structures in *Epithalamion*, "and he thought this morology would make his marriage last a long time." And, of course, Renaissance culture becomes more remote from our students with every passing term, even if many respond to such remoteness with pleasure, finding that it gives texture to the parts of early modern culture that remain familiar. Indeed, some sorts of older thinking now seem less foolish as intervening certainties fade. Unlike educated readers of a century or so ago, we are no longer sure that space is homogeneous; that a single time line is the best mechanism for hanging up historical facts to dry; that human selves surround hard nodes of identity; or that good poets avoid the trivial, the insincere, and the nugatory. Even as in some regards the postmodern curves around to meet the pre- or early modern, though, our pedagogy

62   INTRODUCTION

must remain flexible and complex. Many teachers of Renaissance texts, then, whether neophytes or old hands, will welcome advice, enjoy hearing of others' techniques, or simply wish to know where, pedagogically, the profession finds itself in one not insignificant area of English studies.

Patrick Cheney and I trust that the following essays on shorter Elizabethan poetry (in practice, nondramatic poetry other than *The Faerie Queene*) will be useful in just these terms: individually, they tell how some issues—the introduction of background material, genre, poststructuralism and other uses of theory, and the cultural context—play out in the classroom; suggest some methods that work; and, in the final section, report on larger narratives about the period that might affect how we teach. In putting together this collection, we have been both guided and limited by the identities and interests of those who agreed to write, by the nature of the genres involved, and by considerations of space.

How would this volume have been different had it appeared some decades ago? Probably we would have had an essay on cosmology (and indeed I always show my students illustrations from *Cosmographical Glass*, by S. K. Heninger, Jr., to be sure they know that the universe is based on number, weight, and measure; that the earth occupies the center of the universe unless one takes the paradoxes of Copernicus literally; and that sirens guide tunefully arranged concentric crystal spheres). We might have had an essay on Reformation theological wars (relevant to Spenser's *Amoretti*), and in truth I find that even my irreligious students think them intriguing because the debates have secular analogues and because some students acquire a taste for argument as such. And would there not have been more materials on magic, the occult, and number symbolism? There are books on such topics, of course, and my students welcome with smiles and, I suspect, traces of childhood hope the useful spells for capturing fairies that Katherine Briggs reproduces in her *Anatomy of Puck*.

Here, though, are essays on the transition from medieval to early modern lyric (Anderson), a process that entails consideration of genres and of the self (Fowler). Our authors also deal with language—with flowers and the flowers of rhetoric (Lupton), metaphor (Hedley), and metrics (Woods). The reader will find essays on the pedagogy of many matters currently engaging scholarly interest: gay and lesbian studies (DiGangi); race (Hendricks); readership and reception (McManus, Kennedy); a Renaissance aesthetics of externality, miniature, and decoration (Fumerton); religious attitudes (Shuger); and space—whether a lyric's inscription of locality (Greene) or, quite literally, the place of poetry (Schleiner). The answers to our questionnaires and the essay proposals we received showed a widespread interest in teaching more Elizabethan women writers, so our readers will find essays dealing with Mary Sidney (Hannay), Anne Lock (Felch), Elizabeth I (Mueller), and—with a little chronological reach—Mary Wroth (C. R. Kinney); even the nightingale, or so one hears, was once a woman, although one essay (Lamb) shows how as a bird she often shifted gender. Other essays suggest ways of incorporating information on technology: high-tech (Hulse on the Internet's implications and resources), mid-tech (Marotti on early print culture, Kastan on the material history of the printed book), and surviving low-tech modes (May on manuscript poets).

A number of our essays explore particular genres such as the epyllion (Brown), songs (Ratcliffe), or sonnets (C. R. Kinney); particular texts, such as *The Shepheardes Calender* (Moore), *Amoretti, Epithalamion,* and *Prothalamion* (Cheney and Prescott), Shakespeare's *Sonnets* (Schoenfeldt), Marlowe's and Ralegh's shepherd (A. Kinney), and Gascoigne's and Ralegh's poems (Hedley), and *Astrophil and Stella* (Henderson). Others in this volume take up theory of one sort or another, including new historicism (Fumerton). Is poststructuralism useful in teaching undergraduates (Kuin)? What of genre criticism (Dubrow)? And the Renaissance's own literary theory? Students are often surprised to learn the degree to which many, then and now, have frowned on *poesis*, on making things up (Herman). Other essays focus on suggestions for encouraging students to act, do, or write: students can edit (Cavanagh), record their reactions and notable passages (McManus, Webster), play a manuscript version of the telephone game (May), write sonnets (Henderson), play early modern games (Schleiner), recite (Krier).

Such suggestions accompany a striking taste in many of these essays for the ludic and rhetorical, a tendency that presses against and with one toward remembering what is material: the book trade, manuscript transmission, the specifics of gender or color, actual readers, once-audible voices. Perhaps because our field now stretches into such a range of topics and interests, moreover, and perhaps because the academic world is now so riven that irony has room to seep out of its cracks and seams, many of these essays also show a tolerance for ambiguity and complexity that renders impossible any single "world picture," Elizabethan or otherwise (Tillyard). This is not, I think, a revival of the ambiguities (indeed, seven of them, according to William Empson's famous book on the topic) so dear to the "old new criticism," a bravura play with words confined inside a poem's well-wrought urn, but rather the ambiguity that comes from an increased and not always comfortable recognition of a multiplicity of perspectives (on race, on gender, on genre, on love, on God, on print, on poetry itself) in past cultures and among—and indeed within—ourselves.

Granted this ambiguity and complexity, are coherent stories —or fragments of stories—about Elizabethan shorter poetry possible? We end with several essays on what narratives underlie the authors' pedagogy, or part of it. Inevitably, such narratives note a shift of some sort. ("My dear," says Adam to Eve in a cartoon showing the pair en route out of Eden, "We are living in a time of transition.") Lyric evolves (Greene, Fowler); earlier Tudor poets, so often and so wrongly neglected in courses on sixteenth-century poetry, give way to later Elizabethans (King); and in the larger community one generation yields to another, not without vexation and anxiety on the part of poets and their elders (Helgerson).

The organization of this collection has its own narrative unsettledness, moreover, for there would be many possible ways to order the essays. Nonetheless,

64   INTRODUCTION

we divide the essays into five sections; the first four—and the order in which they appear—will be familiar to readers of the Approaches series: "Teaching Backgrounds"; "Selected Pedagogical Strategies, Courses, Units, Assignments"; "Critical and Theoretical Approaches"; and "Teaching Specific Poems and Poets." The fifth section, "Teaching Critical Narratives of the Elizabethan Age," is new to the Approaches series and will, we hope, provide a precedent for further collections. The idea giving rise to the "Teaching Critical Narratives" section was our belief that students can often benefit from courses structured on clear narratives, and so we called on a generational and ideological spread of well-known Renaissance colleagues to have them tell the story they tell about shorter Elizabethan poetry.

In the collection as a whole, many essays speak to each other across the divide of pages or sections, and we recommend that the reader mentally juxtapose these contributions even when our necessarily linear publication must separate them. For example, Debora Shuger's insights into how Elizabethan religious beliefs related to the lyric gain further specificity when read with Elizabeth Fowler's discussion of Chaucer's palinode (that model of withdrawal so well known to the Elizabethans). And Steven May's ingenious technique for showing students the risks of manuscript transmission will bring home to them the cultural practices of which Arthur Marotti writes many pages later. Our readers, we also hope, will trace other affiliations.

In Utopia this book would have been much longer and, of course, free. We cannot resist fantasizing about such a volume. With more pages to fill, we could have included an essay on teaching modern students about England's class system—its structures, titles, governing laws, and hierarchies. My own students, for example, who often think of class only in American terms of lower, middle, and upper and who call the creator of Astrophil "Sir Sidney," can need reminding that gentlemen were, in the eyes of the law, made not by money or manners but by birth, the monarch, or a bachelor's degree. We have an essay on race, but in a perfect world there would also be one on the island's own tangled ethnicity, on how, for example, the Welsh (neighbors of young Robert and Philip Sidney when the boys were in school) endured English jokes about their thievishness, funny accents, and roasted cheese; Britons were not Saxons. And although readers will find much on Petrarch here, we have virtually nothing on French writers, even though a number of Elizabethan poets owed something to Marot, Bellay, Ronsard, and Desportes and even though many visited France.

Our fancied volume would report further on teaching modern students about Elizabethan poetry and the classics, including ancient mythology (not that in modern handbooks but the heavily allegorized mythology of such Renaissance mythographers as Boccaccio, Cartari, Abraham Fraunce, Robert Stephanus, or George Sandys). And here we neglect some genres: the pedagogically useful emblem (Geffrey Whitney's *Choice of Emblems* is a very pretty trove of illustrations from which to make handouts), the entertaining epigram and ingenious anagram, the difficult but provocatively disreputable verse satire (including Donne's experiments in the genre, when they are not snatched by those teaching seventeenth-century literature, and Nashe's flavorful "Choice of Valentines" for the more worldly students).

Would it help in teaching lullabies and epitaphs to explain a little about early modern child raising, family life, and attitudes toward death? What of medicine and the body? When poems refer to swelling hearts, what did writers think their blood was doing? What does it mean to be "jovial," and what might it be like to think you have emotions emanating from your liver? (On other corporal fragments, see for example, *The Body in Parts*, edited by Hillman and Mazzio.) And sex? Students can be surprised to hear that Elizabethan doctors, far from sharing the Victorian belief that "ladies don't move," could think female orgasm necessary for conception. Moving from the body to the soul, we might also have included essays on religious dissent, for a number of poets were committed to Rome, if only for a time, and some, like Robert Southwell, died for it. As James Shapiro's recent work shows, moreover, England had a few Jews, rendering all the more grievous such poems as the sonnets by Henry Lock, Anne's son, who was able both to imagine himself as various ancient Israelite heroines and to scorn contemporary Judaism. And the Americas, Africa, Asia? We have no essay on colonialism or proto-imperialism, in part because that topic seems less important for Elizabethan shorter poems than for later ones or for the epic, prose, and drama, but our huge, perfected volume would take such matters well beyond anything we offer here. So, too, we would have more on art history, court politics, and popular culture—particularly relevant to prose and drama, but not wholly missing from verse.

So much for dreams (another topic we ignore). Here we present to our readers what we think is a fine set of essays that together make a practical and imaginative guide to teaching some of the most engaging poetry in English. We thank our contributors and those who completed our questionnaires. Working on this volume has reminded us just how much teaching is indeed a collegial enterprise. We hope you will find the following essays as lively, useful, and provocative as we do.

TEACHING BACKGROUNDS

Elizabethan Poetry in the Postmodern Classroom
Clark Hulse

We might, without much elegance, think of the place of Elizabethan poetry in the university as like that of a fly on a mountain. If the teaching of Elizabethan poetry is in any radical sense being transformed, it is because the mountain is in motion, not the fly. Higher education is being restructured, economically and technologically, and few of us, from the isolation of our separate classrooms, feel much confidence about understanding, much less controlling or shaping, those changes. And yet I want to propose in the next few pages that it is precisely in the classroom and (at least in part) by teaching Elizabethan poetry that we can work toward an understanding of those changes for our students and for ourselves and can shape the new university, if ever so slightly, so as to maintain a meaningful space within it for the literature to which we have devoted so much study and care.

At the time I write this, most of us use computers for word processing, we communicate by e-mail, and we probably poke around the Web. We may occasionally show a videotape or some slides in class, and some of us have multimedia classrooms, with Web access, CD-ROM, laser disc, videotape capability, and high-resolution projector systems that descend from the ceiling like three-eyed space monsters. A few are already teaching courses either partially or entirely online.

How far the changes in technologies for teaching will have gone by the time this volume is published is impossible to say, but it is wise to assume that the changes will exceed our expectations rather than fall short of them. All of us will be led, pushed, or dragged through orientation sessions on the use of new media in teaching, both the media I have mentioned and perhaps others I don't

Clark Hulse 67

imagine. Our students will be far more conversant with the media than we are, having used it themselves and having been taught in secondary school by skillful and innovative teachers using diverse student-centered classroom activities. Our students will expect of us something more than the old university classroom, in which the professor is up front professing and the students are lined up in neat rows (or scattered in a more progressive asymmetry), taking notes, filling in the blanks that the professor treats as questions, or occasionally asking questions themselves to prove they did the reading. They will expect us to use the new media in the classroom, to treat it as a way of organizing their work outside class, and to let them use it in their presentations of learning. And they will expect these changes not to be pedagogical parsley added decoratively to the edge of the platter of learning, but to be part of a fundamental reconstitution of what we consider learning to be, how we think learning is acquired, and what the appropriate means are for demonstrating that one has it.

Given the speed of the changes overtaking us, I will not give a lesson plan on, for instance, how to teach Shakespeare's *Sonnets* using CD-ROM or the Web. CD-ROM is already dismissed by many as a transitional technology, and in a year most of the Web addresses will have changed. While I must of necessity give a few Web addresses, I want to focus on a larger strategy, which is to use Elizabethan poetry as a way of understanding cultural transformations in the early modern period—indeed to see Elizabethan poetry as itself a product of and shaper of those transformations—and, reciprocally, to use the study of Elizabethan poetry as a way of understanding the equally large transformations in which we and our students are caught in the postmodern period. This strategy can be deployed in any course setting: a topical course on the Elizabethan sonnet, a focused survey of sixteenth-century literature, or especially a general survey course.

This strategy turns on a simple fact: that the new media, especially the Web, are making available to everyone materials that used to be available to a few, notably the manuscripts and early printed books that have been and still are— in their material states—the treasures of rare book libraries. In their virtual states, they are available to anyone with a modem or Internet connection, but in the transition from material to virtual states they are often sharply decontextualized and stripped of the stabilizing apparatus that has accumulated around them in the past century of learning. The challenge of the postmodern classroom is to acknowledge the accessibility of these fuzzy images and ghostly presences and to work out ways to make them a part of the project of intelligibility that is always a part of teaching.

Making effective use of the virtual availability of such materials has three stages, all involving a shift in emphasis toward the graphical dimension of poetic texts. First is the local use of virtual representations to illustrate and supplement local concepts: seeing, for instance, the woodcuts that accompany the poems in the first edition of *The Shepheardes Calender* (available in the lowtech medium of the *Yale Edition of the Shorter Poetry of Edmund Spenser*) or

68   POETRY IN THE POSTMODERN CLASSROOM

using floor plans of Elizabethan great houses (available in the mid-tech media of photocopying, slides, or videotape) to understand the arrangement of public and private spaces and, by corollary, the generic relation of epic and sonnet. The second stage is the placing of a course on the Web, with syllabi and accompanying illustrative materials (see, for instance, Rebecca Bushnell's interesting Web site for English 30: Introduction to Renaissance Culture at the University of Pennsylvania: www.english.upenn.edu/~bushnell/english-30). The third stage—the one I wish to outline here—is the use of the Web as itself a cultural formation that is inescapably a part of the phenomenological horizon within which Elizabethan poetry is now apprehended and that can be used to make visible the phenomenological horizon within which Elizabethan poetry was created.

A strategy for this third stage requires that a course in Elizabethan poetry not only use the virtual rare materials but also be organized around three concepts: reproductive technology, authorship, and the literary market. In each case, much of the most interesting research over the past two decades in our field prepares us for exactly this reorganization. This organization is perfectly compatible with a conventional use of chronological or generic sequencing as the surface structure of a course and with many of the approaches to specific Elizabethan materials described elsewhere in this volume. What is required pedagogically and supported by new technology is that the issues of reproductive technology, authorship, and the literary market act as the entrance point and continuous substructure to the subject, not as the point of advanced research that we hope to reach at the end of an undergraduate course or hold off for graduate students. And this shift in entrance point and substructure is motivated precisely because these issues form the point of contact between our subject and the present revolution in communications technology.

Reproductive Technology

It is now possible, within a few seconds, to look at a page of a manuscript from around 1405 in which Christine de Pisan shows herself reading from her *Book of the City of Ladies* and helping build the city (Bibliothèque Nationale MS Fr. 607; www.bnf.fr:80/loc/bnf030.jpg), at the beginning of the Wife of Bath's Tale in the Ellesmere manuscript of *The Canterbury Tales* (www.huntington.org/LibraryDiv/ChaucerPict.html), and at printed title pages from sixteenth-century editions of Dante (www.nd.edu/~italnet/Dante). Printed editions of Elizabethan volumes of poetry are less visually exciting than manuscripts and so have been slower to reach the Web archives, but in time they too will be widely available. With these materials accessible in any classroom or dorm room, the otherwise abstract subject of the transition from manuscript to print becomes quickly specific and concrete, if not quite material. Familiar with the frustrating experience of scrolling on screen, students are quick to understand what an incredible technological leap was achieved in the early Middle Ages by the introduction of the codex form for the book. The portability of the codex and the ease with which one could flip around in it are of course traits common to both manuscript and print in the sixteenth century. What surprises students in their first encounters with sixteenth-century printed books, though, is the drabness of these books in comparison with illuminated manuscripts of a century earlier—the very drabness that has discouraged Web designers from using them as decorations for their sites. It is fairly easy to see that the triumph of print initially produced a devisualization of the text, even for a book like *The Shepheardes Calender* that mimics some of the visual qualities of a book of hours. Compare its *Januarye* illustration, for instance, with that of a French book of hours from circa 1525–1550 (Bodleian Library, MS. Douce 135, fol. 2r; www.bodley.ox.ac.uk/imacat/img0025.jpg).

How, one might then ask, does this technological transition affect the specific form of poetry? Of all forms of writing, one might propose, poetry is among those (along with meditational prose) that most resisted this devisualization of the material artifact and, by corollary, of the acts of writing and reading. A natural task, then, is to examine the modes of verbal visualization within the poetic text, especially the use of conceited figures and emphasis throughout the sonnet and other erotic forms on the gaze. From there it is a short step to a consideration of the abashing of the gaze and the defeat of visual pleasure, as in Samuel Daniel's *Delia*:

> All unawares a Goddesse chaste I finde,
> Diana-like, to worke my suddaine change.
> For her no sooner had my view bewrayd,
> But with disdaine to see me in that place:
> With fairest hand, the sweet unkindest maide,
> Castes water-cold disdaine upon my face.
> (poem 5, lines 3–8)

In Daniel's poem, it is the female object of desire who acts as the censor of voyeurism and idolatry. In Pietro Bembo's lyrics, it is the Congregation of the Index that objects, at virtually the same moment Daniel is writing, that Bembo is "mixing holy things with profane" (lcweb.loc.gov/exhibits/vatican/humanism. html; "Congregation of the Index, Censure of Cardinal Pietro Bembo's Poetry").

If the specific materials now easily available help students understand the interaction of the material and metaphoric qualities of a volume of verse, then the structure of the Web itself helps them understand another aspect of the impact of print: its effect on the structure of the poetic anthology. The poetic commonplace book has returned with force as an object of critical attention, thanks to such studies as Arthur F. Marotti's *Manuscript, Print, and the English Renaissance Lyric*. The Web creates an easy way for students to make their own commonplace books simply by browsing, cutting, and pasting at a Web site

70   POETRY IN THE POSTMODERN CLASSROOM

such as Alan Liu's wonderful *The Voice of the Shuttle* (humanitas.ucsb. edu/shuttle/eng-ren.html). Students creating such personal anthologies should be encouraged to rework the material thoroughly—by arranging and juxtaposing, throwing in significant visual material, retitling poems, writing short linking commentaries or fictional biographical vignettes, or even rewriting the poems themselves as it is necessary, useful, or desirable. In short, they should act with all the aggressiveness of Richard Tottel in creating his *Miscellany*, Nicholas Ling in creating *Englands Helicon*, or even Thomas Nashe in gathering together Philip Sidney's and Daniel's sonnets for the first edition of *Astrophil and Stella*. The creation of the anthology is only step 1, though. Step 2 is the writing of a commentary (perhaps comparable to E. K.'s on *The Shepheardes Calender* or Abraham Fraunce's in *The Arcadian Rhetoricke*), in which the student explains his or her selection and arrangement. Step 3 is the leap from criticism into scholarship: the student must now disassemble the anthology and find out where the pieces came from. A list of Web addresses is, at this point, not acceptable, because this exercise is aimed precisely at revealing exactly what the Web had done to the poetry as the latest station in the long train ride of reception and transmission. The student must find out from what edition the Web designer got the text, where that book editor got it, and so on, until there is no place further to go. This means the student will have to leave the Web, go to the library, and spend time decoding the scholarly apparatus at the back of good editions, becoming immersed in the very materials we used to keep them away from until graduate school or later. This tracking of poems back to their first states is often an act of violent recontextualization, since Web texts are often chosen not because of the scholarly rigor with which they have been established but because they are in the public domain. Also, Web texts often exhibit necessary mixtures of modernized and sixteenth-century features, especially graphics (see, e.g., the *Edmund Spenser Home Page*, www.english.cam.ac.uk/spenser/main.htm).

The exercise gives the student the need to uncover the centuries of scholarship that have been swept away by postmodern technology, and in the process the student must confront the long history of reproductive technologies: from manuscript to print to reprint to scholarly edition to school anthology to low-cost paperback to Web. The existence of multiple early texts for the poem (e.g., anything by Michael Drayton) offers students an immediate introduction to the instability of the text. Different versions of the text confront the student with its material history and present specific data around which the student can organize ideas about the history of criticism and the ideology of authorship. And, I find, a good number of students find it a refreshingly concrete project to balance out the heady, if vaporous, joys of criticism.

Authorship

The project of creating a Web commonplace book inevitably assaults received concepts of authorship held by students weaned on modern literature (or rati-

Clark Hulse   71

fies the received concepts of decentered authorship held by their more thoroughly postmodern classmates). It is a simple matter to extend that assault by an exercise in rewriting loosely modeled on Roger Ascham's scheme of double translation. Play a game of Web phone: pass an Elizabethan poem around by e-mail, requiring each student to rewrite a part of it. Then compare the multiple states of the poem with the original. More usefully, compare them with a poem that has multiple text versions: sonnets by Daniel or Drayton are again especially good here. Or compare them with famous instances of poetic answering: Marlowe's "The Passionate Shepherd to His Love," Ralegh's "The Nymph's Reply to the Shepherd," and Donne's "The Bait."

Then ask the central question, who is "author" of each poem or each state, and what does it mean to be "author"? (If the students are simultaneously reading any of the voluminous and wonderful criticism on this subject, from Michel Foucault to Louis Montrose, Richard Helgerson, and David Lee Miller, so much the better.) Link this question back to the issue of reproductive technology: How does the mode of reproduction (in a sonnet sequence, a miscellany, a modern anthology) alter the state of authorship? How do these named authors, so valiantly defined in biographical terms by the editors of modern editions and anthologies, relate to the voices in the poems, voices that sometimes are embedded in very specific social situations and at other times float free of person and embed themselves in their mode of reproduction, masking and revealing the ideology of that mode (especially insofar as the technology of reproduction acts also as a technology of distinction by gender or class).

Literary Market

By now, students should be familiar, even comfortable, with the multiplicative power of Elizabethan poetry, its almost viral ability to inhabit whatever cell will play host to it. It is possible, therefore, to shift the focus to the other side of the equation—from writers to readers. The variability of the text and multiple incarnations of the author can be seen as products not only of reproductive technologies and authorial desires but of the desires of readers, including themselves. Who, at each station of the textual train, has wanted it, who has bought it, and what did they pay for it? (Students—at least my students—are savvy consumers and intuitively understand the various meanings of "pay.") While obviously we don't have sales figures for the sixteenth century, title pages act as interesting indexes of how printers thought their market operated. Each is a kind of advertisement for the work.

Compare, for instance, the title pages of *The Countesse of Pembrokes Arcadia* (1593) with the first printing of the combined Marlowe-Chapman *Hero and Leander* (1598). (Neither title page is, to my knowledge, available yet on the Web, but the low-tech medium of photocopying will suffice.) The Sidney title page (reproduced and analyzed by Margery Corbett and R. W. Lightbown in *The Comely Frontispiece* [58–66]) has family heraldic devices at the top and an

72 POETRY IN THE POSTMODERN CLASSROOM

emblem at the bottom. On the sides are a shepherd and an Amazon, who read-ers will learn are the heroic princes Musidorus and Pyrocles. The elements of the page are tied together with fanciful Italianate strapwork. The effect of the whole is elevated and artful, an effect validated by the leading position of the countess of Pembroke's name as patron of the volume. The genre of pastoral is visually established in the same terms that Sidney uses to describe it in *Astrophil*, "hid-ing royal blood full oft in rural vein" (sonnet 6, line 8). The title page defines the volume as a zone of artistic and class mystery, inviting the reader, in return for the purchase price, to sit at the foot of the table for the poetic feast and glimpse some of its inner significance, though its full import may be disguised.

The *Hero and Leander* title page and preface advertise a contrasting system of inclusion and exclusion. Its motto ("ut nectar, ingenium") and device suggest a hierarchy not of class but of intellect alone. If poetry is again a form of prop-erty, it is a property that establishes a system of inheritance based not on blood but on wit, as Edward Blunt, in his dedication to Thomas Walsingham, talks of the dead Marlowe's "intellectual will," which must be executed by Blunt, Wals-ingham, and Chapman (Marlowe 188). A buyer-reader might, again, be as much shut out as brought in by such rhetorical positioning, but the means of access lie solely in the acts of buying and of reading. What was "begun by *Christopher Marloe*" and in 1598 "finished by *George Chapman*" is implicitly reopened in the late twentieth century to be refinished by our own "intellectual will."

Coda 1: The Student's Tale

The use of the technological resources of the postmodern classroom—espe-cially when it is done with attention to the postmodern aesthetic embedded in that classroom—can help authorize and validate students' responses to the unusual and particular way that they encounter Elizabethan poetry. The poetry is audible primarily as a voice straining to reach students through tiny cracks in a cultural wall: a voice crying faintly under the rubble of Western civilization. This literature does not seem immediately recognizable to them as a central component of mainstream culture or of the historical legacy that has shaped their lives. That legacy is American, capitalist, and postnuclear and has been transmitted by film and television. Yet at least at the urban public university where I teach, students are willing to like Elizabethan poetry: it is neat, weird, different, a graceful and sometimes terrifying message from a distant time and place, a little like a message from space aliens. They are prepared to believe that it is very, very beautiful, and they are prepared to recognize that inscribed within it are recognizable traces of modern forms of oppression, but on neither score are they likely to embrace it as *their* heritage.

Coda 2: The Instructor's Tale

Much of the best scholarship on Elizabethan poetry since the 1970s has de-fined itself by opposition to the New Criticism, specifically in opposition to its claims for the autonomy of the text and for the authority of author and interpreter. Ironically, though, the New Criticism—whatever the conscious ideology of some of its creators—was wondrously democratic as a teaching method. Coinciding with the GI Bill and the rise of the cheap paperback, it made early modern poetry—especially of the early seventeenth century, but of the sixteenth century as well—not only available but seemingly comprehensible to an audience of university undergraduates of unprecedented size. Students held in their brains and hands a way of reading these poems, and though the professor still handed out the grades, the student could compete in spinning out new readings on a field that was tilting toward level.

By an equal irony, cultural and historical criticism, as classroom methods, threaten to work against the democratization of the classroom, despite the conscious democratic ideals of those (including myself) who profess them. They raise the ante of knowledge—one must know more oneself before one can say anything, before one can begin to "read" well, or else one must depend on the professor to formulate, digest, make relevant that knowledge of the past and contextualize the poetic object within it. Postmodern representations of Elizabethan poetic texts of the kind I have described offer to resist that reestablishment of professorial authority inherent in cultural and historical criticism. Not that the Web is, as some claim, nonhierarchical or postideological. (It seems, if anything, to be quite the opposite.) Rather, because the Web allows students to manipulate the poetry (as New Criticism allowed them to) in a context over which the professor does not have a greater claim, it allows for a shared ownership of the material, a reproduction of the poetry within the student that may not necessitate the reproduction there of the professorial ego as well.

But if I am right that the postmodern classroom may allow students to reproduce Elizabethan poetry in their own interest, there is also a specific, pragmatic, and material way in which, by teaching Elizabethan poetry, we may reproduce it in our interest. Much of what I have referred to in this article is already available on the Web, but a great deal is not yet available. It will not become available for free. Someone will have to pay to photograph all those pages, to run them through the scanners, to put in the links and add the routers to the mainframes to handle all the traffic from all our students. Economically, the easiest way for this to happen may be through private vendors, who then tax us—poor scholars, poor teachers, and poor students—for the use of what used to be available free in the library. In the process, the concept of fair use, on which humanistic scholarship and teaching thrive, is squeezed out of the new marketplace.

By the simple act of teaching, we resist this eventuality in two ways. First, each time we use the materials that are already on the Web, we establish and reinforce fair use practices for this new medium analogous to those long established for the medium of print. These established practices then act as a collective legal defense of the sphere of learning as a sphere of public interest. Second, by using the existing materials and desiring and demanding more, we

74   POETRY IN THE POSTMODERN CLASSROOM

create a market for online Elizabethan poetry, a market that libraries and museums then serve by putting more materials on the Web for our use. By bringing the market into existence, we strengthen the hand of libraries and museums with their trustees and with granting agencies when they ask for the money to serve our market, and they, by making the material available, strengthen our hand with university administrations when we ask for money to buy access to them. We create in this new sphere a new space for the past, a new space for poetry, a new space for contemplation, side by side with porn sites and Kai's Power Goo, in the babel of postmodern culture.

Coda 3: The Market's Tale

Technological restructuring acts in the service of economic restructuring. More than one administrator, legislator, or trustee in the land of higher education dreams of the economies of distant learning. They dream that the humanities, which already run for next to nothing and yet generate big tuition revenues, can be made even cheaper with a little capital spending and a sharp reduction in labor costs (this means you). But many economists argue that the late 1980s and early 1990s game of radical downsizing is now largely finished. The key to sustained economic growth now lies in productivity increases by what is already the most productive labor force in the world.

New technology, including classroom technology, means nothing—or worse than nothing—without a smart teacher using it. For technology ultimately rests on techne (skill, craft, knowledge of how to do things), and unlike those who simply wield a new electronic technology, we (the scholars of Elizabethan literature) wield the previous mental technologies: rhetoric, dialectic, disciplinarity, textual exegesis, and cultural analysis. By adding electronic technology to these other technologies we become more productive. To put it crudely, we add value to the product. We have a simple task before us: to demonstrate by the skillful use of the machinery that machines don't teach, we do. The best way to do this is through the artful use of multimedia in preparation for the moment when we turn the machine off and, in the eerie hush that follows, begin the discussion. In that space emerges the ultimate technology for teaching: the dialogue. In whatever form, Socratic or sophistic, small group or large, sustained or intermittent, it is our real inheritance and our real legacy.

The Origins and Art of
Versification in Early Modern English

Susanne Woods

Elizabethan poetry, which established the principal elements of English versification for at least three centuries, provides an excellent site for teaching students about the use of meter and rhythm in English verse. Conversely, Elizabethan poetry becomes more alive when students learn to hear the interaction of meter and rhythm to which the poets themselves paid such careful attention.

I offer here one way I have found useful in introducing students to the subject of English verse and to the genius of the Elizabethan lyric poets who solved the long-standing problem of how to make an art of versification out of the linguistic hybrid that is modern English. I begin with some definitions and a brief history of the formal traditions that lie behind poetry in early modern English, use a few key comments from George Gascoigne's 1575 "Certayne Notes of Instruction on the Making of Verse or Rime in English" (1575) to situate the issues in Elizabethan times, and conclude by scanning a sonnet using concepts and definitions that represent a consensus of modern thinking about how verse moves through time. My object is to show students that scanning a poem is a useful way to understand rhetorical emphases and nuances of tone, to "hear" the voice of the poet.

Philip Sidney was quick to note that verse is not essential to his definition of poetry (as fiction), but that it is an "ornament" particularly suitable to poetry (*Defense* 27). In modern parlance, poets write in verses, or lines, to create and control the pleasures of seriotemporal rhythms common to music and language. For readers to hear those rhythms in their full subtlety, to reenact the voice of the utterance that a poem imitates (B. H. Smith, *Poetic Closure* 5), they need to understand something of what John Hollander has called "the metrical frame" (*Vision* 135).

I define *meter* as the "measure of a line of verse" and *rhythm* as "the movement of a line of verse." Meter is the abstract pattern and measurement of notable phonemic features of a particular language. Rhythm is the way in which a particular line of language is heard in relation to the meter that underlies it. While the first two lines of *Astrophil and Stella*, sonnet 31, are both what we call iambic pentameter, the way in which specific language embodies that meter makes for very different rhythmic movements. The first line is made up of monosyllabic words and several low back vowels—the "ow," long "o," and "oo" articulated through the whole effort of the mouth. The second line moves somewhat more quickly, with a trisyllabic word and more of what we usually call "short" vowels:

> With how sad steps, o Moone, thou climb'st the skies,
> How silently, and with how wan a face.   (180)

76   ORIGINS AND ART OF VERSIFICATION

The meter of these lines is exactly the same: a derivable set of syllabic pairs in which the second syllable is relatively more stressed than the first. This is a simple, easy, and objective derivation, the model with and against which the actual language of the line articulates its rhythm. Rhythm is more subjective, depending on how any given individual would actually say the line. Understanding meter will help any reader speak the rhythm with attention to the poet's intention and artistry, but no sophisticated reader of poetry enacts a line as if the rhythm consisted of merely the two levels of syllabic stress derivable as the meter ("With HOW sad STEPS o MOON thou CLIMB'ST the SKIES").

Some of the mystery of meter and rhythm disappears when we put English verse into a broader picture. Meter is ubiquitous in language, whether it stems from the mnemonic needs of oral narrative, the incantations of magic and religion, or the verbal complement to music, but metrical systems vary from language to language. Greek poetry took conventions of "long" and "short" syllables ("long" defined by the presence of a long vowel or a short vowel followed by two or more consonants), patterned them in relation to each other, and established the notion of the metrical "foot," or group of syllables of certain types (A. Cole in Wimsatt 66–88). Defining the kind and measuring the number of feet became codified as the art of versification in Latin as well as Greek and has provided the terminology and model for describing English verse. Since English verse does not have clear conventions of long and short syllables, the terminology has been translated to describe syllables that are stressed (or accented) relative to one another. The English iambic pentameter of the Sidney lines represents five pairs of syllables whose relation is unstressed-stressed, rather than short-long.

Accentual-syllabic poetry in modern English was invented in the sixteenth century by combining two earlier, local traditions: Old English accentual alliterative verse and romance rhymed syllabic verse from the French-speaking medieval English court. The former measured the number of heavily accented syllables, connecting them within and across half-lines by means of alliteration. So the first few lines of the "Battle of Brunanburh" (c. 937) are careful to connect metrically accented syllables across the caesura, or mid-line pause, by means of alliteration. (By convention, syllables beginning with any vowel alliterate with other syllables beginning with a vowel.)

> /   /   /   /
> Her **Ae**thelstan cing,   **eo**rla drihten
> /   /   /   /
> **b**eorna **b**eagiffa,   and his **b**rothor eac
> /   /   /   /
> **Ea**dmund **ae**theling,   **ea**ldorlangne tir
> /   /   /   /
> ge**s**logan aet **s**ake   **s**weorda ecggum
>
> embe Brunanburh [. . .].   (lines 1–5; Anderson and Williams 253)

In this year Aethelstan the king, lord of earls
son of the ring-giver, and his brother also
Edmund the prince, lifelong glory
won at battle by sword edges
around Brunanburh [. . .] (my trans.)

Romance syllabic verse, by contrast, combined a more precise syllable count
with conventions of elision (counting two syllables as one), other techniques for
varying the count, and rhyme (Woods, *Natural Emphasis* 37–38, 125; Flescher
in Wimsatt 181–83). So a famous early-thirteenth-century reverdi, or spring
song, offers (newly in English) stanzas on the model of the French court lyric,
with refrain and rhyme, and syllables set into regular patterns:

Sumer is icumen in,
Lhude sing cuccu!
Groweth sed and bloweth men
And springth the wde nu.
Sing cuccu!

Awe bleteth after lomb,
Lhouth after calve cu,
Bulluc sterteth, bucke verteth.
Murie sing cuccu!
Cuccu, cuccu,
Wel singes thus cuccu.
Ne swik thus never nu!

Sing cuccu nu, Sing cuccu!
Sing cuccu, Sing cuccu nu!
                    (Haskell 343)

While syllabic verse with clear accentual patterning was long established
in the English lyric by the sixteenth century and Chaucer had written some-
thing that would look to later centuries like iambic pentameter, evidence
from Henrician courtly manuscripts suggests that the sixteenth century began
with some confusion over how to domesticate the French and Italian hen-
decasyllabic line (Woods, *Natural Emphasis* 69–103; Hardison, *Prosody*
16–19). This appears to have been a compound of the desire to imitate Con-
tinental sonneteering and the search for an appropriate English heroic line
(which led, among other things, to the misguided fad for poulter's measure,
as if it could be the stately long line comparable to Latin hexameters). By the
end of the century the longer accentual-syllabic line had become the primary
vehicle for lyric and dramatic, as well as narrative poetry, and English verse
had become graceful enough to tolerate experimentation with classical
meters, which (in Thomas Campion, though not in Gabriel Harvey) expanded

78 ORIGINS AND ART OF VERSIFICATION

the range of phonetic nuance that could vary rhythms in lines still completely metrical (Attridge 173–87).

Gascoigne's "Certayne Notes" provides a clear and still useful discussion of English accentual-syllabic verse, and his fourth point is a summary of good Elizabethan metrical practice (G. Smith 1: 49–51). I find it useful to discuss this section of the treatise with my students, asking what they think Gascoigne means when he says "to place every worde in his natural *Emphasis* or sound," and I spend some time with his example, "I understand your meanying by your eye" which he opposes to "Your meaning I understand by your eye" (1: 51). Although Gascoigne's terminology is slightly different from what we commonly use today, it is clear that he finds the second example unmetrical, suggesting (as he points out) that to fit the iambic movement of the line "understand" would have to be wrenched from its normal pronunciation ("unDERstand").

Time spent with Gascoigne's "Certayne Notes" serves two purposes. It provides a clear, step-by-step explanation of the iambic movement that underlies the Elizabethan lyric, and it answers the common student question whether the poets themselves actually paid attention to such things. To know that they did is helpful when we turn to scansion. If there are variations in the way a poet places the "natural *Emphasis*" relative to the meter of the poem, we may be looking at a special emphasis that affects meaning, or at the very least we may use those tensions between meter and speaking rhythm to hear better the way the poet is moving language through time.

Like most formal constructions, meter creates an expectation that the pattern will continue. A poet controls the feeling a poem conveys in part by manipulating those expectations, either fulfilling or surprising them. When we read the first line or two of a poem, we derive the pattern that we expect will recur, and we become attuned to variations on that pattern. Further, since meter itself is an abstract set of syllabic relations (in an iamb, a disyllabic relation of relatively unstressed followed by relatively stressed), concrete language embodies every metrical line somewhat differently.

I have found two sonnets particularly helpful in showing students something of how the interaction between metrical expectation and the fulfilling language affects mood and meaning: Shakespeare's "When to the sessions of sweet silent thought" (sonnet 30) and Sidney's "Leave me o Love, which reachest but to dust" (in *Poems*; *Certain Sonnets*, sonnet 32). In each case I scan and discuss the lines after the following injunctions: meter is derived foot by foot, rhythm in relation to the whole line.

To derive the meter, I ask my students first to listen for the pattern that emerges from reading a stanza out loud. Is it generally disyllabic or trisyllabic? In the Elizabethan lyric, it is almost always disyllabic at base. We then divide each line into pairs of syllables, starting from the right (and on the alert for the uncounted final syllable of a feminine ending, in which case the first group has three syllables, the rest two). Within each foot, we decide which syllable is relatively more stressed. (I do this second step from right to left as well, to emphasize the act of abstraction.) I then ask them to describe the predominant kind of feet, or syllabic groups or pairs in the line, and their number:

```
      /  x   x   /   x   /   x   /   x      /
When to | the se | ssions of | sweet si | lent thought
  x  /    x  /  x  /     x   /    x      /
I sum | mon up | remem | brance of | things past
```

For purposes of this mechanical scansion, I assume that between any two syllables, one will be relatively more stressed than the other; I leave "pyrrhic" or "spondaic" feet to quantitative meters. What emerges in virtually all Elizabethan poetry is an iambic norm, here a pentameter with an initial trochee in the first line. This is only a crude pattern, but it exercises a pull on how we read the line.

To describe the actual movement of the line, its rhythm, we need a more subtle instrument than the two levels of stress implied by this metrical abstraction. There are a number of potential instruments, including the phonemic alphabet and all the associations of alliteration, assonance, and consonance it suggests, but for a simpler way to begin looking at the interaction between meter and speech patterns, I assume four levels of easily discernible stress in normal English speech. This is a debatable but useful notion originally posited in 1951 by H. L. Trager and G. H. Smith. The tensions between metrical abstraction and fulfilling language—between what the pattern leads us to expect and the actual sounds and words spoken in the context of that pattern— are what create the dynamic movement of a line of verse. An impressionistic reader of this first line of Shakespeare's sonnet might say that the language moves more quickly in the middle of the line, slowing down to emphasize the contemplative "thought" at the end. A scansion that juxtaposes four levels of stress against the derivable meter shows more clearly how this is so (1 = most stressed):

```
When to | the se | ssions of | sweet si | lent thought
  2   4    3   1    4   3     2   1    4     1
```

The entire poem is an exercise in how phonemic features move through time and affect meaning. The predominant slow pace of long vowels, in particular the low back vowels of "with old woes" (line 4), "woe to woe tell o'er" (line 10), and "fore-bemoaned moan" (line 11), comes to a wonderfully appropriate and abrupt "end," with its short vowel and defining dental consonant and its happy rhyme with "friend":

But if the while I think on thee, dear friend,
All losses are restor'd and sorrows end.

80 ORIGINS AND ART OF VERSIFICATION

How meter and speaking rhythms interact to affect pace and meaning is even clearer with the Sidney sonnet, which begins

```
    /   x   x   /   x   /   x  /  x  /
Leave me | o Love, | which reach | est but | to dust
  1   3   2   1   3   1   4  3  4  1

    x   /   x   /   x  /  x  /  x   /
And thou | my mind | aspire | to high | er things.
  4   2   3   1   4 2   3 1  4   2
```

The relatively heavy stresses that launch the first line make the effort at renunciation seem emphatic, while the pull of the stressed position on the normally unstressed "but" marks the contrast between earthly passion and the immortal love to which the speaker aspires.

A similar and even more telling contrast occurs at line 9, the turn into the sestet:

```
    x   /   x   /   /?  x?  /?  x?  x   /
O take | fast hold, | let that | light be | thy guide
```

Because the rest of the poem is iambic, the apparent shift to trochees at the third and fourth feet of this line comes as a wrench and forces a second look at the line. A rereading, trusting in the iambic pattern, gives the line emphatic stress that again forces the contrast between the burning light of earthly love and the beacon light of divine revelation:

```
    x   /   x   /   x  /  x  /  x   /
O take | fast hold, | let that | light be | thy guide
  3   1   2   1   3  1  3  2  3   1
```

While every word is in its "natural *Emphasis*," the normal phrasing of "let that light be" is remolded both by the expectations created from eight previous lines of iambic meter and by the sense of the poem. The poet reenacts the wrenching difficulty of renunciation, and the very energy of the line calls into question the speaker's ability to achieve the renunciation he claims to desire.

Elizabethan poets were the first masters of accentual-syllabic English meters. They not only codified a system for patterning features normal to the spoken language but also tested the uses and limits of tension between those patterns and the various rhythms of the speaking voice. Working through the basic elements of that system will not explain fully the poet's art, but it will give students some sense of what it meant to be, in Sidney's term, a "maker" of Elizabethan poetry.

From Medieval to Tudor Lyric:
Familiarizing Rhetoric

Judith H. Anderson

When I introduce the Tudor lyric, especially the sonnet, to undergraduates in a survey, I have found its highly artificial rhetoric a particular challenge to them. The problem isn't simply that the mode of expression in the sonnet seems alien to them but rather that they aren't even sure why it does, let alone sure how to engage it. The very idea of "rhetoric," except as something vaguely negative and superficial, is unfamiliar to them. Simply to highlight the fact and nature of rhetoric, I therefore employ a comparison between the selection of medieval lyrics offered in *The Norton Anthology of English Literature*, volume 1, and sonnets by Wyatt and Surrey, the two founders of the Tudor lyric tradition. These poets, variously translating and re-creating Petrarchan poems and often glancing at Chaucerian models, serve as a prologue to their successors the Elizabethans in whose writing such roots are present but often less prominent.

Before looking directly at medieval and Tudor lyrics, however, I've found it effective to examine and thus reinforce statements in the introductions to relevant sections in *The Norton Anthology*, which are generally typical of such material. The introduction to the medieval lyric first observes a number of ancient genres, mainly French, to which the lyrics selected belong, and notes the combination of conventionality yet apparent freshness of sentiment in the English lyrics; overwhelmingly, it then stresses the "unself-consciousness and immediacy" of these lyrics, their "naturalness," and their "simplicity" (286–87). Even a glance at the lyrics themselves—for example, "Alison," "Western Wind," "I Have a Young Sister," "Sunset on Calvary," "I Sing of a Maiden," "Adam Lay Bound"—is enough to confirm these impressions, although I postpone this glance, relying on the students' own previously assigned reading of the lyrics to enable their provisional assent.

Instead, seeking a sharp contrast (and risking distortion), I ask them to turn to a section describing "poetic conventions, genres, modes" (406–09) in the general introduction to the sixteenth century, which, like that to the medieval lyric, they have already read. This section, much longer than the one on the medieval lyric, treats the conspicuous concern of the Tudor period with cultural coding and formal structure—with modes like pastoral, satire, and lyric and with forms like the epigram, sonnet, complaint, epic, heroical epistle, epyllion, and so on. Not surprisingly, terms such as "convention," "formal structure," "verse pattern," "genre," and "mode" recur like refrains that are embedded in the expansive paragraphs conveying aesthetic technology. The abiding impact of the section is precisely the Renaissance concern with the character and content of all sorts of form—from the minutiae of blank verse and conceit to the larger contours of pastoral and epic. This is a concern historically attested, of course, in the humanist movement generally and specifically in treatise after

82   FROM MEDIEVAL TO TUDOR LYRIC

treatise on rhetoric. To my reader I would emphasize that, while I could easily tell the students what the anthology sections address, I have found the point I'm trying to make about self-conscious artifice so unfamiliar—indeed, so abstract—to them that the printed word helps considerably to give it substance. I have even found it useful to ask them, flipping pages back and forth from the medieval lyrics to Wyatt's, to notice the difference in their typographical effects—the fact that Wyatt's are simply denser on the page typographically—and to speculate about the implications of such difference.

My next move is to read aloud a few selections from the medieval lyrics and then, again seeking contrast, to read Wyatt's sonnet "My galley charged with forgetfulness." (Students could also do these readings if they have been asked to practice in advance; a spontaneous but halting, unrythmic reading would obscure the contrast, however.) Before reading, I ask the students to listen for differences—any they can hear—between the medieval lyrics and Wyatt's. The first of the medieval poems I read in full is "I Sing of a Maiden," whose understated repetition of a natural occurrence, the falling of dew, delicately suggests the wonder of Incarnation, as in its central stanzas:

> He cam also stille
>   Ther his moder was
> As dewe in Aprille
>   That falleth on the gras.
>
> He cam also stille
>   To his modres bowr
> As dewe in Aprille
>   That falleth on the flowr.   (290–91)[1]

After a brief discussion of the effect of this lyric and the reasons for it, I normally read the first two stanzas of "Alison" in order to have a medieval instance of the love complaint on the table. In isolation, the second stanza carries memories of "hende Nicholas" in Chaucer's Miller's Tale, which the students have earlier read:

> On hew hire heer is fair ynough,
> Hire browe browne, hire yë blake;
> With lossum cheere heo on me lough;
> With middel smal and well ymake.
> But heo me wolle to hire take
> For to been hire owen make
> Longe to liven ichulle forsake,
>   And feye fallen adown.
>   An hendy hap ich habbe yhent,
> Ichoot from hevene it is me sent:

From alle wommen my love is lent,
And light on Alisoun.   (287–88)

Many of the medieval lyrics, such as "Alison," with its four-line refrain following each stanza, are songlike and invite musical accompaniment, and perhaps they should be compared with a Tudor song like Wyatt's "Blame Not My Lute." But given the prominence, if not dominance, of the sonnet, which is generally a lyric form ill-suited to music, in the second half of the sixteenth century, I'm willing—again, risking oversimplification in the interest of dramatic contrast—to move quickly from "Alison" to a reading of Wyatt's "My galley charged with forgetfulness" (440–41).

Now the real discussion of the difference between typical medieval lyrics and a Renaissance sonnet begins, initially with my asking the students for their impressions of "My galley," which often prove lively and interesting. They are likely to notice the elaboration of Wyatt's continued metaphor of a ship, his introspection, the complexity of his syntax and rhythm and their inappropriatenesss for singing, and his studied or crafted, artificial mode of expression. Usually it's possible, following the lead of their insight, also to launch a definition of rhetoric as argument and in this poem also as conceit—at this point a definition that is meaningful, indeed, virtually visible to them. In comparison with the medieval lyrics, Wyatt's poem is a sustained and structured exposition of a situation rather than a celebration or commemoration of one that seems spontaneously additive. As a conceit—the ship steered by love, its oars self-paining thoughts and its sails torn by fearful sighs—it consists of a conceptualized parallel that asks for reasoned interpretation as well as and, perhaps, before emotional engagement.

Once we have talked about general impressions, with some issues likely left provisionally hanging, we proceed to a hands-on, up-for-grabs discussion of Wyatt's sonnet, and, in effect, consider the function of its form, both in the large sense and in terms of stylistic minutiae. Many of the students I meet at the survey (sophomore) level report having had no experience with poetry, let alone with sonnets. We therefore start with basic questions: What is the situation described? What's on the speaker's mind? What sort of thing is "my galley"? Who is "my lord"? What sort of condition or attitude does line 5—"And every oar a thought in readiness"—describe? Where is this happening? What are the stars in line 12, and what is the port or goal the speaker refers to in line 14?

I should note that the last two times I tried some version of these questions, most students recognized that "My galley" is a love poem, but several bright and voluble ones were persuaded that "my lord" was God, and one well-read interpreter even wanted to identify "my lord" with a patron. (Try reading the sonnet again, forgetting your historicized assumption that "my lord" is Love or Cupid and that the stars of line 12 are the eyes of the lady. Lacking such special knowledge, the students who sensed the sonnet's concern with erotic love

84 FROM MEDIEVAL TO TUDOR LYRIC

were not only unable to dissuade those clinging to a religious reading but actually became less secure in their own perceptions.) Since this sonnet by Wyatt was the first of its type the students had encountered in the course, instead of enforcing my reading (and thereby implying their inability to cope with sonnet conventions), I decided to leave the question about the identity of "my lord" hanging, promising to return to it later. Once we had read Sidney's many sonnets about Stella's eyes and other references to Lord Cupid, I devoted another class to Wyatt's "My galley," passing out copies of its Petrarchan original as well as the Petrarchan originals of several Elizabethan sonnets we had read. This class provided a fine opportunity to talk about the force of convention in a credible and persuasive way, since our original reading had been, so to speak, blind to it, and now, informed by the models, the identity of "my lord" and the referent of the guiding stars were clear.

In concluding, I would stress the necessity of dealing in some way with the rhetoric of Tudor writing, whether in lyric, as here, or in another form. Unless it is dealt with directly and as a functional mode of expression, it presents an insuperable obstacle to a historicized understanding and appreciation. Understood, it actually engages students' interest.

NOTE

[1]All poetry quotations in this essay are from *The Norton Anthology of English Literature*.

Framing the Authentic Petrarch:
From the *Rime sparse* to *Astrophil and Stella*
William J. Kennedy

The legacy of Francesco Petrarch (1304–74) will surface early in any discussion of sixteenth-century English poetry. You could routinely explain the form of his sonnet, its topic of unrequited love, and the rhetorical conventions of oxymoron, paronomasia, and catachresis associated with it. But you could also delve deeper into the simultaneous strangeness and immediacy of Petrarch's verse for Elizabethan culture; its tensions and strains; and the hybridity of ancient, medieval, and early modern forms fused in it. To the sixteenth century there was not one Petrarch but many, and Petrarchism hardly referred to a single, stable set of literary practices. This diversity raises the intriguing question of cultural otherness and its absorption into mainstream practices. How and why did such a foreign commodity attract Elizabethan consumers, and what might we understand about it?

Commentaries framing the *Rime sparse* in early printed editions suggest various competing sixteenth-century approaches to Petrarch's poetry (see Richardson; Kennedy, *Authorizing* 25–81). Students may be fascinated to learn that these apparently conventional and, to them at any rate, indistinguishable amatory poems generated so many controversial and discordant interpretations about politics, religion, moral responsibility, gender relations, and social class. The earliest commentators, such as Antonio da Tempo (c. 1420s), Francesco Filelfo in 1448, and Hieronimo Squarzafico in 1484, associate Petrarch (who had lived most of his life near Avignon in southern France) with the ideology of northern Italian despotic patrons (his major supporters after 1353) rather than that of Republican Florence (the place of his father's birth). Later ones, such as Alessandro Vellutello (whose popular edition in 1525 rearranged the order of poems to parallel events in the poet's biography), Giovanni Gesualdo in 1533, Sylvano da Venafro in 1533, and Bernardino Daniello in 1541, focus on Petrarch's rhetorical techniques, his Castiglione-style courtly manners, and his debts to ancient classical texts. A final group that includes Fausto da Longiano in 1532, Antonio Brucioli in 1548, and Ludovico Castelvetro in 1582 claims for Petrarch an emergent Protestantism by associating his ideals with those of Lutheran and Calvinist reform and religious heterodoxy.

From this welter of interpretations emerges a Renaissance Petrarch who could be anything and everything to his readers. Early commentators thought him the greatest of Italian authors, greater even than Dante, whose vulgarity displeased sixteenth-century critics. But Petrarch was hardly a typical Italian poet. His very language would have sounded strange to Italian ears because it is a wholly artificial literary composite of old Tuscan and literary Sicilian forms (derived from the *stil novisti* and earlier court poets), along with classical

86   FRAMING THE AUTHENTIC PETRARCH

archaisms, troubadour Provencalisms, and inventive neologisms (see Hainsworth; T. M. Greene, *Light* 81–146). You could nonetheless mention that in *Prose della volgar lingua* ("Discourse about the Vernacular," 1525) Pietro Bembo went so far as to designate a single line from sonnet 303 as the supreme touchstone for Italian verse: "Fior, frondi, erbe, ombre, antri, onde, aure soavi" (Bembo 98; "Flowers, leaves, grass, shadows, caves, waves, gentle breezes"). Its multiple elisions, consonantal and vocalic variety, and rhythmic pungency exemplify the oral-aural qualities for which later poets and musicians prized Petrarch. (For students who know Spanish you can cite the phonic complexity of Garcilaso de la Vega's "En tanto que de rosa y azucena" [Rivers 37]; for those who know French, cite Ronsard's "Ah! je voudrais, richement jaunissant" [Brereton 53]). If you plan to discuss some Elizabethan ballads and songbooks, you could point out that in mid-sixteenth-century Venice the international madrigal style of such émigré composers as Adrian Willaert and Cipriano de Rore exploits these aural features, anticipating the English styles of William Byrd, Thomas Morley, and Orlando Gibbons. (CD recordings by the Huelgas Ensemble and The King's Singers exemplify Italian and English styles respectively; for development see Feldman.)

You should certainly emphasize that Petrarch's composite language lends itself to rich wordplay. *Laura*, for example, signifies the beloved Laura, who was, despite the impression that Petrarch gives of her virginal aloofness, a married woman with eleven children, but the word also evokes "laurel leaf or tree," *l'aura* ("the breeze" or "breath of wind," "gold," "aura"), or all these things at once, as in sonnets 5, 90, 196–98, 246, 327, and 356. The figure of the laurel in turn suggests poetic victory, but it also evokes the crown of imperial glory in ancient Rome and hence the patrimony of Roman culture in modern Italy. Petrarch's love, personified as Amor, palindromically evokes Roma, the earthly focus of his worldly desires. On the basis of these effects you could explain that commentators assigned to sonnet 27 and canzoni 28, 53, and 128 ("Italia mia") a patriotic significance that affirms the poet's Italian identity and to the "Babylonian" sonnets 136–38 a political awareness that criticizes abuses of the Avignon papacy (see Mazzotta; Mann). You could also point out that, far from being irrelevant to English readers, these readings fueled English protonational Protestant sentiments. Jan van der Noot's *Theatre for Worldlings* (1569), for example, includes a translation of canzone 323 (attributed to the young Edmund Spenser) that patriotically redirects Petrarch's apocalyptic vision against unreformed Roman Catholicism.

To explore Petrarch's diversity you could compare different translations of and modern commentary on his poems. It might be good to start before the Elizabethan period with Wyatt's "The long love that in my thought doth harbour" and Surrey's "Love that doth raine and live within my thought," both of which translate Petrarch's sonnet 140, "Amor, che nel penser mio vive et regna" ("Love, who lives and reigns in my thought"), though each from a different sociocultural perspective (for Surrey, see E. Jones's edition of Henry Howard). Wyatt's brash and adventurous style ("Be reined by reason, shame, and reverence") contrasts with Surrey's elegant, aristocratic circumlocutions ("With shamfast looke to shadoo and refrayne"). Modern translations by Robert M. Durling (1976), James Wyatt Cook (1996), and Mark Musa (1996), fine as they are, blur Petrarch's syntactic density in such lines as "e vol che 'l gran desio, l'accesa spense, / ragion, vergogna, et reverenza affrene" ("and she wishes that my great desire, my kindled hope, reason, shame, and reverence might rein in"; trans. mine), where the transposed word order and archaic subjunctive *affrene* erase usual grammatical markers (see Kennedy, *Authorizing* 5–11; Roche, *Petrarch* 77–89).

To illustrate divergent modern commentaries, you could examine footnotes in widely used modern anthologies. In glossing Wyatt's "Whoso list to hunt," based on Petrarch's sonnet 190, Richard S. Sylvester (131) and David Norbrook and H. Z. Woudhuysen (182) evoke the scriptural subtext of *noli me tangere* ("touch me not") (John 20.17), which earlier commentators had cited to allegorize the deer as the Church of Rome. Both evoke biographical associations of the deer with Anne Boleyn, but neither speculates about potentially discordant linkages of these figures with Rome and the English court. Does Wyatt's translation allegorize church-state relations? Or does it rather represent the poet's dangerous liaison with the king's mistress? R. A. Rebholz explores such ambiguities in his scholarly edition (343–44). Students may judge these associations alien and odd for an amatory poem, but the more you emphasize them, the more you'll be evoking the aberrant (students might say *whacked*) ways in which the sixteenth century actually read Petrarch.

For Surrey's "The soote season," based on Petrarch's sonnet 310, Sylvester (190) notes how the poet formally adapts Petrarch's figures to an English landscape by incorporating "turtle," "hed," "pale," and "brake," while Woudhuysen (Norbrook and Woudhuysen 777) brings up the social context of the poem's publication in Tottel's *Miscellany* (1557) with the caption "Description of Spring, wherin eche thing renewes, save onelie the lover." Neither mentions the contradictory narrative context of Laura's death. Surrey distances his poem from its model by eliminating mythological figures that complicate Petrarch's sonnet. "The nightingale with fethers new she singes," for example, conjures an image of quaint flora and fauna, but Petrarch's "garrir Progne et pianger Filomena" ("chattering Procne and weeping Philomena" [Durling, *Petrarch's Lyric Poems*]) evokes the brutal myth of two sisters' cannibalistic revenge on an offending rapist. Durling interprets the incestuous overtones of Petrarch's "Giove s'allegra di mirar sua figlia" ("Jove takes joy in gazing at his daughter" [trans. Musa]) as "the planets Jupiter and Venus in favorable relation" (Durling, *Petrarch's Lyric Poems*), and Musa gives a similar explanation. Cook recalls the entirely different myth of Proserpina as harbinger of spring: "Jove delights in gazing upon his daughter by Ceres, Proserpina, returned for six months to the upper world" (430). Even this allusion summons a dark, conflictual side of the myth where a father brokers with his brother for sexual possession of his daughter to consolidate family bloodlines. Such allusions seem anything but quaint.

88   FRAMING THE AUTHENTIC PETRARCH

How, then, might students finally assess the imprint of an "authentic" Petrarch in Elizabethan verse? You could direct them to Philip Sidney's *Astrophil and Stella*, for which Ariosto's translator John Harington called Sidney "our English Petrarke" (183). Sidney's own verbal style is dramatic, witty, colloquial, and conversational, aiming to displace Petrarch's artificial composite style (see R. Greene, *Post-Petrarchism* 63–108; for anti-Petrarchism, see Dubrow, *Echoes* 99–119). You could point out that Sidney's *Defence of Poesy* disparages one important example of the hybrid style in English; Edmund Spenser's "gallimaufray" (Brooks-Davies, *Edmund Spenser* 16) of late medieval archaisms; northern provincialisms; and Latin, Greek, French, and Italian borrowings in *The Shepheardes Calender*, which Sidney criticized as an "old rustic language" (*Miscellaneous Prose* 112; see Blank 113–25). Sidney's play with the language of contemporary London and the Elizabethan court nonetheless approximates Petrarchan paranomasia, as in sonnet 62 of *Astrophil and Stella*, with its ingenious configurations of the word *love* as both noun and verb, evoking contrarious meanings of sensual love, spiritual love, and the persons of the lover, Cupid, and the beloved herself.

In a thematic context you could ask why Astrophil censures the ready-made moral lessons of Petrarch's commentators when he decries "allegorie's curious frame" in sonnet 28. Here he is foolishly rejecting the kind of correction that Richard Tottel spelled out in such captions as "The abused louer seeth his folly, and entendeth to trust no more" (1: 33; poem 39) while everywhere giving direct evidence of needing this advice (see Crane, *Framing* 185-96). Sonnet 71, for example, paraphrases Petrarch's sonnet 248, a poem that Italian commentators had allegorized as depicting the brevity of life and insufficiency of art. Sidney's lover, however, concludes with a fatuous, self-absorbed "'But ah,' Desire still cries, 'give me some food.'" For all his direct and indirect Petrarchan echoes, Astrophil claims that he is "no pick-purse of another's wit" (sonnet 74). Here you could explain that he is deriding such poets as Thomas Watson, who in his *Hekatompathia* (published 1582 but circulated earlier) translated whole verses from Petrarch and others and who framed them with elaborate headnotes in the manner of Petrarch's commentators. Even in this respect, Astrophil's attitudes toward hybridity and linguistic contamination evince social change, cultural adjustment, and political development with attendant conflicts, tensions, and outright contradictions in the use of Petrarchism. Because language and cultural assumptions have evolved so greatly over the past four centuries, it may seem difficult to reclaim such authentic historical sentiments of Elizabethan and earlier poets. You can reassure students that those very poets would have felt the same about reclaiming an authentic Petrarch, a figure two centuries distant from them in chronological time and mental space.

Religious Backgrounds of Elizabethan Shorter Poetry

Debora Shuger

With the exception of Edmund Spenser's *Fowre Hymnes*, Elizabethan shorter poetry includes little important religious verse. Its central texts are love lyrics, sonnet sequences, and the like. Not only is this poetry secular, but, unlike the equally secular Elizabethan drama, it is largely untouched by the religious controversies fissuring sixteenth-century culture. For teaching Philip Sidney's *Astrophil and Stella* or Shakespeare's *Sonnets*, Reformation polemics are not, I think, of much use. Yet these poems are shot through with a numinous flickering cast by their myriad references to grace, saints, prayer, adoration, oblation, paradise, heaven. Unless such terms are mere puffery, the habitual recourse to a theological lexicon suggests that religion is braided into the fabric of this predominately secular verse in ways both deeper and more delicate than what is usually meant by "background."

It seems unnecessary to observe that in teaching one often has to begin by simply identifying the religious allusions: that "oblation" in Shakespeare's sonnet 125 echoes the eucharistic liturgy, that Spenser's *Epithalamion*'s rather bizarre portrait of a lady (lines 171–80) derives from Canticles, and so forth. The notes to the standard editions generally provide this information; moreover, pointing out these echoes of biblical, liturgical, and devotional texts does not explain very much. In particular, it does not explain what religious allusions are doing in secular love poems. To make sense of their presence, one must turn elsewhere.

Religion's central and shaping presence in Elizabethan shorter poetry derives from Petrarch, whose sonnet sequence, the *Rime sparse*, wrestles from beginning to end with what the love of Laura has to do with the love of God (Cheney, *Spenser's Famous Flight* 163). There are times when Laura seems to him *mediatrix*—the epiphany of and "faithful, dear guide" to heaven (poem 357; see also poems 29, 333)—but precisely because she resembles all that is sacred, his love for her approaches *latreia*, the adoration proper to God alone (poem 16).[1] In the poems written after her death, it is often not clear whether Petrarch desires heaven in order to behold God or to regain sight of Laura (poems 334, 346, 362). She is—or, more accurately, his love for her is—as much an obstacle to his salvation as its pledge and path (poems 264, 360). Despite Petrarch's anguished effort to reconcile these two loves, in the end—and even before the end—he knows that he is fooling himself, that turning to God means renouncing Laura (poems 62, 355, 363-66).

Spenser's *Fowre Hymnes* reproduces the overall structure of this Petrarchan agon, although in schematic fashion. The Elizabethan sonnet sequences, however, muffle the religious longings that convulse the *Rime sparse*; in these, the relation of human to divine love tends to be handled more lightly, obliquely, implicitly. Thus Sidney's *Astrophil and Stella* secularizes the Petrarchan agon as

90   RELIGIOUS BACKGROUNDS

the conflict between desire and virtue; only two occasional sonnets, "Leave me o Love" and "Thou blind man's marke," specifically address the tension between "eternal love" and its mortal counterpart (161–62). Spenser's *Amoretti* registers this tension mostly in its weird juxtaposition of sonnets celebrating the fully Christian sacrality of human love with those that depict eros as something a good deal closer to idolatry, hunt, conquest, or seduction than "the lesson which the Lord us taught" (sonnet 68). Yet while no Elizabethan sonnet sequence directly engages the relation of sacred to erotic love, the Petrarchan exemplar lingers in the religious images and allusions scattered throughout these lyrics, investing with significance what would otherwise seem hyperbole. Which is to say that in the Elizabethan sequences human love remains, as in Petrarch, entangled with religious aspiration. The beauty of Spenser's "more then most faire" beloved still radiates "living fire, / Kindled above unto the maker neere," which, in turn, kindles "heavenly fyre" in the "fraile spirit" of her lover (*Amoretti* 3, 8). Such lyrics (and there are many of them) articulate the same desire haunting the *Rime sparse*: that the beloved be not simply mortal object of desire but *theotokos*, God-bearer. The beloved need not, of course, be female. Critics have long noted that the young man of Shakespeare's *Sonnets* is loved with a humble and sacrificial adoration bordering on religious worship (Leishman 217–26). His words, the poet tells his master-mistress, "like prayers divine," have daily "hallowed thy fair name" (sonnet 108), for "[y]ou are my all the world" (sonnet 112), "a god in love, to whom I am confin'd" (sonnet 110).

And yet, for all the irradiant holiness of human love, for all its similarity to the love of God, in the end it reaches "but to dust" (Sidney, *Poems* 161; Roche, *Petrarch* 193–97). The crucial truth about Laura is that she is not Beatrice, not, finally, *mediatrix*—and the same holds for all subsequent Petrarchan beloveds. If, in the *Amoretti*, the lady's beauty resembles "heavens glory," it simultaneously entices the lover "with sweet pleasures bayt," so that his soul "unto heaven forgets her former flight" nor "thinks of other heaven, but how it might / [. . .] here on earth to have such hevens blisse" (sonnet 72). And such bliss almost never comes. Most Elizabethan sequences do not conclude with "mutual render" (Shakespeare, sonnet 125). Nowhere in Shakespeare's *Sonnets*, as Leishman notes, "is there unmistakable evidence [. . .] that his friend, in any deep and meaningful sense of the word, loved him at all" (226). Astrophil ends up waiting half the night on a desolate roadside in a futile, final attempt to glimpse Stella as her coach drives past—the typical fate of those who, in Fulke Greville's brilliant phrase, "follow *Cupid* for his loaves, and fishes" (poem 22). Midway through *Caelica*, Greville himself turns in disillusion from the pursuit of carnal beatitude (poem 84); the final poems are almost all religious. In both *Astrophil* and *Caelica*, transcendent yearning collapses under the downward pressure of lust, the desire to get laid proving more than a match for redemptive eroticism. The failure of love's transfiguring promise reveals itself with bitter clarity in Shakespeare's sonnet 129: that which had seemed a stairway to heaven leads in fact to some place not unlike hell. In the Elizabethan sequences, as in Petrarch, the theological valencing that gives love its meaning also works powerfully against happy endings. Human love is not an ordinary means of salvation. (This may be hard to explain to undergraduates.) *Epithalamion*, which manages to combine Petrarchanism with Christian marriage, is thus truly extraordinary.

That Petrarch stands behind the striking interiority of the Elizabethan sonnet sequences is a critical commonplace; this interiority is not, however, generally viewed as part of their religious background. Yet the lyrics of the *Rime sparse* present, as it were, snapshots of the soul, which, taken together nickelodeon-style, constitute an autobiography of inwardness in which the painfully complex entanglements of transcendent and erotic desire weave the deep strata of the self. Petrarch's focus on the stirrings and suffering engendered at the intersection of these two loves—his sense that such movements constitute identity—had a profound influence on the Elizabethan sequences. Sidney's configuration of inwardness as a conflict between platonizing and sexual urges provides the most obvious English translation of Petrarchan subjectivity. Far more subtle (and interesting) are Shakespeare's *Sonnets*. A number of these, some addressed to the young man, some to the dark lady, depict emotional states that seem oddly religious. Sonnet 150 ("O, from what pow'r hast thou this pow'rful might / With insufficiency my heart to sway") thus portrays a love that reaches out to the unworthy and sinful. Sonnets 57 ("Being your slave, what should I do but tend") and 58 ("That god forbid that made me first your slave") register a state of mind that could, in a different context, be termed humility; the description of "patience, tame to sufferance," that "bide[s] each check" (58) without murmuring or daring to question its "sovereign" (57) is strangely reminiscent of Calvin's commentaries on Job. And yet in all three poems the "religiosity" of this love does not sanctify it but rather twists desire into pathology. Sonnet 150 uses the language of *caritas* to describe a tormented infatuation. The humility of sonnets 57 and 58 slides and sickens into abjection. In each case, the spiritualization of eros—the selflessness of this love, its sacrificial, gratuitous character—seems inseparable from its perversity. The psychological complexity of these sonnets derives, that is, precisely from the *complexus* or copula between the sacred and erotic.

Moreover, in contrast to the encomiastic res gestae focus of most medieval and Renaissance life writings, Petrarch's self-renderings limn identity in terms of guilt, misery, desire, and wrenching unsuccess; they give, that is, literary form to the subject produced in confession, a subject individuated not by achievement but by its secret failings and failures. This penitential configuration of inwardness would also seem to lie behind the self-portraiture of the Elizabethan sonnet sequences. These remain, of course, secular lyrics, but like the whispered self-disclosures of the confessional, they depict psychological states usually considered wrong, shameful, and therefore deeply private. Many of Shakespeare's sonnets describe a man's sexual obsession, self-abasement, humiliating neediness, pathetic gratitude for crumbs of kindness, and sense of injured merit. While only his poems risk this much self-exposure, they differ from other Elizabethan sequences more in degree than in kind. The *Amoretti*

92 RELIGIOUS BACKGROUNDS

thus at moments betrays a compromising snarl of piety and tactics. The speaker's opportunistic profanation of Lent in sonnet 22 ("This holy season fit to fast and pray"), like the abuse of devotional topoi for amatory ends in sonnets 27 ("Faire proud now tell me why should faire be proud") and 58 ("Weake is th'assurance that weake flesh reposeth"), raises queasy doubts concerning his motives. There is something about his instrumentalization of religion that calls to mind the scene in Shakespeare's *Rape of Lucrece* in which, as Tarquin forces open his victim's door, "for his prey to pray he doth begin" (line 342). Even *Astrophil and Stella*, for all its lightness of touch, records in mortifying detail the sex-starved fumblings of Sidney's alter ego, his painful lack of success, and his not altogether admirable disregard for either virtue or reason. Both the pathos and edgy comedy of the work depend on these (implicitly autobiographical) confessions of "mangled mind" (161); the poems attest to the courtier's grace, but they also show him begging, gloating, and drooling.

Unsparing self-portraiture has become such a standard feature of modern poetry that it takes some effort to recall how little of this one finds in antiquity or the secular literature of the Middle Ages. The language for exploring "the individual's inner life, affections and [. . .] most intimate movements of thought," as David Aers reminds us, derives from the "medieval penitential tradition" ("Whisper" 185–87). This tradition is mediated to Elizabethan poetry largely through Petrarch—a fact whose pedagogical implications seem uncomfortably obvious: namely, students should be asked to read enough of the *Rime sparse* to get an overall sense of the narrative. I am enough of a new historicist to have been puzzled that I ended up citing as "background" (a term I dislike) a literary work, rather than something more exotic or at least unexpected. I have no interest in reviving old-style literary history. It seemed to me, however, that the religious valencing of the Elizabethan sonnet sequences articulates experiences ranged along an internal fault line where erotic and transcendent desire touch, collide, buckle, and fissure. Yet when I tried to think what other cultural forms registered this sort of inner experience, I came up with zip; one will not find such matters treated in the state papers, Chancery records, or *The Book of Homilies*. They exist only in poetry—not, I think, because there is something peculiarly "literary" (whether aestheticized or make-believe) about these intertangled vectors of desire, but because poetry comes to function in the Renaissance, perhaps for the first time, as the dominant cultural language of inwardness (Shuger, "'Gums'" 16). By approaching the religious content of Elizabethan sonnets through Petrarch, rather than, let us say, Scripture or the prayer book, one encourages students to focus on the experience that these poems articulate—the experience of men who were Christians and in love.

NOTE

[1]All Petrarch quotations in this essay are from Robert Durling's translation.

"Tradition and the Individual Talent": Teaching Ovid and the Epyllion in the Context of the 1590s

Georgia E. Brown

My approach to the 1590s is deliberately perverse: instead of focusing on Shakespeare, Spenser, or Sidney, we examine a deliberately marginal form—the epyllion, or little epic. This works well because young people like to be perverse, and the scandalous nature of a genre favored by an Elizabethan avant-garde appeals to them. The epyllion also helps destabilize assumptions about gender and literature. Self-confident, witty, and critical, it lets poets develop new ideas about authorship, for this "subjective" genre, as I call it, highlights the writer's individual perspective and novelty. Teaching it in turn empowers students to imitate its strategies: to read against the grain, to revel in personal opinions.

Although I teach in the English system, my duties in many ways resemble those of my colleagues in North America. I am responsible for teaching an undergraduate survey that runs from 1550 to 1700 in a mere eight weeks. We cover the epyllion in a two-hour seminar, after we have started *The Faerie Queene* and have done a seminar on *Astrophil and Stella*. I want not only to get information across but also to unsettle their preconceptions, suggest questions, and motivate them. In what is a marketing as well as a teaching job, the epyllion is my secret weapon: it combines sex and even violence with attitude. It speaks to postmodernists, for while self-consciously trivial it shamelessly asserts the value of its prodigality. My hope is that by exploring how the epyllion challenged values in the 1590s we can also challenge our own preconceptions, including our definitions of major and minor, canonical and noncanonical.

Ovid provides the classical sanction for modernity in the 1590s. By comparing epyllia with their Ovidian sources, students explore how writers radicalized the classics and how imitation can be a mechanism for change. Thus we approach the issues that T. S. Eliot raises in his essay "Tradition and the Individual Talent," in which he interrogates individuality. His magniloquently patriarchal opinions have proved accessible and contentious points of departure as we explore one of the ways in which the sixteenth century appropriated classical culture through the rereading of Ovid.

The epyllion is a brief narrative poem, usually about love and often indebted to Ovid for its mythological matter and style. The epyllion vogue was inaugurated by Thomas Lodge with *Scillaes Metamorphosis* (1589) and nurtured by translations such as Arthur Golding's version of the *Metamorphoses* (1567) and the naturalization of Ovidian matter in prose fiction and drama of the 1570s and 1580s. I ask the class to read three epyllia before the session. I always include Shakespeare's *Venus and Adonis* (1593) and Christopher Marlowe's

94   TEACHING OVID AND THE EPYLLION

Hero and Leander (1598), both in Sandra Clark's *Amorous Rites: Elizabethan Erotic Verse.* Elizabeth Story Donno's *Elizabethan Minor Epics* is comprehensive and her introduction excellent, but she omits *Venus and Adonis.* I use Louis L. Martz's facsimile of the first edition of *Hero and Leander,* which does not divide the poem into sestiads, and tell students that modern editions structure the reading experience differently from the first edition. I choose the third poem according to the interests of the students, the issues already discussed in the class, or my own need to stay fresh. I also give the class passages from other epyllia, and some students read further on their own.

Although I use the epyllion in a survey course, the material can be expanded and adapted, and in the past I have included it in a short course on early modern discourses of desire that climaxed, if I can put it so crudely, in John Dryden's portrait of David in *Absalom and Achitophel.* We discuss ways in which parody, generic mixture, and erotic matter can be used to question moral and literary assumptions and to explore such issues as imitation and intertextuality. The epyllion is also helpful in discussing genre criticism (Guillén; Colie, *Resources;* Dubrow, *Genre*). Although a generic approach can schematize texts, the nature of the 1590s requires me to acknowledge the range of particular forms, including work by often neglected writers. Moreover, the decade saw the growth of a literary community as writers, readers, and stationers came to see themselves as a group with its own rules, membership, and history. A generic approach reveals the interplay between individuality and social context. To make this concrete, we look at dedications, always including Shakespeare's dedication of *Venus and Adonis* and Edward Blount's dedication of *Hero and Leander* (rpt. in Orgel, *Christopher Marlowe*). To show that they are more than convention or sycophancy, I introduce anthropological theories of exchange (Mauss; Bourdieu) in which a gift is not a gesture of subservience but a challenge to the recipient's generosity. Is the social elitism of Shakespeare's dedication a way to appropriate for a print culture the gentility created by the decorous exchange of texts in manuscript culture? We note Shakespeare's stress on his youth, a point developed in other epyllia, which were usually dedicated to someone associated with the author's youth (e.g., Lodge's address to friends at the Inns of Court). The dedications express gossipy rivalry and communal self-scrutiny, indicating that literature's meaning derives from both author and community. They are also a way to control the named dedicatee and the anonymous readers who buy or borrow the work and who are to an extent remade in the dedicatee's image. In this way I can also introduce the topic of patronage, print, and the material context that enabled the professionalization of literature.

Students respond well to the epyllion. Certain images or phrases stick in their minds, not least that of Shakespeare's large, fleshy Venus pulling Adonis from his horse, tucking him under her arm, and making off with him (lines 25–36). I encourage them to contribute to a list of comic highlights at the start of the class, as it makes the poems more familiar and attractive. Some students share William Keach's view of the poems, seeing them as poignant explorations of love; others are disturbed by the imagery's fantasies of rape. These disagreements, however, provoke students to realize the poems' ambiguity, one compounded by the compendious nature of the epyllion, a small form that contains other forms—complaint, satire, Petrarchan lyric, epic—within it.

Generic mixture is a rich subject itself, for such mixing allows a writer to display facility and to question the perspectives implied by literary forms or modes. The epyllion is useful for clarifying Petrarchanism, pastoral, and epic: defining these through parody, it throws their features into relief. For example, the epyllion's reaction against Petrarchan idealization provides links among Elizabethan courtly conventions, the ironies of Donne's *Songs and Sonnets*, and the new fashion for verse satire. Thus John Weever's *Faunus and Melliflora* provides a perspective on pastoral and satire, while Thomas Heywood's *Oenone and Paris* contains elements of complaint. The satirical elements in Weever and Marlowe also allow an exploration of poetry's political context: each poet devalues virginity, one basis of Elizabeth's political myth, and attacks the sublimated eroticism that helped fashion political transaction at her court. All epyllia, furthermore, mix epic with Petrarchan and Ovidian elements (Hulse, *Metamorphic Verse*; Keach, *Narratives*; Dubrow, *Captive Victors* 21–79). The epyllion is digressive and unpredictable like Ovid's *Metamorphoses*, while the dedications engage Vergil in dialogue. For example, Shakespeare's dedication of *Venus and Adonis* to the earl of Southampton describes the poem as "the first heire of my invention" (1799). The epyllion can be the inaugural gesture in a writer's career, challenging the graver Vergilian model that starts with pastoral and moves to epic.

After this excursion into genre and our exploration of the epyllion as literary, cultural, and political criticism, we return to the poems' presentation of desire. I may introduce this topic by recalling the image of Venus with Adonis tucked under her arm. We wonder why this is funny or striking and notice how gender expectations have been reversed as the talkative goddess takes an active role with a passive and coy male. We may compare this scene with Neptune's attempt to seduce Leander (*Hero and Leander*, lines 663–80) and discuss the consequence of poems that have both hetero- and homosexual appeal and in which traditionally gendered attributes become fluid. In *Hero and Leander*, for example, Leander is praised for the beauty of his cheeks and lips (lines 65–76), features usually found in blazons of a female object. This can be the moment to introduce some queer theory (Bredbeck; Goldberg, "Sodomy") or feminist theory on female sovereignty (P. Berry) or voyeurism (N. Vickers, "Mistress"). Epyllia elaborate on the pleasures of illicit sights in ways that confuse the hierarchy of empowered male viewing subject and victimized female object. They also explore sexual activity that has been forbidden or marginalized. *Oenone and Paris* is about adultery and betrayal, for instance, and *Venus and Adonis* breaks taboos of gender and age through a figure who is at once erotic and maternal. Through indulging such peripheral sexualities, then, and through the unexpected roles they give the sexes, these poems promote the marginal and transgressive. Discussion can start with students' opinions, as

96   TEACHING OVID AND THE EPYLLION

some find gender bending liberating while others think the epyllion's erotic appeal reinforces patriarchal fantasies. I ask why these poems are so free in their treatment of desire. To get things going, I may mention Madonna, or some similar figure, as the impolite, confident, frankly sexualized female who also likes to hint at lesbianism. What are the consequences of projecting such a persona? (See Sontag's "Pornographic Imagination.")

We then return to the text and to the crux of the seminar. The digressive narrative of the epyllion makes readers self-conscious about their own desires, specifically their desire to find out what happens in the narrative and if the various lovers get together. Will conversation, in the sense of an exchange of language, actually become conversation, in the sense of sexual intercourse? Both meanings were available (see *The Oxford English Dictionary*). Writers of epyllia imply a parallel between reading or writing and desire; they thus challenge views that limit literature's function to the moral and didactic or merely dismiss it as a diversion from better pursuits (Donno, "Epyllion"; Fraser, *War*). I hand out passages from William Webbe's *Discourse of English Poetrie* (1586; G. G. Smith 1: 238–52) and Thomas Elyot's *Boke Named the Governour* (1531; Croft 1: 120–30) to illustrate the humanist insistence on literature's philosophical and ethical value and its utility in preparing readers for public service. In such thinking, a universal truth validates textual authority. But the epyllion, unashamed of immorality and uselessness, flaunts its guilty, errant status.

The epyllion thus also lends itself to a discussion of shame in early modern texts, whether as Christian acknowledgment of sin (Kinney, *Humanist Poetics*; Helgerson, *Elizabethan Prodigals*), as an emotion with a tactical role to play in its transformation into discourse (Foucault), or as a way of figuring authorial anxieties about exposure (Wall). The very shamelessness of the epyllion, its stylistic or narrative extravagance and its eroticism, asserts the author's superiority to social expectations and promotes the writer's individuality. I concentrate on shame's association with exposure because the topic relates to textual transmission and hence to our discussion of dedications. I also relate the epyllion to publication through its exploitation of the image of woman and the dynamics of voyeurism (Wall 169–226). Unlike the sonnet sequence, moreover, the epyllion has survived primarily in printed texts. A good epyllion to use to discuss attitudes to print is George Chapman's *Ovids Banquet of Sence* (1595). Describing how Ovid satisfies every sense as he spies Corinna bathing, it parodies the myth of Diana and Actaeon (*Metamorphoses*, bk. 3). But Chapman's Ovid suffers no punishment for the crime of spying on the emperor's daughter. Rather, Corinna eventually allows him to indulge all his senses, and Chapman's rereading of Ovid serves as an encouragement to those readers, writers, or publishers who would expose what should be kept from view.

At the end of the seminar I move to a brief comparative exercise in which students analyze Ovid's version of a story. For example, if I've been using *Ovids Banquet of Sence* to discuss ideas about publication, I take Elizabethan and Ovidian versions of the myth of Diana and Actaeon, a comparison that brings us back to the relation of reading, imitation, and tradition to individuality. Students can thus start to see what imitating the classics meant to early modern writers (T. M. Greene, *Light*, is useful here). The exercise shows how awareness of convention can paradoxically heighten a writer's sense of individuality and difference. It is also possible to use comparative material to explore competing ways of reading the classics that entail different views of literary function (Alexander 1–24). Chapman's frivolity can be contrasted to Golding's reading of Diana and Acteon as a warning against gambling, hawking, and hunting (in the "Epistle to the Earl of Leicester" that prefaces his translation of the *Metamorphoses*). For Golding, literature serves revealed truth, whereas Chapman places it in an autonomous secular domain, one in which an individual author can claim a reward.

When teaching seniors, I end with a more theoretical discussion. The seminar I have described treats texts in a largely literary context. This is valid because the late sixteenth century was coming to view literature as valuable in its own right. The limits of this approach have been highlighted by the new historicism, though, so we take up that movement's pros and cons. The Eliot essay to which my title alludes can serve as a point of departure, dealing as it does with history and context, albeit in ways uncongenial to new historicists. The question raised in the 1590s of whether literature is a political, civic, and moral activity or, in some degree, a thing apart is echoed in current debates. By acknowledging and analyzing texts' social and political work, new historicism aligns itself in this regard with Renaissance humanism. But early modern writers were also busy creating an aesthetic tradition. I encourage students to wonder how and why such aesthetic idealism begins in late Elizabethan culture.

I have noted some themes and questions the epyllion raises, pressing them into a mythical amalgam of several seminars so as to show the possibilities. I strongly recommend teaching the epyllion: its youthful self-confidence, wantonness, and radical fervor make it exciting for students. It gives them scope to express themselves and allows all of us a flattering sense of our own sophistication as we hear the poetry's witty innuendo. The epyllion appeals to our students for many of the same reasons it appealed to young Elizabethans.

Some examples of the epyllion: Thomas Lodge, *Scillaes Metamorphosis* (1589); Christopher Marlowe, *Hero and Leander* (1598; written by 1593); William Shakespeare, *Venus and Adonis* (1593); Thomas Heywood, *Oenone and Paris* (1594); George Chapman, *Ovids Banquet of Sence* (1595); Michael Drayton, *Endymion and Phoebe* (1595); Thomas Edwards, *Cephalus and Procris* (1595); George Chapman, *Hero and Leander* contd. (1598); Henry Petowe, *The Second Part of Hero and Leander Containing Their Further Fortunes* (1598); John Marston, *The Metamorphosis of Pigmalions Image* (1598); John Weever, *Faunus and Melliflora* (1600). (All these are in Donno, *Elizabethan Minor Epics*, except Shakespeare and Petowe. Petowe is in Orgel, *Christopher Marlowe*. Martz's facsimile of the 1598 *Hero and Leander* should be consulted, as the original differs from most modern editions.)

"The Mushroom Conception of Idle Brains": Antipoetic Sentiment in the Classroom

Peter C. Herman

Teaching the Elizabethan lyric in the context of Stephen Gosson and his brethren's writings (rantings?) against poetry may seem counterintuitive, if not counterproductive. Why give the muse haters any time at all? There are actually many reasons for doing so, not the least being the simple fact of historical accuracy. As G. Gregory Smith notes at the start of *Elizabethan Critical Essays*, "Elizabethan criticism arose in controversy" (xiv), and so did Elizabethan poetry. Furthermore, although it is tempting at this distance to dismiss the muse haters as Puritan zealots and cranks, antipoetic sentiment constituted a mainstream, respectable discourse with deep roots in English Protestantism (Herman 31–59). But most important, the extraordinary number and variety of places where one finds nasty comments about the muses demonstrates the degree to which antipoetic sentiment permeated Elizabethan (and Stuart) culture. In addition to the books devoted exclusively to attacking fictions, one finds examples in sermons, dictionaries, and encyclopedias. Even a humanist defense of women, Thomas Elyot's *Defence of Good Women*, contains a lengthy attack on poetry. Clearly, antipoetic sentiment, as well as its cousins antitheatricalism (Barish), iconoclasm (Gilman), and antidancing sentiment (S. Howard), figured as a constant presence throughout the early modern era, and it needs to be taken as seriously as Neoplatonism or the political resonances of Petrarchan tropes.

What were the charges laid against poetry? And how can we incorporate them into the classroom? First, morality. Gosson and others repeat over and over again that love lyrics are offensive because they incite immorality in others: "pul off the visard that Poets maske in, you shall disclose their reproch, bewray their vanitie, loth their wantonnesse. [. . .] These are the Cuppes of *Circes*, that turne reasonable Creatures into brute Beastes" (Gosson 77). Or, as Richard Brathwaite—despite his own penchant for versifying—later writes,

> Some we have heard, that in reading the strange adventures of *Orlando Furioso*, and conveying the very impression of his amorous passion to themselves, would presently imitate his distraction, run starke naked, make love-songs in commendation of their Angelica, put themselves to intolerable torments to gaine the attention of their supposed mistresses.
> (sig. F2)

I usually distribute to the class a handout containing juicy quotations against poetry from Gosson as well as others (Brathwaite in particular). In graduate classes, I have also occasionally asked a student to prepare a report on Gosson's *The Schoole of Abuse*, since it is one of the few such texts available in relatively

Peter C. Herman   99

accessible modern editions. Before dealing with the attacks, the class has also discussed Philip Sidney's *Apology for Poetry*, taking into account both Sidney's assertions about poetry's superiority to history and philosophy and the cracks and contradictions within the argument (see M. W. Ferguson 137–62; Hardison, "Two Voices"; Herman 61–93; Levao, *Renaissance Minds*). I then ask students to compare and contrast Sidney's arguments in the *Apology* with ideas in *Astrophil and Stella*. Is this the kind of poetry that Sidney is talking about? And if not, why not? At this point, we turn to the attacks themselves and I ask the class if Sidney successfully rebuts the charges of the muse haters in the *Apology*. Students generally pick up that at certain key junctures, Sidney and Gosson actually agree, for example, that poetry in the past was better, that poetry ought to teach virtue, and that poetry can lead to effeminacy. We then turn to *Astrophil*, and I ask what the relations might be between the sonnet sequence and the attacks on poetry. Do the poems confirm Gosson's charges? Do they rebut them? What, for instance, is the meaning of how both Sidney and Gosson conceive of poetry's effect in terms of a ladder?

> Loving in truth, and fain in verse my love to show,
> That the deare She might take some pleasure of my paine:
> Pleasure might cause her reade, reading might make her
>   know,
> Knowledge might pitie win, and pitie grace obtain.
>   (*Astrophil and Stella*, sonnet 1)

> You are no sooner entred, but libertie looseth the reynes, and geves you head, placing with Poetrie in the lowest forme: when his skill is showne too make his scholer as good as ever twangde, hee preferres you too Pyping, from Pyping to playing, from play to pleasure, from pleasure to slouth, from slouth too sleepe, from sleepe too sinne, from sinne to death, from death to the devill.   (Gosson 81)

I also ask students what they make of the fact that far from contrasting Sidney's ladder with Gosson's, Astrophil's desires appear to substantiate the muse haters' charge that the pleasure gained from reading verse will lead to sin.

This question (usually) leads to discussion about the moral stance of the sequence: Is Sidney criticizing Astrophil and possibly the sonnet tradition? What is the relation between the novelty of Sidney's creative theory in this sequence and Gosson's charges? Does the picture change when put in the context of early modern distrust of the imagination? And are there connections between the *Apology's* intermittent agreement with Gosson and other muse haters and the way *Astrophil* seems to confirm rather than deny the charges of the muse haters? In the ensuing discussions, students quickly discover for themselves that Sidney's relations to the muse haters is much more complicated and thought provoking than they might have believed initially. Certainly,

100   "MUSHROOM CONCEPTION OF IDLE BRAINS"

Sidney did not simply ignore the presence of antipoetic sentiment when he wrote *Astrophil*.

Nor did Edmund Spenser when he wrote *The Shepheardes Calender*, which also offers good opportunities for discussing the importance of antipoetic sentiment; it is worth pointing out that the *Calender* and *The School of Abuse* appeared the same year. I usually begin the class by bringing in Spenser's dismissal of *The School of Abuse* in his letter to Gabriel Harvey:

> Newe Bookes I heare of none, but only of one, that writing a certaine Booke, called THE SCHOOLE OF ABUSE, and dedicating it to Maister SIDNEY, was for hys labor scorned, if at leaste it be in the goodnesse of that nature to scorne. Suche follie is it not to regarde aforehande the inclination and qualitie of him to whome wee dedicate oure Bookes.
>
> (qtd. in G. Smith 1: 89)

As I teach Spenser after Sidney, I ask the class to relate this quotation to the *Apology* and *Astrophil*. Does it accurately reflect Sidney's reaction to antipoetic sentiment? This raises the question whether Spenser, who wanted to be England's Vergil, might have his own reasons for publicly trashing poetry's abuser. We also reconsider the matter of the *Calender's* anonymity. There are many explanations for Spenser's refusal to name himself—including political expediency, the medieval tradition of anonymity (D. L. Miller, "Authorship"), and his desire to show that he can keep a secret (Rambuss, "Secretary's Study")—and we discuss if a sense of risk, a sense of doing something not quite acceptable, might also lie behind Spenser's desire for a mask. Is the anonymity, I ask, possibly related to Spenser's description in the *Calender's* envoy of poetry as "base begot with blame" (12), a phrase that among other resonances evokes the charge that poetry's origins are shameful (e.g., John Melton's definition of poetry as "begotte over night in tobacco smoake and muld-sacke, and uttered and delivered to the worlds presse by the helpe & midwifery of a caudle the next morning" [qtd. in Fraser, *War* 9]).

If Gosson's attack on poetry's morality can lead to fruitful discussions about *Astrophil*, the second broad area of concern for the muse haters, the problem of aspiration, which segues into the problem of mimesis itself, provides an excellent ground for looking at several of the eclogues in *The Shepheardes Calender*. Theodore Beza, Calvin's associate whose works were widely read in England, denounces artistic pride in the introduction to his *Abraham sacrifiant* (1550; English trans. 1577): "[they] consecrate this man or that woman to immortalitie, thinges which beare the readers on hand that the authors of them not only are mounted up to the toppe of their Pernassus, but also are come to the very circle of the Moone" (6).

These charges provide a fruitful context for analyzing the *Calender's* pattern of simultaneously announcing and denouncing aspiration. In *Aprill*, for instance, Spenser includes within the lay in praise of Elizabeth an overt retraction of artistic pride:

Shewe thy selfe Cynthia with thy silver rayes,
   and be not abasht:
When shee the beames of her beauty displayes,
   O how art thou dasht?
But I will not match her with Latonaes seede,
Such follie great sorow to Niobe did breede.
   Now she is a stone,
   And makes dayly mone,
Warning all other to take heede.   (82–90)

Significantly, Colin's anxiety directly hinges on Eliza's outdoing Phoebus: "But I will not match her with Latonaes seede." Colin equates his metaphor with Niobe's pride in thinking herself superior to Apollo, for which crime the gods killed all her children and transformed her to stone (lines 138–41). Colin reins in his praise because he fears saying something that will elevate Eliza beyond her mortal station; he wants to avoid saying anything that might put her in danger. At the same time, Eliza represents Colin's art (Montrose, "'Perfecte Paterne'" 40); consequently, praising her implies Colin's praising himself and his craft. Claiming that Eliza outshines the god of light, order, and civilization also means claiming equal stature for the poet. But by raising himself in this manner Colin exhibits the kind of artistic pride that, for example, Beza had in mind when in *A Booke of Christian Questions* he complained about works "invented by artificers for gaine and vaine glory, for to shewe the workmanshipe" (sig. C3^r). In the process of fashioning himself as the Protestant Vergil, Colin seems to realize that his magnification of the poet's imagination clashes with the widespread Protestant distrust of the imagination.

I think, however, that antipoetic sentiment's most important pedagogical advantage is how it aids students in connecting with the early modern period and in reflecting on contemporary issues. When I started working on antipoetic sentiment in 1983, I thought that I was—in good humanist fashion—recovering something from the past. Yet this discourse has returned with a vengeance, and, as in the early modern era, it is very much a part of mainstream culture today. The charges against movies, television, and various forms of popular music repeat almost verbatim those hurled by Gosson and others. Furthermore, when I taught in the South at both an elite public institution (the College of William and Mary) and an urban university (Georgia State University), I found that a significant number, perhaps even a majority, of students accepted these charges as valid. If you ask them, as I have in classes ranging from advanced seminars on Renaissance literature to introductory writing, whether popular music should be censored or whether Hollywood contributes to the decline in family values (whatever that means), generally they answer with a resounding yes. Consequently, by teaching Renaissance antipoetic sentiment, students also reconsider modern antipoetic sentiment. The situation at San Diego State University is different. Most (but not all) students here do not automatically agree with the contemporary attacks on art. Most dismiss them as silly at best. Even so, learning about sixteenth-century antipoetic sentiment encourages my southern California students to take both the earlier and later attacks more seriously. Considering Gosson and company gives them a greater sense of history, of how phenomena they might think exclusive to our era have much longer roots. This fact leads us to ask why antipoetic sentiment revives in both eras, to think about how in both eras the sense of eroding public virtue, of an all-pervasive social and political instability, and the concomitant nostalgia for an earlier, putatively simpler, time seem to instigate attacks on the arts. In other words, the discussion leads to a rethinking of both sixteenth-century and late-twentieth-century musophobia.

SELECTED PEDAGOGICAL STRATEGIES, COURSES, UNITS, ASSIGNMENTS

Sex and the Shorter Poem

Julia Reinhard Lupton

Elizabethan poetry is scattered with references to flowers, most of them sure to stupefy your greener undergraduates in search of more action and less verbiage. Yet these images might not be so dull after all, for a flower—as the biology student in the back row will tell you—is in essence the sexual organ of a plant. Unlike their natural counterparts, however, the flowers of rhetoric display human desire as a response to prohibition and loss (Lupton). The sexual and linguistic life of flowers offers a sensuous, immediately accessible center around which the potentialities of rhetorical, mythopoetic, and psychoanalytic criticism can blossom in any classroom.

I suggest that you start with a simple blazon, a poem that describes the beloved through a list of metaphors comparing her attributes to aspects of the natural world (N. Vickers, "Diana"). Take this famous verse, "There is a garden in her face," by Thomas Campion:

> There is a Garden in her face,
> Where Roses and white Lillies grow;
> A heav'nly paradice is that place,
> Wherein all pleasant fruits doe flow.
> There Cherries grow, which none may buy
> Till Cherry ripe themselves doe cry.   (Sylvester 544)

The first line establishes a metaphoric equation,

garden = face

104 SEX AND THE SHORTER POEM

The equation is then broken into its constituent parts, now in a poetic short-hand that the reader must unfold independently:

> roses = [glow of cheeks]
> lilies = [whiteness of skin]
> cherries = [redness of lips]

Of these, the cherries, which recur at the end of each of the poem's three verses, are the most complex, since they not only continue the pretty description but also signal a certain limit, an element of prohibition, that brings to a close the sequence of analogies.

The cherries, that is, have moved from the safer territory of rosy cheeks and lily skin to the more sexually charged region of the mouth. They have also shifted from lyrical description to the seeds of a micronarrative, that other "heav'nly paradice [. . .] / Wherein all pleasant fruits doe flowe." As in the story of Eden, the cherries name a forbidden fruit: the kiss that the poet's metaphorizing has led him to imagine and then to back away from. Moreover, you can tap your students' own knowledge of contemporary sexual metaphor to make the leap from the cherry lips of the beloved's face to the precious "cherry" of virginity itself. The couplet both enables and prohibits such a leap by rounding off a description that could easily continue downward.

Campion's cherries mark a series of substitutions:

> cherries → lips → [vagina]

Each element in the chain is increasingly illicit; the string of metaphors does not simply picture the beloved's attractions but also protects against them, the theme of the poem as a whole being the guarding of those "sacred Cherries" (line 17) against premature harvesting. As such, the stanza becomes a kind of enclosed garden of chaste beauty, since it at once evokes and blocks off the body of the beloved, effectively sealing all her lips through the closure of the couplet.

Why fruits and flowers? Why does this particular family of images recur again and again in poems like Campion's, repeatedly linking desire, prohibition, and poetic language? Here, an excursus into Ovid's *Metamorphoses* helps spell out in narrative form the logic behind the erotic language of flowers. Recall the story of Apollo and Daphne (*Metamorphoses* 1.452–567): the god falls in love with a nymph who escapes his passion by turning into a tree, the evergreen laurel. The god responds to his loss by reserving her leaves for his commemorative wreaths, the crowns of poets laureate to this day. Another, specifically floral, example is the story of Hyacinthus, a boy loved by Apollo, who accidentally kills him in a game of discus. Ovid describes the boy's death in a simile borrowed from Vergil (*Aeneid* 9.576-81):

> Just as when, in a garden, if someone has broken off violets or brittle poppies or lilies, still hanging from the yellow stems, fainting they suddenly

Julia Reinhard Lupton 105

droop their withered heads and can no longer stand erect, but gaze, with tops bowed low, upon the earth; so the dying face lies prone, the neck, its strength all gone, cannot sustain its own weight and falls back upon the shoulders. (*Metamorphoses* 10.190–95)

The simile bears fruit in the story's conclusion, in which the grieving Apollo transforms Hyacinthus into a flower, writing on his petals "AI AI," letters of lamentation ("funestaque littera" [216]). The tale of Hyacinthus, moreover, appears as one of the songs sung by Orpheus after his fruitless trip to the underworld; alone on a shadeless hilltop, Orpheus, through the power of his music, gathers a veritable anthology (from *anthos*, flower, and *logia*, collection) of trees, each implying a similar narrative of loss followed by vegetal substitution (86–105).

You can sketch the narrative logic of these myths:

desire → frustration → plant → fashioned symbol

The plant stands in for the inaccessible love object, just as roses and cherries stand in for cheeks and lips in Campion's poem. The Ovidian stories narrativize the operation of metaphor as the installation of one image in the place of another, insistently linking such substitution to the experience of erotic frustration. This element of disrupted desire often marks the difference between love poetry and greeting-card versifying; it also explains the element of illicit longing embodied by the cherries in Campion's poem. Desire also distinguishes flowers in the wild from the cultivated flora of poetry, the latter involving an unnatural element of cancellation or prohibition that forces their linguistic blossoming. Hence the corollary to interrupted desire in the first half of the equation is the cutting, marking, or fashioning of the plant into a cultural symbol at the far end of the sequence (Sacks). The cutting and weaving of Daphne's branches to form the laurel wreath, the writing of funeral letters on the petals of the hyacinth, and the Orphic grove of memory all set out the work of poetry as the creation of a substitute object.

If we return to Campion's verse, we can see that it both describes and is a kind of bouquet, insofar as the poem itself is the final substitution in a series of erotic deferrals:

poem → cherries → lips → vagina

In a favorite Elizabethan pun, "poesy" or poetry is also a "posy" or nosegay, a collection of metaphors that figure forth and replace the beloved, who remains in some way inaccessible to the poet-lover, whether dead, virginal, otherwise engaged, or simply bored. The formula for love poetry can be written in this manner:

desire → frustration → poem

106 SEX AND THE SHORTER POEM

The poem itself functions like the metamorphic monuments in Ovid's myths, its lush metaphors springing up at the place where desire has been blocked.

A glance at the social life of flowers in the contemporary world can draw on your students' local knowledge as a resource for reading Renaissance poetry. The floral business depends on love and death. Flowers mark graves: the cut flower is a memento mori, a reminder of death, since its Hyacinthine curls so quickly fade on its broken stem. Living plants, by contrast, symbolize the promise of rebirth implied by seasonal recurrence; hence potted plants are often deposited on graves or planted around them. Yet flowers are also a common romantic gift, and here their link to sexual reproduction is crucial if generally overlooked; I like to tell my students that they can now thank their lovers for "the beautiful bouquet of genitals" next Valentine's Day. But whereas funeral flowers often remain attached to a living plant, the flowers of romance are almost always cut flowers, displaying that element of cultural refashioning which signals the frustration that gives sexual desire its special structure and urgency. (I also like to tell my students that potted plants make good gifts for Mother's Day, but not for Valentine's Day, and that receipt of a living plant from a boyfriend or girlfriend often indicates that the romance itself is dying.)

Having tasted Campion's homely still life, let us turn now to a more elaborate Elizabethan production, Edmund Spenser's *Epithalamion*. The poem begins just before dawn with the poet asking the Muses to turn from elegy to romantic song. He then goes on to compare himself with Orpheus:

> So Orpheus did for his owne bride,
> So I unto my selfe alone will sing,
> The woods shall to me answer and my Eccho ring.   (16–18)

Just as Spenser asks the Muses to put aside mourning for celebration, so he selectively fashions Orpheus into a poet of married love rather than of elegiac tragedy, isolating the moment when through music Orpheus triumphantly regains his bride from death. At the same time, Spenser's image of the woods that echo the poet's final bachelor song recalls the image of the widowed singer-poet sheltered by his poetic grove of memorialized loss. In the *Epithalamion*, the lack most immediately at stake, of course, is not the memory of a dead beloved but the anticipation of enjoying a living one. The Orphic allusion, however—and here lies the interest of Spenser's poem—maps the future promise of desire in search of fulfillment onto the backward glance of regret. This mourning in turn is rooted in the primordial prohibitions of enjoyment that trigger the substitutions of language. In Spenser's poem, anticipation remembers loss.

As the sun rises, the solitary voice of the poet gives way to the task of establishing the bridal couple within the ranks of the celebratory community, with a concomitant tension between the intimate consummation of their union and the public nature of the marriage act. In the third stanza, the poet calls on the nymphs of the neighboring rivers, forests, and ocean to deck the place and person of his bride with flowers:

> And let them also with them bring in hand,
> Another gay girland
> For my fayre love of lillyes and of roses,
> Bound truelove wize with a blew silke riband.
> And let them make great store of bridal poses,
> And let them eeke bring store of other flowers
> To decke the bridale bowers.   (41–47)

The garland of lilies and roses both ornaments and mirrors the attributes of the beloved, an image of erotic readiness woven into a symbol of married love by the blue ribbon (traditional on wedding days). The flowers brought to "decke the bridale bowers"—the bedroom of the bride—anticipate the defloration to come yet situate that act within a socially sanctioned space, insofar as the nymphs represent not only the procreative impulses of the natural world but also the social and political geography of Spenser's Irish union.

The stanza ends with the poet's transfer of his Orphic music to the nymphs: "The whiles doe ye this song unto her sing, / The woods shall to you answer and your Eccho ring" (54–55). The solitary voice of the bachelor poet has given way to the chorale of bridesmaids, the echo now doubling the reflected voice of an unwed Orpheus or Narcissus alone in his self-created forest into the ever-widening circles of a community gathered in celebration of fruitful union: the "handmayds" (103), "fresh boyes" (112), "Minstrels" (129), "merchants daughters" (167), and "yong men of the towne" (261) who meet the bride and groom in subsequent stanzas, a social scene that culminates with the marriage ceremony and festive reception (sts. 12–15).

But perhaps there are just a few too many people here. With the waning of the day, the poet yearns for the fine and private place of the marriage bed:

> Now bring the Bryde into the brydall boures.
> Now night is come, now soone her disaray,
> And in her bed her lay;
> Lay her in lillies and in violets
> [. . . . .]
> And leave likewise your former lay to sing:
> The woods no more shal answere, nor your echo ring.
> (299–314)

The bridal bower of bliss edges closer to the desired act of defloration, the bed of white lilies and purple violets wedding virginity to its vio-lation. The social order that sanctions the union also delays its consummation; from here on, the

108   SEX AND THE SHORTER POEM

Orphic song turned choral lay becomes an insistent request for the peace and quiet that will allow intimacy to bloom.

The *Epithalamion* comes to an abrupt close with a brief concluding stanza that ends, surprisingly, without reworking the poem's familiar refrain:

> Song made in lieu of many ornaments,
> With which my love should duly have bene dect,
> Which cutting off through hasty accidents,
> Ye would not stay your dew time to expect,
> But promist both to recompens,
> Be unto her a goodly ornament,
> And for short time an endlesse moniment.   (427–33)

Although the poet mentions no flowers, this final verse itself bears the structure of a floral gift. Like the drooping head of Hyacinthus, the verse is "[cut] off through hasty accidents," snapped off before its time, before the closure of a final echoing refrain. Spenser explicitly links his song to an act of "recompens," a linguistic substitution that stands "in lieu of many ornaments." It is precisely by marking a debt, however, that the poem can become a "goodly ornament" in its own right, since, following Ovid, the flowers of rhetoric derive their symbolic function and value as place holders for lost objects.

What, in this case, has been lost? In addition to a more complete or satisfying conclusion to the poem, it would seem to be the erotic consummation itself: the unfinished state of the poem figures the lack of a sexual relationship. There are several layers to such a claim: you might lead your class to think of the sexual act as the unnarratable climax of the poem, visible only through the substitutive language of euphemism. We might also imagine a certain drooping of Spenser's flower under the inhibiting pressure of a continued social presence, such as the quintessentially Elizabethan face of the surveillant Cynthia (the moon) peering through the bedroom window (st. 21). Finally, the image of detumesence points to the acculturating function of castration as the necessary cut of prohibition that forever divides the flowers of human desire from the promiscuous productivity of biological plants.

All this loss, however, leads to a gain. The final line of the "Epithalamion" recalls the bold claim that ends Ovid's *Metamorphoses*: "And now my work is done [Iamque opus exegi], which neither the wrath of Jove, nor fire, nor sword, nor the gnawing tooth of time shall ever be able to undo" (15.871–74). Like the flowers of frustration that color the Ovidian landscape, Spenser's poem is an "endlesse moniment" to desire, crystallizing its origin and arc in the very truncation of the stanza. If the *Epithalamion* as a whole is a bridal garland enclosing the marriage couple in the circle of community, the final stanza functions like a wedding corsage or a bachelor's button, a tiny bouquet that bodies forth the "short time," the jump cut, that institutes the daisy chain of love and poetry. In such transactions—between nature and language—lies the key to the myriad floral metaphors of Elizabethan verse.

Giving Voice to Renaissance Lyric

Theresa M. Krier

In spite of strong work in rehabilitating Renaissance lyric in the past decade, it remains a problem to know what to do pedagogically about many sixteenth- and seventeenth-century lyrics conformable neither to New Critical close reading nor to more recent trends in opening up the canon—all sorts of poems categorized as plain style, or Cavalier, and especially the texts set to music for solo song by John Dowland, Thomas Campion, John Wilson, Henry Lawes, and others. When one year I turned to the growing body of recordings of airs, my students all but handed me one path into other kinds of lyric too, and we found ways of talking about them by first working out how to utter them—the more lucid the structure and simple the diction, the more difficult to utter from some position of truth. Air texts and poems like them for which we know of no music inhabit a vibrant space between page and performance. In classes we work on airs and performance in ways that don't require previous knowledge of music, that build bridges between music and poem, that allow music to summon nuance and complexity in our analyses of poems. For upper-level courses, this work also makes it possible to introduce psychoanalysis and social critique, breaking down resistances in students almost before they're aware of having them. The pedagogical ideas outlined here work well in a course called Poetry and Music in the Age of Shakespeare, but they've also adapted to survey courses and to a course with music majors and students interested in early music. The general principle is that lyric poems, which belong to the category of the lively arts, become full, dense, graceful, mobile, subtle when one's work with these poems includes both silent close reading and embodied performances of them, which means speaking them in many ways so that they come to inhabit the mind and issue on the breath. Working through various exercises that posit desiring speakers with many possible stances toward women and sexuality and many kinds of religious intensity makes it necessary for students to find not the kind of close-reading evidence that we often teach them to look for but the kinds of circumstances that could make this utterance true for this speaker—a search conducted by performers as well as social and psychoanalytic critics.

Twice a semester, we have a special evening session during which students who've been working together in small groups for nearly three months perform some coherent combination of English Renaissance poems and music—a conceptual program or a miniature drama using poems and airs as forms of dialogue—lasting twenty minutes or so. No one's required to memorize or to sing or play an instrument. But surprisingly often, students do choose to memorize, to speak a piece as if in the personae of several different speakers, to include live musical performance, to add movement and gesture, even to come up with their own settings of lyrics or play plots.

There are some good things to worry about with this kind of assignment. (There are all kinds of conflicts, and students have to find ways to deal with

110   GIVING VOICE TO RENAISSANCE LYRIC

their differences from one another, which has the effect of making their diversity real to them.) Will the students have too heavy a workload at the end of the term? Can they do all this without direction? (Yes, a good thing for the teacher to remember.) Should I cut down on written work? (No.) Will the performance be torture for the shy ones? Is this going to work for a nondramatic poetry course? (Yes.) Will we get into trouble with the authorities? (I've learned to tell them: No real weapons. No real fire. No real animals.) Every time, in the most unlikely circumstances, this assignment has been a success. Students invite their friends and families. Shy students emerge with unexpectedly public talents. Students show wit in staging and enacting their pieces. They listen to others' performances with attuned hearing. The evening takes on a gala atmosphere. All come to know more poems and to own them more intimately than class work alone allows. In the meantime, students sail through the end of the term with high energy and write beautiful, complex essays, having good reason to appreciate the amount of labor that goes into writing poems at all. Students do well because so many faculties of mind are working, because students have a strong personal investment in the poetry and airs that they find; because the work is physical, emotional, and social, aesthetic as well as intellectual, synthetic as well as analytic.

From the first day of class, students learn traditional things about figures of speech and thought and close reading. Helen Vendler's introductory poetry book (*Poems, Poets, Poetry*) works best in this context, since it so finely mediates between the English teacher's repertoire of figures and tropes and the movements of thought and feeling in a poem. We also listen to recordings of lyrics set to music and start to develop a working vocabulary to describe the emotions and attitudes of the lyric singer. The many settings of Shakespeare's songs through four centuries make a good start: they're often recorded and have the accessibility of charm; the many settings of any one lyric make it easy for students to discover things to say by comparing two or three settings. We go next to Dowland's *First Booke of Songes or Ayres*, the texts of which represent the most attractive qualities of male-lover personae in the period (simple devotion, decency, fidelity, dignity in the face of loss) and introduce students to the attractions of plainness (Graham). From Dowland's songs it's a natural step to more literary and figured texts, like those often anthologized; pieces from Thomas Wyatt, Philip Sidney, John Donne, or Mary Wroth make lively contrasts to Dowland (as do William Lawes's texts and Donne's religious poems).

Students working out how to speak (or sing) a poem necessarily work out a vocabulary for describing how affect and attitude are projected through gesture, voice, and persona in performance. Nearly any set of terms will do, since one pedagogical aim is to amplify students' words for and distinctions among emotions, conditions, and internal movements from one state to another. Students almost invariably classify a poem as happy or sad and then find themselves at a verbal impasse. They aren't aware of needing a range of words for forms of desire, for example. But we work out a rough-and-ready spectrum of descriptors, simple schemes of emotions and personae, on which they can soon elaborate (Rooley 60; Fónagy). Any of these schemes can bear nuancing; others are suggested by writers about music in the period (Donington). Eventually a reader can be both listener and performer of a lyric text: as Douglas Oliver says, this kind of performance is not just reading aloud but the activation of "the reader's whole response to the work of art: intellectual, emotional and sonic" (vii). It requires historical inquiry and analysis. It requires that students become thinking interpreters of "overlays of possible melodies" and intonations (163). Gradually, by means of intensive listening exercises and performing exercises, students become intimate with the texts they've come to sense as their own words for music perhaps.

To develop these skills, some class sessions are given over to trying out manifold ways of taking a lyric. For example, we try out ways of enunciating mere instants of rhythm, tiny delays as expressive of resistance, reluctance, or longing. In those tiny delays, any yearning already evident in the protagonist (speaker, singer, dancer) compounds with the musical rhythm's yearning for its return to stability. More generally, rhythm can release in auditors an array of descriptive words for both timing and emotion, as in all the lively arts: is a passage stately? grave? somber? brisk? spritely? tumbling? spirited? How are the spirits moving in this passage? (Dowland's "Wilt thou unkind thus reave me," first read as a poem and then heard as a song, is a good beginning because of its pronounced and varied rhythmic and emotional motives.) Or again, many airs, like contemporary songs, pull the auditor forward by the desire implicit in, say, a series of rising or falling intervals. Elizabethan musicians were aware of the longings of the interval, the desire of one pitch for movement toward the next, which will give composure. Dowland's "Come again, sweet love doth now invite" is probably the most famous instance, with its five successive leaps of a fourth setting the words "to see, to heare, to touch, to kisse, to die" (Dowland, *First Booke*). There are also contrasting ascents and descents of short melodic motifs, as in "Come away, come sweet love." The arcs and phrasings of melodic lines can convey the play of yearning and reluctance. Thus the delicately linear melody of Dowland's "Can she excuse my wrongs" is punctuated by the setting of two stanzas in which each of the first three lines ("Better a thousand times to die, / Then for to live thus still tormented: / Deare but remember it was I") is set on a single pitch and at a quickened rhythm, and the fourth line returns to the deepened satisfaction of melody and cadence ("Who for thy sake did die contented"). Melody, whether of a single line or of voices in ensemble, is a perfection of call and response. Dowland is also a master of the grave sorrow and tenderness of an honest lover, as in the beautiful, often recorded "Now, o now I needs must part"—which shows with haunting lucidity the potential affective values of long notes united with long vowels, undergirded by the dark, sweet-sharp timbre of the bass viol—or in "Weep you no more" or "Dear, if you change." In lyric poems, much of this emotional weight is carried by caesurae, metrics, syntactic suspensions, and the complex handling of vowels. The songs

112   GIVING VOICE TO RENAISSANCE LYRIC

from *Astrophil and Stella*, for instance, demonstrate these things and make a good transition into the more restless movements of Sidney's sonnets. The same is true of a progression from Dowland's airs to Spenser's spring and Easter sonnets in *Amoretti* to the earlier, more tormentedly Petrarchan sonnets of that sequence.

That a drama of music as well as one of words can emerge even in the miniature space of lyric becomes convincing to students at some point in their vocal work with poems—those exercises that create the possibility of identification with poem, poet, or speaker. One day early in the term, I play a recorded setting of "Sigh No More, Ladies" from *Much Ado about Nothing* and then Emma Thompson's spoken version of it at the start of the 1993 film of the play; music and recitation together easily demonstrate how much a performance can project an emotional stance, how much the lyric's exuberance depends on sheer savoring of sound, and how a tone—amused irony, in this instance—depends upon sonic properties. (There are, of course, good audio and video tapes of recited poetry, but too much exposure to these convinces American students that their non-British accents are wrong.) From that day on, we spend ten minutes at the start of each class with some exercise in speaking. Dozens of these exercises, most of them adaptable to Renaissance lyric and even to reticent English majors, can be found in books on oral interpretation or performing Shakespeare (Rodenburg; C. Berry; Linklater). These exercises work at all levels of students, provided that the teacher is comfortable with the levity and buoyancy that come with this way of embodying sound properties of poems.

By midterm, all these lines of activity converge in students' increased sophistication in speaking of many kinds of achievements of poems. They know that performance can mean how players risk themselves before an audience by enacting forms; what they themselves do physically with poems; what speakers of poems do with language to manifest conditions, moods, emotions. These senses of performance involve a reader's identification with and embodied projection of a speaker. Indeed, working a poem hard enough to give it formal articulation requires alertness to many voices simultaneously: to those of the composer, the poet, the speaker, and the performer (Fischlin 66–67) and to the hypothesized voices of the addressee—beloved, friend, deity. Students will also have an emergent notion of "the performative" in the sense now found in work on rhetoric, subject formation, and gender, that is, in the idea of self-fashioning or of a masculinity that requires repeated enactment. In music, I'm content if students start to develop a feel for rhythm and delay, melodic line, intervals, word painting, and any movements in airs, both affective and musical. (These things seem to come about best when done by ear: written music can intimidate, and in any case transcriptions of Elizabethan vocal music accessible to the lay reader of such music distort both the music and the difficulties of transmission.) It's also productive to think about relations between song and auditor with notions of identification, projection, and enactment; what we can discover in a conversation among these modern terms on the one hand and Renaissance performance ideals of decorum, grace, *sprezzatura*, and mobility on the other; what kinds of desire the song might awaken in its auditors. Then, when we move to what is usually the greater verbal complexity of written poems, we can make a smooth transition to studying the ways that a writer deploys poetic resources to represent a stance, affect, or condition.

Although many readers will already prefer certain recordings, there are more available every month, and readers who don't follow early music may find useful some suggestions of recordings that work well together. Often students have a vague sense that early music is entirely choral and liturgical—or, these days, chant. (This is sometimes a good occasion to introduce them to the language of period liturgy, e.g., in the Book of Common Prayer and the King James Bible; see McColley, ch. 4.) Nonintensive listening to the vigor and directeness of popular recordings of early music clears up misconceptions right away, for example, recordings by the Baltimore Consort, Musica Antiqua, the King's Noyse, the Broadside Band, the Boston Camerata, the Hilliard Ensemble, the New York Ensemble for Early Music, and Circa 1500. Circa 1500's *"New Fashions": Cries and Ballads of London* (CRD Records 3487, 1992) gives wonderful examples of Thomas Ravenscroft's idiosyncratic songs woven out of street cries and country songs and suggests a composer nearly delirious with full-throated voice and rhythm. None of Alfred Deller's recordings of midcentury sounds dated, though introducing students to the countertenor voice may require a full class session. Recordings of Shakespeare songs in period settings are easy to find (the Deller Consort, the Camerata of London, the Folger Consort, the Musicians of the Globe); a few of the many more recent settings need to be singled out: Gerald Finzi's 1942 song cycle *Let Us Garlands Bring* on *Finzi: Dies Natalis* (Conifer Records 75605, 1997); the disc *Sweet Airs That Give Delight: Forty Seasons of Music from the Stratford Festival* (Attic Records ACD 1378, 1993); the hard-to-find jazz settings of Cleo Laine and John Dankworth, *Wordsongs* (Philips cassette 830 461-4 R-1, 1978); and the vinyl recording by torch singer Maxine Sullivan, *Sullivan Shakespeare Hyman* (Monmouth-Evergreen Records). The Consort of Musicke provides *John Dowland: First Booke of Songes* (Decca 421 653-2, 1989; many libraries have vinyl records of the first cutting of this recording in 1976), useful because its texts were joined by the composer and form a tiny, coherent anthology. Recently Joel Cohen and the Boston Camerata, reacting to the ascendancy of the exquisite, intimate lutenist Dowland, have issued a more extroverted recording of the airs, in *Farewell, Unkind: Songs and Dances* (Erato 0630-12704-2, 1996). Surprisingly often, women vocalists record Dowland's amorous laments, as in several by Julianne Baird and Emma Kirkby, who both record many other composers of the period; see, for Baird, *The English Lute Song* (Dorian 90109, 1988) and *Greensleeves: A Collection of English Lute Songs* (Dorian 90126, 1989); for Kirkby, *Elizabethan Songs: "The Lady Musick"* (Decca, L'Oiseau-Lyre D 125296, 1979, 1990) and *Time Stands Still: Lute Songs on the Theme of Mutability and Metamorphosis by John Dowland and*

114   GIVING VOICE TO RENAISSANCE LYRIC

His Contemporaries (Hyperion CDA66186, 1986). Solo and part songs by Henry Lawes, including gorgeous psalm settings and nativity, pastoral, and piscatory songs, can be found in *Sitting by the Streams: Psalms, Ayres and Dialogues by Henry Lawes* (the Consort of Musicke; Hyperion CDA66135, 1994).

This description of a course juggling so many kinds of work may sound unwieldy to those not already convinced by music. The course does require some care in setting a calendar. But once launched, each line tends to float on its own momentum; combined, each way of living with poetry infuses the others and brings focused energy to class sessions. This isn't a course in oral interpretation; students aren't graded on quality of performance; teachers don't need technical or historical expertise in music or performance. The course is more about discovering in Renaissance lyric a pressure to give shape, contour, and weight to inward experience, through words, sensation, literal voice. Luce Irigaray argues for the difficult necessity of creating and inhabiting "enclaves of air [. . .] in which we can breathe and sing freely, in which we can perform and move at will" (66). Breathing sound: the animating gesture that sustains energy for engaging in the more analytic work of a course in lyric.

Philomela and the Gender of Nightingales
Mary Ellen Lamb

Recent editions of texts by women poets—Mary Wroth, Mary Sidney, Aemilia Lanyer, Isabella Whitney—have irrevocably changed the study of early modern lyric poetry. Since the early 1990s, this new accessiblity of poetry by women has led to a harvest of scholarly work legitimating women writers as necessary subjects of academic inquiry. This quiet revolution has also made itself felt in pedagogy. From the sixth edition of the *Norton Anthology of English Literature,* volume 1, to course syllabi in colleges and high schools, lyrics by Mary Sidney and Aemilia Lanyer increasingly appear side by side with those by Spenser, Philip Sidney, Donne, and Marvell. The presence of these texts by women in a primarily male canon forcefully raises important theoretical issues: What is the importance of the gender of a poet? In what way might it matter whether a poem was written by a woman or a man? Ideally, this accessibility of texts by women will create new questions as well as new understandings of the role of gender in the poetry of both male and female poets.

These questions about the role of gender in early modern lyric poetry lend themselves to explorations of a variety of issues: the effect of gender on education, on reading and writing, and on experience in general. There are no easy answers. In this essay, I describe a unit I taught on the voice of the nightingale, as used by both male and female poets, to open up questions for discussion rather than to convey an authoritative knowledge. Running from one to three class periods, depending on how many poems the instructor introduces to the class, this unit was designed to invite a variety of responses from students rather than to work toward a unanimity of opinion.

To begin this unit, I duplicated a selection from the following poems without including the names of the poets or any other markers of gender. The duplicated poems should include at least one poem by a woman and one by a man. (Asterisks indicate poems that I believe work best.)

> Edmund Spenser, from *Shepheardes Calender,* "August," lines 151–89
> Edmund Spenser, from *Teares of the Muses,* lines 235–300
> *Philip Sidney, *Certain Sonnets,* sonnet 4
> *William Shakespeare, sonnet 102
> Mary Wroth, *Pamphilia to Amphilanthus,* sonnet 4
> *Mary Wroth, from *The Countess of Montgomery's Urania,* "O! that I might now as senceles bee"
> *Anonymous poem in a woman's hand (Lamb, *Gender* 207–08; see app.)

First, I asked students to identify which poems they thought were written by men and which by women and to explain their reasons. In the subsequent discussion, students exchanged ideas about stereotypes of gender in lyric poetry. Instead of looking at the nightingale image, at this stage many of them focused

116   PHILOMELA AND THE GENDER OF NIGHTINGALES

on surface features of the verse—style, number of adjectives, length of lines, emotionality. Then I asked them to what extent the gender of a poet mattered to them. Did they tend to read poems by women differently from the way they read poems by men? I was surprised by the amount of disagreement I found on this question. Some students felt that poems existed in a gender-neutral space and that considerations of gender were unimportant or even discriminatory. Others felt that gender influenced language and experience and that poems by women should be read with an understanding of this different discursive place, which often became embedded in the poems' meanings. Both groups admitted, however, that they were curious to see if they were right in their guesses of the poets' gender. (I didn't tell them until the end of the unit.)

Next, I made a presentation on the nightingale as a popular vehicle through which early modern poets considered their own production of lyric poetry. The poems in this unit refer to nightingales as Philomela, whose name means "lover of sweetness." I embarked on the narrative of Philomela, the woman turned into a nightingale in book 6 of Ovid's *Metamorphoses*, a classical source well known to early modern readers. (Other instructors might photocopy the story from Ovid rather than tell it.) In brief, Tereus rapes his wife's sister, Philomela, and then to prevent her from telling of his crime, he cuts out her tongue. Philomela weaves her story in a tapestry, which she then gives to her sister, Procne. In revenge for Philomela's rape and mutilation, the sisters kill and then cook Itys, son of Procne and Tereus, and serve him in a dish to Tereus. When Tereus asks for his son, Procne informs him of the contents of his dinner, and Philomela throws Itys's head at his feet. As Tereus attempts to murder them, all three turn into birds. The nightingale, who flees to the woods to sing her solitary song, is traditionally identified with Philomela.

After students discussed their reactions to this myth, I presented two contrasting models for interpreting Philomela's presence in lyric poems: a displacement model that foregrounds gender and a transcendence model that foregrounds vocation. Both models address the discontinuity between Philomela's rape and revenge and the sweetly sad singing of nightingales conventional to early modern lyric.

According to my own displacement model, the feminine stereotype of Philomela's yearning sweetness enacts a form of cultural violence implicit in the "forgetting" of Philomela's mutilation and revenge (*Gender* 205–28). This forgetting hides the marks of considerable cultural labor invested in denying the legitimacy of women's rage. Like the mutilated Philomela, women who suffered under a patriarchal system were silenced; or if they were to be heard, they were to sing only sweet songs. I have argued that this simultaneous awareness of women's anger and denial of its legitimated expression represented a significant condition of authorship for women (*Gender* 219–24). Instead of preventing women's authorship, this cultural constraint made women's writing different from men's.

The displacement model raises the question why a male poet would appropriate this forgetting as he uses Philomela to express his voice. Does Philomela's sad song aestheticize anger so that a male poet protects himself from retaliation by drawing attention to the sweetness rather than the substance of a complaint? Or is the discursive position of any form of victimhood—whether rape or unrequited love—so associated with the feminine that the poet takes on a woman's voice? The narrator of Philip Sidney's *Certain Sonnets* number 4 provides a paradoxical combination of appropriation and forgetting, as he claims that his pain over unrequited love ("wanting" love) exceeds the pain of Philomela's rape ("too much having" love).

Patrick Cheney's *Spenser's Famous Flight* discusses the implications of Philomela's song in terms of poetic vocation. As the bird of pastoral, Philomela serves as a model for the poet, in this case Spenser, who withdraws into the "otium of the natural world in order to sing a sweet song of love that renders him immortal" (83). For Cheney, Philomela transcends despair to achieve a Christian faith that does not distinguish gender. The very intensity of her loss brings her a poetic fame; the movement of her song from earth to heaven converts fame to Christian glory (83, 86). For George Gascoigne, who influenced this model, Philomela's "harsh rape and subsequent sweet song" represented a Christian's "fortunate fall" (85).

Cheney's transcendent model for Spenser and Gascoigne raises the difficult issue of gender salience. When is pain and silencing necessarily gendered as female, and when may it be just plain pain? Moreover, if a poet choses an avian metaphor to represent himself as a "winged poet," is he obligated to take on the gendered implications of that choice? Must a poet be interpreted in terms of the gendered meanings inherent in a tradition—originary classical narratives and the conventional gendering of songbirds as female—or is a poet free to manipulate a received tradition to his or her own purposes? Is a poet who takes on the voice of the nightingale also bound to take on the nightingale's position in gender?

The last poem on my list, a poem with revisions showing it to be a holograph apparently written by a woman, represents a particularly interesting test case. In its final couplet, "Now Philomela loud and sweetly cries, / Who bides in love lives still and never dies," has this Philomela transcended her pain to achieve confidence in love? Or does the traditional lore that nightingales do not sing in the summer release an ironic reading, which makes visible this forgetting as a hollow fantasy? Is her song gender-specific, or do students' reading strategies remain unchanged by the gender of the author? Instead of providing answers, the goal of this unit is to render students self-conscious about gender decisions they make.

APPENDIX

This holograph poem appears in British Library, Additional MS 15,232, which also includes the most accurate extant versions of poems from Philip Sidney's

Astrophil and Stella. It appears to have been written by someone in the Sidney circle, around the beginning of the seventeenth century. Consultation with paleographers strongly suggests that it was written in a woman's hand (see Lamb, *Gender* 194–228). According to Louise Schleiner (*Women Writers* 2), the first line, water-damaged in the original, may read: "The breath all [Zephyr's blowing ho]ldeth forth." In line 4, "riefs," a variant of *reifs*, means "thefts" (*OED*).

The breath all [   ]ldeth forth
Comforts the flowers which the blasts did kill,
And Phoebus' beams beat back the chilling north
Whose nature's riefs the earth with storms did fill.
Now Philomela sweetly doeth bewail
That falsehood could on true love so prevail.

The buds bound in by hard and massy bark
Softly break forth to blossoms and to leaves.
The cheerful day long lights the drowsy dark;
Who took most care most comfort now receives.
Now in each bush sweet Philomela sings,
True love lasts sweet when sour other things.

The fields do feel no more the biting frost,
The blossoms grow unto their knotted fruit.
Sweet sights, and smells, are sugared of free cost:
All this gives Nature without charge, or suit.
Now Philomela loud and sweetly cries,
Who bides in love lives still and never dies.

The Multiple Readerships of Elizabethan Poetry
Caroline McManus

Anthony Grafton concludes a 1985 essay by describing a dilemma late-twentieth-century professors share with their sixteenth-century humanist counterparts: "We too seek both to interpret texts historically and to make them accessible as classics in the present" ("Renaissance Readers" 649). I would like to suggest that, paradoxically, one of the most effective ways of making early modern texts accessible is to challenge students to interpret them historically. Designed to encourage awareness of the many conflicting discourses that pressured authors' constructions and readers' reconstructions of Elizabethan poetry, the following pair of pedagogical strategies is informed by Robert Hume's call for a "historical reader-response criticism," an "attempt to recapture the outlook of various subgroups of readers in the past" (80). The first strategy, asking students to read through the eyes of a particular early modern English reader, helps students think more critically about the sociopolitical function of Elizabethan poetry rather than assume Renaissance lyrics to be expressive effusions like those of the Romantic poets. The second strategy, having students compile a commonplace book, also makes them more conscious of the similarities and differences between their reading protocols and those of early modern readers.

After selecting one person from a list of names representing multiple readerships (crown, court, country, universities, Inns of Court, city, etc.), students investigate their Elizabethan subject's social and economic status; role in the court, household, or literary marketplace; educational background; library contents and likely interpretive practices; religious beliefs; family, marital, and extramarital relationships; and coterie or factional connections. Students then read and discuss the assigned primary texts from the perspective of the early modern subject, thus generating multiple readings of the same work and dramatizing the inadequacy of generalizations about "the" Elizabethan reader. As John Kerrigan has observed, "When [Elizabethan] authors discuss their audiences at length they tend to distinguish ever more groups and sub-categories, approaching the atomism remarked by Robert Greene: 'no book so yll but some will both reade it and praise it; & none againe so curious, but some wil carpe at it. Wel, so many heades, so many wittes'" ("Editor" 113).

This plurality of meaning forms the basis for Robert Hume's call for further research:

> What reactions did the work generate around the time of its original publication or performance? What audience(s) did the author address? How would various members of the postulated original audience have understood or reacted to the work? What do we learn from parallels to and differences from related works at about the same time? (74)

120 MULTIPLE READERSHIPS

These questions could be used as writing prompts or as a means of focusing class discussion. When reading Marlowe's *Hero and Leander*, for example, Anne Southwell would righteously condemn it as a "busye nothing" (Cavanaugh 177), whereas the earl of Southampton might relish its eroticism, John Manningham commend its wit, George Chapman reflect on its suitability for poetic continuation (and correction), and the bookseller Richard Field assess its marketability. The student playing Walter Ralegh would discover that Ralegh annotated certain passages in *The Faerie Queene* (dealing with Belphoebe and Timias, Marinell, and Sir Calidore), which he read as allusions to himself (Oakeshott 9–20; Cheney, *Spenser's Famous Flight* 112–48). "Queen Elizabeth" could be asked to provide a counterreading of these episodes. The concerns of Spenser's *Maye* eclogue in *The Shepheardes Calender* will seem less esoteric if read from Edmund Grindal's perspective. Additional Elizabethan readers might include Samuel Daniel, John Dee, William Cecil, and Aemilia Lanyer. Working initially in small groups (mixing political faction, or gender, or estate) and then in large group discussion, students could debate what social factors may have most influenced their subjects' interpretive practices.

Students could also share their readings in less conventional ways. Erasmus advocated having students write brief letters in which they adopt literary or historical personae; they might become "the aged and eloquent Nestor" and counsel Achilles, or they might write a letter "dissuading the violated Lucretia from taking her life" (24, 26). So students in this course could be asked to write to one another, still in their personae, about the assigned poems, using Gabriel Harvey's exchange with Spenser (Spenser, *Poetical Works*) or Anne Southwell's letter to Lady Ridgway (Cavanaugh) as epistolary models. The students' commonplace books could be circulated in small groups, thus indicating how different aspects of a given text might be foregrounded by different readers (George Puttenham might admire rhetorical figures, while Margaret Russell might extract stoic sententiae). In fact, one reader might interpret a poem politically one day and morally another, as Harvey seems to have done (Jardine and Grafton). Reading lyrics transcribed in the handwriting of classmates also reminds students that manuscript culture functioned concurrently with print culture (Marotti, *Manuscript*).

Adopting Renaissance personae makes possible another exercise that illustrates the performative, transactional, and often public nature of Renaissance reading: the reenactment of various scenes of reading. For example, Shakespeare might read a sonnet or selection from *Venus and Adonis* to the earl of Southampton, or Mary Sidney might read her dedicatory poem "Even now that Care which on thy Crowne attends" to Queen Elizabeth as she presents the queen with the Sidneian psalm translations, thus generating class discussion of the motives behind the passage selected and the patron's reaction. Sonnets from *Astrophil and Stella* could be read in a variety of contexts to illustrate the contingency of meaning: Philip Sidney to Fulke Greville or to a court audience including Queen Elizabeth or Penelope Rich to Elizabeth Vernon. Students thus learn through active engagement how "reading aloud for another person, or with another, was [. . .] a practice that entailed a host of different relationships: the service due a master, conjugal exchange, filial obedience, paternal education" (Chartier, "Leisure" 117).

Humanist pedagogues expected their students to compile commonplace books; this compilation was, according to a student born in 1583, a "Compendious & Profitable Way of Studying" (qtd. in Sherman 61). Such an assignment could prove equally profitable to our own students, who would be asked at the beginning of the course to copy into a blank notebook one or more brief, personally significant excerpts from each of the texts assigned for class discussion. Juan Luis Vives provides more explicit instructions in *De ratione studii* (1541): his pupil Mary Tudor was to "note down in her own hand any words occurring in her reading of serious authors which are either useful for everyday purposes or unusual or stylish; [. . .] forms of expression which are clever, well worded, smart, or learned; also, pithy remarks which are full of meaning, amusing, sharp, urbane, or witty; also, stories and anecdotes, from which she may draw lessons for her own life" (qtd. in Moss 116). No two books would be alike; as Peter Beal notes, "Every commonplace book is [. . .] a unique witness to the tastes, values, and thinking of a specific person or group" (133; see also Crane, *Framing*). Students could either retain their Renaissance persona (e.g., what might the earl of Essex or Isabella Whitney or John Harington have extracted from a particular poem?) or resume their own identity when gathering quotations. Reading with an eye to compilation, students could be encouraged to annotate their texts in imitation of Renaissance models, summarizing content, drawing intertextual connections, and identifying proverbs and striking rhetorical figures (Kintgen 66, 88). Asking students to familiarize themselves with some of the more common Elizabethan tropes described in Angel Day's *The English Secretary* and George Puttenham's *The Arte of English Poesie* (ed. Arber) might prove useful, especially if students are then asked to identify the rhetorical devices abundantly present in, for example, *The Rape of Lucrece*.

Students organize their quotations topically, adopting at least five of the headings used in Robert Allott's printed commonplace book *Englands Parnassus* (1600). Appropriate headings might include Art, Beautie, Chastitie, Death, Dispaire, Gifts, God, Greatnes, Heart, Honour, Jealouzie, Kisses, Leachery, Love, Marriage, Nature, Night, Pride, Princes, Sleepe, Teares, Time, Treason, and Venus. Near the end of the term, students select one topic and use their collected extracts as the foundation for a comparative paper, just as their early modern counterparts were expected to use their collected commonplaces in compositions and speeches. Like Seneca's proverbial bees, the students thus "mingle all the various nectars [they] have tasted, and turn them into a single sweet substance, in such a way that, even if it is apparent where it originated, it appears quite different from what it was in its original state" (qtd. in Moss 12).

Obviously, students in such a course will never accomplish the (impossible) task of exactly replicating early modern reading experiences, and some of my

122   MULTIPLE READERSHIPS

colleagues might worry that the strategies described above encourage students to read every text as an Elizabethan roman à clef. Yet Renaissance readers were trained to draw parallels between fictional worlds and their own (Kintgen 188) and to exercise significant autonomy in their reception and application of poetic texts (J. M. Wallace). Students are usually fascinated by the multivalent nature of Elizabethan texts, what Annabel Patterson terms the "functional ambiguity" of the poetry (*Censorship* 18)—the political usefulness of pastoral and Petrarchan fictions and the way the poetry operates within broader cultural systems such as patronage. Assignments such as those described above help students discover that the assigned works did not spring Athena-like from the minds of their creators as arcane cultural icons but were instead dynamic texts that helped negotiate specific social concerns. By historicizing notions of reading, we invite students to participate, albeit at a very elementary level, in Robert Darnton's project of developing "a history as well as a theory of reader response" (182).

Placing Elizabethan Poetry:
Some Classroom Ideas

Louise Schleiner

A way to organize work on Elizabethan poetry is to study the scenes where it evolved—the household reading circle of an aristocratic patron, or Paul's Cross and Walk with its bourgeois sermonizing and balladeering and its bookshops and customers, or the halls where courtiers exchanged manuscripts and read personal commonplace books. My students tend to get interested in verse if they can place the poems within the dealings of people who knew one another or at least within a narrative—that is, appreciate the poems somewhat as they were originally known, as works in context, rather than as collected greenhouse rarities. (In fact, assigning some pertinent fiction or letters before coming to the poetry study helps greatly.) Here a sample unit will be suggested from the reading, singing, and sewing circle of an aristocratic woman. Taking Mary Sidney, countess of Pembroke, as part of a group of writers who sometimes visited her in London or at Wilton or sent her manuscripts of verse or music, an instructor can do such a "great-house" unit and include poems by Samuel Daniel, Philip Sidney, Nicolas Breton (one set by the composer Thomas Morley [*Airs*]), and the countess herself. And for contrast students can set her household poetry—itself subtle and often erotic—against the racy, amoral kind portrayed whimsically in George Gascoigne's *Adventures of Master F. J.* (see the "Friday Breakfast" sonnet), against that of the Southampton household as intimated in *Love's Labor's Lost*, and then against some of Shakespeare's sonnets. (If necessary the instructor can suggest these contexts in a half-hour lecture or in readings, without giving assignments in *F. J.* or Shakespeare's play.) Computer assignments with visual and musical materials are highly valuable in making these scenes vivid.

For another unit, say, on bourgeois verse reflecting a quite different setting—workaday London—one could assign readings from Isabella Whitney (in the *Short-Title Catalogue* microfilms); songs, poems, or scenes from Thomas Deloney's *Jack of Newbury* as well as his ballads; readings from Thomas Dekker's *Shoemaker's Holiday*; and readings from the parodic *Willobie His Avisa* (Harrison; about a supposed puritanical alewife).

But I return to the plan focused on the countess of Pembroke, since I have space to develop only one unit. It could organize either a survey segment or a lengthier unit with more readings. Brief lectures about the countess and household reading practices could be interspersed with close work on poems. Whatever the extent of Mary Sidney's patronage, Breton and Daniel speak of being at Wilton, and we see in *The Countess of Pembroke's Yvychurch*, part 3 (1592), by Abraham Fraunce, an allegorical portrait of her circle of ladies-in-waiting, household employees, and visitors, assembled for the deathday anniversary of her beloved brother Philip. Fraunce was a lawyer employed by

124 PLACING ELIZABETHAN POETRY

the earl of Pembroke and a quantitative versifier known for his English hexameter translation of Thomas Watson's neo-Latin *Lachrymae*, or "Sorrows of Amyntas," based on the sufferings of Tasso's pastoral hero. The instructor may not want to assign undergraduates any of Fraunce's or Watson's verse (unless for an optional essay or computer-group topic for musicians on the quantitative movement and its musical connections). But the *Yvychurch* can be usefully described and a few excerpts read out. Fraunce was important to the countess's way of working through her grief over her brother's death in battle, whereby she learned to carry on his identity through her own writing and through editing his incomplete writings: *morientis imago Philippi* ("image of the dying Philip") Fraunce calls her in the dedication to the *Yvychurch*, part 3. His pastoral celebrating her as Phyllis, the female Philip, defined a poetic world of personal and communal grieving where she learned to be a poet and activist for militant internationalist Protestantism. Another household employee, her elder son's tutor Hugh Sanford, was the copy editor of Philip Sidney's works.

So the "nymphs and swains" with pastoral names would be Sanford, Fraunce, her chaplain or doctor, maybe a visiting writer, her ladies-in-waiting and literate serving women, and probably a visiting or resident female relative. Assembled at her Ivychurch estate near Wilton, they take turns performing for her something suitable for the day—a song, a recited poem, a paraphrase of one of Ovid's tales of grief and metamorphosis, or, in Fraunce's case, scholarly comments on what the others have done. In this context the countess conceived her paraphrased renditions of the *Psalms*. Picking up where Philip Sidney left off at Psalm 44, she paraphrased the rest in a variety of meters for reciting or singing. She herself must have sung them at times to her own lute accompaniment; settings of two of them survive (Psalms 51 and 130; B.L. Add. MS 15,117).

Psalm 45 is a glorious royal wedding hymn, in which the poet acquires a lyrical voice by identifying with the well-spoken king and then with the resplendent bride queen, whose very underwear is done in gold. The countess renders the opening lines as follows:

> My heart indites an argument of worth,
> The praise of him that doth the Scepter sway:
> My tongue the pen to paint his praises forth,
> Shall write as swift as swiftest writer may.
> [. . . . .]
> Thy lips, as springs, do flow with speaking grace.   (lines 1–4, 8)

Giving the students a further sample of her psalm renditions—for example, Psalm 73 with its crisp speaking voice lamenting betrayal by a friend, or Psalm 130 in a madrigal meter—the instructor could lead up to the portrayal of the countess's own sense of a calling as a writer in the poem to her brother, "To the Angel Spirit of the Most Excellent Sir Philip Sidney" (Triumph 92–95), which portrays a bold image of her muse mating with his:

To thee, pure spirit, to thee alone's addressed
This coupled work [their Psalms], by double interest thine:
First raised by thy bless'd hand, and what is mine
Inspired by thee, thy secret power impressed.
So dared my Muse with thine itself combine,
As mortal stuff with that which is divine;
Thy lightning beams give luster to the rest.
                    (Triumph, lines 1–7; spelling modernized)

Philip Sidney himself had portrayed the inverse of this cross-gendered inspiration when young Pyrocles cross-dresses and, as Cleophila, infuses himself with the beauty and spirituality of his love Philoclea. Remember that Sidney drafted the *Arcadia* in the company of his sister and her ladies ("you desired me to doo it, [. . .] being done in loose sheets of paper, mostly in your presence" [*Poems* 6]); the writing of it may have begun as part of a parlor conversation game, in which each player took a turn inventing a certain kind of story. Such a game would have occurred when he spent time in her household in 1580, probably cooling his heels in the country after offending Queen Elizabeth by denouncing the royal plan of Catholic marriage to Alençon. Studying this link, the instructor would read with students the sonnet sung by "Lady" Pyrocles in a woodsy bower while Pyrocles's dear friend Musidorus eavesdrops on him and then the blazon poem on the wonders of Philoclea, to which Pyrocles taps his foot on the sandbanks of the River Ladon while he eavesdrops on Philoclea and her ladies bathing naked. (Here it's fun to have a few students imitate Pyrocles practicing how to walk like a woman while reciting the sonnet.)

Transformd in shew, but more transformd in minde,
I cease to strive, with double conquest foild .
[. . . . .]
Thus is my power transformed to your will.
What marvaile then I take a woman's hew,
Since what I see, thinke, know is all but you?
                    (*New Arcadia*, bk. 1, ch. 12, lines 1–2, 12–14)

The blazon poem is "What toong can her perfections tell / In whose each part all pens may dwell," which tells

How all this is but a faire Inne
Of fairer guest, which dwells within,
Of whose high praise, and praisefull blisse,
Goodnes the penne, heaven paper is.   (lines 87–90)

Students enjoy these rhapsodies of the cross-dressed lover's absorption in the female other if they can get caught up in the riverbank scene of peeping from

126   PLACING ELIZABETHAN POETRY

the bushes. Having read a blazon poem also prepares students for later reading of Shakespeare's parodic sonnet "My mistress' eyes are nothing like the sun" (Sonnet 130).

Treating sonnets as part of great-house reading, one can talk briefly about romances such as the cumulative, multivolume *Amadis de Gaule* (which the Elizabethans read in French) or Margaret Tyler's 1579 translation *The Mirror of Princely Deedes and Knighthood* (Ortuñez de Calahorra) and can introduce the sonnet sequence by comparison as an implied narrative, that is, another form of supposed reading for ladies about love (actually, men read these genres just as much). The story is "read" between the poems just as we "read between the lines" of a literary work. At this point the instructor can introduce selected sonnets from *Astrophil and Stella*, extremely erotic poems in which the household of Penelope Devereux, Lady Rich, sister of Sidney's ally the earl of Essex, is portrayed as just such a high-minded, pious scene as that of the Pembrokes.

To offer a few more suggestions: one could treat Daniel's first *Delia* sonnet ("Unto the boundles Ocean of thy beautie / Runs this poore river, charg'd with streames of zeale") in relation to the Ditchley portrait (National Gallery, London), where Queen Elizabeth stands on a map at the sources of the rivers of England, and then to the countess's use of the same imagery—of herself, her spirit, flowing downstream to her brother of oceanic memory—in the 1592 draft "To the Angel Spirit," found among Daniel's papers (cf. Triumph). Recalling the composer Morley's appeal to the countess for patronage, one could study Breton's haunting "Fair in a morn, O fairest morn" (2), probably written in praise of the countess on her "hill" of Wilton; and listen to Morley's setting of it for lute (*Airs*), recorded a number of times; and read other verbally musical Breton lyrics.

Finally, here are some sample topics for computer-networked groups that could also be adapted for the traditional classroom (an enlargeable image would be valuable, especially when the topic is the sonnet in the Ditchley portrait). Each student could choose a topic group; students not liking any assigned topics could form a group and think up their own topic. The parlor game idea below comes from the *Frauenzimmer Gesprächspiele* (Harsdörfer), a book of games long played in aristocratic women's chambers.

> Imagine a possible music video for one of the singable poems and create layout graphics for some scenes, picking up visual hints from the poem. Discuss what constitutes a lyric genre, such as music videos or mood-evoking poems.
> Study the sonnet (attributed to Henry Lee) painted into the Ditchley portrait and mutilated by restorations; use possible rhyme schemes to help puzzle out the missing line-ending words.
> As a game, have each student think up a one-page answer to a love question, such as "Whether in love natural inclination works more than

strategy, intellect, money, or courtesy" or "Whether the greater power in love is of the spirit or of the body"; have one person be judge, who will pose the question and write a ruling on which answer is best.

Compare and contrast Pyrocles's poetry and other ways of wooing his forbidden lady with the strategies of Mrs. Doubtfire in the film of that name.

Collect reproductions and accounts of embroidery and other needlework of the time and study their images in connection with those of selected poems.

Infinite Riches and Very Little Room: Speeding through Some Sonnets in the Introductory Historical Survey

Clare R. Kinney

My focus here is on the challenges of teaching the Elizabethan sonnet in the context of a very large (300-plus students) historical survey for English majors. The course moves at a breakneck pace—*Beowulf* to *Paradise Lost* in thirteen weeks—and I can devote only two lectures and two discussion sections to the sonneteers, making occasional references to earlier sixteenth-century writers of lyric. (Donne's erotic lyrics are addressed in a separate lecture, but by that time we're already moving into the seventeenth century and the poetry of meditation.) I have to work in very broad strokes, trying, in a limited time, to offer as many points of entry into these poems as possible to an audience largely unfamiliar with the conventions and rhetorical strategies of Elizabethan poetry. My teaching assistants revisit and supplement my lectures in discussion sections, but we do not pretend to offer much depth of coverage. We do hope to complicate and historicize, just a little, our students' ideas about a certain kind of lyric performance; we also hope to pique the interest, arouse the pleasure that may encourage some students to take more specialized courses in Renaissance poetry later in their undergraduate careers.

I would like to feel I could balance in my limited lecture space the close reading of particular poems with more historicized accounts of (for example) the cultural poetics of the erotic lyric. By the time we come to the sonneteers, I will have given the students some relevant background in previous lectures— they will have encountered the notion of "self-fashioning"; they'll have heard about the premium placed on the arts of persuasion in Renaissance Europe, about the potential continuum between the strategies of the love poems and the more obviously public and political gestures of artful solicitation, about the particularly charged intersection between courtship and courtiership in a country ruled by an unmarried female monarch. My two lectures, however, tend to treat the poems at a more micro level—at the point of collision, perhaps, between sociohistorical context, literary convention, and poetic syntax— as I attempt to make these lyrics more legible and more pleasurable for undergraduate readers.

My first lecture focuses on the rhetoric and codes of Petrarchism. The students will have read selections from the *Rime sparse* in modern English translation (Durling, *Petrarch's Lyric Poems*, sonnets 3, 132, 140, 164, 302). I spend about half the lecture discussing the Petrarch selections and outlining the larger characteristics and reception history of the *Rime sparse*. I emphasize in particular the innovatory significance of the lyric sequence for the representation of (male) interiority; I also note the multifarious self-fashionings of its poet-lover in the absence of Laura. I point to those elements of Petrarch's poetic vocabulary that are appropriated most enthusiastically by later writers—the externalization of love as a controlling force, the blazoning of the body of the beloved, the deployment of sustained conceit, the use of oxymoron to figure the divided psyche.

In the remainder of the lecture I address my audience's tendency to devalue poetry that works within a visible framework of convention—their vague feeling that when you've seen one Elizabethan sonnet you've seen them all. To clarify some of the ways in which a writer may reinvent or interrogate a conventional discourse, I explore a variety of sixteenth-century Petrarchan appropriations. I'll offer an example of a fairly straightforward recasting of the familiar idiom—for example, Spenser's "My love is lyke to yse, and I to fyre" (*Amoretti*, sonnet 30)—but I'll also glance at both the Wyatt and Surrey translations of *Rime sparse*, sonnet 140, trying to elucidate some of the telling differences between their versions of the lyric. (Both translations are in the *Norton Anthology of English Literature*, volume 1, which is my basic course text, supplemented with occasional handouts.) I like to use Shakespeare to discuss more radical revisions of Petrarchism; the obvious example is "My mistress' eyes are nothing like the sun," but the familiar territory of *Romeo and Juliet* yields a nice comparison between Romeo's pastiche of Petrarchan oxymoron ("O brawling love! O loving hate! [. . .]") before he meets Juliet (1.1.176–82) and the unprecedented "love at first sonnet" encounter of hero and heroine (1.5.93–110), in which the lady is allowed to respond to and reshape the male poet's conceits and the conceits themselves are bodied forth by the hands that touch and the mouths that kiss. (I offer an extended close reading of this exchange.)

By the second lecture, the students will have sampled several English sonnet sequences. I've always taught poems from *Astrophil and Stella* and the *Amoretti* but have recently substituted selections from Mary Wroth's *Pamphilia to Amphilanthus* for selections from Shakespeare's *Sonnets* (in one version of this course, the prelecture readings were *Astrophil and Stella*, sonnets 1, 2, 6, 10, 45, 47, 49, 69, 71, 72, 108; *Amoretti*, sonnets 1, 37, 54, 67, 68, 75; *Pamphilia to Amphilanthus*, sonnets P3, P4, P9, P16, P48, P55, P66, P103 [Roberts's numbering in Wroth, *Poems*]). Wroth is not, of course, precisely an Elizabethan poet, but Philip Sidney's niece is at once the first female English Petrarchist and the most belated early modern English author of a sonnet sequence: it is very helpful to compare her representation of a female lyric speaker with the lyric personae created by Spenser and Sidney.

I start this lecture by reading a passage from Giovanni Pico della Mirandola's oration *On the Dignity of Man*—the lines in which God tells Adam that "Thou [. . .] art the maker and molder of thyself; thou mayest sculpt thyself into whatever shape thou dost prefer" (5). I invite my students to think of these sonnet sequences as performances of the self in which a speaker reorganizes the universe around his or her own desires, constructing microcosmos after microcosmos (I return to this idea when I teach Donne). I offer a brief overview of

130   INFINITE RICHES AND VERY LITTLE ROOM

the putatively informing narratives of the sonnet sequences and then compli-
cate matters with a few remarks on publication history, comparing Spenser's
self-disclosure in the *Amoretti* and *Epithalamion* with the textual history of
Shakespeare's *Sonnets*. (I offer the analogy of cinematic montage—or of shots
in a photographic album—as an alternative to a crudely narrativizing reading
of the sequences' scattered rhymes.) I may also glance at some of the more
striking departures from the *Rime sparse* scenario—the marriage of Petrar-
chism and Protestantism in the consummated desire of the *Amoretti*; the ten-
sion, in Shakespeare's *Sonnets*, between the Petrarchan hyperbole that makes
the male beloved more lovely than a summer's day and the anti-Petrarchism
that insists the mistress's eyes are nothing like the sun.

Narrowing my focus, I might discuss the opening poems of *Astrophil and
Stella* and the *Amoretti*, paying particular attention to the artfulness of the
speakers' preliminary articulation of their agendas, as well as to the manner in
which they insert the female reader within their texts. I note that Astrophil's
climactic "birthing" of a colloquial voice that insists on the authenticity of its
experience is in fact part of his larger scheme to win Stella's "grace." I ask how
we might reconcile the speaker of *Amoretti*, sonnet 1, who places his poems in
"trembling" bondage to his lady's touch and gaze, with the speaker of *Amoretti*,
sonnet 67, who celebrates his own binding of the "yet halfe trembling" deer-
lady. I encourage my students to think about these lyrics as rhetorical perfor-
mances that are intended to solicit (or orchestrate) certain responses; to this
end I might read aloud Shakespeare's "No longer mourn for me when I am
dead" and ask my audience to consider what the poem is trying to do as well as
what it appears to say.

Introducing my students to Mary Wroth in a recent avatar of this course, I
discussed just what it might mean for a woman to invent a (public, published)
voice for a female poet-lover in a society where women were officially and ide-
ally chaste, obedient, and silent. I suggested that when Pamphilia lays claim to
her own desire: "yett love I will, till I butt ashes prove" (sonnet P55, line 14;
Poems), her apparently quite conventional Petrarchan hyperbole signifies *dif-
ferently* (even before we figure in the possible pun on will/ Will[iam] Herbert).
I then raised the question whether the language of Petrarchism can be respoken
by a woman, noting that in the poems of *Pamphilia to Amphilanthus* the body
of the male beloved is never made visible and that it is not his chastity but his
infidelity that creates the state of privation in which the female poet-lover
dilates on her feelings. Since I had emphasized the cultural importance of the
Petrarchan idiom in shaping the way that desire gets talked about in the West-
ern literary tradition, the example of Wroth allowed me to suggest just how
much this tradition is informed by the assumption that the woman is the object,
not the subject, of the lyric text.

Although my lectures offer close readings of particular poems, I must rely
on my graduate assistants for even more tightly focused work in the discussion
sections. In pedagogical conferences with my teaching teams, I suggest partic-

Clare R. Kinney 131

ular poems whose examination might usefully extend or complement the concerns of the lectures, but the final decision about what gets covered in section belongs to the TA. I have sometimes recommended a handout for section use after the Petrarchism lecture—"Looking for Dear Deer in the Hart's Forest"— in which I juxtapose a translation of *Rime sparse*, sonnet 190, with Wyatt's "Whoso list to hunt" and Spenser's "Lyke as a huntsman after weary chace." One graduate assistant reported that his students' exploration of the three treatments of the love-hunt conceit led them to remark on the distinctive use of voice and tone in the Wyatt and Spenser poems; the class was gradually drawn into an investigation of the formal strategies that shaped the poems' voices and created their quite different tonal coloring.

Questions of form tend to be addressed rather parenthetically in my own presentations, although I outline the differences between Italian and English sonnet structure and define some key terms (caesura, enjambment, etc.). Very few students are equipped with the vocabulary to talk about meter or rhyme scheme; I can only glance at these in lecture, but my TAs usually spend some time on poetic form in section (one or two noble souls even scheduled extra meetings to discuss scansion and other technical matters with students suffering from fear of poetry). A perhaps more daunting problem in introducing students to this material is that their previous encounters with the lyric may have privileged models that bear little resemblance to these "old poems," models that may lead them to dismiss our readings as both impenetrable and "unsuccessful." If students are familiar only with the lapidary parataxis of certain modernist lyrics, they may find it difficult to read a short lyric as a sustained act of persuasion or argument and may be impervious to the linear unfolding of its poetic logic. Alternatively (as one of my former TAs cannily noted), if students' uninterrogated model for "real poetry" is a quasi-Romantic, expressive, free-form, ostensibly spontaneous outpouring of emotion, they'll probably resist the potentially multiple agendas, conscious artifice, and serious game-playing of Elizabethan love poetry. Some TAs found it useful to "out" students' assumptions about the aims and values of love poets before getting the class to reconsider just what might be the aims, values, and assumptions informing the Elizabethan lyrics. Others noted that these gestures of demystification are never enough on their own: the section leaders (and the professor) must themselves demonstrate—in the words of another former member of my teaching team—"hearty affection" and "active signs of respect" for the poetry.

Experienced graduate instructors emphasized the importance of steering conversation away from generalized responses to the poems, noting that the very process of teasing out poetic syntax, unpacking the logic of a sustained conceit, and historicizing the connotations of a particularly charged word would return the class to more carefully focused considerations of such larger matters as the speaker's designs on his or her audience. Some TAs suggested that work in small groups might be especially effective in producing a reading of a lyric; if each group was given a few lines to analyze on its own, the semiprivate discussion

132 INFINITE RICHES AND VERY LITTLE ROOM

encouraged students to posit, defend, and refine possible readings outside the
class spotlight. When, moreover, the small groups reunited to share their inter-
pretations, those looking at lines near the end of the poem were able to build
on the comments of earlier discussants.

My own observations of section meetings brought home to me how unprac-
ticed many students seemed to be at considering a lyric as a sustained syntac-
tical speech act or argument, how rarely they were able to connect their
reading of a particular line or phrase to the rest of the work. I liked one TA's
simple tactic of getting a student to read a Sidney sonnet cold and then, after
the class had carefully worked through the poem's complexities, inviting
another student to reread it aloud (with gratifyingly different results). Getting
a sonnet off the page, emphasizing the way that it functions as an imitation of
an utterance seems to me a very helpful pedagogical device (I myself like to
recite Drayton's "Since there's no help" for this purpose). A dynamic and care-
fully paced reading aloud by an instructor can, moreover, do a lot to clarify the
inverted syntax our students often find so baffling in Elizabethan lyric.

My preoccupation with lyric utterance has spilled over into the assignments
I attach to this portion of the survey course. As an alternative to a short writ-
ten analysis of a sonnet not interpreted in either lecture or discussion section,
students may sign up to do a private oral presentation for their TA (or for me,
if they prefer). This assignment requires the memorization and recitation of a
previously undiscussed sonnet, with an emphasis on performance (their recita-
tion should demonstrate that they have made some interpretive decisions), fol-
lowed by a short conversation with the teacher in which they explore the
rhetorical and poetic strategies of the work (and explain why they chose it).
This oral alternative has proved particularly successful with bright, engaged
undergraduates whose prose doesn't always do justice to the quality of their
ideas: such students often offer confident and trenchant accounts of poems
that have come alive for them as texts in performance.

NOTE

I would like to thank the various (current or former) University of Virginia graduate
students who worked with me in ENGL 381 and gave me invaluable feedback for this
essay—in particular, Anne Coldiron, Annie Sussman, Elizabeth Outka, and Neil Arditi.

Incorporating Women Writers into the Survey Course: The Countess of Pembroke's Psalm 73 and *Astrophil and Stella*, Sonnet 5

Margaret P. Hannay

The avalanche of recent research on early modern women writers may overwhelm instructors. How can women writers be added to survey courses when there is already too much to cover? One possible beginning is to incorporate a significant writer like Mary Sidney, the countess of Pembroke, into discussions of genre by focusing on a single poem.

In my survey of English literature course (*Beowulf* to Austen), I have approximately three weeks to cover Elizabethan poetry, a formidable task. To limit the infinite realm of possible discourse, I assign two brief speeches to establish the political and religious context, Lady Jane Grey's scaffold speech and Queen Elizabeth's Armada speech (*Norton*). Then I focus on the Petrarchan sonnet tradition and its political uses. Very few women wrote love sonnets in the Tudor period, but they did write Psalm paraphrases. I devote one class to the intersection of these two traditions in Pembroke's *Psalmes*. After a glance at her straightforward rendition of Psalm 100 as a Spenserian sonnet and Psalm 150 as a modified Italian sonnet, the class focuses on Psalm 73, because it echoes the lines of Philip Sidney's *Astrophil and Stella*, sonnet 5, even as it draws on the Psalm commentary of Theodore Beza.

I briefly discuss restrictions on women's writing; however, since many students now come to this introductory course believing that all women before their generation were passive victims of oppression, I emphasize what Pembroke was able to achieve as the avatar of her brother Philip, who was celebrated as a Protestant martyr. She became a patron to those who honored him, she published his work, she wrote poems to praise him, and she completed the metric Psalm translation that he had begun. She also wrote two original poems in praise of Elizabeth I and translated Petrarch's *Triumph of Death* into terza rima and Robert Garnier's *Antonius* into blank verse. I mention her strong political statements, her importation of Continental literary forms, her biblical scholarship, and her poetic skill in writing 126 different poetic forms in her paraphrases of Psalms 44–150. To give students a sense of her importance I show them the Simon van de Passe portrait (Hannay, *Philip's Phoenix* 59), which signals her rank and suggests the construction of a literary identity independent of her brother; students notice immediately that she proudly holds her *Psalmes* and that the portrait is crowned with the poet's laurel wreath.

I then give a brief introduction to the Psalm genre, noting that Pembroke joined a community of poets who spoke through the words of the psalmist, including not only such men of the church as Martin Luther, Theodore Beza, and Matthew Parker or such famous male poets as Clément Marot and Thomas

134   INCORPORATING WOMEN WRITERS

Wyatt but also such women writers as Queen Mary Stuart, Elizabeth Fane, Elizabeth Tyrwhit, Anne Askew, and perhaps even Queen Elizabeth herself. Pembroke certainly knew the twenty-six sonnets on Psalm 51 composed by Anne Lock, for she quotes from them (Hannay, "Unlock" 24). My students, who are predominantly Catholic in this Franciscan college, know that in addition to the importance of the Psalms in Jewish and Christian public worship, the Psalms have always been considered particularly appropriate for private meditation. Students therefore quickly understand that by speaking the words of the Psalms a person can express his or her own subjectivity (Prescott, "King David" 134; Lewalski, *Protestant Poetics* 301-02; R. Greene, "Sir Philip Sidney's Psalms"). We talk about how Reformation Protestants were particularly eager to translate the Psalms as personal meditation, thereby combining two of their most valued exercises, biblical scholarship and self-examination. Probably the most familiar usage of the Psalms to express subjectivity is Wyatt's paraphrase of Psalm 51 that stresses "Inward Sion, the Sion of the ghost" and the "heart's Jerusalem," a usage highlighted for us by Stephen Greenblatt (*Renaissance Self-Fashioning* 115). Learned women, who were encouraged to confine their writings to translation of godly works, could also find their own voices in the Psalms. In rendering the Psalms, Pembroke speaks through the voice of David like other translators, but she also speaks through the voice of her brother Philip by completing his work (Beilin, *Redeeming* 148–49; Waller, "Countess of Pembroke" 339; Hannay, *Philip's Phoenix* 59–83).

Sidney is invoked most obviously in Pembroke's paraphrase of Psalm 73, a poem that interweaves quotations from *Astrophil* with biblical translation and commentary. A detailed reading of the two poems enables my class to discuss larger connections between gender and genre, observing that Pembroke may have reworked *Astrophil*, sonnet 5, into a Psalm paraphrase rather than a Petrarchan sonnet because a sixteenth-century English woman writer could not afford to admit desire. Pembroke's deliberate revision of her brother's work demonstrates her use of religious discourse to create a public voice. From the psalmist she adopts two strategies for constructing subjectivity. The first is to create an unironic, virtuous self, one that is haunted by God rather than by desire. While her understanding may struggle with a theological problem, her will never quite turns from God; her poem, as Louise Schleiner observes, "creates an effective self-dramatizing of the anguished psalmist in his wavering thoughts" (*Tudor and Stuart Women Writers* 72). Speaking through the voice of David even as she echoes the voice of Astrophil, she thus flattens the comic irony of Astrophil's decision to embrace Stella rather than virtue. A second strategy is to enfold this virtuous self in the community of believers, so that the subject is often constructed by the use of a plural pronoun. Pembroke thereby partially externalizes the struggle between good and evil, and presents it as a conflict between "godly wee" and the "godlesse Crue" (line 34), rather than as Astrophil's internal struggle between reason and desire. This externalization places the struggle between good and evil outside the subject and provides a

Margaret P. Hannay   135

community of support. Because the poet finally chooses to "cleave to god" (line 84) instead of idols, to construct a public voice as a member of the godly community, she is empowered to speak God's praise.

My students learn more by doing than by listening, so I give them a handout with both *Astrophil*, sonnet 5, and Pembroke's paraphrase of Psalm 73. They immediately see that Pembroke, using a technique that Louis Martz calls "sacred parody" (*Poetry* 186), begins with a quotation from *Astrophil*, sonnet 5, "It is most true." Both poems start with a truth statement with which the speaker must struggle and both conclude that reason is inadequate to solve the problem. In Sidney's sonnet, the poet argues that reason is inadequate to conquer love, using his characteristic pattern of thirteen lines of logic undercut by a final ironic statement. It is most true that we should follow reason, most true that Cupid is a false god, most true that Virtue alone is true Beauty, most true that we are but pilgrims who should be on an inward journey to heaven. All this is true, Astrophil concludes, "and yet true that I must *Stella* love" (sonnet 5). Psalm 73 also argues that reason is inadequate while it raises another problem of central importance to students: Why do bad things happen to good people? It is most true that God is good—and yet that goodness is not always apparent in our lives.

Then I give students Beza's version of Psalm 73 so they can see that although Pembroke adapts her brother's phrasing she also relies on her usual scholarly sources. (On her scholarship, see *Collected Works* 2: 10–32.) Beza's "Argument" may have recalled Astrophil's battle with reason, for Beza declares that "nothing [. . .] striveth more against the true wisdome, then doth the very reason of man" when it is "not regenerate" (182). Pembroke's parallel debts to these two sources are most obvious in her first line, which both quotes the opening phrase of *Astrophil*, sonnet 5, and paraphrases Beza's verse 1: "it must needes be true and inviolable, that God can not be but favorable towardes Israel, that is, to them that worship him purely and devoutly." Defining Israel as the godly, those with "undefiled hearts," Pembroke declares that God sends them nothing but good: "It is most true that god to Israell, / I mean to men of undefiled hartes, / is onlie good, and nought but good impartes" (Psalm 73, lines 1–3). Like Astrophil, the speaker is struggling with a proposition that is accepted as logically true but seems experientially false. Like her scriptural originals, however, Pembroke puts the struggle safely into the past tense; the speaker now accepts the truth, although she (the "I" is ungendered, but for convenience I use the feminine pronoun) had struggled against that truth and had almost left the way: "Most true, I see, albe, allmost I fell / from right conceit into a crooked mynd; / and from this truth with straying stepps declin'd" (lines 4–6). These lines rework Sidney's statement that those who struggle against true reason are rebels who hurt only themselves. Sidney's "from whose rules who do swerve" (line 3) becomes Pembroke's "from this truth with straying stepps declin'd" (line 6), using the phrase "straying stepps" from Sidney's Psalm 1, line 2. Yet Pembroke's speaker only "allmost" fell; she never truly falls from virtue.

136   INCORPORATING WOMEN WRITERS

With some guidance students discover additional echoes from Sidney and Beza in Pembroke's opening stanza. "Boiling brest" is quoted from *Astrophil*, sonnet 108, line 2, but it also conflates Beza's image of the soul "set on fire" by doubt (*Psalmes*, verse 3) and his question "Wherefore did I then so sore boyle?" (verse 21). Similarly, that breast "did chafe and swell" in an imitation of *Astrophil*, sonnet 37, line 1: "My mouth doth water, and my breast doth swell." The phrase also recalls Sidney's rendition of Psalm 37.18, a psalm with a similar argument: "Chafe not at some man's great good fortune." In Psalm 37 the speaking voice is an authority admonishing patience: "Fume not, rage not, frett not I say" (line 21), whereas in Psalm 73 the speaking voice does fret and fume as it records an inner struggle against rage that is nonetheless vivid for being self-censored. In Pembroke's version she grew angry when she "first [. . .] saw the wicked proudly stand, / prevailing still in all they tooke in hand" (lines 8–9). Although the speaker's anger is presented—rather unconvincingly—as past, the prosperity of the ungodly is constantly present, emphasized in the repeated use of *still*: they are "prevailing still" (line 9), their "horne of plenty" is "freshly flowing still" (line 29), their riches still increase while "our wealth" (line 36) still grows less in this psychological reading of the verse (Zim 198). Their wealth and power are vividly described: they wear "pride, as [. . .] a gorgious chaine" on "their swelling necks" and are "cloth'd in wrong, as if a Robe it were" (lines 16–18). (Following Schleiner's observation that the phrase is "evocative of some Holbein painting" [*Tudor and Stuart Women Writers* 72], I illustrate it with several portraits that each feature "a gorgious chaine," such as Holbein's cartoon of Henry VII with Henry VIII, Edward VI as Prince of Wales, and Nicholas Hilliard's miniature of Christopher Hatton.) So distressing is this situation that "e'vn godly men" (line 28) are likely to question God.

In stanza 3 the speaker is part of a communal voice, a voice defined by its opposition: the "godly wee" lament together, in the face of the prosperity of "the godlesse Crue." In stanza 4 the conflict is presented as more personal: "Nay ev'n within my self, my self did say." In this passage the repeated personal pronouns stress internal struggle, a conflict that the speaker strives to keep contained within the self. In the conclusion of the poem, looking back on her former struggle with her new understanding of God's presence, she asks a new question: not why the wicked prosper while the godly suffer but why she was so distressed. As in *Astrophil*, sonnet 5, the speaker is a self-admitted "foole" who has been fighting against reason.

Students note that both speakers point out the danger of worshipping lesser gods. Astrophil adores the image of Cupid "in temple of [my] hart." Pembroke's virtuous speaker chooses God and abjures the "whoorish Idolls" chosen by the ungodly, thereby externalizing the problem, projecting it onto the opposition. But the problem is also internal. Pembroke's most significant adaptation of Sidney in this poem may be the "inward part" (line 63), a phrase Sidney uses elsewhere (*Arcadia* 3.50.6 and "Other Poems" 4.543) to stress the theme of interiority, but one that also conflates the description of reason in *Astrophil*,

Margaret P. Hannay   137

sonnet 5, as both "inward light" and "heavenly part." ("Inward light" also recalls "inward sight," phrases that occur frequently in Sidney's works, as in *Arcadia* bk. 2, poem 26, line 2; *Arcadia* bk. 3, poem 39, line 7; *Astrophil*, sonnet 88, line 10; and Psalm 25, line 2.) In this poem Pembroke employs religious discourse to explore knowledge of the self, even as she addresses knowledge of God. Because her "inward sight" has been clouded, she cannot find the answer within herself. Whereas Astrophil recognizes and rejects the guidance of the "heavenly part," Pembroke's speaker seeks such guidance in the future: "then guide me still, then still upon me spend / the treasures of thy sure advise, untill / thou take me hence into thy glories hill" (lines 70–72). In an original addition, she implies that the ascent will be difficult and require a teacher: "O what is he will teach me clyme the skyes?" (line 73). In this final stanza Pembroke adds a coda to her scriptural originals and to Beza. Her plea may well include an admission of her debt to her brother's poems in its allusion to *Astrophil*, sonnet 31, line 1, as Zim suggests (201). It also contrasts the teaching of the godly with the teaching of the wicked who "pronounce as from the skies" (line 23) in her second stanza. The speaker wants to know God. Unlike her biblical sources, Pembroke presents that search for knowledge as a journey to God's dwelling place, perhaps in a conscious echo of Astrophil's statement "that on earth we are but pilgrims made, / And should in soule up to our countrey move" (*Astrophil*, sonnet 5, lines 12–13).

Then, returning to the opening assertion that God is good to those with undefiled hearts, the speaker contrasts earthly goods with God's goodness in a rhetorical repetition that simultaneously expands and builds on the first phrase, seeking "with thee, thee good, thee goodnes to remain" (line 74). God's goodness will satisfy the speaker, so that "no good on earth doth my desires detain" (line 75). Having chosen God, the speaker no longer need fear that her words will betray the community of God's children. Instead, placing her struggle safely in the past, she constructs a virtuous self that is emboldened by faith "to sing his workes while breath shall give me space" (line 84). As the struggle between reason and desire leads Astrophil to choose desire and write of Stella, so in Pembroke's Psalm 73 the speaker's struggle between reason and faith leads her to choose faith and write of God.

Students see that Pembroke's poem has no concluding irony as does *Astrophil*, sonnet 5; there can be no concluding irony for Pembroke's speaker, since ultimately the psalmist chooses the heavenly beauty that Astrophil (not Philip Sidney) spurns. As Astrophil struggles to find a voice that speaks from his heart, so Pembroke's speaker struggles to find a voice that can speak from her "inward part." Instead of seeking to free herself from the influence of predecessors, as Sidney's character does in *Astrophil*, sonnet 1, the speaker enfolds herself in the godly community and positions herself within God's house; from that secure haven she is empowered to speak both for the community and for herself. Religious discourse thus overcomes injunctions to women's silence.

138 INCORPORATING WOMEN WRITERS

I end the discussion of these parallel Sidney poems with a glance ahead to coming attractions: the religious lyrics of John Donne, George Herbert, and Aemilia Lanyer and the sonnets of Pembroke's niece and namesake Mary Sidney, Lady Wroth. Pembroke's metric *Psalmes* both influenced the genre of religious poetry and empowered writers like Lanyer and Wroth to overcome restrictions of gender.

Suggested Reading   Merry Wiesner provides a concise and informative introduction to conditions for early modern women in the first chapter of *Women and Gender in Early Modern Europe*. For additional Pembroke bibliography, see Josephine Roberts, "Recent Studies in Women Writers of the English Renaissance: Mary Sidney, Countess of Pembroke"; Micheline White, "Recent Studies in Women Writers of Tudor England, 1485–1603 (Mid-1993 to 1999)." For general background and a brief introduction to Pembroke's life and works, see the forthcoming MLA volume *Teaching Tudor and Stuart Women Writers* (ed. Woods and Hannay).

NOTE

All quotations from Mary Sidney are from her *Collected Works*. The Penhurst *Psalmes* manuscript is used with the kind permission of the viscount de L'Isle MBE.

Teaching Renaissance Manuscript Poetry
Steven W. May

Students in my undergraduate courses in sixteenth- and seventeenth-century nondramatic literature become acquainted with contemporary manuscripts in facsimile as well as in transcribed and edited formats. I first take the students behind the scenes of their textbook anthologies to see what complicated work must often be done to arrive at the critical texts they are reading. This exercise is easiest with poets whose verse has survived in multiple manuscript copies, such as Walter Ralegh; Philip Sidney; Mary Sidney, countess of Pembroke; John Harington; and John Donne. I bring to class handwriting samples of these and other authors in the facsimile collections edited by P. J. Croft, Anthony G. Petti, and Charles Ryskamp. My students usually agree that the Italian hands are relatively easy to decipher, while proficiency with the secretary cursives would take a good deal of practice.

Meanwhile, I have copied out in my own semilegible longhand four to six lines from a poem on the syllabus; the first stanza of Dyer's "The lowest trees have tops" is a favorite. I give this to a student at random with instructions to copy it on a separate sheet of paper, return the original to me, and pass the copy to someone else in the class. That person, in turn, is to make a copy of the stanza and pass it to someone else while retaining the first student's copy. The last copyist in the class reads his or her work aloud, after which I read the original version. In practice, this exercise always makes its point. If the final text is more or less identical with my version, I congratulate the class on being far more accurate scribes than their Renaissance counterparts, who, in my experience, averaged about two percent substantive errors each time they transcribed a text. When, however, the final text deviates widely (sometimes comically) from the original, I point out that this sort of corruption was the norm for poetry in manuscript circulation during the Renaissance. Once an author's verse began to be passed from hand to hand for entry into the private anthologies, authorial control over the text vanished and a host of mutations ordinarily occurred. The editor's task is to distinguish these corruptions from the original readings to arrive at an authoritative text.

Current disputes about textual theory notwithstanding, I find that my undergraduates are intuitively concerned with what individual poets actually wrote. I touch briefly on the problems of complex variants and the construction of a stemma as illustrated, for example, in William A. Ringler's *Poems of Sir Philip Sidney* or the Donne *Variorum* (Stringer); then, as interest begins to waver, I move quickly to my second objective, familiarity with the vast current of works in manuscript that flowed parallel to and often in overlapping channels with the age's printed literature.

I avoid hands-on work with poetry in manuscript until after we have covered a representative sample of anthologized verse: Wyatt and Surrey in the sixteenth-century course, some Jonson and Donne in the seventeenth-century

140 RENAISSANCE MANUSCRIPT POETRY

course. I may then ask individual students or teams of two or three students to investigate the manuscript anthologies as edited by Edward Doughtie, Ruth Hughey, and me for the Elizabethan period or Ernest W. Sullivan for the later period.

I use this assignment to sharpen my students' recognition of genres as well as to introduce them to manuscript literature by asking them to browse through these anthologies and identify the kinds of verse copied into them. What we are looking for are genres that did not appear in print contemporarily and therefore do not ordinarily appear in modern textbooks. In Hughey's edition of the Arundel Harington manuscript, the long, salacious "Libel of Cambridge" and "Libel of Oxford" are easy finds in this category. The equally substantial attack on Queen Elizabeth's victualler of the navy, Edward Bashe, appears in this manuscript, in Henry Stanford's anthology (May), and even in the Dalhousie manuscripts (Sullivan), where this relic of the 1580s continued to be popular among private collectors well into the seventeenth century. John Lilliat copied satiric and bawdy epigrams and other poems into the Rawlinson manuscript (Doughtie), along with an alliterative tour de force that begins "Ten tough turds did I toss in thy teeth." Stanford preserved unique texts of a number of satiric epigrams, and he reserved the last few folios of the Cambridge manuscript for such taboo works as bawdy riddles. In short, students readily identify many kinds of verse in these anthologies that could not have been safely printed in the Renaissance. Yet they notice simultaneously works by the poets we are studying that circulated in manuscript whether or not they were available at the time in printed editions. A relatively brief sampling from the manuscripts gives my students definite understanding of the concept of manuscript publication, its breadth, and its relative lack of critical or editorial attention as described in current works by Harold Love, Arthur F. Marotti (*Manuscript*), and H. R. Woudhuysen (*Sir Philip Sidney*).

Editing an Elizabethan Poem:
A Course Assignment
Sheila T. Cavanagh

Undergraduate students coming to my Renaissance literature class often arrive in pursuit of a "pre-1660" course to check off their list of requirements for the English major. What they find when they arrive is a course that combines the study of Elizabethan poetry and drama with a practical introduction to research through textual editing, collaboration, and computerized instruction. Throughout the term, our discussions rotate around these topics, as the students develop a deeper understanding of the early modern period through the use of their newly acquired research tools.

The assignment described here requires students to create an edited version of a poem written by an Elizabethan author. They are asked first to choose their intended audience, so that they can gloss the text appropriately. In addition, their final product includes an introduction to the poem, a bibiliography, and an essay detailing "how I edited this poem." Students are allowed to add or change punctuation and spelling, so long as they justify such alterations in their completed presentation. Individual students determine how to incorporate into their texts the historical, mythological, philosophical, biblical, and other information they decide would benefit readers of the poem. More advanced students may explore the poetics of the text.

Students are asked not to consult edited versions of the poem until the end of the term. They are allowed to read criticism of the poem to find particular answers, so long as they cite it appropriately, but only after they have searched unsuccessfully for the information they need. The collaborative design of the project, particularly the time spent raising specific questions about the texts, encourages them to abide by these constraints. Graduate students often avoid the temptation to check other scholars' decisions by choosing poems or plays that do not exist in modern editions, although as more edited texts written by early modern women become available, this option may well become less feasible.

The textual editing project described here can be expanded or contracted according to the level and background of the students. For example, I offer graduate students far less guidance than I offer undergraduates. In a senior seminar, the project is likely to last throughout the semester, and each student chooses a separate poem to work with. In a more general upper-division or lower-level course, I frequently ask students to work in groups, have them work on a shorter poem, and ask them to craft a more modest product. In my experience, students are surprised at how much work a good editing job requires, but they generally acknowledge that this assignment introduces them to resources they can use in other classes or for their dissertation.

Since both computerized classrooms and computer labs are readily available on my campus, students use computers extensively for their work. Each class

142   EDITING AN ELIZABETHAN POEM

has its own discussion group on LearnLink (a campuswide intranet), where they can easily share questions and discoveries online. This technology facilitates regular communication outside the classroom. I began assigning editing projects, however, before our computer facilities were as sophisticated as they are now and found that these projects were equally valuable then. The computer use I describe here makes collaboration, research, and formatting easier, but it is not essential for the success of the assignment.

In my undergraduate courses, I give students a list of poems and allow them to choose one to work with. In an upper-division class, participants also receive an introduction to the *Short-Title Catalogue* microfilm and are asked to begin by making a hard copy of their poem. Lower-division students go to the library and get a copy of an Elizabethan text from the University Microfilms series; furthermore, I give them a modernized typescript, with as much editorial paraphernalia removed as possible. In both cases, we then work together to make sense of Elizabethan orthography, using the overhead projector or the computer so that the entire class can see the same text simultaneously. Once students understand how to read such Elizabethan oddities as reversed *us* and *vs*, they return to their own texts, bringing in further related questions as they arise.

This class period on orthography follows a visit to the special collections department in the library, where students are given the opportunity to see a variety of early modern books and to learn about common publication practices. Seeing actual books from this period clarifies the need for editing and suggests the wide variations in a text that an editor can introduce. Since most of the students have never thought about editing before, this prefatory class session helps them begin to understand the role of an editor and the undertaking that they are about to assume.

Another useful introductory session also takes place in the library, where they meet with the reference librarian who is most familiar with this period. Here, they encounter someone they can consult with for this and future projects; they also learn about print, CD-ROM, and Internet sources for their research. Much more specific than the library tour they probably took as first-year students, this visit is designed to expand their familiarity with the kind of materials that are available to aid their research. Subsequently, students are encouraged to expand their repertoire of reference books and other resources and to share them with their colleagues both in class and on Learnlink throughout the term.

After these initial classes, students begin their editing investigations. Once every week or two, we devote an entire class period (referring to a class that meets three times a week) to discussions of their progress, problems they are encountering, and so on. In addition, they are asked to share discoveries and seek advice from their colleagues in person or online on an ongoing basis. The assignment is designed to make the instructor the last point of inquiry. I certainly read and contribute to the computer discussions, but to support a sense of the students themselves as developing authorities, I do not answer specific

Sheila T. Cavanagh 143

questions unless the students have exhausted other avenues. For undergraduates in particular, I base my assessment on the quality of their pursuit as well as on their final product; therefore, they are urged to view the process, including false starts, as an especially important part of the assignment. Toward the end of the semester, students look at edited copies of the poem and criticism to answer questions falling outside the realm of their expertise. They are assured throughout the term that they are not expected to compress a lifetime of scholarship and reading into one semester. They are asked, however, to keep modifying their glosses as they acquire more knowledge. As undergraduates learn, for example, about metaphor and allegory, they are expected to begin identifying figurative language that they might first have read literally. Here, Learnlink is also quite useful, since it allows students to raise questions with one another about individual words and phrases to determine how they might read them in a particular context.

A broad assortment of Elizabethan poems works well for this assignment. Edmund Spenser's *Fowre Hymnes* and Philip Sidney's *Astrophil and Stella* serve as particularly adaptable texts. These texts divide easily, so that an entire class can work on the same poem, but individual students or groups can focus on different sonnets or stanzas. This approach often encourages the entire class to collaborate, since some of the same questions arise in a number of groups. In addition, lower-division students, who may be daunted by a longer piece of writing, can be assigned a sonnet to edit individually or a sonnet sequence to edit together. For classes ready for a more advanced endeavor, poetry by women writers from the period is especially valuable, since there are few edited versions to refer to. For instance, while Aemylia Lanyer's *Salve Deus Rex Judaeorum* does not readily separate into segments, it offers a challenging text for a graduate student to tackle or for a senior seminar to work on together. The lack of multiple modern editions discourages students from looking prematurely at the work of other editors, while Susanne Woods's excellent recent edition provides an invaluable resource for students at the end of the term.

The editing procedures followed vary according to the poem as well as the style and background of an individual editor. Students working on the Lanyer poem, for instance, might start by working with the dedicatory materials. Having been introduced to the *Dictionary of National Biography* on their library tour, they often begin there to establish the identities of the women honored. Some students then decide that they need to pursue more information about these women, while others begin working directly on the text of the dedications. Here their efforts also vary, in part because of their prior knowledge. For students familiar with classical mythology, the references to Paris, Juno, Pallas, and Venus in "To the Queenes Most Excellent Majestie" (Lanyer 3) provide little challenge. Others need to exercise their research skills but usually identify these figures fairly readily. Concurrently, one student might decide to explore why Elizabeth is called "Empresse" in the first line and another might wonder at her designation as "Mother of succeeding Kings" (line 2). In class and on LearnLink,

144   EDITING AN ELIZABETHAN POEM

students discuss how to answer such questions and explore the rationale for either glossing the terms or not. As they progress through the poem, they continue to share their discoveries, questions, and frustrations, ultimately presenting a polished version of "their" text, complete with a statement of the editorial philosophy they developed and followed. Examples of the finished product by graduate students can be found through the Emory Women Writers Resource Project at abelard.library.emory.edu/wwrp/index.html.

Regardless of the class level or poem chosen, this editing assignment serves as a significant segment of a varied syllabus. Class lectures and discussion help round out the students' editing efforts by broadening their understanding of the historical, philosophical, and religious background of this poetry. Students explore poetics, court politics, Neoplatonism, religious controversies, pastoral, and other unfamiliar terrain and later incorporate any relevant material into their completed texts. They also read and discuss other poetry and drama from the period. By the time the semester is over, they have become experts on a particular piece of Elizabethan shorter poetry within its broader context and have acquired a host of new research skills.

The Elizabethan Age Portfolio: Using Writing to Teach Shorter Elizabethan Poetry

John Webster

After eight years of running a writing program, I returned to the literature classroom wanting to bring my writing classroom experience with me. Writing classes, by their nature, invite active, performance-based learning: writers, after all, have to produce essays, and they have to do so on their own. Indeed, "active learning" had become something of a mantra for me; I found that I wanted my literature students to be active readers no less than I had come to want my writing students to be active writers. My first efforts were not successful. Though I showed students how to notice turns of language in sonnets and poems or how to follow subtextual arguments that work in competition with surface meanings, and though we modeled active reading of passages in careful—even lively—class discussion, when at course end I asked students to do this sort of reading for themselves, the result was disappointing. I clearly hadn't yet bridged the gap between my showing and their enacting some version of active reading. I knew that frequent writing might do that; research has long suggested that students learn better and retain what they learn much longer when they write what they learn. But if constant writing made pedagogical sense, it made no practical sense. My classes generally have from thirty-five to fifty students, and any set of papers will take three to four hours to read even cursorily—far more time and energy than I can add to my workload twice a week for every class I teach. Of course, I could simply assign writing and then either just check it off or not collect it at all. But when I've tried those methods, the quality of writing has quickly degenerated as students begin to think of it as busywork.

So how does one get students to write in a sixteenth-century literature class more or less constantly—at least twice a week—and with care throughout the term and not overwhelm oneself by papers? My answer has become the Elizabethan Age portfolio. If it does not by itself make my students active readers, it certainly has for me established the preconditions for that progression. Moreover, though its main purpose has been to solve the problem of being overwhelmed by papers, the effects of putting this method into practice have gone well beyond that initial benefit.

I introduce the assignment by explaining that a portfolio for a literature class is like many other portfolios: a collection of work done, together with an essay reflecting on one's experience in doing that work. As the assignment has evolved, it has just three elements: a detailed listing of the portfolio's contents; all the writing done for the course (including exams and formal papers) neatly organized and paginated; and a two- to three-page self-reflective essay.

Originally, the point of the contents listing was only to make my end-of-quarter review of students' work easier: from the contents page I could see at

146   ELIZABETHAN AGE PORTFOLIO

a glance how complete the portfolio was. Its second, unintended effect, however, has been to define a level of care in the putting together of a student's material. For I don't just want a requirement-fulfilling sheaf of pages. I want students to produce a body of work that they themselves will recognize as a substantial contribution to the success of the course. Indeed, the assignment's function has by now gone well beyond my first intention of paper-reading management. For I now think of the project as offering students the opportunity to pull together, document, and review their whole term's thinking.

It is with these goals in mind that I explain for them the self-reflective essay:

> The self-reflective essay should be about your experience in this class. It may take a number of different forms. It may, for example, be a narrative of your experience in this course—why you took it, what problems and challenges it presented to you as it progressed, and what you did to address them. Or it may discuss how your attitudes about reading Elizabethan Age literature have developed, changed, or not changed during quarter: what were you thinking when you came in, and how has that changed in the ten weeks since? Or it may be a letter to prospective students—from one who now knows what to expect and can offer advice whether or not to enroll at all. What should students be prepared for? What might they know going in that would make the experience of taking the class better than it otherwise might be?

Although I find myself interested in just about any essay students give me in response to this assignment, the prompt quite obviously invites them to think about their experience of the course and to find some way to turn that experience into a narrative account. The resulting essays are varied; I've found particularly useful those in which students have reflected on the way various pedagogical devices have affected them.

As for reviewing these projects, it goes remarkably quickly. *Review* is the key term—at thirty-five to forty pages each I certainly couldn't read them all. I do, of course, read the self-reflective essays, but the reading goes very fast; they are, in fact, among the most interesting and entertaining papers I receive.

And I have learned a great deal from them. I've learned how effective my students generally feel group work to be, for example; I've also learned to avoid certain exercises that nobody liked. I've learned as well what has made reading Elizabethan lyrics difficult for many students and how much they have struggled just to be able to paraphrase. Indeed, I'm no longer annoyed when students turn in papers largely made up of paraphrase. To be sure, I still want more sophistication than that, but with my better sense of where paraphrasing papers come from, I also feel better able to help the students who write them.

The portfolio counts for fifteen percent of the course grade—half of that for the essay, the other half for writing assignments. That's not a lot, but it's been enough to keep most students concentrating. I only sample any one portfolio's

John Webster 147

collection of papers; I scan for completeness as well as for the level of intellectual engagement in the writing. It takes me four to five hours to review, grade, and mail back a set of fifty portfolios. (I have students submit their portfolios in stamped, self-addressed mailing envelopes.)

I have already described one major benefit of this assignment: portfolios allow me to use daily writing as a primary means by which to help my students become active readers. I do collect and respond to some of their work as they write it, especially in the early weeks of the quarter, but as much as three-quarters of their writing just goes straight into the portfolio. Students know it counts to have done the work, and most put a good deal of effort into doing it well, even if I don't read it then and there.

There are other benefits, some minor, some major. A minor one is the assignment's organizing function. If students write often and if all that they write must appear at course end in the portfolio, I can see at a glance who has been in class and doing work. I don't need to take roll or check off daily assignments. Since I am not ordinarily good at such matters, this benefit helps me greatly. The major benefits of portfolios all follow from being able to ask for regular and responsible writing, and perhaps the most obvious of these benefits is the enormous difference in the quality and quantity of daily student participation in class. I call the actual papers that students write "response papers"; I explain on day 1 that none of the daily writing has to be "right"—that would defeat the purpose. Just as one can't make an omelette without breaking eggs, neither can one become an active reader without making mistakes. Works by Wyatt, Sidney, or Queen Elizabeth herself will all survive whatever students do to them. Indeed, worse has already happened many times before and often in print. So instead of rightness, the point of these papers, I tell students, is to help them create for themselves an active relation with what they read. For as I have already suggested, my classroom goal no longer is simply to have students discuss intelligently and receptively my readings of texts. Rather I want students to be actively generating their own readings—even when the texts they are studying are the very challenging ones of sixteenth-century lyric poetry.

To help students write, I give topics; I gear them to helping less-experienced readers develop a method for first noticing and then exploring poetic language. With my prompts I try to break the process of reading into discrete steps: early in the quarter the tasks run heavily toward locating effects to explore; later I ask for more sustained exploration and argumentation. I follow the same principle in individual units as well. When I teach sonnets, for example, though my large-scale goal will be to leave students able to develop readings of sonnets as compressed, miniaturized plays, each with characters, a dramatic situation, and a plot, my first prompt is very simple. Because most of my students find the compression of sonnet language almost impenetrable, for their first response paper I only ask that they notice and explore three to five words that seem to have a special role in the poem. Only after students have gotten better at noticing poetic effect do I up the ante by asking them to write about a particular

148   ELIZABETHAN AGE PORTFOLIO

sonnet's dramatic elements. With those, I again go step-by-step. I focus first on the speaking voice: What adjectives best describe the speaker of this sonnet? (Angry? Guilty? Confused? Resolute?) Why do you think so? What, specifically, about the language of the poem leads you to think this?

It will only be the fourth or fifth response paper before I ask students to sketch the full dramatic situation, describing speaker, listener, and plot. For that is a great deal to be able to do. Indeed, that paper will in fact constitute a dry run for the formal writing for this unit, a four-to-five-page paper explaining as specifically and fully as students can the dramatic structure and purpose of one of the sonnets we have read.

Response papers have several benefits; though my principal interest in them lies in encouraging students' intellectual engagement with their readings, I also expect that the writing that students do will bring them to class already having thought about those readings and already having worked out responses for at least some of the questions I will be asking during the class hour. And because of the higher level of class discussion that results from this daily work, I feel I can promise students when we begin the course that they themselves will find the class more relevant and interesting for having written as much as they will.

But beyond these classroom matters, students also benefit greatly from the portfolio's providing a concrete place in which they can see their own work grow. This is true literally: by course end students will have accumulated thirty to forty pages of writing about Elizabethan poetry, all of it produced by their own hands. But the sense of a student's work growing has a more abstract force, for as students review their work to write the self-reflective essay, they can see for themselves how much more sophisticated their thinking has become.

As a teacher I like this, since I have found that what students learn in English classes is sometimes hard for them to measure, hard even to see, with the result that some students don't think much has happened at all. They thus may not much respect the work we've done in the course, and they may not particularly respect themselves for having done it. The Elizabethan Age Portfolio offers them something visible and touchable and by that benefit alone confers a value on the work they've done. I know that sounds like pop psychology, but I do believe that this assignment helps students respect the work they do and makes them better students. I can see this growth in the self-reflective essays; most tell the story of their experience in the course, and though some of these essays do tend to drift into the "why I think you are a great teacher" genre, their more dominant themes are those of discovery and confidence (the anonymous course evaluation comments make a pretty good check on the extent of sycophancy). Rhetoric and composition instructors often talk about helping students take ownership of their writing, and those instructors suggest writing portfolios as one way to encourage this assumption of ownership. The same applies to the Elizabethan Age Portfolio: when students see how much they have done with the literature they are studying, they are much more likely to have a sense of control as well.

In closing I describe one last benefit of the course portfolio—though it is perhaps also a drawback in a collection of pedagogical essays on sixteenth-century lyric: the portfolio assignment is portable. With adjustments it can be used in virtually any course. I note, though, that the project is most effective in courses where students feel themselves highly challenged by the material. The best set I've yet received was from a history of criticism (Plato to Nietzsche) course. But owing to the difficulty many of my students have with sixteenth-century language, the Elizabethan Age Portfolio has run a close second. Essay after essay in the portfolios describes both the demands of this poetry and the enormous sense of achievement students feel from having to write constantly about texts they almost without exception find very, very difficult. After reading responses to the portfolio assignment from students themselves, I cannot now imagine ever teaching another undergraduate course without it.

CRITICAL AND THEORETICAL APPROACHES

Teaching Genre

Heather Dubrow

Shakespeare criticism, as its practitioners frequently observe, provides a convenient microcosm of shifts in critical practice. So too, one might add, do the various fortunes of the sections of *The Faerie Queene*: witness how our profession's turn to feminism intensified the long-standing interest in book 3 and how the study of colonialism increased, if not inflated, the value ascribed to book 5. But in fact no area of inquiry better demonstrates changes in critical methodologies and ideologies, assumptions and agendas than the shifting position of genre in the study of early modern literature.

The centrality of that subject in the decades before 1970 is evident. Major scholars regularly engaged with questions about literary form, and major studies regularly resulted; witness, among a host of other possible examples, Rosalie L. Colie's *Shakespeare's Living Art*. During this period the significance of genre variously was justified by—and, not coincidentally, helped justify—the study of formal patterns and classical sources.

Genre got a bad press in the years after 1970, not only in Renaissance studies but also across the profession. Spearheaded by Derrida, the poststructuralist attack on genre attributed to it a rigidity that has in fact been present only rarely (even the stricter neoclassical statements on genre sometimes admit to exceptions to its norms) and that has been regularly challenged by practitioners and theorists of genre criticism. Similarly, the many opponents of formalism during this period often wrongly assumed that the study of genre necessarily encourages ahistorical approaches to literature. Indeed, in a profession that not only studies but also so often practices synecdoche, genre came for many Renaissance scholars to represent the bad old days of conventional criticism.

During the period since 1970, however, such attacks have coexisted with a renewed interest in literary form and with many fruitful approaches to it. Feminism of course encouraged the study of that fortuitously euphonious duo "gender and genre." Certain Marxist studies, notably the essay on romance that Fredric Jameson includes in *The Political Unconscious*, demonstrated that far from being ahistorical, the examination of genre can crystallize crucial cultural shifts. Two early essays by a leading new historicist, Louis Montrose ("Eliza," "Of Gentlemen and Shepherds"), by precept and example advocated reexamining pastoral from a historical perspective. To be sure, in practice most new historicists, Marxist critics, and fellow travelers devoted little attention to literary types. But the subject remained the focus of attention for a handful of scholars involved with those and other contemporary forms of historical inquiry; witness, for example, Thomas O. Beebee's *The Ideology of Genre* and Annabel Patterson's *Pastoral and Ideology* and witness as well how their titles insist on the congruence of genre and current critical preoccupations. At the same time, the final decades of the century saw incisive reexaminations of genre from more traditional perspectives, notably Alastair Fowler's *Kinds of Literature*.

Even so brief a history of the fortunes of genre criticism gestures toward the pressures militating against extensive attention to this subject, the challenges of teaching it to our undergraduates, and the overwhelming reasons for doing so. To begin with, if an interest in the subject is contagious, so too is a suspicion of it, and many teachers need to confront their own ambivalence about genre to teach it effectively. Those who equate it with a happily discarded, old-fashioned approach to early modern literature would find it useful to rethink their strategically useful but intellectually shallow division of the profession into a dull older generation and exciting young turks: the work of the critics classified in this binary way is typically more varied in quality and assumptions than such a divide acknowledges. But in any event the connections of genre to cutting-edge issues in contemporary scholarship, such as the workings of ideology and gender, also rebut any impulse to undervalue this mode of analysis as outdated. Indeed, genre can reveal the complex and dynamic relation between aesthetic decisions and cultural attitudes, as I've argued elsewhere (*Happier Eden* 268–70), and there is some evidence of a renewed interest in studying genre from that and other perspectives.

How then should one teach genre when engaging with lyric poetry, and how can one teach it well? One of the most extreme answers is to focus an entire course or, failing that, an entire unit on it. For example, when I taught sixteenth-century poetry and prose to Carleton College undergraduates, I organized the course sometimes by writers, parading in historical sequence, but sometimes by genre. Both approaches, of course, have trade-offs: the first encourages sustained involvement with—and hence often excitement with—the corpus of particular writers, and the second redirects some of that attention to questions of form.

152　TEACHING GENRE

However one structures the course, one has to work out strategies for reversing many students' sense that genre is both an unfamiliar and an uncongenial concept. The problem is intensified by and must be addressed through a broader context: undergraduates at all but the most elite institutions (and sometimes there as well) often find early modern literature profoundly alien and hence threatening. (Notice undergraduates' telling phrase "early literature," a category that on occasion includes, say, Dickens.) Raised on a nourishing but insufficiently varied diet of novels and short stories, they may also find lyric poetry foreign and intimidating. These types of discomfort and distrust increase the challenges of introducing yet another apparently foreign concept, the workings of literary form.

I have adopted two opposite but interwoven strategies for the broader challenge of teaching unfamiliar concepts and cultures, both of which are particularly relevant to genre. First, I often make a point of acknowledging the threatening otherness of the material I teach. I festooned one syllabus, for example, with the opening sentence of L. P. Hartley's *The Go-Between*: "The past is a foreign country. They do things differently there." Similarly, building on rather than denying the alienness of the texts covered in my survey of British literature, I suggested on the first day of one course that this course was like foreign travel—disorienting, exhausting, yet exhilarating—and as the term progressed I returned to the metaphor regularly. The concept of genre can be readily integrated with this master trope: one might compare cognate ways of studying the distinctive characteristics of a foreign country with the process of determining what the popularity of a literary form not currently in vogue shows about the distinct characteristics of the culture that adopted it. For example, why do medieval writers so often turn to the dream vision? And, more to our purposes here, why did the country-house poem flourish in the seventeenth century?

But if in some ways I acknowledge and even celebrate the foreignness of the texts and cultures I am teaching, I also attempt to lessen it in others, suggesting that from certain perspectives the material is really very familiar. Thus, in teaching lyric and other genres, I attempt to assure students that they understand more about the concept of literary form than they may have realized. In particular, in several of my courses I hand out a sheet on which the following paragraph (borrowed from my book *Genre*) appears at the top of the sheet labeled *Murder at Marplethorpe* and at the bottom under the title *The True History of David Marplethorpe*:

> The clock on the mantelpiece said ten thirty, but someone had suggested recently that the clock was wrong. As the figure of the dead woman lay on the bed in the front room, a no less silent figure glided rapidly from the house. The only sounds to be heard were the ticking of that clock and the loud wailing of an infant. (1)

I insist that the students fold the paper so that they can read only the top half at first: the contrast between this game of concealment and the usual examination of handouts creates a lighthearted mood from which we segue into the very serious literary issues at stake. Predictably but reassuringly, when the title flags a mystery the students assume the dead woman is the victim and the silent figure the murderer; the bildungsroman title, in contrast, leads most of them to expect that our unfortunate corpse is David's mother. Thus students not only realize that genre guides their interpretive procedures even if they are not familiar with the term; they also begin to think about such issues as generic expectations and the workings of formulaic literary types.

Also valuable in the process of making genre seem more familiar and accessible are parallels with popular forms, including versions in media other than print. Thus I encourage undergraduates to identify generic norms and expectations in sitcoms, cowboy movies, and police dramas. One of my graduate students, Braden Hosch, reports success in using popular music to teach lyric poetry in general and genre in particular; students are, as he points out, already very familiar with the genres of this music. To spark discussions of it, he supplies photocopies of the lyrics and plays the songs in question on a portable machine. Similarly, I discovered that students are pleased and intrigued to find that many popular songs, notably Bob Dylan's "Lay, Lady, Lay," are versions of a genre they would have thought they had never encountered, the persuasion poem. Undergraduates are also likely to become excited with pastoral elements in science fiction (a topic that can generate fruitful discussions about how pastoral changes when developed in narrative as opposed to lyric).

An equally valuable way of making genre a more accessible concept, even perhaps an English-speaking guide in the sometimes foreign world of early modern texts, is by tracing parallels between literary genres and social experiences. The different expectations attendant on two apparently similar occasions, a birthday party for an elderly relative and a birthday drink for a contemporary, can aptly represent the workings of genre. Not the least advantage of this perspective is that it allows students to apply the work of the classroom to their daily lives, a particularly valuable process for those undergraduates to whom the life of the mind still itself seems to be a foreign country, visited only at one's peril and only for as short a time as possible. For example, after introducing the concept of genre for the first time, I sometimes assign my students the task of interpreting some conversation in which they participate later the same day in terms of generic expectations.

Once students become comfortable with the concept of genre, they are in a position to investigate its workings in lyric poetry more deeply. It can be useful to challenge them to think about what cannot happen in a given genre and what the answers show about both generic expectations and the particular form in question: why, for example, do sonnets include so many metaphoric murderers but few if any literal ones? Writing assignments that involve actually composing a text in a genre, though difficult and even upsetting for some students, prove stimulating for others; I know that some colleagues ask their classes to turn out entire sonnets, though I myself have had success in encouraging them to think

154 TEACHING GENRE

about that genre by simply creating a couplet. Genres are, of course, shaped and even on occasion defined by the responses of readers and critics, not just those of writers; it can be fruitful to introduce the definitions and descriptions crafted by Philip Sidney and George Puttenham after the students have themselves struggled to define a genre or to juxtapose those early modern discussions of genre with a few sentences by a twentieth-century critic in order to encourage the class to think about the aims and problems of the process of literary categorization.

But it is pastoral more than any other literary form that variously exemplifies and justifies the challenges of teaching lyric poetry from the perspective of literary types. This is one of the best, arguably indeed the very best, form to use when encouraging undergraduates to think about and in terms of genre. To begin with, since pastoral is, I maintain, metalyric (its inset songs draw attention to the songlike elements in lyric, its refrains to lyric temporality, and so on), studying it can enrich discussions of the lyric mode as a whole. Sidney's "Ye goteherd gods" and Spenser's *Prothalamion* crystallize debates on such issues particularly effectively. The radical distinctions among definitions of pastoral, pivoting on issues as central as whether it represents an escapist fantasy or, by contrast, a judicious engagement with central ethical and political issues, demonstrate the challenges of defining literary types. And because critics as varied in their approaches and as incisive in their respective modes of analysis as Paul Alpers, Louis Montrose, and Annabel Patterson have all recently written on pastoral, it also provides a convenient test case for evaluating different takes on literary form.

Pastoral also responds particularly well to several other techniques useful in teaching genre. That valuable if predictable pedagogical strategy of juxtaposing two instances of the same literary form works splendidly with the several versions of and reactions to Marlowe's "Passionate Shepherd to His Love"—a comparison that now can be further enriched by allusions to or even perhaps a viewing of Ian McKellan's cinematic version of *Richard III*, in which that poem is sung by an entertainer. Not the least virtue of such juxtapositions is that they can encourage students unaccustomed to reading texts closely to do so. What better example of the need to think intensely about nuances of language than the opening of Donne's "Bait," which recasts Marlowe's "all the pleasures" ("Passionate Shepherd," line 2) as "some new pleasures" (line 2)? Because classical literature offers versions of pastoral that are as intriguing as they were influential, studying this genre can introduce those literatures and cultures to undergraduates who have little Latin and less Greek; when I have been fortunate enough to teach students who do in fact have some knowledge of either of those languages, I have encouraged them to examine the texts in question in the original. (Not only collegial generosity but also enlightened self-interest should encourage all of us to counter the declining interest in several foreign languages, notably Latin and Greek, by stressing their importance in these and other ways: the survival of those departments contributes to the health of the university, while taking courses in them can contribute to the intellectual health of our students.)

Pastoral also lends itself to those juxtapositions of its literary versions and what some would term its subliterary or nonliterary avatars—and hence to the reexamination of those categories. For example, I have found it fruitful to show students connections between the norms of pastoral in a poem like Sidney's "Ye goteherd gods" and the reincarnation of these norms in the literature of roguery, such as Dekker's cony-catching pamphlets. And it is harder to think of a more complex or more intriguing example of the relation between a genre's popularity and a culture's preoccupations than pastoral. Many critics have already traced its relation to politics (Montrose, "Eliza," "Gentlemen"; A. Patterson, *Pastoral*). And, like Dutch landscape painting (a parallel I often adduce), it flourished in a period of urbanization. Moreover, I suggest that by recasting time in terms of continuities and repetitions figured by songs repeated by a second poet and by refrains, pastoral offers a model of temporality in revealing and reassuring contrast to the models of rupture represented in the Renaissance by events and myths ranging from the Fall to the Reformation to the death of Elizabeth.

I argued earlier that pastoral is metalyric. Among the most self-conscious of all literary forms, pastorals are typically metapastorals as well (thus *The Shepheardes Calender* famously and repeatedly engages with the problematics of its own literary type), and as such they incorporate discussions of literary form that can spark similar discussions in our own classrooms. And in another sense pastoral is metagenre, another point one can productively explore when teaching. For in the recurrent and telling episodes in which its shepherds sing a song composed by another denizen of the pastoral world, this literary type engages with the complexities of rewriting what has already been written—singing again notes that have been heard before—and thus invites students and teachers to engage with the complexities of how and why genre itself does so.

Impressions of Poetry:
The Publication of Elizabethan Lyric Verse
David Scott Kastan

> If we wish to understand the appropriations and
> interpretations of a text in their full historicity we
> need to identify the effect, in terms of meaning,
> that its material forms produced.
>
> —Roger Chartier

Teachers of Elizabethan poetry have, understandably, tended to pay little attention to the material forms of the poetry they teach. It is difficult enough to find decent editions to teach from and to inspire (if not merely require) students to read with care; adding a layer of bibliographic sophistication seems an unnecessary and perhaps impossible task and in any case not one apparently crucial to the study of the poetry itself. But of course the poetry itself is the very issue. It isn't clear what this could mean apart from the materializations that make the work present. The material forms in which poetry circulates, its modes and mechanisms of transmission, are what shapes its intelligibility, and a consideration of them is necessary to clarify what that poetry is, as both utterance and artifact.

For most of the sixteenth century, at least in England, print was not the natural environment of lyric poetry. Lyric, usually composed as occasional verse, was for the most part written, read, and retranscribed in manuscript. The customary means of textual production allowed lyric gradually to escape the circumstances of its writing, as it was absorbed, precisely as it circulated, into new contexts. Readers actively engaged it, personalizing it, as they recopied it into commonplace books and manuscript collections, in the process denying the original both textual authority and fixity but ensuring it a vital social existence. Only slowly did lyric take to print as its characteristic medium of transmission—though print was the medium that would return the poem to the poet and, largely by virtue of its ability to unify and stabilize texts, make possible lyric poetry's eventual absorption into the literary culture (Marotti, *Manuscript*; Wall; Woudhuysen, *Sir Philip Sidney*).

It was not, however, until the end of the sixteenth century that the transition was largely accomplished. The so-called stigma of print (Saunders; May, "Tudor Aristocrats"), which worked to prevent aristocrats (or those who pretended to gentility) from seeking publication for their poetry, was only then sufficiently overwhelmed by the dignity of lyric's newly emergent literary status. "'Tis ridiculous for a lord to print Verses," wrote John Selden in an extreme expression of the social prejudice; "'tis well enough to make 'em to please himself, but to make them public is foolish" (135). Though a coterie manuscript system thrived well into the seventeenth century (Love), increasingly authors did make their verse public, discovering cultural and even financial advantage in the medium of print. John Harington observed somewhat ruefully that "Verses are growne such merchantable ware, / That now for Sonnets, sellers are, and buyers" (*Letters* 164).

Verses did indeed become "merchantable ware," and various moments can be seen to mark the shifting consciousness—the publication in 1557 of what gets called *Tottel's Miscellany* (actually somewhat gracelessly entitled *Songes and Sonettes, Written by the Ryght Honorable Lorde Henry Hawarde Late Earle of Surrey, and Other*), the 1568 publication of the collected works of John Skelton, the 1579 publication of Spenser's *The Shepheardes Calender*. Arguably, however, it is only with the appearance of Philip Sidney's *Astrophil and Stella* (in two editions in 1591, one in 1592, and again in 1598 in the collected works published as *The Countesse of Pembrokes Arcadia*) that the prejudice against printed poetry largely disappears, Sidney's massive cultural presence (as a Protestant martyr-hero) lending lyric itself something of his own prestige.

Gabriel Harvey, perhaps surprisingly, caps a string of epithets in praise of Sidney by calling him "the Paragon of Excellency in Print" (G. G. Smith 2: 265), and poets, following Sidney's example (or, more properly, the example of his publishers, Sidney having died in September 1586 before any of the verse was published), began eagerly to seek print publication as the necessary form for their literary ambitions. Samuel Daniel allowed his *Delia* to be published in 1592, though he felt obliged to protest in the dedication that it was only because he had been "betraide by the indiscretion of a greedie Printer" that he was "forced to publish that which I neuer ment" (Delia, sig. A2r). Daniel explains, somewhat disingenuously, that it was the unauthorized appearance of twenty-eight of his sonnets in the first edition of Sidney's *Astrophil and Stella*, published by Thomas Newman in 1591, that led him the next year to see his poems into print and dedicate them to Sidney's sister.

But others seemed less apologetic about their poem's appearing in print, and single-authored collections suddenly exploded on the scene. Henry Constable's *Diana* was also published in 1592. Thomas Lodge's *Phillis*, like Barnabe Barnes's *Parthenophil and Parthenophe*, appeared the following year. In that same year, 1593, Giles Fletcher's *Licia* was published, and 1594 saw Michael Drayton's *Ideas Mirrour*. (Both poets invoke Sidney in their prefaces; Fletcher refers to "that worthie Sidney"; Drayton to the "Divine Syr Phillip.") Spenser's *Amoretti* and *Epithalamion* were published together in one volume in 1595, as was Richard Barnfield's *Cynthia*. Verse miscellanies had been published (or republished) in virtually every year of Elizabeth's long reign (Pomeroy), but clearly it was in the 1590s, with the publication of these individual sequences and collections, that lyric poetry became a significant literary form, no longer merely occasional verse written by gentlemen-amateurs and circulated among a coterie audience but—precisely as the poetry gets organized into fixed, coherent (and commodifiable) structural units—a part of an established literary institution that offered the increasingly professional

158   IMPRESSIONS OF POETRY

poet visibility, if not financial reward, and substantial cultural prestige (Marotti, *Manuscript* ch. 4).

It should be obvious that any study of Elizabethan lyric poetry should attend to the material forms in which it circulated, if only to complicate and clarify the idea of the literary that lyric comes triumphantly to represent, as well as the very notion of subjectivity that lyric seemingly unproblematically asserts; but in truth sensitivity to the material text should be central to our task as teachers of literature. We do, after all, have to read *something*, and that something, as it makes available the poem's syntactic, formal, and ideational units, is inescapably part of the poem's meanings rather than a neutral and somewhat embarrassing conveyor of them. To ignore this fact is to idealize the poem as autonomous and self-sufficient, to deny it any effective principle of realization, as well as mistakenly to universalize the contexts in which it is written and read.

Literature exists only and always in its materializations, and a focus on the material forms in which the verse circulates and is presented to the understanding (not least of which are, of course, the modern anthologies in which we usually encounter this poetry) has several important advantages for our students. First, it usefully demystifies the poetry, clarifying the conditions of creativity, recognizing it as a product of an author writing and being read within specific (if changeable) material, commercial, and institutional conditions; or, put differently, such attention is precisely what allows the poetry to be restored to its animating histories.

Thinking about the early printed forms in which Elizabethan lyric poetry appeared enables the poems to be understood as both historical objects and historical events, enables us to see that their meaning and value are produced (and constrained) by determinate material commitments. The book formats themselves reveal much about the cultural status of poetry in the period; the shift from the small octavo and quarto publications in the 1590s to the impressive folios later on (Sidney in 1598, Daniel in 1601, Spenser in 1611, Jonson in 1616, Drayton in 1619, Fulke Greville in 1633) itself marks the trajectory of poetry's prestige. Title pages display a set of relations among authors, publishers, printers, booksellers, and, implicitly, book buyers. Prefaces and dedications articulate a network of dependencies between publishers and poets, poets and patrons, and poets and their hoped-for readers and inevitably express some anxiety on the part of these poets about exposing their work, their "priuate passions," as Daniel terms them (Delia, sig. A2r), to the eyes of a reading public. "How hard an enterprise it is," writes John Dowland, "in this skilful and curious age, to commit our priuate labours to the publike view" (*First Book of Songs or Ayres*, sig. °1r).

But it is the poem itself on the pages of the early printed texts that most tellingly reveals "the effect, in terms of meaning, that its material form produced" (Chartier, *Forms* 2). The physical features of the book, as Wendy Wall has argued, establish the poetry's autonomy and authority, divorcing it from its extraliterary, occasional origins and locating it in fixed relations with other poems that resist readers' ready appropriation (Wall 71–89). Individual poems gradually come to be consecutively numbered, one to a page, the work as a whole achieving a unity and stability of structure unusual, if not impossible, in manuscript. And the verse forms themselves are reinforced, if not actually established, by the coherence permitted and emphasized by print; the sonnet, for example, becomes legible *as a sonnet* as it is increasingly isolated on a single page. In the early printed verse collection, the collaboration of poet and publisher "makes an art of technology and creates a book out of disparate poems" (Newton, "Making" 255) and, it might be said, identifies and secures the verse form through the creation of the book.

If, however, early printed editions structure and fix the poetry as both form and artifact, they also reveal a fluidity of language and syntax that is usually lost in modern editions. Many, if not most, modern texts have chosen to modernize ("normalize" is the usual, tendentious word for the practice) spelling and punctuation, but, for example, a Shakespeare sonnet read in any modern edition will necessarily suppress possible meanings available on the page of the original. Whose meanings these are is, of course, one of the questions raised by an early printed text: Are they authorial or compositorial? The uncertainty itself usefully exposes the network of dependencies needed to produce a book, but, whatever their source, there is a density of significance on the page of the 1609 edition of the *Sonnets* that modern editions usually restrict. Sonnet 63, for example, speaks of the devastating effects of time on the youth, the hours that have "fild his brow / With lines and wrincles." The 1609 edition's "fild" is, not unreasonably, usually rendered as "filled"; the youth's now smooth brow shall in time be "filled" with age lines and wrinkles. But his brow could as well be "filed" (or defiled) by time's sharp scythe, a reading no less possible of the "fild" of the original (Duncan-Jones, *Shakespeare's* Sonnets 236). A modern edition has to choose, but for a Renaissance reader both meanings were visible and in play. Or, in line 2 of sonnet 27, the poet takes to his bed "with trauaill tired." The early modern spelling, "trauaill" encapsulates an ambiguity unrenderable in modern English. Editors today must select as the cause of the poet's weariness either his "travail," echoing the "toil" of line 1, or (as most editors do) his "travel," anticipating the "journey" of line 3. Once we commit to modernization, we must choose between alternatives that were happily to Renaissance readers—and obviously to Renaissance poets—simultaneously available. As a pedagogical exercise (and one indeed that I regularly use and encourage others to try), the modernizing of an early text is unquestionably valuable, forcing students to discover the richness in the unfamiliar orthographic conventions; as an editorial practice, it is arguably less defensible, closing off meanings that the poem's earliest readers had before them on the page.

Attention to the material forms in which the poetry was circulated and read is, then, necessary if we are to understand what that poetry was at the end of the sixteenth century, as a verbal structure, as a cultural gesture, as a material artifact, and as a commodity. (Such attention is, of course, made easy by microfilm

160   IMPRESSIONS OF POETRY

and photocopying; nonetheless, two caveats should be noted: facsimile, for all its ability to reproduce the early text easily and cheaply, in fact fully reproduces only the codes structuring the verbal medium; other material aspects of the text—the quality of paper, for example—are necessarily absent. And the duplication of facsimiles has the odd effect of producing multiple copies of a book that was, on account of early printing-house practice, more likely than not unique.) Today we inevitably read this poetry, in a sense, backward, seeing it clearly as literature and reading it as it has crystallized under the pressure of its success. The story of that success, in fact unpredictable and hard won, has, however, largely been forgotten; but the poetry's complex relations to the culture in which it was produced—and the plenitude of meanings and intentions it can therefore speak—are still visible on the pages of the early printed texts and should be kept in view.

New Historicism and the Cultural Aesthetics of the High Elizabethan Lyric

Patricia Fumerton

This essay employs a version of new historicism to read Elizabethan lyrics as not only aesthetic but also cultural artifacts. Already, however, I am deviating from the party line. Most new historicists shun the word *aesthetics* because the term, they argue, implies belief in Art, that is, in rarified objects that transcend their historically specific time. In literary studies, they contend, such a vision of transcendent art characterized formalist or, more precisely, New Critical readings of Renaissance poetry, against which new historicism has also defined itself. It is a credo of new historicism that texts do not transcend their time but instead are produced by and productive of their culture. It is a further maxim that cultural contexts—the loose amalgam of assorted facts, artifacts, and practices that make up an age—are themselves texts that can be read critically like a literary text. I accept these tenets of new historicism. However, I still insist on the term *cultural aesthetics* when addressing the Elizabethan era because this was a period in which, among the court elite at least, society became uniquely and intensely artful. Seemingly inconsequential or trivial artifice—the pretty, the florid, the ornamental—saturated all areas of high Elizabethan court life: art, architecture, cuisine, dress, language, poetry, and the like. The aesthetic, in this context, was quintessentially historical or cultural.

This is a social fact that students do not easily see or value. For many undergraduates, the high Elizabethan lyric exists in a social vacuum—as so many fancy poems about love that seem to be saying little in a whole lot of impenetrably highfalutin, conventional language and, in the sonnet sequences, to be saying it (i.e., nothing) over and over again. My goal in teaching these lyrics is to contextualize the poetry within social practices of ornamentation in such a way that students see they are absolutely right (although their view of "nothing" significantly differs from that of Elizabethan readers). I bring the students to realize that much of this poetry is precisely about nothing, or what I call the x of truth, which is hidden within and discovered through layers of figuration or metaphor, fashionable guises, and ornamental covers (with specific analogy to miniatures). As my argument suggests, the new-historicist methodology I here employ has been greatly influenced by poststructuralist theory (as has new historicism generally). But I would argue that any destabilizations I elicit in class readings were also available to readers of the time, living as they did when social, economic, and spatial mobility was especially profound and when new physical and intellectual discoveries shook the old order on a regular basis. In a kind of sympathetic mimesis of such exciting disruptions, which also characterized Elizabethan artifice generally, I structure the class's uncovering of meaningful pretty nothings in the high Elizabethan lyric as a Socratean discovery; it unfolds surprisingly. This surprising and unsettling

162   NEW HISTORICISM

process of discovery can be accomplished in three or four fifty-minute classes. We begin with concrete analysis of one poem and only gradually move outward to cultural artifacts through stylistic fashions (though one could proceed in the reverse direction).

I first elicit from the students a close reading of Thomas Wyatt's "They flee from me." After reading the poem out loud, I proceed through the stanzas, beginning in each case with a simple question: "Who are 'they'?" for the first stanza; "What is 'this'?" for the second stanza; "What is 'what'?" for the third stanza. Follow-up questions on the first stanza are designed to confuse as much as clarify. I ask students what they imagine is the literal situation in the stanza and what clues there are to whether we should take things in a literal or figurative sense. As we proceed from such posited identifications for "they" as "deer," "squirrels," "women," "courtiers," it becomes clear that we cannot be at all certain of the literal situation. I go on to ask them to try to settle on the speaker's tone, and that proves equally problematic. In the second stanza, the students gather more confidence. "*This* is definitely about a woman," one invariably asserts. "The writer is fondly remembering a past moment," another might claim. But then we focus on troubling words in the stanza. "What does 'heart' mean?" I ask, and the connotations of "hart," that is, a male deer, soon surface. I ask, "What does 'caught' mean?" and the fear of being a captured animal, captured by the woman in her unnervingly exposed "guise," comes out. In the final stanza, as we ponder "what" the speaker thinks "she hath deserved," these complications take on an even knottier guise. What does she deserve for "so kindly" serving him? Does "kindly" mean "considerately"? Is the word spoken in bitten irony? Or is it spoken thankfully because his "gentleness," his gentility and gentleman's way of life, embraces the fashion of change or "new-fangleness" and he fears being "captured" by women? Or does "kindly" mean "in kind," that is, "in like manner" or "tit for tat"? Is he getting back some of his own fashionable changeableness? Or does it mean "in the same nature" ("kind" here meaning "nature" or "natural")? Men, then, are of the same nature as women, not so different after all; or are they?

The students soon get the point. This poem is tremendously evocative and mysterious: evocative because it is mysterious. The mystery is structured in a way paradigmatic of the poems of the later Elizabethan period. First, there is a center of obscurity that is the algebraic function, the x of truth: "they," "this," "what." Second, there is the actual text describing or limning the truth, which turns out, on close inspection, to double the truth. The poem tends to double up on itself, to repeat words in a way that creates two contradictory meanings ("seek"/"seeking"; "gentle"/"gentleness"), to use meter and rhyme to split open a seemingly univocal phrase or idea (as in the irregular meter of the last line of the first stanza: "Busily seeking with a continual change"), to create images out of dead clichés ("dear heart"), to use the displaced language of figure. The great cultural coordinates along which truth is doubled in the poem are human versus animal, male versus female (in Petrarch's son-

Patricia Fumerton 163

nets, also human versus divine). Third, we assume that one aspect of each of these polarities is the truth, and the other, the like-truth of figure. But we don't know which is which, with the result that—relative to the plain truth under the x—both seem displaced figuratively. Both are a "strange fashion" of truth.

Still holding my cultural cards close to my chest, I then provide some background on the tradition of English lyrics—one of the most popular forms from 1500 to 1630—to set this poetic structure in perspective. I state that background in terms of stylistic levels, outlining the shift from the plain or native style (with its roots in English poems of the fourteenth and fifteenth centuries) to the Petrarchan or high style (which began with Wyatt's return from Italy in 1527, became fashionable in the 1570s and 1580s, and remained so for the next twenty to thirty years). A poem in the plain style, I note, is a short poem of broad human significance, spoken by a rational, self-knowing "I" attempting in no uncertain terms to speak truth. This plain speaker employs logical structures as well as rigid meter and stanzaic forms and avoids figures. In short, the plain-style poem is one person (usually a man) talking to another (for example, Wyatt's "Madame, withouten many words"). A poem in the Petrarchan style, by contrast, is a short poem in which all human significance is compressed into the adoration between the poet (usually a man) and his lover-muse, compressed to such an extent that the truth becomes unutterable (a premise built on the Petrarchan situation itself as the untouchability of the loved one). This poem is spoken by a slightly irrational "I" who uses elaborate metaphors and conceits that often exert an independent or duplicitous logic seeming to diverge from the truth—a logic, indeed, of self-conscious reflection on figures. In short, the high-style poem is not one person talking to another but one person talking to himself and trying to make the words come out right.

To set the small argument within the larger: just as a poem such as "They flee from me" is structured as a dialectic between the inexpressible truth ("they," "this," "what") and the self-doubling figure for the Truth, so the lyric impulse of the age is structured as a dialectic between the inexpressible truth (the plain style, which goes out of fashion) and the self-doubling figures for truth (the Petrarchan style, which comes into fashion). To put it in the vocabulary of "They flee from me," plain style is the "naked" truth, and the Petrarchan style is indeed "fashion" ("guise," "newfangleness"). Of course, what may lie behind the fashion of inexpressibility (paradoxically expressed through endless elaboration) might be an epistemological uncertainty about the very possibility of truth. This is an idea I pursue but never resolve for the students (as it may not have been resolved for Elizabethans).

At this point, I begin to open up the question of figure and fashion as cultural phenomena and ask, "What is fashion?" "Do we need such fashions as metaphors or Calvin Klein jeans?" This gets the students thinking about the implications of style for cultural practices, then and now. Leaving this question still open, I then reverse the field and ask not about the nature of fashionable

164 NEW HISTORICISM

dress but about that of naked truth. I do so by looking at another poem, Shakespeare's sonnet 20:

> A woman's face with Nature's own hand painted
> Hast thou, the master mistress of my passion;
> A woman's gentle heart but not acquainted
> With shifting change as is false women's fashion;
> An eye more bright than theirs, less false in rolling,
> Gilding the object whereupon it gazeth;
> A man in hue all hues in his controlling,
> Which steals men's eyes and women's souls amazeth.
> And for a woman wert thou first created,
> Till Nature as she wrought thee fell a-doting,
> And by addition me of thee defeated,
> By adding one thing to my purpose nothing.
> But since she prick'd thee out for women's pleasure,
> Mine be thy love, and thy love's use their treasure.

Here I ask, "What is the 'thing' in line 12?" "Why can't the poet (or we) say the 'thing'?" "What, then, is the 'naked' truth?" The idea here is to reveal that the Petrarchan sonnet is all about the discovery of the naked truth, but the discovery proceeds as covering: a redefinition of truth as concealment, as presentable only in some "guise" or "fashion." Indeed, in Shakespeare's sonnet 20 we have a whole series of coverings: face (heart (eye (thing))). The poem moves and points to the "thing" (the x of truth) but can only get there by the configuration face $\rightarrow$ heart $\rightarrow$ eye $\rightarrow$ thing $\rightarrow$ truth.

If time permits, the instructor may here turn to some of Sidney's sonnets, such as sonnet 3 in *Astrophil and Stella*, where the face itself is the x of truth dis-covered within a series of rhetorical fashions—face (truth)—or sonnet 1, where the truth, arrived at through consideration of others' "inventions fine," lies not in the face but in the "heart" (see my discussion of these poems in *Cultural Aesthetics* 91–95, 102–03). In each of these poems, in brief, we again witness the poet trying to discover or recover a naked truth (whether in the heart or face), yet again each production is nothing but the fashionable dress of truth. Or, to expand the range of the reference to include such "dresses" as the face or heart (the body itself), each is a grand cover-up. The poems discard cover after cover in their effort of discovery but then, when they get to the locus of truth, stop (we never see what lies in Stella's face or heart).

I then posit to the class that we think of these poems not as "dress" but as "covers"—a slightly more general concept that allows us to generalize even further about the nature of metaphor in the Renaissance. Now cultural aesthetics can boldly enter. As a method of illuminating the nature of metaphor as rhetorical cover, I propose we look at a concomitant fashionable form that was quite literally encased in covers: the miniature portrait or limning. Much of this part of the class draws on my chapter on miniatures (and sonnets) in *Cultural Aesthetics*, which provides many black-and-white prints of miniatures and their cases (67–85). Other helpful resources, which include abundant color illustrations, are Roy Strong's *The English Renaissance Miniature* and his coauthored *The English Miniature* (Murdoch, Murrell, Noon, and Strong).

Pursuing this tack, I first provide the students with a brief history of the English miniature. I note that miniature painting was a tradition in England that began under Henry VIII and peaked in Elizabeth's reign with the artists Nicholas Hilliard and then Isaac Oliver. (The craze for miniatures thus occurred at almost the exact same time as the fashion for Petrarchan sonnets.) As Eric Mercer notes, the tradition began in association with illuminated books and goldsmithing. Portrait miniatures separated from books circa 1500, at which time portraits began to be placed in jeweled reliquary lockets previously used for religious miniatures. Mercer speculates that part of the miniatures' popularity or fashionableness was directly related to the increasingly public and state nature of large-scale portraiture. Everything the public portraits could not express found release in miniature.

Most important, the miniature expressed private love. Hilliard (c. 1600) wrote that miniatures should "catch" the "lovely graces, witty smilings" and "stolne glances" of the sitters (77). Such pictured intimacies were exchanged between lovers or relations (even the queen's miniature resembled a mistress more than a sovereign) and were shown in secluded places, such as the bedchamber, where they were only reluctantly and secretly unveiled. Finally, these intimate pictures were ornaments: they were intricately painted on a typical background of ultramarine blue with jewel-like colors (ruby reds, emerald greens, and the like) and set in gorgeous, jeweled frames or lockets. Instructors can show slides of some miniatures and their cases, such as Hilliard's *Armada Jewel*, which contains a miniature of Elizabeth I, or the *Gresley Jewel*, which holds miniatures of Thomas Gresley and Catherine Walsingham (Murdoch, Murrell, Noon, and Strong 50). Other telling miniatures are Hilliard's *Unknown Man* (c. 1590–93), in which the figure presses his hand—only half seen under his jacket and shirt—against his heart; his *Man against a Background of Flames* (c. 1595; sometimes ascribed to Oliver); his *Unknown Lady* (c. 1585–90) (Strong, *Miniature* 94, 167, 19); his *Man Clasping a Hand in the Clouds* (1588), which displays the puzzling motto *Attici amoris ergo* ("for the sake of Athenian love" or "because of classical love"); and his *Young Man among Roses* (c. 1587–88) (Murdoch, Murrell, Noon, and Strong 42, 43).

We might make our entry into these miniatures by way of a close reading of the *Roses* miniature (beautifully photographed in color in *The English Renaissance Miniature*). "What," I ask, "is represented in this miniature?" "What do you see in the face?" Not much. "Where, then, do we get the sense of melancholy from?" Color, line, motto. "What is the significance of the cloak in the miniature?" "What is the effect of painting the thorny eglantine directly onto the lover's cloak, without the use of three-dimensional perspective?" "How can you

166 NEW HISTORICISM

relate the ornamental 'cloaking' to the use of crossed lines in the picture, such as the crossing of the lover's arm over his chest?" "So what does the motto 'Praised faith brings sufferings, or penalties' mean?" Such questions elicit the discovery that what is imaged in this miniature, as in Wyatt's poem, is a mystery. We get the sense of thwarted or crossed love, but the exact nature—the ultimate truth— of that love, like the golden motto, like the lover's blank, nearly expressionless face, like the heart within his breast that lies under the hand, under the cloak, under the decorative eglantine, remains concealed within ornamental layers.

Now we might return to the larger question of fashion, rerendering it in terms of covers. "Why, in the expression of the ultimate truth (which in the Petrarchan mode is love), are covers needed?" The man among the roses, like the man against the background of flames (with his bared breast and his hand holding a miniature over his heart), appears to want to represent or expose his love. "Why would they not uncover their intent (open the locket; discard the cloak)?"

All these questions take us back further to the meaning and purpose of rhetorical figures or, more broadly, ornament. Miniatures, such as the *Unknown Lady*, are gorgeous with ornamentation both within the frame (the jewel-like colors and lacy patterns) and outside the frame (their settings and covers). The Petrarchan sonnet may also be seen as centrally preoccupied with ornaments, as in Sidney's sonnet 3. This is the age of elaborate ornamentation. "What is ornament?" "What is the relation of ornament to its object of beauty?" "What is the effect of opening the jeweled case or looking through layers of ornament?" Finally, "If something is the ne plus ultra of beauty—a face, a pair of eyes, a jewel—why does it need an ornament (mascara, a setting, metaphor)?" At this point, we can blow the cover on the whole discussion and note that the Greek word for *ornament* is *kosmos*. "Does this help us understand the role of ornament in relation to the truth it adorns?"

The revelation: ornaments are covers or veils, but they are also marks of truth. Indeed, without the cover, there would be no discovery. Put another way, ornaments may distract from the beautiful, but they are also signs: signs that the beautiful is part of a class or cosmos of beauty not visible here. Augustine, whom Petrarch much revered, defended allegory along similar lines—as a visible sign system pointing to spiritual truth—in his *De Doctrina Christiana*. The nagging question, however, which, once again, I usually leave hanging, is whether that cosmic, allegorical truth of self or love cannot be seen because it is invisible (Augustine's position) or, much more unsettling, because it is not there at all. In summary, is the ornamental chain of being a connected meaningful whole, or is it a parcel of superficial fragments that finally—as the students have suspected all along—represent the truth of nothing?

Poststructuralism: Teaching the *Amoretti*

Roger Kuin

Those of us who have encountered and practiced what used to be called, for lack of a clear term, "all that modern stuff" in our own reading and writing and found it an enlightenment and a joy may have been surprised? intrigued? disappointed? when we tried to communicate it to undergraduates. The experience leads us to analyze its pros and cons, and I try here to do so on the basis of my work with sonnet sequences in general and with the *Amoretti* and *Epithalamion* in particular.

Poststructuralist criticism broadly falls into three categories: the formal, the psychoanalytic, and the political. Under formal I should place all semiotics/semiology, the school of Derrida (misnamed deconstruction[ism]), and some early followers of Foucault; under psychoanalytic, principally the influence of Lacan; and under political, most new historicism, feminism, and what is currently called cultural studies.

Teaching the Renaissance by way of these critical currents involves opportunities and problems, none of which are to be underestimated: all too often English departments blithely adopt course proposals on "theory," on the unproved assumptions that it is important to move with the times and that today's students demand it. Such a practice neither serves the pleasure of contemporary criticism nor avoids the problems of its application to undergraduate teaching.

In the case of the *Amoretti* and *Epithalamion*, the pleasures and opportunities of modern critical practice stem in great part from the fact that sonnet sequences are mysterious beings entirely lacking in contemporary theories about their nature and structure. While sonnets receive some brief mention in works ranging from Antonio da Tempo's *Summa Artis Rithimici* (1332) to Puttenham's *Arte of English Poesy* (1589), about sonnet *sequences* all Renaissance theory is silent. The closest term used is Sidney's "other kind of songs and sonnets," doubtless derived from a study of Petrarch's practice and reflecting only the fact that in a paradigmatic Italian sequence the sonnets were interspersed with *canzone*. The lack of any other formal model presents the modern scholar-critic with rich opportunities for speculative conclusion. That these have not been left unexploited can be seen in such political approaches as Ann Rosalind Jones and Peter Stallybrass's "The Politics of *Astrophil and Stella*" and Arthur Marotti's "'Love Is Not Love,'" psychoanalytic works such as Mariann Sanders Regan's *Love Words*, and more formal studies such as my own *Chamber Music*. The lack of theoretical, generic material contemporary with the texts themselves, in fact, enables them to be treated, to a certain extent, as natural or social phenomena and thus opens them up to the kind of scrupulous but irreverent analysis favored by contemporary critics.

My own experience, which has been mainly in Barthesian and Riffaterrean semiotics and some Derridean practice, has shown such analysis to be exciting

168   POSTSTRUCTURALISM

and rewarding. Roland Barthes's work is the more artistic: it reflects the confrontation of texts by a quirky, original, and extremely bold mind willing and able always to think a matter, or a text, *differently*, and to let the form as well as the content of the resultant criticism be influenced by that difference. Barthes provides us with no method to follow—the ones he tried to construct in midcareer were unconvincing (in *Système de la mode*) or unadaptable (in *S/Z*) and soon abandoned—and thus stimulates us to search our own minds for their own surprises.

Michael Riffaterre, by contrast, has, in *Semiotics of Poetry*, created a method of extreme rigor, based on the idea that a poetic text is a series of proliferating variants of and around a repressed matrix and that it has not only a (heuristic) meaning but a (semiotic) significance. Following his method allows one to progress from the former to the latter through the praxis of what Riffaterre calls "semiosis"—roughly, the (re-)creation of this significance within the reader. A poetic text is frequently related to an "intertext" (not the same as a source), which it transforms either by expansion or conversion.

Both these authors teach critics who will learn from them that there are radically different ways of reading a text that, experienced in addition to the traditional or straightforwardly heuristic ones, vastly enrich the critical and the reading processes. To those brought up on what Derrida might call "metaphysical" reading (a text "reflects" what the author "means"), discovering these alternative ways of reading can be revolutionary.

When one reads Spenser in this way the *Amoretti* and *Epithalamion* begin by showing themselves even more clearly than usual as the conversion of a cumulative intertext. They cannot be read apart from Petrarch, the Pléiade, Sasso, Tasso, and Sidney, but they yield their true riches when read together with these (as well as with *Faerie Queene*, books 1 to 3 and the Bible). The first tension exposed in Spenser's sequence is thus similar to that experienced between the two (and sometimes three) texts in Derrida's *Glas*: a bouncing back and forth between the several poles of an urgent but undecidable relation.

Moreover, when reading in this way one learns to see the stresses within the text itself, which allows it to demonstrate its nature as texture, a woven structure of inner tensions. The relation, for example, between sonnets 10 and 68 in *Amoretti* ("Unrighteous Lord of love" and "Most glorious Lord of life") can be more clearly understood in its tension with Sidney's sonnet 5 ("It is most true") and in the retrospective light of Cupid's subsequent dismembering into amoretti, while the "venemous toung" of sonnet 86, which is the Blatant Beast's envoy within the sequence, is reduced to a choir of croaking frogs in the marriage ode. In this same ode, however, Cupid reasserts his role as the myth that fights back: the attempted repetition of the coup from sonnets 10 and 68 in the parallel between the angels' flight around the altar and the amoretti's fluttering about the nuptial couch is much less obviously triumphant and leaves in the reader's mind a kind of creative unease that favors continued thought.

Third, these critical practices also affect our reading of individual poems.

Sonnet 15 in *Amoretti* ("Ye tradefull merchants"), for example, is certainly not, in a "normal" reading, one of the strongest, but it shows, when looked at in the light of Riffaterrean semiotics, an extraordinary double curve of search and reward and disappointment and lessons learned. Applying the concept of "ungrammaticalities," and then tracing their relations, reveals the text's structure of significance. The octave links semes of trade and weariness and vanity. The phrase "all this world's riches" functions as the interpretant: it suggests the simultaneous presence of a number of biblical intertexts that remind us, by the naming of "this world," of the riches of the *other* world, which neither merchants nor readers of sonnets are expected to forget. The sonnet's first part is thus a text produced by expansion of the matrix "the values of wealth are false values" through the model of a *structure of false solutions*. However, the sonnet has a double structure, and a further dual sign is provided by the curiously weak blazon. Line 13, which in most blazon catalogs introduces the hidden but quite physical core of the woman's attraction, here uses a moral topos to defeat an immoral one. By so doing, it denies the experienced blazon reader's expectation. It also retroactively criticizes the whole of the blazon: the conversion is overdetermined by the blazon catalog's own ungrammaticalities. Its lameness now appears as a sign of the falseness of its values—the values, by extension, of all blazons. The second part of the text, converting its hypogram,[1] is generated by the matrix "values of the body are false values," and its model is that of the *denied* (or *altered*) *climax*. To find the unifying element, we must return to the closing of the problematic circle: the connection between line 14 and line 1. The poem's two halves are then shown to be two hemispheres, meeting not only at lines 5 and 6 but also (like east and west) at the extremities. The denial of our expectation by line 14 places us in the position of the merchant, who has with "weary toil" found the riches of the blazon yet found them in vain, because line 14 has exposed our values as false, just as the merchants' were.

Whom does the sonnet address? Apostrophically, the merchants. Yet every poem addresses the reader. In this case, the text's significance lies in the fact that we as readers, avidly following the blazon catalog to its expected conclusion, find ourselves rebuked and our values equated with those of the merchants. The two addressees, reader and merchant, become, ruefully, one.

Completing the analysis, we find in this circularity of problematic the key to the unifying structure of significance. The invariant of which the two substructures are variants is the matrix "*material* values are false values," whether of wealth or of the body. The method of overall text production is expansion; the second part's conversion is built into the larger movement as a variation. The model that unites the submodels of false solutions and denied or altered climax, as well as the circularity of the total structure, actualizes the matrix through the pattern of the *fruitless search*.

Finally, what Paul Ricoeur in *Time and Narrative* calls the "downstream" aspect of the text, the mimetic reaction of the reader to the text ("Mimesis III"), is not left unaffected by such a poststructuralist reading. Perhaps only a

170   POSTSTRUCTURALISM

reader used to discerning and analyzing structural factors can look at Shake-speare's *Sonnets* and become aware of their vast and all-permeating enterprise of transforming and converting the *Amoretti* and *Epithalamion*'s intertext. The key—the "interpretant"—lies in sonnets 153 and 154, which form the only (other) genuinely "anacreontic" interlude in what John Kerrigan (in the intro-duction to his Penguin edition of the *Sonnets* and *A Lover's Complaint*) calls the "tripartite Delian structure" (13) and thus lead us to consider the Spenser-ian text in tension with the Shakespearean. What then emerges is stupendous, and extraordinarily subversive: a sequence that celebrates its triumph over the Petrarchan tradition by moving from tigerish, blood-embrewed tyrannesses to the cosmic mutuality of a married love and procreation is deconstructed by and in a second sequence that begins with procreation, moves steadily to suspicion, reproach, lust, and despair; and culminates in banalities strutting in the stan-zaic form of the *Fowre Hymnes*.

The genuine and intense pleasure, then, of what I prefer to call a modern critical practice concerning a Renaissance text like the *Amoretti* consists in the intellectual excitement generated, the reader's cocreativity, and the sense that the text is yielding reserves of meaning and significance of which the nature is not always explicable in detail but the presence is wholly convincing.

There are also, however, serious questions about this practice as a method of teaching, which should not be underestimated. In the first place, and most the-oretically, the practices under discussion largely reflect, indeed are, personal revolutions on the part of their practitioners. These critics were themselves trained in the rich and scrupulous school of what we may call old historicism, whether of the British humanist, the German *wissenschaftlich*, or the French neoclassicist variety, which in any case included a considerable grounding in what used to be called "Western civilization." This background the scholars came, in various ways and for various reasons, first not to take for granted, then to regard with suspicion, subsequently to treat as an adversary, and eventu-ally—at least in and for themselves—to subvert or to overthrow. In each of their cases, the process of revolution is an integral part of the critical practice. Now if such practices are taught, as they usually are, to undergraduates either as part of a smorgasbord of "critical approaches to literature" or as the new orthodoxy, almost everything that gives them life and makes them moving and convincing is lost, and indeed their very nature is subtly but effectively subverted.

A related and complementary problem is that today's undergraduates increasingly lack the background knowledge that would enable them to see these practices in any kind of perspective. Even those students entering senior-year (fourth-year) courses in Renaissance poetry now generally have no prior knowledge whatever of either European history or literature before 1700, lit-tle geography, no foreign languages, and very little sophistication in the active or passive use of their own tongue. These deficiencies often prevent them from even understanding the highly sophisticated texts of contemporary criticism.

Third, in such conditions, emphasis on critical practices is apt, for those students who *can* understand them, to deprive them of one of earlier (indeed, all) literature's greatest pleasures: that of *submitting* to the text, of absorbing it, being carried away by it, and then learning it and slowly understanding it—of becoming, in other words, an intelligent, sensitive, and unassertive traveler in the foreign country that is the past. Many current critical practices emphasize the equality of the reader with the text; they teach readers to be "resisting readers," to look the text squarely in the eye, to mistrust it, to interrogate it, and (often) to judge it. Such an approach is dangerous even when practiced by the learned: for them, indeed, the danger is part of the attraction. When uncritically absorbed by the ignorant, however, it becomes unlovely and counterproductive.

How, then, do we avoid the pitfalls while maintaining and enhancing the pleasure of a modern criticism? My own solution is fairly radical: I explain to my undergraduates broadly what I have written here and persuade them that they need first to know and absorb a little of what they will later perhaps be taught to subvert. Following this, I teach them "the Renaissance," quite traditionally, meanwhile acutely aware that, as in Borges's "Pierre Ménard, Author of the *Don Quixote*," the Renaissance I teach them will not be the same as the one I learned. (I use the term *Renaissance* advisedly, alerting them to the existence of its current adversary *early modern* as part of the spectrum the exploration of which I encourage them to defer.) When I feel that they have begun intelligently to enjoy the texts with a certain background of learning, I may try out with them various modern readings, but initially I introduce such approaches without labels and always with as much sensitivity as possible to the students' own reactions and readiness.

Insofar as secondary education no longer communicates what used to be considered the heritage of Western civilization, I do believe some such introduction to literature needs to be accomplished at undergraduate level before modern critical practices can be addressed with any validity or intellectual honesty. Even young revolutionaries must be taught what it is they will later be permitted or encouraged to subvert. If revolution becomes orthodoxy, if revolutionaries become conservatives, any revolutions will have been definitively betrayed.

This is not, emphatically, to deny the value of such practices. They can be immensely liberating intellectually; they can release huge riches in texts such as the *Amoretti*. They have opened up whole areas of attention—the constitution of the speaking subject, the situation of lover and beloved within a wider and more public world, the recognition of tensions within the text, the constitution of new sorts of relevance to our own time—and Anglo-Saxon readers especially have occasionally been taught a new and salutary emphasis on thought as not synonymous with research. I am convinced that our own minds (and therefore our teaching) can only be enriched by the pleasure of a continuing engagement with such critical practice in our scholarly and critical work.

But we should never forget that in today's undergraduate teaching we are dealing with the vulnerable, the open, the intellectually virginal, the easily

172 POSTSTRUCTURALISM

bewildered, the preoccupied, who have little background, little time, and little money. We should ask ourselves, continually, what our goal is in teaching them the Renaissance. What do we want to accomplish? My own answer is that I should like them to have learned the informed pleasure of intelligent travel in its country. Some knowledge, much humility, and a great deal of delight. The *Amoretti* and *Epithalamion* have been for most of us a discovery of enormous joy. The pleasure of modern criticism has, for some of us, been the same. If we can transmit both these pleasures to our students without betraying either, we shall have built the narrow, swaying bridge that is the goal and the reward of our profession.

NOTE

[1]A hypogram is "a text not present in the [poem's] linearity. [. . .] The significance is shaped like a doughnut, the hole being either the matrix of the hypogram or the hypogram as matrix" (Riffaterre, *Semiotics* 12–13).

"Love Is Not (Heterosexual) Love": Historicizing Sexuality in Elizabethan Poetry

Mario DiGangi

To teach Renaissance poetry is to teach some of the earliest and arguably some of the most compelling male homoerotic verse written in the English language. As recent lesbian and gay scholarship has demonstrated, representations of homoerotic desire can be found in all the major Renaissance poets and dramatists—Marlowe, Spenser, Shakespeare, Donne, Jonson, Milton—as well as in lesser-known writers like Richard Barnfield.[1] One need not be familiar with the theories and premises of lesbian and gay studies, however, to incorporate a discussion of homoeroticism into the teaching of Renaissance poetry. As I hope to show, the fundamental theoretical issues can be introduced through the standard practices of close textual explication and historical contextualization.

In my experience, approaching Renaissance poetry through questions of sexuality can be a highly enjoyable and productive venture. The differences between modern and Renaissance notions of eroticism, gender, and anatomy readily capture students' interest. Moreover, students generally appreciate being considered mature enough to handle such material, as this unsolicited student response to my teaching of Shakespeare's *Sonnets* indicates:

> It's fascinating to discover and discuss sexuality, an aspect of life that's everywhere yet so infrequently discussed as such. Never in a literature class has anyone interpreted Shakespeare's sexuality in this way and it's so refreshing to have a new outlook on this after getting the same dry interpretations since eighth grade.

Focusing on sexuality can generate genuine engagement with texts often perceived to be dry. Finally, I find great value in conveying—especially to lesbian and gay students, whose perspectives are often ignored or disregarded—the conviction that sexuality is a legitimate and worthwhile subject of intellectual inquiry.

Aside from the pedagogical value of refreshing the undergraduate English classroom, I would argue that issues of sexuality can play a vital role in successfully teaching Renaissance poetry. In Renaissance England, homoerotic relations did not constitute a separate linguistic, social, or geographical sphere, as the modern ideas of gay sensibility, gay lifestyle, or the gay ghetto imply; instead, they pervaded all levels of cultural and social life (Bray; Bruce Smith, *Homosexual Desire*). A focus on homoerotic relations in Renaissance poetry can therefore provide the basis for a discussion of ideologies of gender, sexuality, and status in sixteenth-century England; Elizabethan transformations of literary conventions and discourses (Petrarchan, pastoral, Ovidian, satiric); and the politics and pragmatics of editing Renaissance texts. My strategies for addressing

174   HISTORICIZING SEXUALITY

these topics were developed in a sophomore-level survey course for English majors, yet they should be appropriate for more advanced courses as well.

My course unit on Renaissance lyric, which begins with Wyatt and Sidney, stresses the importance of resisting anachronistic assumptions about love poetry as a heterosexual, private, and genuinely emotional form of expression. Despite the current divergence of opinion on important issues in the history of sexuality, many scholars agree that concepts of sexual orientation (e.g., heterosexuality) and sexual identity date from the nineteenth century. Social historians have argued that modern notions of privacy were only emerging in the sixteenth century. And whatever emotional sincerity we might attribute to courtly lyric must be measured against the self-fashioning practices of courtly culture: namely, the circulation of poems in manuscript and the code of artificiality, imitation, and display advocated in books like Castiglione's *Courtier*.

For these reasons, I locate Wyatt's depiction of male-female relations squarely within the context of male-male relations, particularly the social rivalries and patronage networks of the Henrician court. Wyatt's poetry illustrates Eve Kosofsky Sedgwick's theory of "male homosocial desire," which posits that in patriarchal cultures men typically bond with one another through the bodies of women (25). While homosocial desire is not necessarily sexual, it can be, and even nonsexual male bonds can be erotically charged. Sedgwick finds a model homosocial triangle in Shakespeare's sonnet 144 ("Two loves I have of comfort and despair"); similarly, Wyatt often triangulates the male speaker's courtship of a mistress with one or more male figures: a personified Love, an implied auditor, rival lovers (as in "Whoso list to hunt"), or even his own lute. In "The long love that in my thought doth harbour," for instance, Love is portrayed as a military captain to whom the speaker owes allegiance. Unlike the Petrarchan source, which ends with the rejected lover's declaration that it is good to die loving well, Wyatt's poem concludes with the speaker's asserting his loyalty not to his mistress but to his "master" Love (line 12), for "good is the life ending faithfully" (line 14). The lover recuperates from the loss of his mistress by reaffirming a more stable bond with another male.

The homosocial dimensions of sixteenth-century love lyric are also evident in Sidney's *Astrophil and Stella*. Astrophil's courtship of Stella is hardly an intimate affair: his ostentatious passion affects his performance at public tournaments (sonnets 41, 53), distracts him from social and political duties (sonnets 18, 21), and becomes intelligible through the political discourse of "Tyrannie" and "monarchie" (sonnet 2, line 11; sonnet 69, line 10). I approach these issues by asking students to explicate sonnet 9, in which Astrophil compares Stella's face to "Queene Virtue's court" (line 1), and to consider how this comparison might serve Astrophil's interests. Exorbitantly flattering Stella, Astrophil simultaneously objectifies her, and his rhetorical mastery belies his claims to powerlessness (see N. Vickers, "Diana"). Sidney's erotic politics are further illuminated by Arthur Marotti's influential essay "'Love Is Not Love': Elizabethan Sonnet Sequences and the Social Order," which argues that Elizabethan courtiers expressed their professional anxieties and aspirations through Petrarchan poetry. As the elaborate Petrarchan conceit of sonnet 9 suggests, Sidney's negotiation with his poetic predecessors and rivals extends the notion of male homosocial desire to intertextual as well as interpersonal relations.

Historicizing sexuality in the poetry of Wyatt and Sidney sets the stage for a discussion of the provocatively open and ambiguous poems in Shakespeare's *Sonnets*. The first sonnet of *Astrophil and Stella* clearly establishes that the male "I," Astrophil, writes poetry to obtain "grace" from his mistress Stella (line 4). In the first sonnet of Shakespeare's sequence, by contrast, an unnamed speaker employs a universal "we"—"From fairest creatures we desire increase" (line 1)—and identifies an unnamed addressee only as "thou" (line 5). Notwithstanding the strong imperative of the final couplet ("Pity the world" [line 13]), the speaker does not reveal any personal motives for urging this mysterious addressee, who might be either male or female, to reproduce.

Although the enigmas of the *Sonnets* are palpable and immediate, many students will have been guided by previous teachers or textbooks to regard these poems as transparent yet profound expressions of heterosexual love. They may be surprised to discover that the "mistress" praised in the oft-anthologized sonnet 18 ("Shall I compare thee to a summer's day?") is actually the young man addressed in the early poems. The first twenty sonnets, which establish the speaker's "love" for this youth, deserve close attention. In class, I approach this set of poems through the following questions: Why, and through what rhetorical strategies, does the speaker urge the young man to reproduce his beauty? Does he have a personal interest in making such an argument? And why does he eventually shift his emphasis from sexual reproduction to poetic reproduction?

Initially taking a paternal stance, the speaker urges the wasteful youth to find a "mother" to bear his child (sonnet 3, line 4). Significantly, he directs the youth not to find a suitable partner in romantic love but to imitate a farmer's thrifty tillage by producing his "posterity" on a female body (sonnet 3, line 8). Having reduced this woman to a merely reproductive and dynastic function, the speaker eliminates her altogether when he exalts the ability of his own verse to reproduce the youth's "image" (sonnet 3, line 14). A direct comparison between sonnets 12 and 15, which employ the same "When [. . .]" (octave) / "Then [. . .]" (sestet) structure, emphasizes the speaker's shift from male-female sexual reproduction to male-male poetic reproduction. Whereas in sonnet 12 the speaker advises the youth to defeat time by "breed[ing]" (line 14), in sonnet 15 he himself battles time by "ingraft[ing]" the youth poetically (line 14) and all "for love of you," as he proudly declares (line 13).

But what kind of love has the speaker declared? The question is most provocatively explored in sonnet 20, which introduces a playful and frank eroticism into the sequence. While the octave's portrait of an androgynous young man seems to resolve the initial mystery about the speaker's "master mistress" (line 2), the sestet introduces a new, distinctly sexual, mystery. The traditional interpretation of the sestet's argument can be paraphrased as follows: "When

176   HISTORICIZING SEXUALITY

Nature 'prick'd thee out for women's pleasure' (line 13), the penis she supplied destined you for sex with women, but you should love me (emotionally) nevertheless." Because the speaker's homoerotic desire cannot be physically consummated, the story goes, he renounces it and settles for a nonsexual love.

But this most enigmatic and punning of poems should not be reduced to a single interpretation, let alone such a conventional one. At least two alternative readings of the sestet are possible: "You were originally created for a woman (as a sexual partner), until Nature added one thing (your self-love) that defeated my purpose (to convince you to preserve your beauty through sexual reproduction)"; or "You were originally created as a woman until Nature gave you a penis, a 'thing' that has 'nothing' to do with my sexual purpose (which may involve a different part of your anatomy ['nothing' = hole]) but that deprived me of you nonetheless by giving you the desire and the ability to please women sexually." The speaker's sexual desire for the youth is thus thwarted by the youth's exclusive attention either to his own "thing"—hence the masturbatory indolence implied by "self-substantial fuel" (sonnet 1, line 6) and "self-love" (sonnet 3, line 8)—or to the "nothing" of women.

How does the couplet resolve this impasse? Modern editions typically repunctuate the poem's final line to read, "Mine be thy love, and thy love's use their treasure"; yet the 1609 quarto reads, "Mine be thy love and thy loves use their treasure." Providing students with a photocopy of the sonnet from a facsimile edition of the quarto, I ask them how the grammar of the unedited couplet might suggest a different resolution than that prompted by the edited version. Whereas in the edited line the speaker appears to accept that the youth's nonsexual love for him will not involve the sexual activity ("love's use") the youth enjoys with women, in the unedited line he appears to insist that the youth take him as a lover ("Mine be thy love") and reject all his other "loves" or suitors. In other words: "Since Nature 'prick'd thee out' (pierced you, leaving a hole) for 'women's pleasure' (i.e., the pleasure of being sexually penetrated), love me sexually and let your lovers 'use their treasure' (expend their own sexual resources without you)." Having demonstrated that the youth is anatomically equipped to enjoy sex with a man, the speaker ultimately reasserts his sexual designs on him (for a similar reading, see Orgel, *Impersonations* 56–57).

To counter skepticism about the plausibility of such a reading, I remind students that ideas about sex, gender, and sexuality are historically and culturally variable. Distinctly modern understandings of sexual identity and orientation were not available to Shakespeare and his contemporaries. The goal, of course, is not to convince students that Shakespeare was "homosexual" or "gay" (which are modern identity categories) but to establish the historical distinctness of Renaissance sexual ideologies and to convey the idea that multiple, contradictory understandings of same-sex desire existed in Shakespeare's culture, as in our own.

The *Sonnets* themselves present multiple perspectives on the speaker's desire for the youth. By describing himself as a patient and neglected slave, the speaker of sonnet 57 expresses the more painful consequences of his devotion. I ask my students to consider why the editors of *The Norton Anthology of English Literature*, the text I use in my survey course, might have excluded this particular sonnet from their selection and whether or not that exclusion seems justified. Whereas some students predictably claim that the editors may have deemed the sonnet's masochistic language too overtly sexual, others offer various ideological, aesthetic, and pragmatic explanations for its omission. This assignment always generates a valuable range of responses and a lively debate. The abject tone of sonnet 57 can also provide an effective transition to a discussion of the "dark mistress" sonnets (127–54), in which the speaker expresses his resentment toward an alluring yet sexually threatening woman (sonnets 129, 135, 144). Notably, Shakespeare associates disease and disorder not with male-male but with male-female sexual relations.

Despite their obvious importance, Shakespeare's *Sonnets* need not be the last word on the place of male homoerotic relations in Elizabethan lyric. Richard Barnfield's sonnets (1595) provide a valuable contrast to Shakespeare's more tempered, resonant expressions of same-sex love. Barnfield's poems are playful, unambiguously sexual attempts to seduce one "Ganymede"—in classical mythology, the beautiful shepherd boy Jove brought to Olympus to be his cupbearer and lover (Barkan, *Transuming Passion*; Saslow). In Renaissance England, *ganymede* could be used colloquially to signify any dependent (and presumably sexually available) young man, like a page or player. As the presence of Ganymedes in Barnfield's sonnets, Marlowe's *Hero and Leander*, and Shakespeare's *As You Like It* indicates, Elizabethan authors used pastoral and Ovidian conventions to explore erotic desires outside the boundaries of Protestant marriage and reproductive sexuality. In *Hero and Leander*, for instance, Neptune, mistaking Leander for Ganymede, aggressively woos the reluctant and confused youth, who can imagine only Hero as an appropriate sexual partner for himself. Marlowe's representation of homoerotic courtship hence provides a logical transition from a discussion of Shakespeare's *Sonnets* to a unit on erotic verse narrative.

Unlike Ovidian poetry, Elizabethan verse satires openly attack same-sex desire. Deriding the London gallant who enjoys a "plump muddy whore" as well as a "prostitute boy" (40), John Donne's satire 1 (1593–94) evokes an image of "sodomy," a predominantly legal and religious category that identified certain acts (e.g., same-sex prostitution) deemed socially or politically transgressive (Hiller). Yet in various other poems Donne aligns male homoeroticism with friendship, romantic love, and religious devotion (Klawitter; Rambuss, "Pleasure"). It is therefore imperative to understand that in the Renaissance only disorderly manifestations of same-sex desire were branded "sodomitical." Moreover, "sodomy" could name a variety of socially transgressive behaviors (e.g., bestiality, adultery, heresy, witchcraft) that did not involve a same-sex component (Bredbeck xi–xii).

This distinction between orderly and disorderly forms of homoeroticism

178 HISTORICIZING SEXUALITY

reveals why love in Renaissance poetry is not heterosexual love. Sexual ideologies and practices were no more monolithic in early modern culture than they are in our own, where, to cite just one newsworthy example, a movement to legitimize the same-sex "marriage of true minds" currently struggles against sodomy laws and homophobic counterefforts, in Shakespeare's words, to "admit impediments" (sonnet 116).

NOTE

[1]See, for example, Bredbeck; DiGangi; Goldberg, *Sodometries*; Klawitter; Orgel, *Impersonations*; Bruce Smith, *Homosexual Desire*; Traub.

What's Race Got to Do with It? Teaching Shorter Elizabethan Poetry

Margo Hendricks

The emergence of a body of scholarship concerned with race in early modern English culture has generated much interest in pedagogical strategies for teaching race in literature classes. Newly available documents and changes in historiography have sparked debates about the "semiotics of race" (Hall, *Things* 10) in the canon of early modern English literature. Students and scholars of Elizabethan literature not only have a wide range of critical studies to draw on but also have access to manuscripts and printed texts whose existence has been either unknown or elided. This expanded textuality has produced revisionary reinterpretations of canonical works in the light of the myriad textual and visual representations of Africans, Indians, and Native Americans.

Often contrasting the beloved's whiteness against the darkness of the Moorish, Indian, or Ethiopian body, a number of Elizabethan poems illuminate the significance of ethnicity and race to early modern English literary culture. These early modern lyrics frequently draw on different tropes (exoticism, blackness, whiteness, barbarity, savagery, and the erotic) to adumbrate idealized notions of Englishness, love, and beauty. Ultimately, these lyrics, as Kim Hall suggests, warrant "more sustained attention" (*Things* 269) than they have been given not only in scholarly studies of Elizabethan poetry but also, more crucially, in the teaching of early modern English literature.

In this brief pedagogical essay, I offer a framework for teachers interested in fostering discussions about race and shorter Elizabethan poetry. In doing so, I hope to illustrate that considerations of race in sixteenth-century English literature can be fostered through an examination of lyrics. In effect, this essay seeks to encourage teachers of Elizabethan literature to incorporate what is not always "black" and "white" in the Elizabethan conceptualization of racial identity. In what follows I outline a number of useful strategies to introduce students to the semiotics of race in early modern England. The course that provides the pedagogical context for this essay is titled The Idea of Poetry. In this course, students read a range of late sixteenth- and early-seventeenth-century lyrics, traversing a variety of modes (odes, elegies, sonnets, and verse satires), Philip Sidney's *Apology for Poetry*, and a number of critical essays on race. Over the course of ten weeks, students write four to five analytical papers (3–5 pages in length) and an original lyric. For the purposes of this essay, John Donne's elegy 19 and Everard Guilpin's *Skialetheia*, satire 5, will illustrate the ways in which race can be made part of the study of Elizabethan poetry.

Introducing Race

One of the difficulties in teaching race as an aspect of shorter Elizabethan poetry is that students often protest the interjection of "politics" into what they

180   WHAT'S RACE GOT TO DO WITH IT?

see as an aesthetic appreciation of a literary work. Encouraged to appreciate the imagery, wordplay, assonance, and form of a poem, students view any attention to social or cultural issues as detracting from the beauty of the work and, in their writings or comments, often appear openly hostile to considerations of race. For these students, race evokes sometimes painfully contradictory and burdensome emotions. Is there no place where the complex social injustices or problems that shape much of their social consciousness can be set aside and the literary work appreciated solely on its own merits? Can we not read literature for its own sake without dragging into it the current polemics? Why can't we just view art as art without complicating it with all this social baggage? These and other questions have surfaced in my courses whenever the issue of race (or gender or class) is raised vis-à-vis a literary work whose imagery is not obviously racial, that is, in texts where characterizations or references are not of Africans, Indians, Moors, or Native Americans.

In these instances, works such as the poems reproduced in Hall's appendix can be introduced as depicting images of race, but texts such as Edmund Spenser's *Epithalamion* or William Shakespeare's *The Rape of Lucrece* cannot. Thus the first order of business in getting students to consider race in relation to Elizabethan poetry is to help them reevaluate their assumptions about the relation between art and ideology. In The Idea of Poetry, students are invited to reframe the question of race so that the complexity of early modern notions of race is not occluded by modern ideologies. To stimulate their efforts, I give students a photocopied handout of the *Oxford English Dictionary*'s entry on race, photocopies of entries from sixteenth- and seventeenth-century dictionaries (Richard Percyvale's and John Minsheu's bilingual dictionaries are two favorites), and a brief lecture on lexicography. Students are asked to select a synonym of race (kind, lineage, nobility, and stock, for example) and to trace its lexical genealogy. This exercise encourages students to focus on the etymological origins and extant definitions of the word *race* and simultaneously destabilizes assumptions about the fixity of meaning. It is important that students become sensitive to the historical specificity a word may have in the sixteenth century that, as centuries pass, becomes occluded or even effaced.

Students are divided into small working groups and are given secondary readings that offer an overview of the concept of race in Western culture. In this particular course, I have found chapter 2 of Michael Banton's *The Idea of Race*, Kwame Appiah's entry on race in *Critical Terms for Literary Study*, and chapter 1 of Benedict Anderson's *Imagined Communities* quite useful. Each group is asked to summarize the arguments of these chapters, to assess their usefulness in relation to early modern English literature, and to ascertain whether the information provided by the students' examination of early modern dictionaries complicates these very modern theoretical considerations. Each group then is asked to produce a brief position paper, which is circulated among the class for later discussion. Central to the strategies suggested here is a notion of race broadly construed as signifying not only color or phenotype but also nationality, ethnicity, genealogy, or typology. It should be noted that students have not engaged in readings of any lyric as yet. This is done deliberately. In other early modern English literature courses where the topic of race is introduced, I have found that the greatest resistance comes when students see themselves as having been forced to turn from aesthetic considerations of a work to political readings. The activities deployed in this course before close reading aid students as they examine theoretical and cultural assumptions about race, its meaning, and its historicity. Such strategies redefine the critical terrain so that when an intersection is postulated between a notion of race and early modern aesthetics students are less hostile to the idea.

Pleasures of the Text

Teaching John Donne's elegy 19 has long been both a pleasure and a bane. On the one hand, the lyric's evocative sensuality and imagery provide an excellent example of the complexities and logic of Petrarchism—Donne's opening exhortation is nothing more than an elaborate blazon. On the other hand, when read against Nancy Vickers's cogent essay "Diana Described: Scattered Woman and Scattered Rhyme," for example, Donne's elegy engenders in its readers a heightened sensitivity to the disturbing paradox produced by the blazon. Add to this mixture Donne's use of the trope America (usually figured as a site of enormous wealth that is female, chaste, and unguarded), and one finds a lyric that traverses the aesthetic-political divide that students often insist is necessary to appreciate a literary work.

In a carefully structured writing assignment, students are asked to make sense of Donne's request that his mistress "licence [his] roving hands, and let them goe / Behind, before, above, between, below" (lines 25, 26)[1] in the light of the previous image in which she is likened to "Mahomets Paradise" (line 21). Students quickly comprehend that there are frequent shifts in Donne's imagery—from angelic to terrestrial to textual. In discussions about the imagery, I guide students over Donne's highly attenuated exotic landscape as the lyric's argument turns from the mistress's body to overt ethnic loci—Islam and America. As the lyric unfolds and the imagery of one stanza flows into the next, defining the mistress's body first as "Mahomets Paradise" and then as the speaker's "America, [his] new found lande" (line 27), the mistress subtly becomes identified with non-English and non-European cultures and spaces that, typically, are represented as alien, dangerous, exotic, and barbaric in early modern English writing.

Edward Guilpin's satire 5 similarly deploys non-European spaces and cultures as a point of departure for his satire on London. The poem invites its readers to accompany the satirist-narrator as he exposes the dis-ease that has infected London (and by extension England). The satirist guides the reader along a "flower bespangled walk," where he "may heare / Some amorous Swaine his passions declare / To his sun-burnt Love" (lines 33–35). The poet

182   WHAT'S RACE GOT TO DO WITH IT?

then describes London as the "mappe of vanities, / The marte of fooles, the Magazin of gulles" (lines 66, 67). And if the reader does "but observe the sundry kindes of shapes," he would "sweare that London is as rich in apes / As Afrricke Tabraca" (lines 68–71). A few lines later the poet observes that the city is overwhelmed by a "hotch-potch of so many noyses, [. . .] / That Chaos of rude sounds, that harmony, / And Dyapson of harsh Barbary" (lines 37–44). Throughout this section of the satire, Guilpin works with a dichotomy presumably familiar to his readers—Africa, with its "sun-burnt" women, apes, and "harsh Barbary," on one side, and London, with its "flower bespangled walk," on the other.

What becomes apparent to students is the subtle ways in which a very specific type of racializing begins to emerge in the two poets' use of imagery. In both texts, Africa, America, and Islam provide Donne and Guilpin the means to deploy a hierarchical system of contrasts based on a coded lexicon that defines each of these terms as barbarous and exotic and as sites of sensuality and sexuality. Furthermore, as I suggest to my students, such lexicons are implicated in the formation of a concept of race as they allow hierarchies of difference to be adumbrated, constituted, and reaffirmed. In the moment that Donne's mistress becomes "America" and Guilpin's "apes" appear in London, the poems cease to concern just a man's desire for his mistress or a satirist castigating his fellow citizens and become an evocation of a racializing discourse intended to foster early modern England's developing sense of racial identity.

In arguing that these two poems contribute to early modern conceptualizations of race, I endeavor to highlight the complex aesthetic, moral, and political dimensions invoked by the lyrics' associative juxtapositions of non-English and non-European geography and cultures. Students are encouraged to consider in their written assignments the ways Donne's elegy and Guilpin's satire create or add to a semiotics of race through the figurative use of terms such as "Barbary," "hotch-potch," "America," "sun-burnt Love," and "Afrricke." As part of their reflections on the poems, students are asked to identify and discuss, especially in Guilpin's work, other possible racializing terms or images and to relate this to the lexicographical and theoretical work done at the beginning of the course.

What transpires in the students' engagements with the poetry is a growing appreciation for the complexity of early modern conceptions of race, the contribution made by poetic writings to these conceptualizations, and the complex intermingling of social and aesthetic cultural assumptions attendant on the formation of racial identity. In the current academic climate, teaching race as integral to an understanding of Elizabethan poetry can be fraught with obstacles. For those of us whose scholarly writings seek to highlight the issue, teaching race to undergraduates can challenge even the most experienced. The strategies in The Idea of Poetry course provide students a matrix for examining both their presumptions about the function of literature and those of early modern English poets.

Margo Hendricks   183

Not surprisingly, these strategies have their genesis in a traditional pedagogical technique—close reading. Once students discover that the language used to create images of pleasure in Elizabethan poetry is also the language used to create racial ideologies, they are more willing to consider the possibility (and plausibility) of reading race in works such as Donne's or Guilpin's. Moreover, students are more willing to assume responsibility early in the course for the pedagogical imperatives and strategies that will guide them through a work's racial inscriptions, and in doing so they also take responsibility for beginning the process of redefining what race means.

Ultimately, students must approach "the texts of Western culture as equals" and the professoriate must forego "the role of Prospero-teacher to passive students" (Hall, *Things* 268) when treating issues of difference (whether race, gender, sexual orientation, class, or religion) in the classroom.

As teachers of Elizabethan poetry we must begin to rethink our own assumptions about what constitutes a meaningful engagement with Elizabethan poetry, an inquiry that may perhaps be the most useful framework for introducing race into the classroom. For, as the poetry of Donne and Guilpin highlights, the lexicon of race recognizes few borders—whether temporal, historical, aesthetic, political, or philosophical. Our responsibility is not merely to teach the techniques of close reading but to "licence" our students' "roving hands" to begin the difficult work of uncovering the literary history of race in Western culture.

NOTE

[1]All Donne quotations in this essay are from his *Poems*.

TEACHING SPECIFIC POEMS AND POETS

Motives for Metaphor in Gascoigne's and Ralegh's Poems

Jane Hedley

A good way to teach George Gascoigne's and Walter Ralegh's lyrics is to call attention to the way both poets use metaphor as a rhetorical strategy, a strategy of persuasion. For the most part neither poet uses metaphor suggestively or "darkly"; both of them spell out and play out the correspondences between tenor and vehicle for whose sake the metaphor has been constructed. I have found that George Puttenham's discussion of the "courtly figure" (299; ed. Willcock and Walker) of allegory helps explain this way of using metaphor, since for Puttenham this trope is just as much a social or political as it is a literary gambit.

In *The Arte of English Poesie* Puttenham cites *allegoria* as "the chief ringleader and captaine of all other figures, either in the Poeticall or oratorie science" (186). To be able to say one thing while intending or meaning another is an important social resource, especially at court; for indeed, as Puttenham wittily asserts, it is "the profession of a very [that is, a true] Courtier [. . .] cunningly to be able to dissemble" (299). While Puttenham's treatise is ostensibly and primarily a glossary of poetic devices, "it is at the same time," as Daniel Javitch points out, "one of the most significant arts of conduct of the Elizabethan age" (68). Nowhere is this more apparent than in the discussion of *allegoria*, which Puttenham terms "the Courtly figure" and commends to the queen in his final chapter with a facetious encomium to all those practices of indirection that enable the courtier to "dissemble not onely his countenances and conceits, but also all his ordinary actions of behaviour, or the most part of them, whereby the better to winne his purposes and good advantages" (299).

Puttenham's characterization of courtliness suggests a relation between poetic and social artifice that will enable Gascoigne's and Ralegh's poems to begin to be read as politically and psychically motivated stylizations of social life. But what is most conspicuous about the figurative strategy of "Gascoignes Woodmanship" or "Lullabie" or "Good Morrow" and Ralegh's "The Lie" or *The Eleventh and Last Booke of the Ocean to Scynthia* or "The Passionate Mans Pilgrimage" is not the cunning use of *allegoria* to keep the speaker's meaning "dark" but the way in which, having chosen a particular metaphoric vehicle to carry his meanings, each poet is constrained to work within its limits and thereby to make those meanings more and more obvious and predictable. By the time we reach the end of a poem like "Gascoignes Woodmanship" or "The Passionate Mans Pilgrimage," in which a single metaphor has been used to structure an entire narrative (of a courtier's progress to disaster, of a dedicated soul's journey from this world to the next) or else, as in Ralegh's "The Lie," to catalog an extensive inventory of social evils, the tenor-to-vehicle relation has come to seem all too predictable and procrustean. The difficulty of such poems for students, in my experience, is not so much what they mean as why the poet chose to develop his meaning in such a way. In teaching these poems I therefore find it especially important to highlight the relation between poetic device and social context, inviting students to discuss the choice of metaphor and the way it has been developed in relation to the author's social or political purposes.

For *The Ocean to Scynthia*, I know of no better way to do this than by assigning the first and third chapters of Stephen Greenblatt's biography of Ralegh, which assimilate Ralegh's poems to an elaborate enterprise of "self-fashioning" and tell an exciting story about how this one came to be written. In lieu of assigning Greenblatt, the instructor can tell students the story of how the poem's author fell out of favor with a female ruler whose favorites were encouraged to publish their devotion to her in the idiom of romantic courtship. It is worth explaining that *The Ocean to Scynthia* was not published in our modern sense but circulated at court as a desperate bid to make amends for having secretly married without the queen's permission. (That Ralegh's poem and plight became notorious within the courtly inner circle can surely be inferred from his cameo appearance as "the Shepheard of the Ocean" in *Colin Clouts Come Home Againe.*)

After a context of publication for the poem has been established, it is important to affirm students' first impression of the poem's incoherence and amorphousness: I warn them before they read it, lest otherwise it seem they've been given an unreadable assignment. The fun begins when students see how the poem's formal incoherence advances the poet's allegorical project. If the ocean could speak to the moon, if indeed the ocean as we know it can be imagined to be already speaking to the moon, what would that speech be like? Because the poem offers itself as a possible answer to this question, the next step is to wonder what Ralegh's purpose might be in speaking as the ocean and what can be learned from the ocean's predicament about the political and behavioral

186   MOTIVES FOR METAPHOR

dynamics of a courtier's relationship to his queen. As a perspective on that relationship the metaphor is not just psychologically but also politically suggestive: the political work it does is to naturalize their relationship by depicting the queen's power over her courtiers as an irresistible part of the divinely sanctioned order of the cosmos.

Turning to Gascoigne, we find him doing a lot of this work of contextualization for us. I like to play "Gascoignes Woodmanship" off against Ralegh's "The Lie" or "The Passionate Mans Pilgrimage," inviting students to decide which they prefer: the spectacular impersonality of Ralegh's allegorical role-playing or the canny self-interestedness of Gascoigne's. It is tempting to do some very particular biographical backlighting with Ralegh's poems (no one busier, it seems, with quill and parchment on the eve of his execution!) but preferable to highlight the way in which Ralegh (if he is the author of these poems) has used the allegorical metaphor to submerge his individuality in a drama that lifts away from specific contexts to emphasize the human condition as such. Gascoigne, on the other hand, often stages a highly self-interested process of turning his life into poem fodder. Both in "Woodmanship" and in *The Adventures of Master F. J.*, *allegoria* becomes a social gambit for furthering particular purposes in dialogue with others or with a particular other. Often what it amounts to is an opportunity for role-playing whose purpose is to transform an event or interaction into a readable text with a more or less hidden subtext. The man or woman who proffers the allegorical figure is inviting his or her interlocutor to become party to a process that by its indirection gives them both a measure of protection while fostering intimacy between them. In such cases, the figure's "darkness" or difficulty will vary circumstantially with its author's ultimate goal and his or her motive(s) for indirection.

Mocking himself in the third person, Gascoigne confesses to the Lord Grey of Wilton in "Gascoignes Woodmanship" that he did not learn fast enough how to thrive and prosper at court:

> He thought the flattring face which fleareth still,
> Had bene full fraught with all fidelitie,
> And that such words as courtiers use at will
> Could not have varied from the veritie.   (lines 45–48)

He has recourse to the courtly figure not to show that he has learned to dissemble with the best of them but to persuade his interlocutor (apostrophized as "My worthy Lord" in the poem's first line) that from now on the knowledge Gascoigne has gained from experience will enable him to prosper and yet stay honest. The woodmanship metaphor is in keeping with the appearance of down-to-earth practicality he seeks to project—not a piece of poetic finery but a tool that lies to hand. But his allegorical strategy is in its own way cunning, after all: the series of seemingly artless confessions that "your woodman" failed again and again to "hit the mark"—first at college and law school, then at court and on the battlefield—turn out to be more and more beside the real point of his story, which is that such targets as these institutions present to a man's ambition are not worth hitting after all. At the end of the poem he gives the woodmanship metaphor a surprising twist by producing a carrion doe who offers herself enigmatically to him as an easy target with a difficult lesson to teach—that if a fool will persist in his folly he may become wise. As it moves from *allegoria* to *ironia* to *enigma*, the poem's trajectory will help the inter-relatedness of these figures emerge.

One way to make the seeming heavy-handedness of the controlling meta-phor interesting in Gascoigne's poems is to raise the issue of control—an issue that often emerges within the poems themselves as their overt or covert theme. It can be asked whether such poems leave us with the impression that the poet is in control or, alternatively, that he has let the metaphor itself determine what he could say and mean. His metaphor may even tell us things about him that he didn't entirely mean to say. Take "Gascoignes Lullabie," for example, a poem whose masculine speaker calls attention to his masculinity even as he takes on a female persona: "And lullabie can I sing to / As womanly as can the best" (line 4). This poem's allegorical strategy is interesting to discuss because it is unmistakable yet ambiguous: Is the poem's speaker using this device to tell us he's a "sensitive male" or to mock his own impotence or what? Pretty clearly, the poem's message is that finally you have to give up control of your life to the aging process. The speaker's meaning is scarcely in doubt from one stanza to the next—except that I find I need to gloss the apostrophe to "my little Robyn" in the penultimate stanza—but his motive for metaphor is eminently discuss-able. Lullabies are not only women's work, they are servants' work—it is his nurse, presumably, who sang this man to sleep the first time he was a child. One possible way to motivate the poem's allegorical device is to see it as enabling a very macho man to acknowledge and come to terms with a shaming sense of powerlessness.

When I teach a course called Allegory in Theory and Practice that takes on *The Faerie Queene* and other allegorical works, such as *The Play of Everyman*, Hawthorne's *The Scarlet Letter*, and Melville's *The Confidence Man*, the theo-rists we read call attention to the very active role an allegory calls on the reader to play. With the allegorical lyrics of Ralegh and Gascoigne I like to emphasize that the courtly figure gave people a way to say readable things to one another in particular contexts. My favorite examples of this occur in Gascoigne's shrewdly realistic depiction of the game of sexual courtship in *The Adventures of Master F. J.* When the married woman F. J. is pursuing decides it's time to let him catch her, we are told that she "[falls] to flat and playn dealing" with him: drawing him aside, she asks him "secretly & in sad earnest" who is the author of the love poem he has just performed to music for her and her friends:

My Fathers Sisters brothers sonne (quod F. J.) His Mistresse laughing right hartely, demaunded yit again, by whom the same was figured: by a

188 MOTIVES FOR METAPHOR

> niece to an Aunt of yours, Mistres (quod he). Well then servaunt (quod she) I sweare unto you here by my Fathers soule, yt my mothers youngest daughter, doth love your fathers eldest son, above any creature living. (67–68)

It's a notable oddity that this kind of riddling exchange is what passes for "flat and playn dealing" between the would-be lovers. When the other lady who is interested in F. J., Lady Fraunces, says she dreamed she saw him coming toward her in a gown all covered with naked swords (73) or when she offers to be his Hope if he will be her Trust (66), we begin to see that these young people's conversation is rife with allegorical devices. Their appetite for these devices is related to the sexual aggression and rivalry the devices assist them to sublimate and civilize (and which "Gascoignes Lullabie" suggests Mother Nature takes care of in another way, as part of the aging process).

In the Lady Fraunces we can also discern an appetite for authorship, in the sense that the allegories she concocts give her a role to play in F. J.'s affair with her rival and a way to involve F. J. in turning that affair into a readable text—an object lesson in what happens when one goes after a woman like her sister-in-law. Like Shakespeare's Rosalind, Lady Fraunces hopes to cure the man she cares for of a certain way of being in love by assisting him to play the lover's role for all it's worth, but to do so self-consciously, as an "experiment." The point I like to make by calling attention to Fraunces's strategy is that even though most of the poetry that survives from this period was authored by men, the women they interacted with were probably just as adept at using allegorical devices to further an interpersonal agenda. Arguably, indeed, a woman would be likely to have an even greater aptitude, as well as appetite, for the self-detachment and self-protection such devices would afford her.

Allegorical role-playing can be undertaken, says Puttenham, "in earnest as well as in sport" (186): in the case of Lady Fraunces we can infer a complex and subtle blending of the two. The allegorical mode is less ironic, and in that sense more in earnest, when it assists the allegorist to make a commitment or to express a heightened sense of purpose:

> Giue me my Scallop shell of quiet,
> My staffe of Faith to walk vpon,
> My Scrip of Ioy, Immortall diet,
> My bottle of saluation:
> My Gowne of Glory, hopes true gage,
> And thus Ile take my pilgrimage.
> (Ralegh, "Passionate Mans Pilgrimage" lines 1–6)

Here in the opening stanza of Ralegh's "The Passionate Mans Pilgrimage," what Puttenham calls a "mixed allegory" (188) leaves no doubt about the speaker's intentions; as I read his rhetorical motive for making them so explicit

Jane Hedley   189

it is indeed to express that he knows where his commitment will take him. That a heightened sense of purpose may come along with the choice to use an allegorical device is more obvious when the commitment is explicitly religious or spiritual, as in this instance, than it is in "The Lie" or "Gascoignes Woodmanship." But all three poems are uncannily similar in that their speakers seem progressively emboldened by their own activity of playing out a chosen metaphor, to the point where in each case a final, explosive twist takes both the metaphor and the maker to another level of commitment or of insight:

> Seeing my flesh must die so soone,
> And want a head to dine next noone,
> Just at the stroke when my vaines start and spred
> Set on my soule an everlasting head.
> Then am I readie like a palmer fit,
> To tread those blest paths which before I writ.   (lines 53–58)

This passage is comparable, surely, to the moment in "Gascoignes Woodmanship" when "Jehovah" produces a carrion doe for the woodman to kill ("I saye Jehovah did this Doe advaunce, / And made hir bolde to stande before mee so" [lines 136–37]) or to Ralegh's triumphant assertion in the final stanza of "The Lie" that having his soul throw down the proverbial gauntlet ensures that he won't be able to lose his grudge match with the World.

A heightened sense of purpose may also be problematic, however, for the one who has purchased it thus. Like a costume that restricts its wearer's freedom of movement and limits the range of activities in which it will be comfortable or appropriate to engage, the metaphor limits the range of gestures and story lines available to the one who cloaks himself or herself in it. Having outfitted himself for pilgrimage, Ralegh's "passionate man" has undertaken to suffer: "Blood must be my bodies balmer" (line 7) is the line that immediately follows his explicit commitment "thus [to] take my pilgrimage" (line 6). By the same token Lady Fraunces, in offering to play Hope to F. J.'s Trust, takes on a role she is ultimately powerless to abandon when Suspicion takes her partner captive. In the second version of the *Adventures* Gascoigne plays out the inexorable logic of the metaphor on which both F. J. and Fraunces have staked their future happiness, dooming F. J. to spend the rest of his days as a dissolute cynic and Fraunces, his Hope, to suffer death by "consumption" (231). Angus Fletcher suggests that insofar as the protagonist of an allegorical fiction is doomed or fated by his metaphor of purpose, he will behave, as it were, neurotically: he will resemble the victim of an obsessive-compulsive disorder. Fletcher's insight can give us a way to motivate the relentless refrain of Ralegh's "The Lie" or the claustrophobic obsessiveness of *The Ocean to Scynthia*. In these instances, arguably, the decision to adopt an allegorical persona has proved to be a Faustian bargain.

A Week with the *Calender*
John W. Moore, Jr.

Let us place ourselves in the following situation: we are teaching a one-semester undergraduate survey of Renaissance poetry, and we have set aside three fifty-minute class periods to introduce *The Shepheardes Calender* to students reading Spenser for the first time. How can we best use those three class periods? First, to teach the *Calender* well, one must have a passionate commitment to some personal, deeply held, and clear explanation of the poem's worth. Current analyses of the *Calender* stress new-historicist perspectives and emphasize Spenser as a poet primarily concerned with the uses of court power. Perhaps it is time to view the *Calender* as the work of a Protestant poet who seeks to establish for poets and poetry a position of public spiritual leadership. Since I teach the *Calender* the week after Philip Sidney's *Defence of Poesy*, I link the works as two discussions of the same issues. Both works inaugurate a new generation of poets and poetry, and both make serious claims for poetry's central role in the moral development of the citizens of the Reformation state. Whereas Sidney claims that poets teach moral wisdom better than philosophers and historians do, Spenser equates poets with priests and bishops as the moral leaders of society and, in effect, concludes that poets are the better teachers, thereby confirming in advance Milton's later shrewd assessment of his achievement. The *Calender* stands with the *Defence* as a manifesto of the new Protestant poetry, the poetry of virtuous instruction.

Second, the *Calender* is a pastoral poem. In the *Calender* one finds a variety of pastoral perspectives, all being contested, debated, and explored. No one definition of pastoral works well in all cases; in the house of pastoral there are many rooms. Vergil, Horace, and Hesiod, Sannazaro, Mantuan, and Marot, among others—each with a distinctive attitude toward pastoral—make appearances here. The *Calender* is not a pastoral like *A Midsummer Night's Dream* or *As You Like It*. It most resembles *Lycidas*. Like that poem, the *Calender* pits differing views of pastoral against one another. One view pursues the ancient dream of humankind living in harmony with nature and finding satisfaction in the golden age, the unfallen world. Another view flows from the Christian ecclesiastical word *pastor*, or shepherd. Priests and bishops are pastors, or shepherds of their congregations or flocks. Many of Spenser's shepherds are ecclesiastical pastors whose task is to lead their flocks to the Christian goal of heaven. That interpretation of *pastor* explains why so many of the eclogues are given over to discussions of how to be a good clergyman or pastor, that is, how to be a good shepherd. Poets are also pastors within the Sidney-Spenser system because they speak the words that lead men to their final end and highest good. Which paradise does one seek: the earthly or the heavenly? That question divides the speakers within the debates.

Third, *The Shepheardes Calender* consists of twelve eclogues, in the middle

John W. Moore, Jr.   191

ten of which various speakers debate topics of interest to shepherds and each speaker tries to state his position effectively. No debate ends with a clear winner, and the whole series of debates has no resolution. However, readers inevitably find one side in each debate more attractive. By the end of the debates, each reader knows what all the debates were really about. However, the basic rule of *Calender* interpretation is that no two persons will ever agree about what they have read. As a result, the poem becomes a personal possession and a site for passionate argument, as Spenser surely intended.

The interpretation of the *Calender* I love best tells the story of Colin Clout's journey toward understanding his role as a pastoral poet, the poet as England's pastor. I therefore focus on seven eclogues, which I divide into three sets: day 1, *Januarye* and *Aprill*; day 2, *June*, *August*, and *October*; and day 3, *November* and *December*. That grouping tells a story about a wonderfully gifted poet named Colin Clout, who allows his disappointment in love to cause him to abandon his public role as a poet (*Januarye* and *Aprill*). Subsequently, he comes to an important realization about the relations among love, poetry, and audience and about the nature of great poetry (*June*, *August*, and *October*). Finally, he sings the great song that his flock requires (*November*); here at last he becomes the poet who functions as the good shepherd. Illuminated by his journey from misunderstanding to understanding, he leaves the pastoral world of personal ambition, the golden age and earthly paradise dreams of his youth, to take up his public task as a poet who will function as a pastor or moral leader (*December*).

That version of the *Calender* tells us about people who have assumed responsibility for the spiritual well-being of others: priests, poets, and governors. If the Reformation state exists to facilitate the individual Christian's passage from earth to heaven, then, asks the *Calender*, what role do shepherd-poets have in this supreme enterprise? That journey to understanding the role of poets begins with the *Januarye* eclogue, which makes even more sense when coupled with *Aprill*—the task of day 1.

What do we learn about Colin from reading the *Januarye* and *Aprill* eclogues? To answer that question I ask the students to write out their answers to the following question: Why does the poet of *Aprill*'s "Lay to Faire Eliza" (lines 37–153) react as he does to Rosalind's *Januarye* rejection of him as a lover and a poet? That question allows us to see that the *Calender* opens with a crisis. The young shepherd-poet Colin Clout addresses a complaint to the gods of love and to Pan in which he tells them that Rosalind has rejected his love and his love poems; he wants their help. Sung on the pipe that has won him the great fame described in *Aprill*, those compositions have won only her scorn. Astonished and deprived of her love, Colin feels that the winter he sees in the external world has entered his soul. He works out in great detail the parallels between the bleakness of his inner state and the wintry condition of the trees, the ground, and the flock. Unable to find any consolation or hope for a better future, Colin breaks the pipe with which he had earlier served the commonwealth. I liken that action to the priest's initial fury in George Herbert's

192   WEEK WITH THE *CALENDER*

"The Collar": service to others seldom provides the pastor with the inner contentment he seeks. Colin now rejects any further public service and resolves to devote his energies to solacing himself.

That decision reveals Colin's true motive for being a pastor and a poet. Colin is not yet fit for the role he has undertaken, because he seeks the shepherd's post primarily to benefit himself. Self-exaltation and self-aggrandizement really drive him. The early statement of this theme of the proper motive for the pastoral life introduces a major topic for the debates that follow. *Februarye, Maye, Julye,* and *September* discuss the tension between service to the flock and service to oneself, the ecclesiastical desire for greater wealth and position.

The opening crisis also announces the theme of romantic love as a possible impediment to effective public service. Whom do pastors serve? Why do we need pastors at all? Colin's disappointment comes from his inability to win a woman's love. Finding no romantic love in his private life, he repudiates his public role. That theme of romantic love—the Rosalind theme, the desire for erotic satisfaction—dominates *March, Aprill, June,* and *August.* These eclogues debate the tension between the desire for romantic love and the obligation to fulfill the public demands placed on the poet-pastor. If in the first eclogue he breaks the pipe, his instrument of service, then in *Aprill* we hear the song that won him his initial greatness.

"The Lay to Faire Eliza" celebrates the political harmony that Queen Elizabeth has brought about; it makes the nation conscious of its well-being. The blazon describes a community of reciprocal gift giving in which the citizens bring the queen gifts in return for the blessings of peace and prosperity that she has given them. That song of political well-being, with its ritual of political harmony, provokes a conscious sense of shared good fortune and communal happiness. As in Jonson's "To Penshurst," the monarchical hierarchical system is here seen to work, for it is driven by mutual love and not by fear of authority or political oppression. The lines that frame this delightful lay tell a different story. Never again will Colin sing such a song of public inspiration or see the state so happily constructed. The fragile *Aprill* vision collapses when challenged by one romantic setback. Defeated personally, Colin refuses any further service to others. He retreats to what most concerns him: an analysis of his own woe.

On the second day, I ask the class to consider *June* in the light of *October* and to answer the following question: Is the Colin of *June* prepared to accept Piers's challenge to "rayse one's mind above the starry skie" (*October*, line 94)?[1] In *June,* Colin progresses and retreats. On a positive note, when Hobbinoll claims to have found an earthly paradise where Colin can join him, Colin decisively rejects any such possibility and labels that idea a youthful folly enjoyed by those who have not yet encountered love, a response similar to that of Polixenes in the second scene of *The Winter's Tale* (1.2.59–86).

Hobbinoll also retains Colin's pastoral dream of an earthly harmony in which desire finds fulfillment. Hobbinoll announces excitedly that he has found the

John W. Moore, Jr. 193

paradise lost by Adam. Colin now knows that no such place exists. He inhabits a fallen world that cannot provide him with what he most desires. We must admire his control when he appears amused by Hobbinoll's naïveté. Colin now accepts a world of limits, one not designed to meet human expectations for happiness. In addition, he no longer seeks poetic fame or prominence. He no longer believes in his early songs. He now lives solely to cure the pain of disappointed love. But no song can cure that grief (lines 65–96). To our surprise, his wise and stoic acceptance collapses as his desire for revenge breaks through his new facade. He wants to injure Rosalind and to make her suffer for his woes. He also wants to harm Menalcas, who helped turn Rosalind against him. As we see in the *August* sestina, Colin is now trapped within his own self-absorption (*August*, lines 151–89).

As we reach the midpoint of the *Calender*, Colin stands revealed as an inadequate poet. The sequence from *Januarye* through *August* has stripped Colin to his primary concern with himself. He cannot possibly serve others because he has no wisdom that will benefit anyone. If the *Calender* were to end at this point, the poem would have to conclude that poetry can make no claim to a serious role in the Reformation state. The golden-age pastoral world of endless summer and contentment has turned out to be a delusion, a literary and psychological hoax. Colin has found life too harsh, too bitter, and too disappointing to believe any longer in that pastoral perspective.

Discussion of the relation between poetry and teleology becomes explicit in *October*. The greatness of this eclogue lies in its analysis of poetic motivation and poetry's subject matter. Cuddie, "the perfect patterne of a poete" (argument, line 1), asks that question several times: "What I the bett for thy / They han the pleasure, I a sclender prise" (lines 15–16); "What good to Cuddie can arise?" (line 18); "But who rewards him ere the more for thy? / Or feedes him once the fuller by a graine? / Sike prayse is smoke" (lines 33–35). Cuddie resembles Colin in his preoccupation with the poet's salary and not the poet's task. Piers counters that the task well performed improves civic virtue. Cuddie asserts the primacy of self-interest. Piers reviews the four social uses of poetry that poets like Cuddie and Colin have abandoned: "to restraine the lust of lawlesse youth with good advice" (lines 21–22); to "sing of bloody Mars, of wars, of giusts" (line 38); to sing "[o]f love and lustihead" (line 51); and to "make thee winges of thine aspyring wit, / And, whence thou camst, flye backe to heaven apace" (lines 83–84). To the lack of a reward, Cuddie adds the further impediment of an uninterested audience, an aristocracy given over to ease: "And mighty manhode brought a bede of ease" (line 68). Poets refuse to sing, and the audience turns away. Piers plaintively asks, "O pierlesse Poesye, where is then thy place?" (line 73). He sees before him a society bereft of moral leadership.

For the third class, I ask the students why Colin appears so despondent in *December* when in *November* he has just discovered the source and nature of enduring human happiness. Happily, *November* also resolves the impasse of *October*. When Thenot asks Colin to sing on the occasion of the death of Dido,

194   WEEK WITH THE *CALENDER*

Colin accepts this gloomy topic; it suits his dreary mood. As he proceeds through the expected catalog of mourners and depicts a world given over to grief caused by this young woman's drowning, Colin reaches a grim *de casibus* and *contemptus mundi* conclusion (lines 153–62). The line "nys on earth assuraunce to be sought" (157) restates Colin's *Januarye* complaint and terminates all hope of ever finding any enduring, golden-age delight. However, this act of renunciation also cleanses his soul of radical error. Thus prepared for vision, he suddenly sees Dido in heaven and joy fills his soul. Dido walks among the saints and is installed "in heavens hight" (line 177). That heaven, Colin realizes, is the pastoral place that he has long sought: "Fayre fieldes and pleasaunt layes there bene, / The fields ay fresh, the grasses ay greene" (lines 188–89).

This moment of transition from woe to joy, brought about by visionary experience, constitutes the climactic moment of the *Calender*. Colin discovers the subject matter needed for the poetry that can make the highest claims in a Protestant community: presenting heaven as the goal of human striving. He has discovered the source of assured human joy and happiness. Colin finally knows what will truly feed his flock's spiritual needs. He feeds them with this poem and thereby fulfills his personal pastoral responsibility. The poem also identifies the process of composing a poem as a mode of knowing, an experience that enables the mind to transcend its limits and to open all heaven to the poet's eyes and thereby to the eyes of the readers. Others may believe in the existence of heaven; Colin knows it exists. Poetry has brought him sure understanding. Through poetry, he has gained supreme knowledge without the aid of a church or a Bible and without reliance on faith. As a result, he can now speak with exceptional authority. The search begun in *Januarye* is over, but there is one more eclogue.

Filled with this new and inspired knowledge, Colin now views with bitter clarity his long and misdirected search for fulfillment. *December* makes best sense if we read it as Colin's farewell to false pastorals, the errors of his youth. The tone is one of intense self-accusation for past mistakes. The poem flows from the comprehension gained in *November*. Colin is no longer bewildered; he knows well how wrong he was. He now knows what is true and right, and he can judge his past correctly. How foolish he was to seek on earth what Dido possesses in heaven! The despondent and bitter tone resembles that of Red Crosse during his penitential experience in the House of Holiness in *The Faerie Queene*. Confrontation with his past mistakes fills Colin with the same bitterness and self-loathing—a very human response.

Having rewritten his own story, Colin hangs up the pastoral pipe and renounces his role as a poet who derives from the world of nature the truths that the poet-pastor must sing to feed the souls of his flock. In having him do so, Spenser completes his investigation into the nature and role of poets and poetry within a community that regards heaven as the final end of human striving. By the time we close the *Calender* we know the proper motivation for becoming a poet-pastor, we comprehend the crucial social role of that poet-pastor, and we understand the proper subject matter for such serious poetry. Best of all, we know the process one must undergo to reach these understandings.

The *Shepheardes Calender* is therefore a great poem because it announces the arrival of a new generation of poets who will take leadership in the formation of the nation's values and whose poems will address its audience's deepest concerns. The *Calender* promises its readers great joy.

NOTE

[1] All Spenser quotations in this essay are from *Spenser's Minor Poems*.

Learning to Love the Star Lover:
Teaching *Astrophil and Stella*

Diana E. Henderson

Philip Sidney's *Astrophil and Stella* sometimes surprises the teacher by failing to engage the student. Turning to this dashing, doomed icon of Renaissance courtship, this learned, worldly model of authorial *sprezzatura*, I have sometimes presumed that students would find the cult of Sidney's personality as intriguing now as his contemporaries did then and that the wit and complexity of his sonnet sequence would speak for itself. But for those untrained in the rhetorical pyrotechnics and elegant variations within the love-sonnet tradition, Sidney's facility may seem facile. Even when alerted to his formal control, students who value sincerity and sentiment in their poetry find *Astrophil and Stella* too arch, too artificial. And—like other pre-Shakespearean poets—Sidney lurks in the shadow of the Bard, sometimes regarded as if he were an inferior warm-up act.

I have taught Sidney repeatedly as part of an upper-level undergraduate course on sixteenth-century poetry and have analyzed individual poems from *Astrophil and Stella* in introductory contexts as well. Perhaps the most fruitful analogy I have found to initiate the discussion is a comparison with the blues. Like the sonnet, the blues stanza is a tight form that might seem limiting but on closer examination turns out to be useful to the performer in shaping deeply emotional lyric material; from Robert Johnson to Robert Cray, the predictable form and its subtle variation become an essential part of the game, the tradition in which the blues performer situates his or her particular version of a self— a voice, a subjectivity—as a style.

The emotional pain plus the formal game create a balance, allowing passion and despair to become art. I come back around repeatedly to this balance, trying to challenge student assumptions that only directness of style gives credibility to assertions of strong emotion. Self-conscious performance, as in the blues, is not inherently negative, but it nevertheless challenges easy notions of authenticity and sympathetic identification that seem commonsensical to many poetry-reading students. Yet formality, wordplay, rhetorical shaping, and irony can also signal just how raw and extreme are the subjective states being dramatized in the sonnet. The feelings seem so intense that they require the poet to find rigid structures and strategies to gain control, to go beyond a howl or a grunt. Or so would be the poetic performer's sense of the situation; this need for structure provides him or her with a reason (beyond the obvious ones of fashion and literary self-promotion, which I also mention) for bothering to write a lengthy series of sonnets. The verbal game thus creates an opportunity for the poet to locate himself or herself critically and to examine the workings of desire and the self rather than simply to express their effects. No one makes more of this potential for self-conscious construction than Sidney.

Diana E. Henderson 197

When introducing Sidney's sonnets within a broader survey course, I have chosen his programmatic sonnet 1 and placed it in dialogue with Shakespeare's sonnet 73 ("That time of year thou mayst in me behold") and Lady Mary Wroth's "Come, darkest night" (sonnet P22) from her sonnet sequence *Pamphilia to Amphilanthus*. All three love lyrics share the familiar pun on leaves (as natural objects, as pages of writing), through which they call attention to both literary imitation and mimetic representation. The speakers' various relations to these imaginary landscapes allow us to discuss in specific terms the ways in which an inherited vocabulary or metaphor can be crafted to a poet's particular ends. Shakespeare uses his poetic line "When yellow leaves, or none, or few do hang" to revise—at least momentarily—nature's linear sequence, recoiling from "none" to hover at the moment when precious little remains to be cherished; the line thus epitomizes his poem's wistful attempt to make the most of his own natural decay as an incentive for love. Writing later, Sidney's niece Mary Wroth also finds herself in a subordinate position to her beloved, but understandably (given her gender) with less sense of irony. For her, the "distressed" trees have shed their "dead leaves," becoming "leafless, naked bodies, whose hues fade": the similar analogy between poet and natural landscape leads her to a far bleaker conclusion, the very redundancy of expression echoing her despair. By contrast, Sidney's poem approaches frantic, frustrated comedy, dramatizing the speaker as a confused seeker of "fruitful showers" amidst "others' leaves." Whereas Shakespeare uses the comparatively loose English sonnet form, Sidney manages the much tighter Italianate rhyme scheme yet modifies the form by adding an extra foot. He thus sends a typically double message: he will use and adapt, be Petrarchan and anti-Petrarchan, play the fool and demonstrate his artistic command simultaneously.

By discussing these three sonnets together, students can gain a sense of the shared patterns and ironies of love sonnets (all three, typically, present the poet as lover rather than the beloved as the predominant poetic subject), but they can also see the range of effects and moods the patterns produce. Usually students vary in their preferences among these sonnets and are eager to debate the poems' comparative appeals. Even when they tend toward Shakespeare, they become aware that his poem is a product of certain conventions and choices that carry no more transparency or sincerity than do Sidney's fireworks.

Is Sidney mocking Astrophil's misguided attempts to find inspiration in stale places? Is the poem itself "bad" if we are not moved by the speaker's plight? If such questions do not arise in connection with sonnet 1, they soon surface in courses where we read more of the sequence. (Given time constraints, I now assign a maximum of about twenty-five poems, including several of the songs—enough to give students a sense of the narrative shape without creating a weighty blur in which the particular poems are forgotten.) To discuss the ways in which Sidney clearly signals his interest in text as performance—the way he makes explicit gestures at himself as an autobiographical subject but always teases the relation between life and fiction—we turn to sonnet 45, in which

198   TEACHING *ASTROPHIL AND STELLA*

theatricality takes center stage. As in sonnet 1, Sidney makes the fourteenth line a punch line, one that approaches metaphysical inquiry into the nature of the subject even as it allows the possibility of a bawdy "bad" pun on "tail": "I am not I, pity the tale of me." The range of interpretations encouraged by Sidney's poem once again provides a specific route into larger debates about the functions and uses of poetry, especially as they tie with Sidney's cultural moment. My understanding and contextualization of the sequence draws on new historicist and postmodern psychoanalytic discussions of the development of the modern subject (Barker; Reiss; Fineman, *Eye*), as well as on scholarship that places the Elizabethan lyric within its own court and manuscript contexts (Jones and Stallybrass; Wall; Dubrow, *Echoes*; Henderson, *Passion*). I call attention to *Astrophil and Stella*'s self-conscious allegorizing and dramatization to raise questions about students' own ethical and aesthetic assumptions regarding poetic self-presentation. To the extent that students can articulate their principles for evaluating poems, they tend to be informed by Romantic notions of the lyric. While Sidney cuts a proto-Byronic figure in his struggles with competing forms of authority and originality, the obvious differences in his cultural position and his poems from the solitary meditators of high Romanticism allow students to consider the historical factors involved in developing a framework for interpretation.

To address these issues, we not only consider the narrative dimension of *Astrophil and Stella* as a tale of courtly love (why does Astrophil briefly "get" and then lose Stella? what are we to make of the stages and changing perspectives on this story provided by the interweaving of songs with the sonnets, of lyric with narrative?); we also compare Sidney's own theory with his practice. Having assigned the *Apology for Poetry* for the class after our discussions of the sonnet sequence, I divide the class into groups (about five students in each group) to compare Sidney's essay with *Astrophil and Stella* and to decide on their disjunction or fit. Is Astrophil a poet who imitates what should be, rather than what merely is? Does Sidney then represent a "brazen" world rather than the "golden" one he posits as the proper poet's domain (*Apology* 15)? The references to lead and iron in the concluding sonnet (108) suggest Astrophil's location far from realms of gold; but perhaps, despite his being a biographically linked persona for Sidney, his descent into lust and frustration should be read as a negative exemplum showing how infected will thwarts erected wit. If the "skill of the artificer standeth in that *Idea* or fore-conceit of the work, and not in the work itself" (*Apology* 16), what is the "fore-conceit" of Sidney's sonnet sequence, and how should we evaluate his skill? Is Sidney a poet who "coldly" makes "fiery speeches" (81) in the voice of Astrophil, or is he distinguishable from those love poets Sidney disparaged? The *Apology* does not serve as a key or simple explanatory guide, students soon discover; rather, they find that the playful, ironic tone they have studied in Sidney's sonnets extends to the conventionally somber genre of poetic theory. In addition, reading Sidney's comments on the proper use of love poetry recalls the allegorical potential of

Astrophil and Stella's title, reminding students that even while Sidney puns on Penelope Rich's name he might also be deploying his beloved as a symbolic abstraction. I encourage the groups to decide which of the arguments in the *Apology* they find persuasive and which outmoded or faulty. Whatever their conclusions, the exercise provokes them to think about the moral responsibilities of a writer in different historical contexts.

In my sixteenth-century poetry course, Sidney provides a fulcrum as we turn from the lyric tradition of songs and sonnets to longer narrative forms, including Spenser's epic and a lyrical play by Shakespeare. Having already learned something about the Petrarchan tradition and the courtly contexts of Wyatt and Surrey, students can see how Sidney enlarges the scope and claims for poetry. In addition, I present a brief history of his advocacy for militant Protestantism at court and his subsequent rustication, anticipating the concerns and difficulties with Protestant poetics in *The Faerie Queene*. I also suggest that the rise of the author in which Sidney participates is a compensatory strategy for ineffectuality in the political arena (see McCoy, *Sir Philip Sidney*). After his dashing but not very useful gesture of riding without proper leg armor at Zutphen and his subsequent gangrenous death at age thirty-one, Sidney's posthumous elevation into a courtly and poetic ideal carries obvious irony as well as cultural power. We consider both aspects by looking at several elegies in his honor by Fulke Greville, Walter Ralegh, and Mary Sidney. Fulke Greville's "An epitaph upon the Right Honorable Sir Philip Sidney" serves double duty, its poulter's measure demonstrating that iambic pentameter was but one among several options for serious poetry and reminding students of Sidney's major role in establishing metrical norms during this formative period for modern English. Ralegh's epitaph illustrates the uses to which Sidney's figure, like his poetry, was put by those interested in advancing their courtly or poetic stature; after acknowledging a rivalry in life, Ralegh soon resorts to familiar conceits and a rhetorical torrent that supplants his putative subject in an effort to further the living author's position. The pastoral elegy usually attributed to Mary Sidney, "The Dolefull Lay of Clorinda," reinforces once more that an aesthetic strategy of distancing and formality may not be at odds with deep feeling: despite her closeness to her brother, this poem is not particularly personalized. The difficulty of definitively establishing her authorship arises as well, encouraging discussion of literacy, the social conditions of writing, and the role of gender and class in understanding sixteenth-century authorship (see Henderson, "Female Power"). Carrying on her brother's legacy gave Mary Sidney a particular license to write despite her gender; the 1591 publication of *Astrophil and Stella* similarly provided an incentive for others outside the male aristocracy to circulate and publish their sonnets, producing the sonnet craze of the 1590s. Sidney thus also serves as a pivotal figure for considering shifts in who wrote and how their work was distributed, including the movement from immediacy and performance at court to the wider social circulation of poetry as published text.

200   TEACHING *ASTROPHIL AND STELLA*

Several assignments are linked to these class discussions. If class size permits, I have each student begin discussion of one of the assigned sonnets with a five-minute oral presentation. Throughout the semester, I ask students to compose their own commonplace books, handwritten rather than typed, in which they may include their meditations, verse, and illustrations, as well as passages they found memorable in our reading. Besides reminding them of the technological changes in how we read and write, this exercise is enjoyable for most students, allowing some creativity and personal connection with what often seems (at least at first) remote material. I also have students write a five-page paper in which they focus on the most interesting distinction between two comparable sonnets (either two Sidney sonnets or one by Sidney and one by another author on our syllabus).

Along with the paper, I ask students to submit a sonnet of their own composition. They have total freedom of topic and tone but are to make sure the poem is in sonnet form. I encourage them to exploit the potential of working with an established form, using word placement and metrical variation to signal points of emphasis. This exercise always reveals that some have either not made the effort or else not understood the discussion of metrics, so I try to follow up with personal conferences for those students. At the other end of the spectrum are those who not only manage the assignment but show flashes of wit or craft:

> I've read of lust and Cupid's dreadful dart,
> Of Wyatt's deer and also of his lute,
> I've been amazed by Stella's barren heart:
> She spurned her love and left him destitute.
> [. . . . .]
> I've scanned complete a thousand lines and more
> Of damn[ed] iambic metered dysphony,
> I've been bemused by antique metaphor,
> But well esteemed their grave morality.

To which another budding poet replied in "The English Major's Lament":

> But I, alas, have no such muses' spark
> To brighten that which churns within my brain,
> And I am left with words but not with art
> And to my keyboard must return again.

With the experience of composition comes some humility and less dismissiveness of the sixteenth-century sonneteers' achievements. I type up all the offerings without attribution, and circulate this sheaf of sonnets to the class.

My farewell to Sidney brings us back to the modern world, to reconsider the legacy and distance of *Astrophil and Stella*. I end by comparing Sidney's sonnet 31 ("With how sad steps, O moon, thou climb'st the skies") with Philip Larkin's "Sad Steps." Larkin laments his belated, aged position, looking back in history to a time when formal poetry felt as vital and new as does young love for others now. For the late-twentieth-century writer, the moon

> Is a reminder of the strength and pain
> Of being young; that it can't come again,
> But is for others undiminished somewhere.

Yet for all his distance, Larkin still uses a tight metrical form (six three-line stanzas, with the rhyme scheme *aba bba cdc ddc efe ffe*) even as he mocks rhetorical excess in describing the moon:

> High and preposterous and separate—
> Lozenge of love! Medallion of art!
> O wolves of memory! Immensements! No,
>
> One shivers slightly, looking up there.   (169)

Sidney's sonnet ends with a question (only partially rhetorical) concerning the correspondence between sublunar love and cosmic order; for Larkin, the gap has widened into an abyss. I ask the students to consider where they locate themselves in relation to Sidney and Larkin—as youths, as readers of poetry, as participants in their culture.

Other modern poems influenced by Sidney might work as well: John Berryman's *Dream Songs* offers an obvious alternative. The point is to acknowledge the temporal and cultural distance of Sidney's sonnets without making them museum pieces, and then to return to the present to consider how students as well as poets can still find something vital in this encounter. As my many questions embedded throughout this essay imply, I am not interested in defining one line of interpretation or one function for Sidney's *Astrophil and Stella* in my courses. Rather, I want to provide students with some tools for becoming more familiar with sixteenth-century poetry, and through it with writing and culture more generally. I also want them to enjoy it, just as they enjoy listening to modern forms like the blues (even when they are aware of ideological and experiential gaps between themselves and the performers). We attempt not so much to master material as to wrestle with it, recognizing those aspects that are recalcitrant and mysterious, as complicated as living, as well as those seemingly beautiful, immediate, and comprehensible dimensions of poetry that nevertheless often turn out to rely on an understanding of form and context. If the engagement does not come with a first reading of *Astrophil and Stella*, yet it will come—at least for enough students to make the labor worthwhile.

Elizabeth I: Poet of Danger

Janel Mueller

Surviving portraits of Queen Elizabeth I show a figure of majestic serenity and regality who rivets attention with her heavily embroidered and bejeweled gowns and headpieces, the keen glance from her otherwise impassive face, the graceful ease of her long, tapering fingers. When a class on her poetry opens with slides or book illustrations of some of these paintings, students easily pick up on the paintings' grandiose, idealizing, iconic tendencies. The most striking and most frequently reproduced are the Darnley, Sieve, Ermine, Armada, Ditchley, and Rainbow portraits, where Elizabeth appears as a goddess or otherwise celestial being (Strong, *Gloriana* 84, 100, 112, 130, 134, 154). Such an entry will enable a direct turn to her verse, which registers very differently. Its voice reflects on the quandaries that stem from limitations on human agency and knowledge; these are not the moods or perspectives of a detatched, remote divinity.

The known verse compositions of Elizabeth I resonate with wry observations on life's chanciness, starkness, and obliquity but simultaneously reach for equanimity—or the appearance of equanimity—in a spare, understated style that draws heavily on aphoristic, witty modes of formulation. The forthcoming edition of Elizabeth's works on which I am collaborating (Marcus, Mueller, and Rose) ascribes fifteen poems to her, eleven of which appeared in Leicester Bradner's edition (3–10), one in Steven W. May and Anne Lake Prescott's edited transcription, two more in a sixteenth-century compilation that has never been reprinted (*STC* 6428; Richard Day sigs. Ii.iiiv, Ll.ir–v), and a final poem preserved on a detached manuscript leaf at the National Maritime Museum, Greenwich, England, as MS 5NG/4. Six of these poems are in Latin or French. A course unit devoted to Elizabeth will probably focus on—or select from—her nine poems in English.

If class opens with the superhuman impression created by Elizabeth's portraits, the more ordinary (in the sense of representative and period) character of Elizabeth's English verse can be made striking by means of the contrast. Judged on the basis of her known surviving compositions, Elizabeth Tudor offers an instructive case of how poetry came to be written in mid- and later-sixteenth-century England. Any prospective poet would need to be familiar with the applicable conventions and expectations for composing verse in the Renaissance, which in turn required both formal education and cultural exposure to contexts where verse was routinely present. But to proceed from reading or hearing poetry to writing it, the prospective poet also required the opportunity and the incentive to internalize this social experience of conventions, expectations, and contexts and to make it his or her own, ready to be used, developed, and extended. Only through such combined acculturation and appropriation could a poet turn conventions, expectations, and contexts into the means and substance of self-expression, of registering a voice and a style in verse. The following discussion outlines a developmental case for Elizabeth as a poet formed within this Renaissance mode and setting.

Using her French, Latin, and Italian as well as English, Princess Elizabeth did considerable amounts of prose translation and letter writing. But she composed no poetry, as far as we know, until she became politically suspect to her half sister, Queen Mary, and was imprisoned summarily at Woodstock Castle in 1554–55, without provision for any judicial review. Elizabeth's lot was confinement, solitude, and enforced idleness; her physical surroundings were the castle walls and her chamber's windows. As many timeworn monuments attest, the writing of graffiti has immemorial beginnings. In that time and place it was ordinary social behavior for prisoners and castle guests alike to scratch their names, mottoes, and other messages on walls and windows. This is the experiential context in which Elizabeth produced her first known verse.

The genre she chose—and never abandoned—was the epigram, a verse form with strong classical and Renaissance associations

> which makes a satiric or aphoristic observation with wit, extreme condensation, and, above all, brevity. [. . .] Tone defines it better than verse form. The etymology of the term—Greek epigramma (inscription)—suggests the brevity and pithiness. [. . .] The major epigrams in the Western tradition run a gamut of tones from biting to sharp to gentle, [. . .] which lets us distinguish the epigram from the proverb and apothegm, which are impersonal and gnomic in tone.　　　　　　　　　(Warnke 375)

Elizabeth wrote one epigram of two cross-rhymed quatrains and a couplet on a window frame at Woodstock. She wrote another epigram—understandably shorter, a single couplet—by scratching it on a window pane with a diamond. She signed both epigrams, expressly claiming them as hers. The longer one reads as follows (Platter 220–21; cf. Hentzner 144; Groos 117, 119):

> Oh Fortune, thy wresting, wavering state
> Hath fraught with cares my troubled wit,
> Whose witness this present prisoner late
> Could bear, where once was joy, flown quite.
> Thou causedst the guilty to be loosed
> From bands where innocents were enclosed,
> And caused the guiltless to be reserved,
> And freed those that death had well deserved.
> But all herein can be nothing wrought,
> So God send to my foes all they have taught.
> Finis. Elisabetha the Prisoner, 1555.

When Elizabeth's shorter epigram was transcribed, its context was fortunately preserved. "In her imprisonment at Woodstock, these verses she wrote with

204 ELIZABETH I: POET OF DANGER

her diamond in a glass window," recorded John Foxe (Foxe 1714; cf. Holinshed 1158):

Much suspected by me,
Nothing proved can be.
Quod Elizabeth the prisoner.

These two epigrams are thoroughly characteristic of the genre in their verse form, their terseness, their premium on wit, and their personal tonality. Here and throughout, wit in Elizabeth's verse invariably stakes its ground in antithesis: sharp registration of contrary experiences, thoughts, or emotions. In the Woodstock epigrams, antithesis is thematic and situational but equally conventional: Fortune once gave Elizabeth joy but now threatens death; justice has turned into injustice. As verse, students can compare these formulations productively with Thomas Wyatt's "The pillar perished is whereto I leant"; Henry Howard, earl of Surrey's "So cruel prison, how could betide, alas": and George Gascoigne's "Woodmanship." To add tonal coloration to antithesis, Elizabeth may resort to punning—in which likeness in sound triggers perception of unlike meaning—or to irony, which she understood (by way of Cicero and Quintilian, those supreme authorities in the Renaissance) to involve the cloaking of a speaker's intent by words that can have double meanings. In the first epigram, Elizabeth ironizes in the next-to-last line, which can read as helpless resignation ("In all here, nothing can be wrought," i.e., "nothing can be done") or as dark prediction ("All in here can be wrought nothing," i.e., "made nothing of"). The last line, a lesser instance of irony but a greater instance of wit, projects either reading, or both, on Elizabeth's "foes" as their just deserts ("all they have taught"). In the second epigram, Elizabeth ironizes in the first line, which can be taken to mean "Much is suspected by me" or "Much is suspected to have been done by me." She complicates the irony in the second line, which registers total impasse: neither she nor her accusers can prove their suspicions.

What above all imbues the two Woodstock epigrams is Elizabeth's intensely conveyed sense of her extreme personal danger: all is unpredictable, unwarranted, uncontrollable, and unavoidable. Will she come through? She inscribes her epigrams in and from her state of extremity: her mortal danger compels her to self-expression in verse, which may prove a self-recording, a self-memorializing. She may not get out alive. On the evidence of the much greater bulk of her girlhood letters and translations from religious works, before her life hung in the balance, the serious-minded, prose-inclined princess—like many mid-century intellectuals—had shunned poetry as a toy for the idle. But in isolation at Woodstock, with writing materials denied her, Elizabeth discovered a means of coping with endangerment and its forceful emotions by composing epigrams. If this began as a last resort, it would become a lifelong habit.

The next epigram that we know Elizabeth composed survives in her highly legible italic handwriting of the 1560s, on the last leaf of her French psalter.

This may be the "obscure sentence" reportedly written by the queen in "a book at Windsor" when she was "much offended with the earl of Leicester," her earliest and most durable favorite, in 1565 (John Nichols 1: 198). The text is a single, cross-rhymed quatrain that Elizabeth again signs:

> No crooked leg, no blearèd eye,
> No part deformèd out of kind,
> Nor yet so ugly half can be
> As is the inward, suspicious mind.
> > Your loving mistress,
> > Elizabeth R (Elizabeth I, Windsor)

Antithesis—outward ugliness, inward ugliness—constitutes the theme and grounds the judgment in the wit of a precise proportional relation: an inwardly suspicious mind is twice as ugly as a deformed body. Here, however, the danger posed by inward, suspicious minds is under much more control than in the Woodstock epigrams; Elizabeth can calculate it as a ratio of two to one. There is more tonal lightness, too, in the pun on "so ugly half," which conducts the calculation while it images the body and soul as each "half" of a complete person. An altogether new dimension, moreover, appears in the subscription accompanying the signature. It locates this epigram in a context of address and (possible or necessary) reply, that is, in a situation ready to become dialogue. Verse dialogues, a prominent Renaissance genre, typically develop contrasting characterizations or attitudes by means of opposed speakers. Here, though, the opposition is contained within the single speaking figure of Elizabeth, who pronounces severe moral judgment but subscribes herself "Your loving mistress," the first explicit instance of self-gendering in her verse. Significantly this feminine self-identification does not simply register affection but conveys a full quota of superiority in status and in affect. "Your mistress" has spoken lovingly, in chastisement and in deep knowledge of her addressee, who could quite plausibly indeed have been Robert Dudley.

Elizabeth's contemporaries considered her to have registered her finest achievement in her chosen genre of the ironic, antithetical epigram when in the early 1570s she composed "The doubt of future foes," the most frequently recopied of her known poems. It is also the one given pride of place in George Puttenham's *Arte of English Poesie* (1589) as an example of the "gorgious," "the last and principall figure of our poeticall ornament," which consists in "copious & pleasant amplifications and much varietie of sentences all running vpon one point & to one intent" (247; ed. Willcock and Walker). "Gorgious," which we understand to mean "showy," "magnificent," has a still obscure etymology, as the *Oxford English Dictionary* records. I suggest to my students that Puttenham's spelling alludes to the famous late classical Greek sophist and rhetorician Gorgias of Leontini, who held Athenian audiences spellbound with his political eloquence decked out in runs of antitheses, full of metrical patterning and

206   ELIZABETH I: POET OF DANGER

sound play that confounded ordinary distinctions between verse and prose. Elizabeth's poem can be termed "gorgiastic" in its array of antithetical constructions, its highly insistent verse rhythms, and its assertion of complete political competence and awareness. According to Puttenham, Elizabeth wrote it in the wake of the Northern Rebellion and the Ridolfi plot to wed Mary, Queen of Scots, to the duke of Norfolk and set the pair on the throne of England; her purpose in writing it was to signify to questionably loyal factions and subjects that "she was nothing ignorant of these secret practices, though she had long with great wisdom and patience dissembled it" (207).

The eight quatrains of "The doubt of future foes" make up an epigram too long to quote in its entirety, but the poetic structure can be clearly characterized: it is an unfolding series of antitheses figured and reemphasized by the use of ballad meter and cross-rhyming ($a_6b_6a_8b_6$). The framing antithesis evokes an endangered, pensive Elizabeth in the first stanza and, in the last three stanzas, an energized Elizabeth who wields her sovereign prerogatives to detect the treacherous, punish the guilty, and set her realm on a stable course. The transition from quandary to triumphant reaffirmation of queenship proceeds by way of other antitheses presented as Elizabeth's unfailingly clear perceptions (denoted by the rule of reason and the weaving of wisdom's web) that challenge the delusions and deceit that "cloak aspiring minds" (line 10; "Verses"). The midsection of the poem deals vigorously in irony as hidden, doubled meaning that requires to be unmasked, especially in the fine fourth stanza, in which open vowel sounds betoken her adversaries' reckless ambition ("top," "hope," "-posed"), closed vowel sounds ("root," "rue," "fruit-") betoken the dashing of their prospects, and the final futility is figured in the grafted stock (Norfolk as would-be king of England) that will bear no issue:

> The top of hope supposed
>> The root of rue shall be
> And fruitless all their grafted guile,
>> As shortly you shall see.   (lines 13–16; "Verses")

The fifth stanza compounds the queen's own perspicacity with that of certain loyal subjects, "worthy wights / Whose foresight falsehood finds" (lines 19, 20). This augmentation of her personal agency swings "The doubt of future foes" into its climactic close. There is, first, the containment of "The Daughter of Debate / That discord aye doth sow" (lines 21, 22; a long-recognized allusion to Mary, Queen of Scots). Then there is the withholding of residency in the realm from dangerous persons: "No foreign banished wight" and "no seditious sects" (lines 25, 27; the vocabulary evokes England's insularity—"anchor," "port," a possible pun on "brooks"). Effectual royal agency culminates in the stanza-long development of the image of the sword of state as a personification—"prosopopoeia" in the terminology of Renaissance poetics and rhetorics —but the image is presented in such general and abstract vocabulary that only the pronouns ("my," "his," "their," "who") sustain any sense of persons. The effect is, however, purposive, for Elizabeth's justice takes on a thoroughly objective character and light:

> My rusty sword through rest
> Shall first his edge employ
> To poll their tops who seek such change
> Or gape for future joy.   (lines 29–32)

The Folger manuscript whose version I have cited and modernized adds a tag after the last line: "Vivat Regina" (Long live the queen).

Later epigrammatic compositions by Elizabeth can be profitably analyzed for their skillful deployment of antithetical structure so as simultaneously to image and express a poetic speaker enmeshed in the divided pull of contrarious feelings. One such composition in three stanzas of sixains—a verse form of French origin that nevertheless retains the marks of the epigram in its cross-rhymed quatrains followed by a concluding couplet—is "I grieve and dare not show my discontent." In all probability this poem was written out of painful disillusionment in 1582, when the queen parted with her last prospective husband, François Hercule de Valois, successively duke of Alençon and duke of Anjou (often called simply by his royal title, "Monsieur"). The self-divided, erotically yearning, extravagantly despairing speaker of "I grieve and dare not show my discontent" invites comparison with Donne's speaker in "The Broken Heart." Both poems permit the interesting classroom exercise of seeking a possible vanishing point of gender differentiation or gender saliency in Petrarchan hyperbole. Any such finding carries theoretical as well as practical significance, for if we can identify some abjected state of extremity in love that leaves gender out or behind when it reaches expression, then gender is not always the secure determinant of a writer's stance, concerns, and vocabulary that we nowadays take it for in literary composition. Here is an opportunity to tease a deep implication out of a focused comparative discussion of Elizabeth and Donne as love poets.

Another question that might be raised about Elizabeth's verse of the early 1580s concerns her very deliberately chosen and defended status as England's Virgin Queen: Are there expressions or intimations to be found of any second thoughts of regret or self-recrimination about her choice of celibacy? "When I was fair and young" is another poem from circa 1580 that exists in a three-stanza and a four-stanza version with the recurring refrain, "Go go go seek some otherwhere, importune me no more." Here Elizabeth compounds dialogue and refrain with epigram to narrate the comeuppance visited on the first-person speaker, a scornful "mistress" to many would-be suitors, whose heart Cupid wounds with such unquiet, day and night, that she is brought to "repent that I had said before, / Go go go seek some otherwhere, importune me no more" (May, *Anthology* 129). Antithesis and irony, the undergirding staples of

208   ELIZABETH I: POET OF DANGER

her verse composition, significantly redound to the discomfiture and discredit of the poet here, not of her adversaries; it is she who repents of what she has done and who she has been.

If Elizabeth is in her origins and in much of her practice a poet of danger, do her verses "I grieve and dare not show my discontent" and "When I was fair and young" repudiate "danger" in another period sense—that of female sexual standoffishness, as influentially introduced in the figure of Daunger in the *Romance of the Rose*? The subtle handling of past time and memory in both poems invests this question with great potential poignancy. For if there is repudiation of "danger" as a strategy of feminine comportment, this comes too late, after the fact, when all the consequences of saying no are in full view and irreversible in the patterning of Elizabeth's personal life. Once again, students' understanding of gender dynamics in Renaissance verse can be enriched by comparing Elizabeth's first-person representation of female sexual standoffishness with that of a male poet who describes his self-enclosed, exquisitely remote female subjects in the third person; a useful example is Edmund Spenser's evocation of the pair of swan brides in *Prothalamion* (Berger, "Spenser's *Prothalamion*"; Cheney, *Spenser's Famous Flight*).

Whatever readers decide regarding the interpretive implications of antithesis and self-division in Elizabeth's epigrams of the early 1580s, by the end of that decade it is clear that danger presents itself to her in a third form for poetic recognition and articulation—the danger of failing to reckon with her mortality and failing to keep her reason, desire, and will fixed on virtue as her ultimate joy and reward. As in her case, so too generally: the turn from secular to more loftily moral or religious verse becomes conventional in English poetry writing after 1600. It is not yet conventional, however, in the decade when Elizabeth, like Philip Sidney in "Thou blind man's mark, thou fool's self-chosen snare" and "Leave me O love that reachest but to dust," writes "Now leave and let me rest; Dame Pleasure, be content" (Stanford 155-56), engages in a verse exchange with Walter Ralegh in which she affirms the triumph of Virtue over Fortune (Black 535), and continues to employ an epigram-like stanza for the allegorical vision poem she composed in French sometime after the English deliverance from the Spanish Armada, in which she imagines the death of her old, internally warring, sinful self and her renewal as an equilibriated and equable, celestial being (May and Prescott).

What I have presented here as a developmental trajectory for Elizabeth's compositions in epigram form (using a standard author-centered focus) could conduce equally well to newer interpretive emphases—for example, to class discussion of the ways and means that might be taken by poetry writing in a cultural context where poetry does not command high cultural esteem. Under one lens, the epigram form will appear as an authorial choice; but under another lens, that of Elizabeth's age, it will be evident that poetry mostly had to be kept short, artful, and moral to justify its existence at all. John Harington, the queen's godson and favorite, tells a story about how "The doubt of future

Janel Mueller 209

foes" came to circulate at court: "My lady Willoughby did covertly get it on her majesty's [writing] tablet and had much hazard in so doing, for the queen did find out the thief and chid for spreading evil bruit of her writing such toys when other matters did so occupy her employment at this time, and was fearful of being thought too lightly of for so doing" (Harington, *Nugae* 1: 58). Here is direct contemporary testimony to a fourth and final danger that Elizabeth faced: disparagement as a queen if she were known to be a poet. This danger "of being thought too lightly of for so doing" may seem utterly groundless today. Yet, in applying historical perspectives in teaching, I consider that my obligations to the materials themselves and to the cultivation of an informed sense of the past require me to signal the possibly severe constraints that this danger could have put on Elizabeth's compositions in verse. Even though we will probably never be able to reckon the toll imposed by her monarchical status on her slender poetic corpus, the case of Elizabeth I remains a striking and suggestive instance of the double face—of accessibility, of alterity—that texts and writers from the past are always presenting to us and our students.

Teaching Noncanonical Poetry to Undergraduates: The Sonnets of Anne Vaughan Lock

Susan M. Felch

> Lo straining crampe of colde despeir againe
> In feble brest doth pinche my pinyng hart,
> So as in greatest nede to cry and plaine
> My speache doth faile to utter thee my smart.

These lines—apparently the complaint of a lover to his cruel mistress—no doubt sound familiar, although readers may have trouble locating them in their favorite anthology. Despite the poem's seeming familiarity, however, the complaint comes not from a frustrated lover but from a penitent sinner, the biblical King David. It is part of a poetic paraphrase of Psalm 51, one of the seven traditional penitential psalms, believed to have been penned by David after the prophet Nathan rebuked him for committing adultery with Bathsheba and arranging the murder of her husband. In the paraphrase, this psalm, with its underlying story of lust, sex, murder, sorrow, and shame, is cast in the genre we associate with despairing lovers and cold-hearted mistresses—the sonnet sequence. Indeed, the twenty-one poems of the paraphrase, along with five prefatory sonnets, constitute the first known sonnet sequence in English (1560). This fact alone would be reason enough to include these poems in courses that study the sonnet form. But our interest should be piqued further when we take note of the poems' author, Anne Vaughan Lock (c. 1534–c. 1590), and the context of their composition. These sonnets, in fact, provide a window through which we may glimpse the complex dynamics at work in mid-sixteenth-century poetry, particularly the centrality of religious issues, the development of literary texts and genres, and the role of women authors.

I teach Lock's sonnets in three different settings: an introductory world literature course, a British survey course (*Beowulf* through Samuel Johnson), and an upper-division course on sixteenth-century British literature. Although I spend only one period on Lock in the introductory and survey courses and up to a week in the upper-division course, my pedagogical approach in all three situations combines formal, historical, and cultural analyses. I introduce her poems in the context of the sonnet genre: in world literature, students have already looked at Petrarch's sequence; in the British literature classes, they have read Wyatt and Surrey. I include a biography of Lock with the initial assignment but avoid making extensive prefatory comments. On the first day, I engage the students in a close reading of one sonnet or more, compare these poems with what students already know about the genre, and begin to explore the poems' implications for understanding the sixteenth century. While it is tempting to teach Elizabethan poetry almost exclusively from the perspective of the 1590s, Lock's poems allow access to the earlier period on its own terms.

One practical barrier to teaching noncanonical texts is that the photocopied pages on which they are printed simply look different from the professionally published anthologies to which students are accustomed. A critical edition of Lock's works is now available (Felch), but previously her writings have been available only in microfilm, online transcriptions (Brown University Women Writers Project, www.wwp.brown.edu), or facsimile (Garrett). The discrepancy in format can lead to skepticism: if this stuff is so important, why does it resemble a throwaway handout? I have two strategies for overcoming this initial resistance. First, I try to present the poems as attractively as possible: on heavy cream paper with wide margins and clear print for the survey and world literature classes and as a bound, desktop-published booklet for the upper-level course. Second, I don't call attention to the disparity between my homemade text and the anthology, nor do I comment on the exclusion of Lock's work from the canon. In other words, I use strategies of inclusion that encourage students to approach these poems as they would any other sonnet.

I also find that students are fascinated by Lock's eventful life, which shatters some of their preconceptions about sixteenth-century women (Collinson, "Role"). I explain that Lock was born into a London merchant family that was well connected to the court of Henry VIII: her father, Stephen Vaughan, was a diplomat, and her mother, Margaret Gwynnethe, served as silkwoman to both Anne Boleyn and Catherine Parr. The family also maintained a vigorous allegiance to the "new religion," Protestantism: Vaughan, a friend of Thomas Cromwell, wrote letters in support of William Tyndale, who was later burned as a heretic; Anne's tutor, Mr. Cob, was examined by the conservative bishop of London for his nonconformist religious views; her stepmother, Margaret Brinkelow, previously had been married to a radical Protestant pamphleteer.

Anne herself embraced Protestantism fervently. With her first husband, Henry Lock, she hosted the Scottish reformer John Knox in their London home, even after he became persona non grata to the newly crowned Roman Catholic queen, Mary Tudor. Later, fearing persecution in England, Anne traveled to Geneva with her two young children (but without her husband) and spent nearly two years there until the accession of Elizabeth. After returning to London, Lock busied herself promoting nonconformist Protestantism in England. She acted as an intermediary for Knox at court; she wrote a Latin poem that was included in an elegant manuscript intended to win back the queen's favor for Lock's second husband, the Puritan preacher Edward Dering; by 1583, when she was married to her third husband, Richard Prowse, she had become a figure of such importance that the Puritan printer John Field dedicated one of his books to her (Field sig. A2r). She wrote two books herself: a translation of four sermons by John Calvin, dedicated to Catherine Brandon Bertie, the dowager duchess of Suffolk (1560), and a

212 TEACHING NONCANONICAL POETRY

translation of Jean Taffin's *Of the Markes of the Children of God*, dedicated to
Anne Russell Dudley, the countess of Warwick (1590). Both books conclude
with original poems.

With Lock's biography in mind, the class turns to a close reading of the son-
nets themselves. Students are often shocked, but also intrigued, by Lock's
forceful language. Given their expectations for sonnets, they ask, Where are
the elegant wordplays, the courtly lover, the compliments and complaints?
Here the opening sonnet is simply one long, despairing sentence:

> The hainous gylt of my forsaken ghost
> So threates, alas, unto my febled sprite
> Deserved death, and (that me greveth most)
> Still stand so fixt before my daseld sight
> The lothesome filthe of my disteined life,
> The mighty wrath of myne offended Lorde,
> My Lord whos wrath is sharper than the knife,
> And deper woundes than dobleedged sworde,
> That, as the dimmed and fordulled eyen
> Full fraught with teares and more and more opprest
> With growing streames of the distilled bryne
> Sent from the fornace of a grefefull brest,
> Can not enjoy the comfort of the light,
> Nor finde the waye wherin to walke aright: (62)[1]

The language itself provides some challenges; we deal first with unfamiliar
orthography by reading the poem aloud. Two words require recourse to the
Oxford English Dictionary: "disteined" means "defiled" or "stained"; "grefe-
full" means "sorrowful," as in "full of grief." The entry for *distain* indicates that
the word was used first as a participle in 1590; since it obviously occurs thirty
years earlier in this sonnet, students learn, much to their surprise, that the
authoritative, multivolume *Oxford English Dictionary* is incomplete. The sim-
ple task of deciphering the words on the page alerts them to the significance of
texts as physical artifacts and disabuses them of the notion that textbooks and
reference works are infallible.

Returning to the sonnet, I point out that the narrator is paralyzed by two
appalling sights: one internal (a stained life) and one external (the wrath of
"myne Lorde," represented as a double-edged sword). The language and
imagery are urgent, dynamic, and horrifying, dramatically capturing that
moment after the pleasure of eating the forbidden fruit has vanished, when the
eyes are open and the realization of guilt has created a gaping hole in the soul.
Such knowledge turns the body into a distilling furnace, which fills the eyes
with briny tears that first diminish and then totally eradicate the sense of sight.
By this point, students are usually hooked on Lock's graphic imagery—dazzled
sight, a stained life, knife-edged anger, and a boiling cauldron of tears. Susanne

Susan M. Felch   213

Woods similarly remarks on the second sonnet, "My students respond viscerally to the physical passion" ("Body" 138).

If students are puzzled by the colon that ends the first poem, they soon notice that the initial five poems of this sequence constitute a continuous narrative. The second poem focuses on the body of the narrator, who is unhorsed in an uneven jousting match. With God's shining light only a distant memory, the speaker's blind body is shown in incessant motion, groveling, groping, and finally gathering up enough breath to cry, "Mercy, mercy." The intensity of the voice, characterized as a shrieking cry and a braying inarticulate noise, is amplified in the middle poem. A personified Despair prosecutes the speaker, using the admission of guilt to argue that she be banished from God. In the fourth poem, however, Despair is no longer necessary, as the narrator's conscience becomes prosecutor, jury, and executioner. Disabled, insentient, dragged into the very throat of hell, the narrator finds her voice only at the end of the poem, although it is a voice drained of any right to speak. In the fifth sonnet, the faint cries for mercy are accompanied by sighs, groans, faltering knees, and hands that collapse in the very act of supplication. And yet, despite—or rather because of—this pitiful state, the narrator is able to articulate a prayer of repentance, the paraphrase of Psalm 51 that follows.

These five prefatory sonnets introduce two potent forces in sixteenth-century literature: biblical allusions and Calvinist theology. The two are closely intertwined. An emphasis on the Bible was central to Protestant thinking in the sixteenth century, as Lock's allusion to the "dobleedgcd sworde," a common reference to God's word (Heb. 4.12; Rev. 1.16, 2.12), illustrates. The biblical imagery also enlarges the scope of Lock's sonnets; she is imagining not merely a distressed individual but a representative sinner threatened both by a righteously angry God and by a guilty conscience. At the same time, the allusions provide a subtext of hope. The despairing narrative prefaces the penitential psalm of David, a sinner but also an esteemed king who was commonly held to be a model for the Tudor monarchs. The blind, unhorsed narrator of the second sonnet recalls the apostle Paul, knocked from his horse on the road to Damascus and blinded, but restored to both sight and salvation within three days (Acts 9). In the fifth sonnet, the narrator sends "confused crye, / To crave the crummes of all sufficing grace" (63), an allusion to the Syro-Phoenician woman who persisted in asking Jesus to heal her daughter even after she, an outsider, had been rebuffed (Matt. 15.21–28). These three images, which illustrate the abject helplessness of sinful human beings and their relationship with an absolutely holy but also gracious God, accurately depict the main tenets of Calvinist theology, namely the total depravity of human beings and the sovereign choice of God either to condemn them or to show them mercy.

Lock's sonnets thus provide an introduction to the Protestant beliefs that helped shape England throughout the sixteenth century, but they also lead to an exploration of other cultural forces. The occasion for the publication of these

214   TEACHING NONCANONICAL POETRY

sonnets—the entire volume was a New Year's gift to the duchess of Suffolk, another Marian exile and a confidant of Catherine Parr—shows how tightly religious issues were intertwined with political concerns (Donawerth). Lock's gift to the duchess may have been intended to encourage the new queen Elizabeth to imitate the royal David by bending her knee in penitence for the sins of England. The final two sonnets anticipate the blessings attendant on a nation that honors God as they seek his mercy not just for the narrator but for all of "Sion," a reference both to biblical Israel and sixteenth-century England.

Thus a courtly genre, the sonnet, is shaped into a didactic sermon, possibly continuing the princely instruction begun by William Baldwin's *Mirror for Magistrates*. Certainly Lock's sonnets show evidence of two distinct literary sources: the sonnet with its elaborate rhetorical code and the plain-speaking Bible translations and paraphrases that proliferated throughout the first half of the sixteenth century. Lock's images of the penitent sinner as a complaining lover, pierced by wounds and consumed by tears, and her puns on her own name ("Loke on me, Lord: but loke not on my sinne" [Paraphrase 11.6; 68]) argue for a sophisticated handling of the Petrarchan tradition (Dove). At the same time, Lock strips down her language to imitate the simplicity favored by English translators of the Bible. In the upper-division class, I bring in several translations and metrical paraphrases of Psalm 51, among them Lock's own prose translation, which is printed in the margins alongside the sonnets, and compare them with her poetic paraphrase.

In addition to helping students become more aware of the theological dimensions in sixteenth-century literature, the persistent entanglement of religion and politics, and the complex development of literary forms, Lock's sonnets raise the issue of gender. Her poems lead naturally to a consideration of other women writers from this period, including Anne Askew, with whom Lock's mother may have been acquainted, and the four well-educated and well-connected Cooke sisters whom Lock herself knew. All these women were prominent participants in the political and religious affairs of their day, despite strictures against women holding official positions in either the court or the church. Their activities suggest the need to redefine notions of public and private, formal and informal, when assessing the extent and significance of women's work (Harris).

At this point in the class, I return to the issue of canonicity. Why don't Lock's sonnets appear in early modern or twentieth-century anthologies, although her book itself was republished in 1569 and 1574? For the early modern period, I point out the hybrid nature of Lock's genre: the paraphrase of a psalm in a sonnet sequence was suitable neither for public singing in the churches nor for inclusion among amatory courtly poems. In twentieth-century anthologies, her exclusion probably can be traced to a literary bias against religious poetry, the small number of poems, and possibly her lack of status as a woman writer, although, since the sonnets were not attributed to Lock until recently, gender discrimination may not be a significant factor.

As teachers, however, we often forget that most Elizabethan poetry is unfamiliar to undergraduates, so they are not as likely to emphasize the distinction between canonical and noncanonical texts. Consequently, I find that students tend to integrate the noncanonical poems into their own canon. They easily make connections between Lock and other writers whom we read and are as likely to choose her sonnets as those of Sidney or Shakespeare when asked to write an explication paper or to discuss the importance of the sonnet in the sixteenth century. When they later encounter Despaire in Spenser's *Faerie Queene*, students remember Lock's image of Despair and thus are keenly aware of the deadly threat he poses to Redcrosse, the knight's inability to help himself, and his need for the "unmerited grace" of Una's rescue as she snatches the suicidal knife from his hand (1.9.33–54). They also respond directly to Lock's powerful language. Unbiased by academic strictures about what constitutes "good" or canonical poetry, one of my survey students wrote, "I identify with these sonnets because they are filled with such raw, human emotion. I love them!"

NOTE

[1] All Lock quotations in this essay are from Felch, *Collected Works*.

Words and Music:
Campion and the Song Tradition

Stephen Ratcliffe

At least one composer, Thomas Campion, wrote both the
words and the music of his songs; and there are no sweeter
lyrics in English poetry than are to be found in Campion's
song-books.

—A. H. Bullen

The remarkable beauty of Campion's words is generally explained by noting the
equally remarkable fact that Campion was a poet-composer who wrote not only
words but "ayres," or songs—words and music together: "In these *English* Ayres,
I have chiefely aymed to couple my Words and Notes lovingly together, which
will be much for him to doe that hath not power over both" (Davis 55). In the
editions of his works, for example, Percival Vivian, who prints none of that
music, finds that "the extraordinary fluidity and lack of stability in his rhythms
[. . .] is referable to the purpose of musical composition with which they were
written" (lvi); Walter R. Davis, who includes modernized transcriptions of the
scores of 26 of the 106 songs originally published in Campion's five songbooks,
claims that Campion's distinction as "the primary poet of the auditory imagina-
tion is due to his combining the roles of poet and composer in a manner unique
in the history of English literature" (xxiii); and W. H. Auden, who prints 21 fac-
simile reproductions of the original scores and 18 modernized transcriptions,
argues that Campion's songs "would not be what they are or sound as they do if
he had not, when he wrote them, been thinking in musical terms" (9). Thus we
are told to pay attention to the word half of "poems" whose other half (the miss-
ing music) is not only the source of what we find so appealing in those words but
also nearly impossible to find, let alone study and analyze.

Fortunately, while we can't easily *see* Campion's notes on the page, we can
nonetheless *hear* them sung—and thus also hear their effects on Campion's
extraordinary words—in the single currently available recording of Campion
songs, which, alongside recordings of contemporary composers of madrigals as
well as airs, can give us an "ears-on" experience of what makes the Elizabethan
song tradition so special.

I've found it useful in my English Renaissance poetry class, which focuses on
classic short poems from Thomas Wyatt to Andrew Marvell, to introduce stu-
dents to the pleasures of the song tradition and of Campion in particular by
including a midsemester transitional unit on madrigals and airs. I start with a
few songs by Thomas Morley, perhaps "Now is the month of maying" from *The
First Booke of Balletts to Five Voyces* (1595), "Miraculous love's wounding"
from *The First Booke of Canzonets to Two Voyces* (1595), and "Arise, get up,
my dear" from *Canzonets or Little Short Songs to Three Voyces* (1593), whose

Stephen Ratcliffe   217

words can be found on the jacket notes to the Deller Consort *Madrigals of Thomas Morley* album (cond. Alfred Deller, LP, Vanguard, 1972) as well as in E. H. Fellowes's monumental *English Madrigal Verse, 1588–1632*. Hearing these songs performed while looking at the text of their words will show students how music "works" in songs written for multiple voices (i.e., madrigals). For example, while Campion's songs foreground the text by presenting it in a single voice (plus instrumental accompaniment) or several voice parts acting as one (each voice singing the same syllable at the same time), the complex overlapping of Morley's several voices simultaneously singing different syllables to different notes tends to foreground music ahead of words. Thus listeners who hear line 3 of "Arise, get up, my dear" ("Spice-cake, sops in wine, are now a dealing!") sung to three quick-paced voices may well not know quite what they have heard:

Soprano.	deal - ing			spice cake	sops	in wine
Alto.	spice cake sops		in wine, O fine,	spice	cake sops in	
Tenor.		spice cake	sops in wine,	sops	in	wine

Soprano.	sops	in wine are now a	deal - ing		
Alto.	wine, O fine,	are	a	deal - ing	
Tenor.	are	a deal - ing,	are a	deal - ing	

Similarly, the apparently simple text of "Miraculous love's wounding,"

> Miraculous love's wounding!
> E'en those darts, my sweet Phyllis
> So fiercely shot against my heart rebounding,
> Are turned to roses, violets and lilies,
> With odour sweet abounding,   (Fellowes 145)

becomes, when sung, decidedly indecipherable, as the following transcript of the soprano part alone will suggest:

> Miraculous love's wounding, love's wounding, miraculous love's wounding, miraculous love's wounding. Miraculous love's wounding, miraculous love's wounding, miraculous love's wounding. E'en those darts my sweet Phyllis, E'en those darts my sweet Phyllis, So fiercely shot against my heart rebounding, rebounding. Are turn'd to roses, violets and lilies, violets and lilies, with odour sweet abounding sweet abounding, with odour sweet abounding. Miraculous love's wounding, miraculous love's wounding, miraculous love's wounding, miraculous love's wounding, love's wounding, miraculous love's wounding, miraculous love's wounding.

To follow the text of these words being sung (on top of an equally circular and overlapping text of words in the tenor part: different notes for each part, sung

218   CAMPION AND THE SONG TRADITION

simultaneously) will be to see and hear how crucial a role music plays in any listener's experience of a song's words.

Looking at madrigals by Morley will help show students how music and words interact in songs generally: how music dictates the repetition of words, how the length of syllables may be drawn out over several notes, how different syllables may be sung to the same notes or the same syllables sung to different notes. (In Morley's "No, no, Nigella" [Fellowes 149; *The First Booke of Balletts to Five Voyces*, 1595], for example, we hear five voices singing the word "no"— soprano on high D, second soprano on B, alto on G, tenor on D, bass on the G below C—followed by three more intonations of that same "no," which, multiplied by five, comes to twenty times "no" in a fabric of sound so insistent, how could Nigella, whoever she may be, think to resist?)

Written for a single voice, the songs of John Dowland and Campion seem simple by comparison. But they are not simple, of course, since Dowland's emotionally charged expressions of melancholy ("semper dolens, semper Dowland") are driven by a highly complex interaction of music and words whose sense can be understood—and therefore felt—because their musical settings place them squarely at the center of a listener's attention. Campion's power, while of a different order from Dowland's, derives from an equally complex interaction of multiple systems of order—syntax, substance, and the phonetic and rhythmic structures of words coupled to metrical, rhythmic, melodic, and harmonic structures of notes—as my analysis of Campion's "Now winter nights enlarge" in *Campion: On Song* has shown. I begin with Dowland's "In Darkness Let Me Dwell" (available on a New York Pro Musica Antiqua album, where it is read first by Auden and then sung by Russell Oberlin):

> In darknesse let mee dwell, The ground shall sorrow be,
> The roofe Dispaire to barre all cheerfull light from mee,
> The wals of marble blacke that moistned still shall weepe,
> My musicke hellish jarring sounds to banish friendly sleep.
> Thus wedded to my woes, And bedded to my Tombe,
> O Let me living die, Till death doe come,
> In darknesse let mee dwell.   (Doughtie, *Lyrics* 351–52)

This song demonstrates several characteristic features of the English air's marriage of solo voice with lute accompaniment: a musical "prelude" that establishes mood, lengths of syllables drawn out or shortened beyond what a reader of the words alone might expect, and musically dictated repetition of words that the text by itself doesn't suggest. (When these words are sung, we hear "the ground the ground," "my music my music," "jarring jarring sounds jarring jarring sounds," "O let me living die O let me living let me living living die," "Till death Till death do come Till death Till death do come Till death Till death do come.") For something less depressing I also play "Come Again" and, if time permits, "Come Away, Come, Sweet Love," both of which are available on the album *Ayres for Four Voices* and both of which present an equally rich display of examples of how music in interaction with words changes those words—changes, that is to say, a listener's experience of words that, without their music, are simply poems. In "Come Again," for example, the syncopation of overlapping voice parts ascending a scale of notes on the words "To see, to hear, to touch, to kiss, to die" creates a sense of musically dictated climax that a reader of those words by themselves will not hear.

Which brings me back to Campion's songs, those "eare-pleasing rimes without Arte" as Campion calls them in the preface to *A Booke of Ayres* (1601; ed. Davis), whose multifaceted relation of complex identities—one made of words and one of notes—yields what amounts to "complexity squared" (Ratcliffe ix), which nonetheless depends on that genuine simplicity inherent in the combination of its two primary parts, words and music. If there is any time left in my interlude on Elizabethan madrigals and airs, I try again to show the principles of simultaneous co-operation between any song's independent and interdependent systems of order—words and music—by playing a recording of the first song in Campion's *A Booke of Ayres*, "My Sweetest Lesbia," which is alas no longer available.

Reading Marlowe's Lyric

Arthur F. Kinney

The sharp tonal discrepancies of the four lines opening the first sestiad of Christopher Marlowe's *Hero and Leander* prescribe a distanced reading for students while telling them what they can properly expect:

> On Hellespont, guilty of true love's blood,
> In view and opposite two cities stood,
> Sea-borderers, disjoin'd by Neptune's might;
> The one Abydos, the other Sestos hight.   (Orgel, *Marlowe* 17)

Lines 1 and 3 are elaborate if not hyperbolic in their expression, forcing a sense of mythic importance through the exaggeration of diction and sound; lines 2 and 4, contrarily, clump along with a kind of straightforward notation that at once reinforces and deflates their rhyming partners. *Hero and Leander* begins bifocally, asking students to engage with high passion and romance and at the same time to be carefully, realistically critical of such posturing. Lest students fail to see or accept this, the poet continues by describing a masculine Hero whose pictorial dress is stained "with the blood of wretched lovers slain" (line 16) in contrast to a veil of "artificial flowers and leaves" (line 19) and shoes of shells and coral "[w]here sparrows perch'd, of hollow pearl and gold, / Such as the world would wonder to behold" (lines 33, 34)—she is at once startling, seductive, and silly. In summary, "So lovely fair was Hero, Venus' nun" (line 45), she remains equivocal and equivocating—both a naive virgin serving the goddess of the household and of love and a prostitute whose chief interests are carnal. She is, moreover, paired with an effeminate Leander whose smooth breast and white belly surpass "[t]he white of Pelops' shoulder" (lines 66, 65). As Hero and Leander initially exchange genders, so they court each other by teasing, avoiding, seducing, and fleeing from each other. Every tradition of romance is both followed and inverted, and love is presented sympathetically and comically, dramatically and satirically. Deflating lines are transformed into authorial commentary that injects a new voice into the poem that must itself be characterized, assimilated, and then interpreted and judged. For students, reading Marlowe's *Hero and Leander* draws on the traditions of romance learned throughout the years of schooling, but students must apply these traditions to a plot of such twists and turns amid a tonal variety so kaleidoscopic that critical awareness is always being alerted. Even the ending—which may or may not involve a consummation of love; which may or may not treat Hero with cruelty; which may or may not even be the ending of the story as the final line, "*Desunt nonnulla*" ("something is wanting"), would insist—keeps raising doubts and asking questions that will elicit lively classroom debate.

Next to such a lively, forceful Ovidian overture, the pastoral poem called

*"The Passionate Shepherd to His Love" seems limpid and transparent (from *Englands Helicon*, 1600):

> Come live with mee, and be my love,
> And we will all the pleasures prove,
> That Vallies, groves, hills and fieldes,
> Woods, or steepie mountaine yeeldes.
>
> And wee will sit upon the Rocks,   5
> Seeing the Sheepheards feede theyr flocks,
> By shallow Rivers, to whose falls,
> Melodious byrds sing Madrigalls.
>
> And I will make thee beds of Roses,
> And a thousand fragrant poesies,   10
> A cap of flowers, and a kirtle,
> Imbroydred all with leaves of Mirtle.
>
> A gowne made of the finest wooll,
> Which from our pretty Lambes we pull,
> Fayre lined slippers for the cold: 15
> With buckles of the purest gold.
>
> A belt of straw, and Ivie buds,
> With Corall clasps and Amber studs,
> And if these pleasures may thee move,
> Come live with mee, and be my love.   20
>
> The Sheepheards Swaines shall daunce & sing,
> For thy delight each May-morning,
> If these delights thy minde may move;
> Then live with mee, and be my love.

I introduce this poem to my class by way of *Hero and Leander*, rather than move from the shorter poem to the longer one, because I think some of the same discrepant tonalities as well as some of the same themes are lurking here, but many of them more subtly and deeper below the surface of the language. Whereas *Hero and Leander* provides some of its own running commentary and interpretation, this shorter poem, a mere six quatrains, makes its readers work harder. Working harder, they learn more about how lyrics—and Marlowe's especially—function.

I begin discussion by asking what the speaker in the poem is attempting to do. For one thing, he is describing a pastoral life in which nature is seen as simple, peaceful, fulfilling, and even providential. It is enabling; it allows the shepherd

222   READING MARLOWE'S LYRIC

and his love to be self-sufficient while living a life of reflection and contemplation. The countryside has "all the pleasures" (line 2), and the wool of the sheep provides clothing and slippers both (lines 13, 15). The poet describes a prelapsarian existence, a song of innocence. This existence is also static, we learn on closer examination; even love itself is a condition rather than an act.

Perhaps so, but it will not be long before someone will argue that art vies with nature in this poem—or at least in the conceptualization of the persona. Birds don't sing something as complex as a madrigal (line 8), while the fancy embroidering of caps (line 12) is an active rather than a conceptual interjection of art into nature, suggesting that nature is by itself imperfect and incomplete. The static quality of the poem is now in question. We then read of using wool pulled from lambs (line 14), so the intervention of humanity in nature can be forceful; further on, the desire for "buckles of the purest gold" (line 16) like "Corall clasps and Amber studs" (line 18) places an exchange value on the material of nature—gold, coral, amber—that, whether or not grossly commercial, nevertheless gives a priority to certain parts of nature that reconfigures the natural scene as it reemploys what is found there. The portrait of nature is no longer one of a countryside in active repose but rather a finding place for an inventory of what is valuable, what is tempting, perhaps even what is seductive.

A descriptive poem has turned into a dramatic one, and at this point I usually ask the class to interpret the force of the first line, which is both invitation and command, a line in the imperative mode. Does the imperative suggest that the shepherd feels the need to argue his case rather than present it, and, if so, what is the mode (and what are the terms) of the argument? Are the proven pleasures (line 2) he urges those of witnessing nature rather than appreciating it? using nature for adornment rather than contemplating the natural state of things? Are we to read "purest gold" as the loveliest metal found in nature, the most valuable, the most glittering, or (following alchemy) something to be turned into all wisdom and all treasure? Are coral and amber pleasures consonant with belts of straw and ivy buds (line 17) or in conflict with them? Do seeing and appreciating these pleasures, in short, equate with being the shepherd's love (line 1), with being in love? Could nature be equally pleasurable if it remained valleys, groves, hills, fields, woods, and mountains (lines 3, 4) or are those merely introductory, a come-on finally insufficient? In what ways are such pleasures similar or dissimilar to the May dancing and singing of the shepherds' swains (line 21)?

Just as the poem turns on key words such as the straightforward "Come" that opens the poem and the "Madrigalls" that complicate it, so I think the poem, like any invitation or seduction and like any argument or act of persuasion (for that is what the poem actually is), must take its final step in the final lines. The last two lines of the poem make another turn (or counter-counterturn, as in the sonnet form) with still another, briefer proposition. But unlike the rest of the poem, it is suddenly hypothetical rather than prescriptive. The poem argues, in effect, that the invitation holds only so long as the beloved finds delightful the various attractions presented in the course of the poem. Moreover, they are not necessarily meant to be physically delightful but they are meant to be mentally so: "*If* these delights thy *minde* may move" (line 23), then and only then "live with mee, and be my love." The poem is not about the countryside at all, then; it is about a series of values metaphorically expressed through the pastoral mode. It is about attitudes and concepts, not things, that are pleasurable. What the passionate shepherd is asking is that his beloved share his passions and his outlook, which renders the ideal mental state as one that mingles and finally marries nature and art, much as Polixenes will urge in *The Winter's Tale* of Shakespeare: "[. . .] nature is made better by no mean / But nature makes that mean. So over that art / Which you say adds to nature is an art / That nature makes" (4.4.89–92).[1]

In much briefer compass but with no less art, "The Passionate Shepherd" enters into the same fundamental Renaissance dispute over nature versus art that *Hero and Leander* does, asking repeatedly whether art perfects or contaminates nature and whether one or both is preferable—whether, in fact, they can ever be separable, considering that all our thoughts and awareness must necessarily combine sensory data and conceptualization, perception and interpretation. What appear to be poetic statements by Marlowe are also arguments that use metaphor to heighten the conscious awareness of the world and how poetry both reflects and shapes it. Lyric for Marlowe never means, simply, song.

We know *Hero and Leander* had an effect on the Renaissance because George Chapman thought it necessary to complete the poem in a severely monotonal continuation that belies both Marlowe's purpose and his achievement. We also know that "The Passionate Shepherd" had an effect because two later lyrics—"If all the world and love were young" attributed to Walter Ralegh and "The Baite" by John Donne—attempt to answer the shepherd on the nymph's behalf. All three poems are the subject even later on of part 1, chapter 4, of Izaak Walton's *Compleat Angler*. I conclude this brief, but always appealing, segment on lyric, voice, and tone by examining one or both of these later lyrics. Here is the poem attributed to Ralegh (the fifth stanza, from Walton's 1655 edition, is found in one manuscript):

> If all the world and love were young,
> And truth in every Sheepheards tongue,
> These pretty pleasures might me moue,
> To liue with thee, and be thy loue.

> Time drives the flocks from field to fold,   5
> When Riuers rage, and Rocks grow cold,
> And Philomell becommeth dombe,
> The rest complaines of cares to come.

> The flowers doe fade, and wanton fieldes,
> To wayward winter reckoning yeeldes,   10

224 READING MARLOWE'S LYRIC

A honny tongue, a hart of gall,
Is fancies spring, but sorrowes fall.

Thy gownes, thy shooes, thy beds of Roses,
Thy cap, thy kirtle, and thy posies,
Soone breake, soone wither, soone forgotten: 15
In follie ripe, in reason rotten.

Thy belt of straw and Iuie buddes,
Thy Corall claspes and Amber studdes,
All these in mee no meanes can moue,
To come to thee, and be thy loue. 20

[What should we talk of dainties then,
Of better meat then's fit for men?
These are but vain: that's only good
Which God hath blest, and sent for food.]

But could youth last, and loue still breede, 25
Had ioyes no date, nor age no neede,
Then those delights my minde might move,
To live with thee, and be thy love.

Tonally, this put-down is perhaps even more forceful than the original poem,
and its clear-eyed sense of reality is both humorous and convincing. Or is it?
Once the initial joy in the poem has worn off the class, I ask them to look at it
more carefully. Does the parallel set of responses actually demolish the origi-
nal proposals in the passionate shepherd's invitation to the nymph? In some
ways, as in the progressive ideas in stanza 3, the answer is clearly yes. At other
times, as in stanza 4, the response is merely an unsubstantiated remark. In fact,
such remarks outweigh, in number and force, the substantiated ones, and
Ralegh's poem seems at some level to be inadequate. Yet my keen students,
who see poetry as process rather than proclamation, jump to the final stanza
here as we earlier did with Marlowe. There is a strong counterturn in "But"
(line 25) that shifts both tone and attitude. The joking of the previous stanzas
is set aside and the poem returns to the first line (though not the first stanza).
Now the ideal enters, and a whole new conception of life and love enters this
poem. Moreover, this ideal of permanent youth would seem, alone, to have the
capacity to "breede" love (line 25). Such a delightful situation (line 27) pro-
vides ageless joy (line 26), surely a desideratum, and, logically, the second
poem moves on to the last line, arguing, in agreement with Marlowe, that such
pleasures are sufficient to make the invitation good: "To live with thee, and be
thy love" (line 28). Has the poet totally reversed himself? Or is he using this
extension ironically, to show in some finally demonstrative way how impossible,
and so how silly, Marlowe's initial proposition is? While I let the class debate
this—and they do—the poem will actually support both positions, as Marlowe's

will not. The response poem, then, enters more openly, with more awareness, into the debate between nature and art that we have seen is a central concern of the English Renaissance.

Each of the three poems we have discussed raises issues of voice that demand a close reading of poetry; students must note texture and tone, stance and development. Each work stands alone and often has. But my final point with the class is that all three poems yield even more benefits when read in conversation with one another. Anchored in the same period, addressing the same issues, aimed at similar audiences, they speak to one another and across one another, as testimonial, gloss, argument, and reply. As a unit they not only show how contextualizing poetry often enriches each constituent member of study but also help us through accretion of shared purpose and accumulation of detail to a fuller, more enhanced, more reliable sense of the attitudes, values, and debates that characterized the heightened moment of literary culture that first produced them.

NOTE

[1]All Shakespeare quotations are from *The Norton Shakespeare* (Greenblatt et al.).

Teaching Spenser's Marriage Poetry:
Amoretti, Epithalamion, Prothalamion
Patrick Cheney and Anne Lake Prescott

Although *Amoretti, Epithalamion,* and *Prothalamion* are rarely grouped as a topic of modern criticism, Spenser's marriage poems work well together in the classroom. In 1595, Spenser published *Amoretti and Epithalamion,* complementing a Petrarchan sonnet sequence on the courtship of his wife, Elizabeth Boyle, with a Catullan ode on their marriage, all lodged within the reformed English Church. Then, in 1596, England's national poet published *Prothalamion,* creating a generic and conceptual echo between *Epithalamion* and this betrothal poem on the Somerset sisters, who were chaperoned by Queen Elizabeth's favorite, the earl of Essex. Each marriage poem begins with the poet's presenting himself and his literary career to the public, and this self-presentation in turn forges a link with *Amoretti,* in which Spenser also presents himself and his literary career in relation to his beloved and his queen (sonnets 74, 33, 80) and to Christ (sonnet 68). One way to connect all three poems, then, is to foreground Spenser's circumstance: a late Elizabethan poet charts Protestant marriage as an institution vital to his nation. In this essay, we reenact our own conversations on teaching these poems. We start with Prescott on *Amoretti* and end with Cheney on *Prothalamion*; in between, we talk together about *Epithalamion.*

PRESCOTT: *Amoretti* is enjoyable to teach, although in anthologized fragments it loses coherence and symbolic force. After giving some facts (the lady is Elizabeth Boyle, who, like Spenser, lived in Ireland; they married, we think, on 11 June 1594; he was over forty and a widower; he wrote at least one sonnet, sonnet 8, before they met), I outline Spenser's design (Dunlop, "Drama," "Unity"; W. C. Johnson, *Spenser's* Amoretti): twenty-one sonnets; then sonnet 22 on the "holy day," Ash Wednesday; next, forty-five sonnets (as many as the forty days of Lent plus the Sundays, including one, sonnet 62, welcoming the new year, that probably alludes to 25 March, the legal new year); then sonnet 68 on Easter; and finally twenty-one more sonnets. What other patterns there are or how they relate to *Epithalamion* is debatable, but this basic shape is clear enough. Student reactions vary; my students usually think number symbolism so alien as to be weird and hence cool. If there's time, I bring in the 1559 Book of Common Prayer (Booty): it has the same number of "days" with assigned readings—eighty-nine—as Spenser has sonnets, and its wedding vows are what the lovers will say when they reach the altar in *Epithalamion* (as of course they never do in the sequence—any more than Easter prevents the absence and dark that come later in the liturgical year). The poetry's religious dimension has a polemical significance that parallels its erotic argument. Some readers think of the lover as learning, as becoming worthy, but the sequence indicates something else: just as grace is undeserved, so the lady yields to her lover's desires only when he gives up. It is bad Reformation theology, I remind students, to suppose that virtue or prayer will earn salvation, and it is bad Spenserian erotics to suppose women winnable by moans, pleas, flattery, reproofs, metaphors, or theatrics of the sort parodied in *Amoretti*, sonnet 54.

Amoretti has delicious sweetness. For once, the lover wins the lady, even if there is separation and slander to endure before the "Anacreontics" that follow and the wedding after that. Even the sonnet's most exaggerated lamentations and reproaches, moreover, may be meant more to entertain than to unsettle the beloved. And yet, complicating and deepening the witty charm and (temporary) joy are energies that demand attention. Like *Epithalamion*, *Amoretti* is not unproblematic (Loewenstein, "Echo's Ring"; Kuin in this volume and in *Chamber Music*). The tensions that ruffle the marriage poem ruffle the sonnets.

First, I take up Spenser's relation to Petrarch. *Amoretti* can be loosely Neoplatonic, if finally critical of such idealism, but for the most part this is a Petrarchan sequence. Like many who write "after" Petrarch, though, Spenser has a problem: how to follow a powerful tradition without becoming its slave. Spenser's solution is clever. If the default position of the Petrarchan lover is fruitless longing, why not love a woman who can decently be won? True, poets thrive on pain, so it is not surprising that Spenser's lover loses her again; but for a moment he can relish victory and we never hear that the betrothal is broken; we hear only that the pair is separated and evil tongues are wagging somewhere. To love a marriageable woman is thus not only good Protestant ethics (Reformers, I remind students, privilege marriage over celibacy) but also a way to outdo Petrarch, Ronsard, and Sidney. The lover can go and catch *this* star without her falling into sin. Earlier in the term the class has read Petrarch (in Wyatt's English) on the lover's "galley charged with forgetfulness" and on a deer whose collar says "Noli me tangere"—do not touch me. When Spenser "descries the happy shore" or when his deer allows herself to be tied, he achieves a literary as well as amatory triumph. Even the victory prayer in *Amoretti*, sonnet 68, is post-Petrarchan in ways the Ash Wednesday sonnet (22) is not. To see the lady on a holy day was a cliché, but here sexual and divine love no longer jar. Petrarch's deer recalls the risen Christ who said, "Noli me tangere," but Spenser's dear/deer, although also associated with Christ in some fashion (e.g., Prescott, "Thirsty Deer"), may be handled.

A second energy is the violence of a sequence fascinated by cruelty, wild animals, trembling captives, bondage, prey, and murder. Such savagery has led one of my graduate students, James Fleming, to argue in a fine paper for echoes of the Irish wars. Certainly the poetry has political resonance. A male student once told me he "could not forgive Spenser for what he did to women." "Did you ask him," a colleague laughed, "what women did to Spenser?" Since then I have seen some uncomfortable humor in sonnet 74, with its lover surrounded by Elizabeths—mother, beloved, and queen—not unlike the shepherd lass amid the Graces in *Faerie Queene*, book 6, canto 10. *Amoretti* is bloody enough, despite its wit and affection, to be rated PG. Spenser is for

228   SPENSER'S MARRIAGE POETRY

grownups, not adolescents, and since I teach adolescents I give them some parental guidance, if not always the guidance they expect from a professor.

Sex can be a messy and predatory business, I say, with more to it than good folks—good like the traditionally proper or good like love's new thought police—can always bear. My students know this, but they don't always know that I know or that Spenser knew. Given permission to enjoy and encouraged to drop the illusion that the dead can obey our own culture's dictates, many relax their principles a little (and better—or perhaps merely more worldly—students relax them a lot). Yes, love should be mutual, and no, one shouldn't hound women or "pen" them like Busirane (*Faerie Queene* 3.11–12) in Petrarchan tropes. But to imagine Eros as a presentable youth, looking dependable with his crew cut and varsity letter or spectacles and Microsoft job offer, somebody whom one could introduce to one's great-aunt, will not work for lyrics that take desire and its complexities seriously. Eros will keep misbehaving himself, spilling the wine and writing naughtily in it like Ovid's Paris, or turning suddenly into Priapus (piercing through his toga, as Catullus puts it somewhere, asking us to pity his "tale") like the lover in *Astrophil and Stella*, sonnet 45), or bursting unexpectedly into tears or laughter. And, although Eros may lie about this, he will never, ever make somebody love you just for your mind and character. True, Spenser's lover praises the lady's inwardness. I sometimes show students sonnet 15's likely source, a sonnet by Philippe Desportes (*Diane*, bk. 1, sonnet 32) that tells how merchants can find treasure right at home in the lover's lady; Desportes ends there, but Spenser adds that his beloved's mind is "adornd with vertues manifold."

A related issue is the lover's self-absorption. Ego is what lyric poetry is good at, I tell students, who again can, if encouraged, welcome a chance to soften their political or moral rectitude. Petrarch watches himself loving, I say. Spenser does it. Donne does it. Gaspara Stampa and Louise Labé, too. Labé adores her man's brown eyes, but she doesn't explore his personality or let him have his say. Sure, Spenser has a male perspective—he's male. If you don't want to read about the poet's self or its literary simulacrum, I suggest cheerfully, try something more dialogic like the novel. Indeed, good lyric poets are aware—often self-mockingly—of their narcissism, which may be one reason Spenser repeats his poem on Narcissus (35 and 83). Then, having lingered over a few sonnets (1, 22, 54, 67, and 68 are my favorites to teach, although the image in 89 of Spenser as a moping dove is nearly irresistible), we are ready for *Epithalamion*.

CHENEY: In *Epithalamion*, too, I find that students often focus on the relation between groom and bride. This widely admired text—"Spenser's greatest poem" (Warkentin, "*Amoretti*" 38), "one of the great poems of English literature" (Clemen 569)—offers a chance to debate how a gifted late-sixteenth-century male poet represents female identity. Unfortunately, many students are now less concerned with some features of *Epithalamion* that earlier gener-

Patrick Cheney and Anne Lake Prescott 229

ations recaptured: the poem's genre (T. Greene, "Spenser"; Tufte, *Poetry*; P. Miller; see Puttenham, *Art of English Poesy* in G. Smith 2: 52–55), its famed numerology (Hieatt, *Monument*; A. Fowler, *Triumphal Forms* 161–73; Fukuda; Chinitz; Gleason), its harmony and joy (Cirillo; Hill), its church calendar (W. C. Johnson, "Sacred Rites"), its truncated tornada (Neuse, "Triumph"), its integration into the 1595 volume (Kaske; Thompson; King, *Spenser's Poetry* 160–77), and even its "teaching" (DeNeef 7–10).

PRESCOTT: Yet my students often enjoy hearing about some such findings. Number symbolism seems to grab them, perhaps because its precision is in such tension with poetry's ambiguity. Similarly, some love the architectural symmetry that doesn't quite parallel that of the number system (Wickert). I quote the Apocrypha's Book of Wisdom on how God created the world by "number, weight, and measure" (The Wisdom of Solomon 11.17) and tell them that the Renaissance found numbers—which by now included that Indian invention, the zero—so compelling that one Frenchman wrote a whole ode to "One" (one line begins, "O Un!") and Pietro Bongo wrote a long book, *De mysteria numerorum*, on what numbers mean. For the intrigued, I recommend work by Christopher Butler. The Book of Common Prayer is seldom familiar to my students, so I remind them that Spenser's prayer for posterity comes from the wedding service, boldly taken from the priest at the altar and given to the poet-husband in bed with his bride. And students are surprised to hear that the prayer in stanza 19 against scary fantasies and "deluding dreams" (line 338) appropriates a (Catholic) tradition by which the priest would accompany the couple and their friends to the marriage bed and pray that it be free from the "demons of illusion." Indeed, old marriage customs can shock students because their rowdy earthiness violates modern notions of privacy or decency, and many students are startled to know Protestants do not, technically, think marriage a sacrament.

CHENEY: Students are also startled by a pressing problem in *Epithalamion*: "where we might anticipate a celebration of 'mutual good will' [as in *Amoretti*], we find rather a demonstration of mastery" (Spenser, *Yale Edition* 590). The problem—a loving groom masters his bride on their wedding night—makes for good discussion. My students are often disappointed in the bride and anxious about the groom; she is too quiet and submissive, he too controlling. Above all, my students are troubled by the poet's "idealizing" of the female, even as they complain that he is too preoccupied with his own fears. For many, *Epithalamion* is a poem less about marriage than about maleness—the man's use of eloquent rhetoric to manage female identity: "let this day let this one day be myne" (line 125). Recent criticism echoes these concerns: *Epithalamion* "celebrates a moment of social and sexual appropriation in which the female body is passive, available, exposed to view, and noticeably silent" (Bates, *Rhetoric* 143; see D. Anderson; Loewenstein, "Echo's Ring"; Mazzola).

230 SPENSER'S MARRIAGE POETRY

PRESCOTT: Yes, this is true: some students are vexed by Spenser's mastery, his male arrogance. Recently, though, I have had fewer students like the one who raged that Spenser makes his bride an object by, for example, comparing her lips to rubies. "Look again," I said. "See? Spenser says cherries." The point is not a picky one: cherries are to be tasted (and, sure, eaten). Perhaps such anger will wane when sophisticated and confident women can find male strutting and crowing, even male focus on one's body parts, more endearing than otherwise, especially if one loves the guy doing the crowing and focusing. But I can say this more easily than you, because I am a woman. What we can tell students depends in part on our own gender, age, race, religion, location. My hope, one that teaching Spenser's poetry facilitates, is to provide the young women I teach with a model of feminism that is psychologically on top, so to speak: not angry (Spenser is out of earshot), unthreatened (he can't exert mastery over us, at least not in bed), and—in spite of the risks—willing to imagine attitudes I cannot share (gender condescension, sexual boasting, monarchism). As our world becomes more just, the agitation that Spenser produces may fade into an urbane but clear-eyed resignation that does not spoil our pleasure in his poetry. I'm more interested in recent attention to the poetry's darker moments.

CHENEY: Indeed, whereas older studies "typically emphasized [*Epithalamion's*] serenity," "more recent criticism [. . .] has drawn attention to its anxieties" (Dubrow, *Happier Eden* 35–36). For me, Spenser's masculine representation of his bride here is the central issue, and the best way to enter it in class is to return to the text. The famous blazon (167–203) warrants careful analysis, especially the elaborate metaphorical description of her physical beauty. My students are generally unimpressed: for them, the poet's association of a real woman with precious stones, fruit, cream, flowers, and architecture, rather than an artful reworking of the stunning blazons in the Song of Songs or an association of a young woman's beauty with the highest values of nature and art, inscribes an oppressive dehumanization of the female.

PRESCOTT: Wouldn't you find it helpful to bring in the Song's headnote in the Geneva Bible to explain the allegorical overtones?

CHENEY: Yes, but I withhold analysis of the blazon until I explain why Spenser's representation of the bride is the central issue. I mean *central* quite literally (though not numerologically). *Epithalamion* means "before the bedchamber," so if the poem has a center, the title locates it in the domestic space of stanza 17. Structurally, this stanza registers a turn in the poet's mind ("Now ceasse ye damsels your delights forepast" [line 296]) and in his refrain: "The woods no more shal answere, nor your echo ring" (line 31). The stanza also superbly focuses the problem of representing female identity, for here the loving Christian groom views his naked bride lying in their flower-decked bridal bower, and the male poet shockingly resorts to a pagan myth of forced sexual entry:

Patrick Cheney and Anne Lake Prescott 231

> Now night is come, now soone her disaray,
> And in her bed her lay;
> Lay her in lillies and in violets,
> And silken courteins over her display,
> And odourd sheets, and Arras coverlets.
> Behold how goodly my faire love does ly
> In proud humility,
> Like unto Maia, when as Jove her tooke,
> In Tempe, lying on the flowry gras,
> Twixt sleepe and wake, after she weary was
> With bathing in the Acidalian brooke.   (lines 300–10)

Students can be troubled by the Maia simile, even indicting Spenser for voyeuristic lust. They see the myth as representing his consciousness: he imagines himself a god eyeing an exposed female.

PRESCOTT: Yet students shouldn't confuse "lust" (physical urges pure and simple) with loving sexual desire—or think Spenser and their professor separate "pure love" from what sonnet 67 calls the lady's "will." Medical theory held that conception requires orgasm: ladies were not to shut their eyes and think of England, as one Victorian mother supposedly advised her daughter to do.

CHENEY: Even for sympathetic critics the passage often shows "the bride as an object" and "emphasizes Maia's sexual passivity" (Dubrow, *Happier Eden* 67, 38). If we look again, we see something quite different. Spenser foregrounds a complex process of perception, but not just his own perception. He begins by activating the reader's perception—and the attendant damsels': "Behold." He asks others to share his intimate view of his naked bride, hidden beneath her "odourd sheets, and Arras coverlets."

PRESCOTT: Indeed so, because early modern weddings, even more than our own, were public affairs: the bride and groom entered their bridal chamber not alone but with often mirthful friends and family.

CHENEY: In this public affair, what do we see? First, we see a woman lying on the marital bed in a certain posture: "Behold how goodly my faire love does ly / In proud humility." The word "goodly" and the phrase "proud humility" convert a physical posture into moral character. Just how is a "goodly" bride lying when she lies in "proud humility"? Evidently, she is presenting herself. Spenser's language reveals that even though she is lying down, naked, hidden under cloth, and vulnerable, she is occupying a position of some strength. The conversion of physical posture into moral character reveals that she is looking at him. How is she looking? The word "goodly" suggests beautifully, favorably, virtuously. The phrase "proud humility" is an oxymoron that here "represents

232   SPENSER'S MARRIAGE POETRY

mutuality of desire, the bride humble in her surrender to her husband, but the groom also now a servant to her awakened desire" (Kaske 282). We see more than a woman in bed; we see her consciousness (John Buck and Dominic Delli Carpini, personal communications). Centering his poem on the bedchamber, Spenser foregrounds female interiority at the impending moment of penetration: "Twixt sleep and wake, after she weary was." "Weary" suggests a condition at once physical and mental; "Twixt sleep and wake" locates the condition on the threshold of consciousness. Grammatically speaking, the goodly bride lying in her proud humility is like Maia when Jove takes her. The simile pertains directly to her, not (only) to him.

The terms of Spenser's simile show the bride's consciousness to be internally divided. The pastoral landscape of a golden world like Tempe, with its "flowry gras" and "Acidalian brooke," and Maia's relaxed nudity and sparkling purity after her bath, suggest the bride's pleasure, comfort, and moral ease at her impending intercourse. "The simultaneous surrender to a divine lover and repose in a pastoral pleasance implies a conjunction of the natural and the supernatural" (Bernard, *Ceremonies* 178). Yet Jove's forced entry into this landscape also suggests the bride's fear, while the emphatically placed "tooke" captures both Jove's theft of Maia's virginity and her sense of losing a valued possession. Spenser recalls a masculine rape, but his sweetly erotic poetry counteracts the violation. The counteraction also emerges in the peculiar agency of the actors. Jove may do the taking, but he gets only one verb to do it with; by contrast, Maia, for all her relaxation, was weary, presumably with exercise; she bathes in the Acidalian brook; and she lies on the flowery grass. Spenser's active syntax conditions her passivity.

Once students see the Maia simile as representing the bride's divided consciousness, we return to what initially struck them, except that now they perceive a complexity that alters their original response: a male poet describing female consciousness is also representing his own consciousness. He presents himself not as a lustful voyeur but as fearful that he is a lustful voyeur, even as he enjoys his gaze. That one simile could represent both masculine and feminine inwardness is evident in the syntactic slippage of a key verb in line 308: "lying." Presumably, Maia is "lying on the flowry gras"; the syntax, however, says that Jove is "lying." The two lie together. Some literary historians think a modern subjectivity was merely nascent in late-sixteenth-century England (Barker; cf. Maus, *Inwardness*), yet we might say that here Spenser is pushing the barriers of subjective language itself.

If so, students now have a useful lens for viewing the rest of the poem. They can peer through it during a class exercise, alone or in collaboration. For instance, they can return to the opening sequence, in which the groom tries to awaken his bride from her sleep, using the word *awaken* and its variants nine times: from "Bid her awake" (line 25) in stanza 2 to the complaint in stanza 5: "Wake now, my love, awake. [. . .] / Ah my deere love, why doe ye sleepe thus long, / When meeter were that ye should now awake" (lines 74, 85–86). Stanza

Patrick Cheney and Anne Lake Prescott   233

6 then shows the bride awakening: "My love is now awake out of her dreames" (lines 92–94). Spenser expresses his impatience over the day's promise of pleasure, but he also makes the bride's dawning consciousness the day's inaugural event.

In the blazon of stanzas 10 and 11, Spenser reveals the ethical and religious character of the bride's awakening: "So sweet, so lovely, and so mild as she, / Adorned with Beauty's grace and Virtue's store" (lines 160–70). If "sweet," "lovely," "mild," and "grace" take us inside the bride, "Virtue's store" tells us what we find: "honors seat and chastities sweet bowre" (line 180) and "that which no eyes can see— / The inward beauty of her lively spright" (lines 185–86). When the merchants' daughters stand astonished "lyke to those which red / Medusaes mazeful hed" (lines 189–90), Spenser tropes more than chastity (Young) or male anxiety (Loewenstein 291–92); he offers a spectacular representation of the bride's complexly "amaz[ing]" (line 181) inwardness. Since Pegasus sprang from Medusa's blood, Spenser is also identifying his bride's "inward beauty" as the very source of his poetic inspiration.

He cannot physically see his bride's interiority, but he can "read" what Shakespeare calls "the story [. . .] printed in her blood" (*Ado* 4.1.122). In stanzas 9 and 13, the bride blushes three times, indicating the complexities of "the interior affective life and the subjectivity of the beloved woman" (Krier 186). Spenser does not explain these complexities away; he externalizes them in the "crimsin" of her "cheekes" and in her "sad eyes" (lines 226, 228, 234).

Spenser ends *Epithalamion* with an imperative: "Song made in lieu of many ornaments, [. . .] / Be unto her a goodly ornament, / And for short time an endlesse moniment" (lines 427–33). The poem is a gift to Elizabeth Boyle. What is that gift? It is the gift of "solace" (line 35). Spenser is awake to the suffering his wife will endure, in the bedchamber when she loses her virginity amid "lamenting cryes" and "dolefull teares" (line 334) and later, on the childbed, when she becomes a "woman in [her] [. . .] smart" (line 395). My colleague John Buck remarks that he knows no poet through the eighteenth century who registers more sympathy for the consequences of sexual intercourse than Spenser does in *Epithalamion*.

PRESCOTT: I agree (although I think the same sympathy informs *Amoretti*). Any wedding is a liminal moment, and as such dangerous. I ask my students if they remember the three billy goats Gruff. There can be trolls under a bridge. No wonder grooms used to carry brides over the threshold: thresholds are scary, for something may have to die that something new may come. Hence, it has been argued, a great epithalamium needs a touch of elegy (Schenck).

CHENEY: Nowhere is the touch of elegy more poignant than in the Maia simile, where the male poet's Orphic mastery of the female metamorphoses into an Orphic charm protective of female identity, integrity, and life. As the poem's penultimate stanza especially reveals, Spenser's gift to his bride is a song fully

234   SPENSER'S MARRIAGE POETRY

aware of sexual love's role in their shared destiny: more than procreation or pleasure, their act in the bedchamber is the vehicle of salvation itself, as man and woman join in body and in mind to raise a "large posterity" destined to "inherit" the "heavenly tabernacles" (lines 417, 422).

PRESCOTT: Since Jove and Maia produce Mercury, "god of language, interpretation, [. . .] musician, shepherd god" (Brooks-Davies, "Mercury"), Spenser is self-conscious in his choice of myths.

CHENEY: He mythologizes the genealogy of a couple's shared consciousness and of his own art. Here Jove's descent to the pastoral world mirrors the progression of Spenser's literary career—from epic to love lyric—as indicated in stanza 1, when he identifies with Orpheus (Cheney, *Spenser's Famous Flight* 187–88).

PRESCOTT: And this, I think, brings us to *Prothalamion*.

CHENEY: Yes, and if the Orpheus, Maia, and Medusa myths in *Epithalamion* help explain why some readers view Spenser as the "poet's poet," one way to teach *Prothalamion* is as the poet's poem.

The notion of Spenser as the poet's poet is under attack, in part because it worsens Spenser's standing as the most neglected major poet in English and in part because it effaces his other career as a colonial administrator (Rambuss, *Career* and "Spenser's Lives"; Alpers, "Poet's Poet"). But before surrendering the poetical to the colonial Spenser, we may wish to register that the poetical Spenser is *dulce et utile* in the classroom. By classroom, I mean (admittedly) a space for teaching poets and writers. In such a space, this poet's poet can acquire a pleasing utility, because he can do well what many of our students require most: the telling of a clear and moving narrative about literary history. He is the poet's poet because he looks back across literary history to his multiple origins and, through a fortune not independent of this gaze, he appears beyond the grave in the works of later poets.

Prothalamion presents a good opportunity to get such a version of literary history into the classroom quickly. In 180 lines, Spenser writes a literary history (Herendeen, "Spenserian Specifics"), with allusions to his own poetry (*Shepheardes Calender*, *Ruines of Time*, *Faerie Queene*, *Epithalamion*) and to the poetry of others: English river poetry (Camden, Leland, Vallans), medieval dream vision (Chaucer, Langland), and classical poetry (Catullus, Vergil, Horace, Propertius, Ovid), including such arresting myths of male mastery, rape, and loss as Daphne and Apollo, Leda and the swan, Proserpina, and Orpheus and Eurydice (Spenser, *Works* 8: 495–505, 667–73; D. Norton; Wine; Woodward; Rogers, "Carmina" and "Proserpina"; A. Fowler, "Spenser's *Prothalamion*"; Cain). Then many later poets write his poem as a moment in their literary histories (Hollander, "Spenser's Undersong" 148–63). Like an exquisite floral chain, *Prothalamion* links past with future.

Patrick Cheney and Anne Lake Prescott 235

Teachers can get this chain into the classroom in two ways, both naturally linked. The first is to interlace students in a striking paradox: a poem that many readers find beautiful has glaring narrative disruptions. Students usually sense the poem's "exquisite courtliness and appearance of easy power," its "deliberate and disciplined joy" (Bloom, *Spenser* 3–4), and their awareness of these qualities will make it easier to ask about what has long troubled readers like John Hughes, who in 1715 criticized the "Spousall Verse" for transgressing an "essential property" of allegory adhered to by *The Faerie Queene*: utter self-consistency. "[T]he two brides," he wrote, "are figur'd by two beautiful swans sailing down the River Thames. The allegory breaks before the reader is prepar'd for it; and we see [. . .] [the "birdes"], at their landing, [. . .] [as "brides"], without knowing how this sudden change is effected" (qtd. in Spenser, *Works* 8: 666). More recent readers ask, "[I]n a poem of ten stanzas nominally celebrating [a] double marriage, [. . .] why are two stanzas devoted to the poet's own life and troubles, and a third to some patron-seeking praise of Essex?" (Berger, "Spenser's *Prothalamion*" 509; see Lewis, *English Literature* 373).

For some critics, these stanzas show Spenser's disillusionment at the end of his career (Cain 46; D. Miller, "Spenser's Vocation" 219–21; Helgerson, *Laureates* 88). Yet some recent analyses contradict this oddly Romantic reading of the bard withdrawing from the world, suggesting rather that *Prothalamion* "advertises Spenser's patriotism, his epic ambitions, and his continued willingness to serve his queen and her favorite" (Oram 290; see Manley, "Spenser"; Eriksen). The question makes for engaging class discussion: in his last published poem, is Spenser withdrawing from history or reentering it? An answer is of importance in any postcolonial culture where Spenser's cultural authority is debated (McCabe, "Spenser"; Hadfield, *Experience*; Maley, *Salvaging*). If Spenser is withdrawing from history, some will be comforted by his detachment from his "imperialist" project; if he reenters history, others might applaud his engagement. Yet such bifurcation is at best reductive. What teachers need is not an ideological machine that closes the poem down but a hermeneutic strategy that opens it back up. Such a strategy is right at hand. When we return to the verse, we discover that Spenser reenters history, but hardly to champion imperialism.

I begin by suggesting that the poem's peculiar narrative movement—from autobiographical images of pastoral retreat in stanza 1 to allegorical images of idealized nature in stanzas 2–7 to realistic images of history and politics in stanzas 8–10—looks very much like an enactment of the program informing Spenser's earlier poetry, especially *The Faerie Queene*: human beings overcome disillusioned withdrawal into pastoral *otium* through a vision of wedded love that motivates ethical action in society. Stanza 1 presents the first stage of a poetic process, in which the poet leaves "Princes Court" (line 7) for pastoral *otium* to "ease" his "payne" (line 10). Stanzas 2 through 7 trace a second stage: the poet "chaunce[s] to espy" an idealized vision in which a "Flocke of Nymphes" (line 20) deck "two Swannes of goodly hewe" (line 37) with "Flowers" and "Garlands" (lines 74, 83). Through grace augmented by faith, the poet

236   SPENSER'S MARRIAGE POETRY

sees an imaginative vision in which he symbolically witnesses the effect of his own poetry, figured when the swans overcome their fear of marriage thanks to a "Lay" of wedded love sung by one of the nymphs (line 87). Stanzas 8–10 present a third stage: the swan procession enters "mery London" (line 127), prompting the poet to celebrate the national ideal seen in Essex's Arthurian service to Gloriana (Hieatt, "Continuation," "Passing"). Inspired by the vision, the poet and his readers (the swan brides) return to actuality transformed, and the "Birdes" suddenly become "Bryde[s]" (lines 176–78). The narrative disruptions signal a meta-allegory of the allegorical process, by which the poet can "fashion" virtuous readers (*Works* 2: 485 [*Letter to Ralegh*]).

Yet *Prothalamion* registers some significant changes from *The Faerie Queene*. The poet foregrounds a female identity and agency now independent of the queen and even initially of her archpoet. His role as a national love poet praising the queen appears at first to be appropriated by a totally female ritual in service of "the companionate condition of marriage" (Montrose, "Spenser's Domestic Domain" 115). This ritual, with its garden imagery of flowers, baskets, swans, and garlands, looks conspicuously like the process of creating allegorical images out of the garden of allegorical forms and then of activating those images for some artistic cultural service. Spenser redirects the flow of English history, not outward to politics in Ireland or riches in the Americas, but back into another feminine force right at home: "mery London, my most kyndly Nurse, / That to me gave this Lifes first native sourse" (lines 128–29). The progress of the feminine ritual measures a voyage from Greenwich to London, court to city, queen to aristocrat, suggesting that Spenser may be turning from a nationhood of royal power to a nationhood of aristocratic power (Helgerson, *Forms* 55–59). Yet Spenser's new aristocratic nation does not exclude his old one, as "Great England's glory" rings "great Elisaes glorious name" (lines 146–57). Finally, however, this newly conceived "England," with its cultural value lodged in the domestic space of marriage itself, is literally housed in the poet's place of birth—"Which some brave muse may sing, / To ages following" (lines 159–60). In this last published poem, the hierarchy of Spenser's emphases is complex, but the poet appears to be foregrounding a nationhood of artistic power, in which his art channels the flow of aristocratic and royal energy into the institution of Protestant marriage.

The second way to get the floral chain of *Prothalamion* into the classroom is to give students samples of later poets who felt it necessary to come to terms with the "Spousall Verse." For instance, Shakespeare's 1609 *Lover's Complaint* disperses language from the second stanza of *Prothalamion*, including the behavior of his young woman: "A thousand favours from a maund she drew, / Of amber chrystal and of beaded jet, / Which one by one she in a river threw" (lines 36–38; Jackson). Drayton's 1619 *Pastorals* imitates *Prothalamion*'s refrain: "Stay Thames, to hear my song, thou great and famous flood" (3: 49; A. Fowler, "Spenser's *Prothalamion*" 65n21). Similarly, Milton's 1623 *Lycidas* and 1629 "On the Morning of Christ's Nativity" are indebted to Spenser's strophes

Patrick Cheney and Anne Lake Prescott   237

(Spenser, *Works* 8: 675; Gross 29). Like Drayton, Pope in his 1709 *Pastorals* imitates the refrain: "Fair Thames, flow gently from thy sacred spring" (qtd. in Spenser, *Works* 8: 497). In the early-nineteenth-century "To the Morning Star" and "To Morning," Blake draws on *Prothalamion* (Gleckner, *Blake* 5, 27, and *Blake's Prelude* 76, 176–77), while in April 1802 Wordsworth read *Prothalamion* with his sister Dorothy, and in his 1807 "Intimations of Immortality" and "Resolution and Independence" he offers elaborate imitations of *Prothalamion's* language and imagery (Schulman; Hartman 267–68). In 1827, Coleridge was even moved to tears by the poem, referring to "the swanlike movement of [the] exquisite *Prothalamion*" (qtd. in Spenser, *Works* 8: 660), and Charles Lamb said that he could "repeat, to this day, no verses to [himself] more frequently, or with kindlier emotion, than those" on the temple (qtd. in Spenser, *Works* 8: 502; Eaves 424). In contrast to Pope and Drayton, Dante Gabriel Rossetti echoes the first line of the refrain in "The Stream's Secret"— "Between the lips of the low cave / Against that night the lapping waters lave" (qtd. in O'Donnell 187)—and Yeats is indebted to the "Spousall Verse" in both his 1919 "The Wild Swans at Coole" and his 1928 "Leda and the Swan" (Bloom, *Spenser* 34). Most famously, T. S. Eliot gives *Prothalamion* a role in literary history by quoting the last line of the refrain twice in his 1922 *Waste Land* (lines 176 and 183) and then by rewriting it: "Sweet Thames, run softly, for I speak not loud or long" (line 184). Thereafter, Gertrude Stein, Edith Sitwell, and May Sarton all pen twentieth-century prothalamia (Tufte, *High Wedlock* 253–55, 266–67, 279–80, and "Stein's Prothalamion"), while our own contemporary poet John Hollander writes that Spenser's "magnificent spousal verse [. . .] is a poem that descants upon itself obliquely, but with a sad power that not even Spenser's earlier *Epithalamion* [. . .] could summon up" ("Spenser's Undersong" 148, 153). More than any late-twentieth-century poet, Hollander himself summons up the poignantly soft flow of Spenserian literary history: "All the singing rivers commend our rivery songs: / The estuary at New London hummed an old theme / Softly in the revised standard version of the Thames" (*Powers* 41 ["Principal Reivers"]; see also *Powers* 35 ["One of Our Walks" and "Where I Work"], "From the Ramble" in *Visions*, and "Asylum Avenue" and "A View of the Ruins" in *In Time*). By adding to this list, teachers can record just how in *Prothalamion* the poet's poet writes the poet's poem.

Such a list raises the question that leads back to the text: Why would so many gifted and influential poets imitate this Spenser poem (rather than, say, *Epithalamion*)? W. B. C. Watkins provides only a hint when he claims that if forced to choose between *Epithalamion* and *Prothalamion* most poets would prefer the latter for its "rare quality of a dream, grave yet joyous and tender, set to incomparable music" (*Shakespeare* 222). The sample list also allows teachers to identify Spenser's vital part in the trajectory of English literature, which can be useful in many kinds of courses, especially surveys. Finally, the list allows us to counter a commonplace about *Prothalamion* as the final register of Spenser's literary career: that because within five years he had died and Essex was

238   SPENSER'S MARRIAGE POETRY

beheaded, "the beseeching voice of the *Prothalamion* fades into the background of history, of forces which the poet cannot shape" (Burrow, *Spenser* 25). In fact, Spenser's song continues to shape history because he once wrote history so powerfully. Sweet Thames, run softly, for you speak both loud and long.

Whichever strategy teachers use, they will find that the standing of *Prothalamion* in literary history makes it a moving work in the classroom. Its breathtaking floral beauty; its swanlike grace and power; its famous refrain, with a river running through it; its intrusive portrait of the woeful artist as an old courtier; its youthful Orphic charm against the ruins of time; its challenging myths of seduction and rape in a courtly betrothal poem under the gaze of the Virgin Queen; its perplexing narrative disruptions and metamorphoses; its fusion of history and vision, politics and poesis, the real Essex and the literary Arthur: these are some of the links that bind the poem to "Sweet Themmes"— to literary time itself: past, present, future.

Making Shakespeare's *Sonnets* Matter in the Classroom

Michael Schoenfeldt

In my many attempts to teach Shakespeare's *Sonnets* to undergraduates of different levels, I have found that I must do battle with an infelicitous combination of familiarity and estrangement that my students bring to these poems. The familiarity derives from the capacity of certain parts of selected sonnets to furnish in isolation terse statements of proverbial wisdom or limpid expressions of love. This mining of sonnets for sage quotations blends perniciously with the awed bardolatry that far too many students seem to think is the zenith of Shakespeare studies. The estrangement derives from the profound differences that emerge between Shakespeare's account of the self and our own post-Cartesian, post-Freudian presuppositions about selves and desires. This psychological strangeness only confirms students' prejudices about the irrelevance of past utterances to their own concerns. In this essay I want to suggest that we can begin to make the *Sonnets* work in the classroom by engaging with rather than fighting against the material underpinnings of the poems. Close attention to the editorial decisions that have produced the poems as we know them and exposure to the medical, ethical, literary, and psychological regimes under which these remarkable poems were written can give students a meaningful purchase on them. I propose, then, that we can make the *Sonnets* matter by emphasizing in our pedagogy the formal and cultural matter from which they are made.

This material is first of all the medium of the sonnet, a taut structure demanding the formal confinement of a vocabulary of extravagant longing. Shakespeare's *Sonnets*, in particular, break from the standard octave-sestet form in favor of three quatrains and a couplet. This arrangement enhances the capacity of the sonnet to function as a machine for logical argument. The poetic and architectonic structure of each sonnet, particularly as it is based on the unit of the quatrain, has recently been impressively explored by Helen Vendler in *The Art of Shakespeare's* Sonnets, a book I will certainly consult in my future class preparation as well as in my scholarship.

The *Sonnets*, though, come down to us not as isolated poems but rather as a sequence, however unauthorized. Implicit in the notion of a sonnet sequence is a pronounced tension between the formal constriction of the individual sonnet and the narrative distension of the larger collection, between the verbal quantum of a single poem and the resonant linearity of the longer narrative. I explain to my students just what we know and do not know about the 1609 *Sonnets*, using the fine work by Margreta de Grazia and Peter Stallybrass on the editorial construction of the *Sonnets* (see de Grazia, *Shakespeare*, "Scandal"; de Grazia and Stallybrass; and Stallybrass). Of particular interest here are the mysterious dedication of the 1609 volume and the editorial revisions of John Benson in 1640 (who converted masculine pronouns to feminine in one sonnet,

240 MAKING SHAKESPEARE'S *SONNETS* MATTER

changed masculine nouns to neutral ones in two others, and arranged the *Sonnets* into groups) and of Edmund Malone in 1780 (who identified the mysterious Mr. W. H. with the addressee of the first 126 sonnets and argued that the final twenty-eight were addressed to a woman). I expose the students to this material to show them just how impure and tentative any presuppositions we hold about the *Sonnets* are, and to demonstrate thereby a requisite skepticism about any implicitly teleological or autobiographical interpretation of the poems. This can be a salutary lesson for undergraduates raised on romantic notions of the total authorial control of the printed text. I agree with Stephen Booth that for all its inadequacies the 1609 quarto provides the best available text, and I often show students his splendid edition, where they may view facsimile pages facing a modernized text. This gives students a graphic representation of some of the signal continuities and striking differences between Renaissance and modern books. I usually have them look at the facsimile of sonnet 146, "Poor soul, the center of my sinful earth," since it contains one of the few textual cruxes of the sequence, when the beginning of the second line repeats the end of the first: "Poore soule the center of my sinfull earth, / My sinfull earth these rebbell powres that thee array" (Booth, *Shakespeare's* Sonnets 125). I use this poem not just to give students a clear example of the vagaries of textual transmission but also to encourage students to supply their own possibilities for the elided words. This requires them to read the poem closely and frequently elicits spirited and intelligent discussion. I do not use Booth's edition as a text with undergraduates, however, because its fanatically close readings are usually imitated to bad effect by inexperienced students; I prefer instead John Kerrigan's judicious Viking edition (and look forward to trying out the new Arden edition, edited by Katherine Duncan-Jones).

Since students are typically unfamiliar with the genre of the sonnet sequence, I emphasize the stunning difference between this sequence and all previous sequences. Whereas most sonnet sequences since Petrarch were dedicated to the articulation of unrequited heterosexual love, Shakespeare's *Sonnets* begin by imploring a young man to reproduce himself through heterosexual intercourse and conclude with a series of poems that affiliate consummated heterosexual passion with incurable disease. These poems must have struck the 1609 reader as a radical disruption of the conventional narrative of erotic courtship. In the early sonnets, woman is not the idealized recipient of the erotic aspirations of a male speaker but rather a means of biological reproduction, to be frequented so that men may lay claim to the fragile immortality of progeny; in the later poems, woman, now identified with a culturally derogated darkness, is the object of a wasteful, enervating, uncontrollable desire that contrasts markedly with the idealized love of a young man. I try to get my students to see the very different sexual economies that provide the bookends of the 1609 sequence: although both the early and late poems involve love triangles, the early poems urge a young man to "give away [your]self" through the reproductive expenditure of semen to "keep [him]self still" (sonnet 16), while the later poems describe such expenditure as "th' expense of spirit in a waste of shame" (sonnet 129), a completely unproductive depletion of vital energy.

Whenever I teach the sequence, I make a point of calling attention to the elusive sexuality of the young man in sonnet 20, a poem that has been invoked to prove both that Shakespeare was, in our modern sense, gay and that he most certainly was not. The poem's bawdy wordplay and its gender-bending eroticism fascinate modern students. The androgynous "master mistress of [the speaker's] passion" is in this poem praised for possessing an almost feminine beauty, but in terms that also perform ritual antifeminism—the young man has "A woman's gentle heart, but [is] not acquainted / With shifting change, as is false women's fashion." In these lines lurks a pun on "quaint," the available word for female genitalia, but the force of the pun is not fully realized until the corollary pun on male genitalia is made in the poem's penultimate line: "pricked thee out." The poem indicates that the young man was intended to be a woman until a feminized and heterosexual Nature "fell a-doting" and gave him a penis, "adding one thing to my purpose nothing." The speaker certainly finds this sex change a source of some frustration—"by addition me of thee defeated"—indicating that the young man's penis frustrates the speaker's erotic desire. But the couplet, although viewed as a clinching point by those critics who want to save Shakespeare from the "taint" of same-sex desire, leaves open the dispensation of the young man's erotic attentions: "But since she pricked thee out for women's pleasure, / Mine be thy love, and thy love's use their treasure." Coming after nineteen poems in which a speaker urges a young man to engage in the usury that is heterosexual intercourse—investing one's spirit with interest in the body of a being who may thereby produce other beings—sonnet 20 suggests either that the speaker and the young man will have a nonsexual but fervently emotional relationship or that they will have a sexual but nonreproductive relationship. This poem, one of only two composed exclusively of feminine rhymes, typically proves a good occasion for student discussion and for demonstrating the power of the presuppositions, about Shakespeare and about sexuality, that we bring to the poems.

In the sequence as it comes down to us, this scenario of triangulated love mutates into the poems we have come to call the dark lady sonnets, poems that allow the situation comedy of the opening poems to issue in sexual nightmare. Although the darkness invoked in these poems refers to dark hair and coloring in an age that idealized fair skin and light hair and so cannot be precisely aligned with what we in the twentieth century mean by race, I argue that these poems nevertheless bespeak a hierarchy of color that underpins Western racism (see Hall, *Things*). These poems practice a sometimes playful dissent from poetic tradition; "My mistress eyes are nothing like the sun" is a poem students seem particularly to like, in part because its jocular flouting of convention is so easy to comprehend. But this playful distortion of poetic tradition issues ultimately in an alarmingly divided self, one that desires uncontrollably

242   MAKING SHAKESPEARE'S *SONNETS* MATTER

what it knows is unattractive and injurious. In a dense and subtle argument, Joel Fineman has located the emergence of modern poetic subjectivity in the lyric effects produced by just this division (*Shakespeare's Perjured Eye*).

The notion that emerges in these poems of erotic desire as a disease fascinates and disturbs our students, perhaps because AIDS has folded its own malignant truths into the insight of sonnet 147 that "Desire is death." But the poem is based on a notion that runs contrary to our own presuppositions about the relation of identity and desire. Whereas we tend to imagine that identity emerges from a person's particular configuration of desires, early modern accounts of the self assume that all persons are afflicted by a wide range of desires. What individuates is one's success at controlling these desires. The speaker of sonnet 147, for example, depicts desire as a perverse yearning for what at once precipitates and prolongs the illness of desire:

> My love is as a fever, longing still
> For that which longer nurseth the disease,
> Feeding on that which doth preserve the ill,
> Th'uncertain sickly appetite to please.

The poem depicts a medicalized allegory of the self in which "reason" the physician has abandoned the patient out of anger "that his prescriptions are not kept." The speaker is consequently "frantic mad" without reason and "Past cure" without a physician. I link this poem's account of the disease of desire to the situation of the final two sonnets (153 and 154), whose speaker is likewise "sick," "a sad distempered guest." This speaker, though, seeks a "sovereign cure" for "love's fire" in the baths. (Venereal disease, a malady of love often likened to fire [as in sonnet 144], was thought to be ameliorated if not cured by baths, in part because the profuse sweating they produced resembled the purgative effect of mercury, another "cure" for venereal disease, which worked by precipitating massive salivation.) This speaker, though, learns only that "Love's fire heats water, water cools not love." Desire is a contagion that is spread by the very act of trying to treat it.

I then use this account of unregulated desire as a disease to confront one of the more troubling sonnets for twentieth-century readers, sonnet 94. This sonnet has proved difficult in part because it idealizes a discipline we tend to pathologize. It imagines self-control as a prophylactic against the diseases of desire and indicates that the deliberate disjunction between inner compulsion and outer demeanor that we construe as hypocrisy is the epitome of civil, and even religious, conduct. Discipline in this regime functions as a fragile bulwark against both the internal festering of human flesh and the contagion of social disease. The poem's urgent endorsement of cool stability can only be understood against the unstable, overheated self, susceptible to the insanities of insubordinate desire, that is depicted in the other sonnets. I use this poem to measure the greater emphasis on self-control that marks early modern psychology; under this

Michael Schoenfeldt   243

earlier regime, modes of constraint we might construe as unhealthy repression are coveted as salutary acts of self-government necessary for the protection of self and other.

What has most troubled modern readers of sonnet 94 (Empson; Hubler, *Sense*; Booth, *Essay*) is the apparent disparity between the emotional coldness of the figures being praised and the divine praise they merit:

> They that have pow'r to hurt, and will do none,
> That do not do the thing they most do show,
> Who moving others are themselves as stone,
> Unmoved, cold, and to temptation slow—
> They rightly do inherit heaven's graces,
> And husband nature's riches from expense.

It has proved particularly difficult for modern readers to see how the cool remove of one who cultivates a disjunction between action and desire can be imagined to merit the graces of a heaven theoretically dedicated to the emotion of love. But against the volcanic instability of unregulated desire articulated in "My love is as a fever," the stony dispassion of sonnet 94 assumes a profoundly positive valence. Whereas the speaker of sonnet 147 is "frantic mad with evermore unrest," the speaker of sonnet 94 articulates a mode of conduct intended to resist the innate tendency of the body to such febrile insanity by cultivating a necessarily chilling self-control.

Whereas most Shakespeare sonnets divide into three quatrains and a couplet, sonnet 94 offers an atypical break between octave and sestet whereby not only the imagery but also the ethical thrust of the poem seems to change. The purpose of the sestet, however, is to demonstrate how the rigorous self-control the octave endorses not only delimits a superior's efforts to hurt others but also inoculates such a superior against harm from base infection. The sestet, that is, moves from the sturdy, inanimate world of stone to the delicate, ephemeral world of flowers to stress the hygienically prophylactic rather than the socially strategic uses of the imperturbable self-absorption the poem praises:

> The summer's flow'r is to the summer sweet,
> Though to itself it only live and die;
> But if that flow'r with base infection meet,
> The basest weed outbraves his dignity.
> For sweetest things turn sourest by their deeds;
> Lilies that fester smell far worse than weeds.

I contrast this surprising idealization of self-enclosure to those early sonnets that urge a young man to abandon his sterile self-absorption in order to mate. I then proceed to link this strategic solipsism to sonnets 33, 110, and 111, in which the speaker laments the processes by which subjects expose themselves

244 MAKING SHAKESPEARE'S *SONNETS* MATTER

to a social stain by contact with the base. Sonnet 33, for example, "Full many a glorious morning," blames the sun for allowing "basest clouds to ride / With ugly rack on his celestial face." I argue that whereas the larger sequence seems divided between the expression and the suppression of emotion, sonnet 94 comes down firmly on the side of suppression, but in terms that show such suppression to be at once unattractive and necessary. A tension present in the comparatively constricted form of the sonnet—that the vehicle for expressing erotic desire becomes a vessel for attempting to contain it—thus is seen to resonate with one of the central ethical dilemmas of Western culture since Augustine: whether desire is something to be eradicated or just redirected. Relatedly, the poem queries whether a despised hypocrisy is just a prized civility from a different angle. Whereas other sonnets express in manifold ways the involuted curves and wrinkles of the desiring self, sonnet 94 offers a strategy for ironing out these curves and wrinkles in terms that record the immense human costs and surprising social benefits of following this strategy.

I thus aspire in my classroom to display the *Sonnets* not just as wonderful poems in their own right but also as occasions for discussing some of the central continuities and signal differences between the early modern period and our own. The students invariably find their expectations disturbed, both about Shakespeare and about the English Renaissance, but in ultimately salutary ways. Emerging from very different notions of authorship, poetic form, and self from those shared by most of our students, the poems nevertheless manage to excite the notice of students and to reward proportionately the efforts students are willing to make to understand them.

TEACHING CRITICAL NARRATIVES OF THE ELIZABETHAN AGE

A Story of Generations
Richard Helgerson

The story I tell when I teach Elizabethan poetry repeats a story the poetry tells, a story of generational conflict and solidarity.

In Edmund Spenser's self-consciously inaugural work, *The Shepheardes Calender* (1579), solidarity stands out. The book is dedicated to Philip Sidney, a young man of nearly Spenser's age. It has an introduction and notes by another young man, a certain E. K. And the introduction is addressed to E. K.'s—and the poet's—"verie special and singular good frend" Gabriel Harvey (Spenser, *Yale Edition* 13). A year later, a set of "proper wittie familiar Letters" between Spenser and Harvey appeared "with the Preface of a wellwiller to them both" (Spenser, *Poetical Works* 611, 609). These letters identify still other members of this circle of friends; intensify the sense of age-based, ingroup solidarity; and even give a name to their society. Together these young men constitute an "Areopagus," a senate modeled on the ancient Greek senate and bent on the reform of English poetry. As the centerpiece of this shared activity, *The Shepheardes Calender* repeats in its very structure the pattern of in-group solidarity. Though the first and last of its twelve eclogues are solo pieces, the others are all dialogues, most of them between shepherds of roughly the same age. And as one of those shepherds, Colin Clout, is revealed to be a mask for Spenser and another, Hobbinoll, is identified with Harvey, the circle of friends outside the poem and the circle of friends inside it merge.

The Shepheardes Calender thus represents the generational cohort from which it arose. But the poem also gives voice to a nervous defensiveness that points toward generational conflict. The dedication calls on Sidney to protect the poem from envy, E. K.'s introduction admits the role "unstayed yougth"

246 STORY OF GENERATIONS

had in producing it (*Yale Edition* 17), the *Februarie* eclogue stages a debate between youth and age, and the *October* eclogue "complayneth of the comtempte of Poetrie" (*Yale Edition* 170). Seventeen years later, in the opening stanza of the second installment of *The Faerie Queene* (1596), Spenser locates that contempt more precisely:

> The rugged forhead that with grave foresight
> Welds kingdomes causes, and affaires of state,
> My looser rimes (I wote) doth sharply wite,
> For praising love, as I have done of late,
> And magnifying lovers deare debate;
> By which fraile youth is oft to follie led,
> Through false allurement of that pleasing baite,
> That better were in vertues discipled,
> Then with vaine poems weeds to have their fancies fed.   (4.proem.1)

The owner of this "rugged forhead," William Cecil, Lord Burleigh, was Queen Elizabeth's chief minister and a man widely recognized as *parens patriae*. His antipathy to the "looser rimes" of amorous verse clearly mattered, not only because of who he was but also because that antipathy represented attitudes Spenser and his generation had been brought up to share. In making themselves poets, these young men rebelled against a heavy burden of paternal prohibition.

Such rebellion is the subject of the *Old Arcadia* (1580), the book Philip Sidney was writing at just the time that Spenser dedicated *The Shepheardes Calender* to him. The *Old Arcadia* tells of the abandonment of heroic endeavor by its two princely heroes, Pyrocles and Musidorus, who, in pursuit of love, disguise themselves as an amazon and a shepherd. In the book's searing final scene, the young men are set in judgment before Euarchus, the "good ruler" who is Pyrocles's father and Musidorus's uncle. Not recognizing them, Euarchus condemns both to death, and, when told who they are, he denies all relation: "Nay, I cannot [. . .] acknowledge you for mine; for never had I shepherd to my nephew, nor never had woman to my son. Your vices have [. . .] disannulled your birthright" (Robertson 411–12). Sidney's own father, Henry Sidney, who bore a striking likeness to Euarchus and who was both Burleigh's friend and himself a leading figure in Elizabeth's government, would perhaps not have cast off his son merely for turning poet. But his son never gave him the chance. While Philip Sidney shared his fiction and poems with his sister and brother and with other friends of his own age, he kept their existence a secret from his father. The poems themselves, not only the pastoral poems in the *Arcadia* but also the sonnets of *Astrophil and Stella*, are shot through with anxieties that would explain his reluctance. They struggle repeatedly to make a place for their own disruptive desire against voices of fatherlike admonition. No wonder Sidney wrote a defense of poetry. From his generational perspective, poetry needed defending.

When Philip Sidney was twelve, his father sent him a solemn letter of advice, a letter that was later printed as "most necessary for all young gentlemen to be carried in memory" (H. Sidney, title page). Scenes in which a father or father substitute gives just such advice to a soon-to-be-wayward young man appear regularly in Elizabethan prose fiction, as they do in Sidney's own verse and prose. Both parts of John Lyly's enormously influential *Euphues* begin that way, and so do nearly two dozen other fictions by such writers as Robert Greene, Thomas Lodge, George Pettie, George Whetstone, Barnabe Rich, Brian Melbancke, and Austin Saker. And, like Spenser, Sidney, and Lyly, many of the others make clear that their heroes' willful neglect of precept was also their own. Just as the fictional young men—Colin Clout, Pyrocles, Musidorus, Astrophil, Euphues, and many others—leave the path of well-doing, as that path was defined by paternal advice, to pursue the wanton pleasures of love, so their authors wandered from the path set out for them, to write the books in which these stories are told.

But what was the expected path? Why was there such tension between Elizabethan fathers and their sons? Both generations were raised in a tradition of civic humanism that coupled classical learning with the goal of service to the state. Their training and ambition were thus much the same. But whereas the state needed the fathers, unemployment was often the lot of the sons. In a letter to his humanist mentor, Hubert Languet, Philip Sidney defined both the aim of the education he had received and the frustration attendant on it: "To what purpose should our thoughts be directed to various kinds of knowledge, unless room be afforded for putting it into practice, so that public advantage may be the result, which in a corrupt age we cannot hope for?" (Pears 143). And two years later he was still lamenting that "the unnoble constitution of our tyme [. . .] doth keepe us from fitte imployments" (Osborn 537). As the son of a high-ranked government official and as heir apparent of two earldoms, Sidney bore a heavier weight of expectation than most. But, at different levels of intensity, his experience was widely shared. He and his fellows were brought up to do one thing but found themselves doing another. Instead of serving the state in positions of honor and responsibility, they were writing amorous poems and fictions. Such experience inevitably drew them closer to one another, even as it set them at odds with the generation of their fathers.

The great outpouring of Elizabethan poetry and fiction that began in 1579 and 1580 with the work of Spenser, Sidney, and Lyly was thus the product of frustration and owes much of its extraordinary vitality to a rebellious redirection of youthful energy. But, oddly, even as the poetry declares its own waywardness, it manages to satisfy paternal expectation. Not only does it rehearse those precepts it repeatedly transgresses but by its very existence it also fulfills one of the great aims of such humanist precepts: it, too, serves the state. In reforming English verse and prose, Spenser, Sidney, Lyly, and the other young writers of their generation performed a patriotic act. They gave England a language and literature that might rival the accomplishments of antiquity. "Our

248 STORY OF GENERATIONS

Mother tonge," E. K. sadly declared in his introduction to *The Shepheardes Calender*, "which truely of it self is both ful enough for prose and stately enough for verse, hath long time ben counted most bare and barrein of both" (Spenser, *Yale Edition* 16); and, in his *Defence of Poesy*, Philip Sidney regretted that "England [. . .] should be grown so hard a stepmother to poets" (*Miscellaneous Prose* 110). Remedying these defects transformed poetry's self-acknowledged vice into patriotic virtue. For the men who wrote it, Elizabethan poetry turned out to be a way of being good by being bad, a way of repairing the breach between generations even as they widened it.

Chaucer and the Elizabethan Invention of the "Selfe"

Elizabeth Fowler

> Uncouthe unkiste, Sayde the olde famous Poete
> Chaucer: whom for his excellencie and wonderfull
> skil in making, his scholler Lidgate, a worthy scholler
> of so excellent a maister, calleth the Loadestarre of our
> Language: and whom our Colin clout in his Æglogue
> calleth Tityrus the God of shepheards, comparing hym
> to the worthines of the Roman Tityrus Virgile.
> —*The Shepheardes Calender*

Poets like Edmund Spenser did not break from their English forebears but saw themselves as the students of such "olde famous" masters as Geoffrey Chaucer, John Lydgate, and John Skelton. Both the envoy and the epistle that open *The Shepheardes Calender* begin by quoting Chaucer; in *The Arte of Rhetorick*, Thomas Wilson reports that "The fine Courtier wil talke nothyng but Chaucer" (qtd. in Southall 13); the single poet that Henry Howard, earl of Surrey, mentions in his adoring "Epitaph on Sir Thomas Wyatt" is Chaucer. Much has been said about the Continental influences on, say, *Tottel's Miscellany*, but it is salutary to remind ourselves that Francis Petrarch is a fourteenth-century poet—a *medieval* poet on the English timeline: Tudor poets knew Petrarch's poetry through Chaucer's example. The "envoy" of The Clerk's Tale makes explicit Chaucer's pervasive rivalry with Petrarch, a rivalry that shaped Spenser's own revisions and rejections of Petrarchism. The Continental and classical inheritance of the Elizabethan poets is best understood as passing through Chaucer, Lydgate, and the other late medieval English poets who were even more prolific translators than were their heirs.

The continuity of the English tradition is especially fruitful to stress in introductory survey courses, which often include Chaucer and are, of course, seldom able to include Continental or classical lyric. The achievements of the Tudor lyric poets are unintelligible without an understanding of the strategies and tools that they inherited. In a process begun by Chaucer and consolidated by Spenser, English lyric developed a sophisticated technology for representing and producing interior, subjective experience. This essay sketches a medieval background to the early modern configuration of interiority that Spenser calls the "selfe." In the classroom, this outline can be enriched by recent literary scholarship on Renaissance subjectivity (e.g., Fumerton; Gregerson; Maus, *Inwardness*; Porter; Selleck; Shuger, *Renaissance Bible*). My aim is near to the aims of Elizabethan lyric: it is to make us and our students skilled analysts and chroniclers of the technologies that produce interior experience.

Lyric poetry claims special access to intense forms of subjectivity, appeals

250   ELIZABETHAN INVENTION OF THE "SELFE"

strongly to the passions of modern readers, and is brilliant and brief. It there-
fore makes an excellent occasion for improving students' historical precision
about the forms that are taken by subjectivity. Elizabethan lyric falls largely
into three modes: the devotional, the amorous, and the petitionary. All these
kinds of poetry seek to define the meaning of interior experience—the experi-
ence of spirituality, of the passions, of cognition, of subordination, of need.
Each of the three modes elaborates a concept of the person that shall occupy
our attention here: the meditative, impassioned thinker of the religious lyric;
the enthralled speaker of the amorous lyric; and the sophisticated authorial
voice that solicits patronage. Each of the three makes an important contribu-
tion to Spenser's notion of the "selfe." I call such paradigmatic concepts or
models of the person *social persons* (see E. Fowler, "Rhetoric").

The devotional, amorous, and petitionary modes of lyric all rely largely on
using second-person address (and thus on rhetorical figures such as apostro-
phe), on emphasizing the affective experience of the first-person speaker (and
thus on literary forms such as the prayer, the sonnet, and the complaint), on
slowing down plot to a state of near stillness, and on speeding up metaphor to
a state near allegory. How can students learn to recognize features of early
modern poetry that seem to them both invisible and obvious? Earlier English
poetry can help students see how Tudor lyric, that most intimate of forms, has
a social history. What kinds of cultural practices were available to enhance and
structure people's experience of themselves as interior, feeling beings? How
did those practices change over the centuries? A few of Chaucer's poems can
quickly show how he helped later English writers invent the social person of
the "selfe."

After the Fourth Lateran Council, which in 1215 prescribed annual confes-
sion to all believers, penitential theology produced a refined notion of the inte-
rior of the person. By developing an alternative (if often compatible)
understanding of the interior of characters throughout *The Canterbury Tales*,
Chaucer shows that fiction can be a powerful way to describe interior experi-
ence. Students may have encountered his experimental uses of voice in the
prologues of the Wife of Bath and the Pardoner. These texts display paradoxi-
cal psychological experience "within" fictional characters—an influential new
way of using fiction in English. Chaucer closes *The Canterbury Tales* with The
Parson's Tale, a retreat to penitential ways of understanding character, but at
the last minute he recoups his brief for fiction in the Retraction. There the per-
son who confesses in response to the Parson's "litel tretys" is Chaucer the
author, not Chaucer the dying man who presumably had sins more rankling
than poems to confess. He stresses the way that our sense of the verbal repre-
sentation of intention (that key aspect of interior experience) becomes ambigu-
ous and complex in fiction. The Retraction replaces the social person of the
"penitent" with those of the "makere" and the "compiler," two influential
medieval forms of authorship (see Minnis 207–09). English Protestantism cre-
ated new institutions and practices to explain and shape people's experience of

Elizabeth Fowler 251

their interiority and further altered the relation of poetic fiction to theological writing. Mary Sidney and Philip Sidney's translations of the Psalms, for example, richly recover a penitential devotional practice for lyric poetry by making the Psalms available in an intimate English plain style removed from the sacrament of penance and its institutions and social persons. Like Chaucer, they associate vernacular poetry with penance in order to expand the capacities of poetry: their Psalms move lyric further toward a new devotional configuration of interiority.

A second mode of lyric is the amorous poem—no doubt the most popular part of the Renaissance syllabus. Here, too, Chaucer provides some historical correctives. The theme of mutuality in love and heterosexual relations is an ideal usually explained by means of the "companionate" mode of marriage praised by Protestant preachers (e.g., Sinfield, *Literature*). It may be more intelligible to students when introduced as an ideal brought into poetry before the Reformation by the Franklin, the Wife of Bath, the Nun's Priest, and others among Chaucer's personae. The Shipman's Tale wittily draws our attention to the commercial diction that will accompany this notion of marriage and its "sexual debt" into the Reformation; connecting Elizabethan lyric with Chaucer can help guard against a sentimental isolation of Protestant marital ideals from the other economic and political institutions of English society. Perhaps the more prevalent configuration of sexual relations in the Elizabethan lyric involves less mutuality and more tyranny. The violent images and political diction of lyric not only are intensifying metaphors but also deserve cultural explanation (see R. Greene, "Colonial Wyatt"). Chaucer's short roundel "Merciles Beaute" makes a good foil for Elizabethan amorous poems, because it contains the themes of murder, monarchy, slavery, imprisonment, food, mercy, and cruelty that continue unabated into Renaissance writing about love. The Knight's Tale suggests a political origin—their conquest—for Palamon's and Arcite's use of such a fantastically brutal vocabulary of love in the set pieces of their lyric complaints (E. Fowler, "Afterlife").

A third mode of lyric—the mode of writing for patronage—liberally mixes the devotional and amorous postures. At its core lies the speech act of petition, which can be a starting point for in-class discussions of the financial support and circulation of art in English culture. Questions about the status of satire, the political suppression and commission of texts and ideas, and the erotic and gender configurations of patronage are all likely to arise. The twenty-six-line begging poem "The Complaint of Chaucer to His Purse," with its oblique address and suggestive erotic accusations, makes a good comparison with the epideictic mode of Elizabethan complaints, dedications, elegies, and epistles. Fruitful examples are Walter Ralegh's complex *The Ocean to Cynthia* and Spenser's weighty apparatus to *The Faerie Queene*, including the proems. If there is time for John Skelton, the vaunting "Garlande or Chapelet of Laurell" embeds a series of eleven lyrics addressed to women patrons. It features an aggressive representation of laureateship and includes cameo appearances by

252   ELIZABETHAN INVENTION OF THE "SELFE"

John Gower, Chaucer, and Lydgate, the reigning triumvirate. The social person of the poet-petitioner has its opposite in Colin Clout, the ragged shepherd "under whose person the Authour selfe is shadowed" in Skelton and Spenser (*Shepheardes Calender*, epistle 141), and who more often flouts his patrons than petitions them.

The "Selfe"

All these long-standing lyrical modes (devotional, amorous, petitionary) make possible the invention of a new configuration of interiority in the sixteenth century. Sonnet 45 of Spenser's *Amoretti* contains the best title for this most influential social person of Elizabethan lyric: the "selfe" (cf. *Faerie Queene* 2.12.47). Ask students to identify the term Spenser uses to describe the poem's paradigmatic representation of the person:

> Leave lady in your glasse of christall clene,
> Your goodly selfe for evermore to vew:
> and in my selfe, my inward selfe I meane,
> most lively lyke behold your semblant trew.   (lines 1–4)

Does Spenser use the word "selfe" the way we do? (See Selleck 33–36.) How does he suggest the "selfe" is made, discerned, and practiced rightly and wrongly? What kind of body does it have? What social practices and environments are evoked by the poem's images of the "selfe"?

With help finding which are the ripest words to choose for study, students can discover a lot about literary history on their own. The entry for *self* in *The Oxford English Dictionary* shows how philological change is a sign of larger cultural change: students should study its dense pages. Reading the entry is worth an hour or more of class time, because it will teach them to think about how language changes in time and about the intellectual and affective content of grammar, syntax, and metaphor. The largest-scale division is according to part of speech. (Teachers will need the list of abbreviations from vol. 1, pp. lxvi–iii, and perhaps the entire "General Explanations" section.) The consequential difference between the roles of the reflexive pronoun and the substantive proper noun is well demonstrated in the change suffered by the word *self*, which expands over centuries from a merely reflexive, emphatic feature of sentences to an independent entity with a philosophical tradition behind it. As students come to grips with the differing senses of the word, they will find sonnet 45 cited under definition C.I.4.b, and they will see that Spenser's substantive use of the word to convey a particular kind of interior experience is, according to the *Oxford English Dictionary*, originary.

In addition to historical dictionaries, concordances can be good sources for investigating the explicitly curious and archaic words in Spenser's lexis. It is always worth looking up Spenser's archaisms in the abbreviated concordance

Elizabeth Fowler 253

that is the glossary of *The Riverside Chaucer* (or in the best Chaucer concordances, also by Larry D. Benson). Consulting Chaucer tells us a lot about Spenser's synonym for "selfe," the phrase "semblant trew." A student might want to work out the connections between sonnet 45 and Chaucer's translations, *Boece* and *The Romaunt of the Rose*, in which the word "semblant" appears prominently. Spenser's phrase "semblant trew" allusively opposes "Faus-Semblant," the character in the courtship story of the *Roman de la Rose* that so influenced Chaucer's criticisms of the devotional and sexual uses of representation.

Many studies have clarified how profoundly the Reformation affected lyric modes of writing and reading (see especially Lewalski, *Protestant Poetics*; Shuger, *Renaissance Bible*). When an instructor has only minutes to present a historical brief, he or she cannot rely on students' familiarity with Tudor ecclesiastical politics. Look to the poem: the hyperbole of Spenser's second quatrain raises the problem of representing divinity and is an occasion for the discussion of Reformation iconoclasm and the relation between the devotional and amorous modes:

> Within my hart, though hardly it can shew
> thing so divine to vew of earthly eye:
> the fayre Idea of your celestiall hew,
> and every part remaines immortally [. . .].   (5–8)

Protestant iconoclasm should be seen, paradoxically, as one among many styles of representation; like the speaking lover, iconoclasm prefers the symbolic to the natural likeness, the "Idea" to the material image. Spenser's recourse to a Platonic diction softens the devotional topos of the stanza, which suggests a shrine for the adoration of a divine beloved—perhaps something like the chantry chapels destroyed in the Reformation, where her "every part remaines immortally," though "dimmed and deformd" (line 10) and in need of restoration. Spenser's adoring lover effects a reworking of the medieval topos of the shrine that recalls Chaucer's reworking of the topos of confession: the lover appears in the position of the worshipper (and the heart in the place of the architectural chapel) just as Chaucer's "makere" appears in the position of the penitent (and his curriculum vitae in the place of a penitential schedule of sins).

The appearance of the divine icon of the lady within the chantry chapel of the speaker's heart raises theological questions, but it also wittily proposes to transfigure such weighty matters into the lighter stuff of aesthetics. What kind of icon is the lady's "semblant trew"—religious or aesthetic? According to the *Oxford English Dictionary*, the word *trew* can describe religious faith or precise rendering. An aestheticized practice of self-correction is urged on the lady by the set of words that includes "clene," "goodly," "deformd," "playne," "fayre," and "darkned." This penitential, erotic, and deeply aesthetic notion of the care of the "selfe" is given two alternative futures by the speaker of the poem: it may

254   ELIZABETHAN INVENTION OF THE "SELFE"

be pursued narcissistically in the mirror, or it may be pursued through love and obedience to the speaker's demands. That this set of alternatives has a special, gendered force can be brought out by treating the emblematic episode devoted to the torture of Mirabella in *The Faerie Queene*, book 6, or by examining John Milton's use of the topos in Eve's description of her birth and turn to Adam in *Paradise Lost* (4.440–91).

What is the dominant image in *Amoretti*, sonnet 45, for the "selfe"? It is the face in the mirror ("in your glasse of christall clene, / Your goodly selfe for evermore to vew" [1–2]; "the goodly ymage of your visnomy" [10]). The reflected face allows us to connect Spenser's social person, the "selfe," to a constellation of images made by other arts in other media: the portrait, the miniature, the frontispiece, and the view of heavenly bodies taken by astronomers (line 14). Behaviors performed by the face are crucial to the amorous Elizabethan lyric and its representations of sexuality: seeing, breathing and speaking, kissing, suckling and eating, expressing emotion, grooming. Why do the Renaissance arts choose this particular part of the early modern body to represent interior experience and identity? What kind of interior experience does it represent? To answer these questions, it is helpful to compare the modes of representing the face (such as the blazon) elsewhere in the *Amoretti* and *Epithalamion* and in other Elizabethan poems. Rather than mere descriptions of appearance, these representations are practices that structure relations among the "selfe" and other social persons. Spenser himself unpacks the simile's appeal to action in lines like "Her lips lyke cherryes charming men to byte" (*Epithalamion* line 174).

The representation of the face in frontispieces and other portraits of poets and patrons gives us a visual image for the social persons native to the petitionary mode of lyric. This image is part of a process of reciprocity: poets offered to immortalize patrons in exchange for preferment. The petition of sonnet 45 relies on this mode when it tells the beloved to choose between the face she can produce in her mirror and the immortal face that is made in the poet's "inward selfe." The "likeness" is a surprisingly recent invention in which the face becomes an expression of a newly interior identity. Though impermanent wood, plaster, or wax likenesses were used in a few fourteenth-century royal funeral processions, medieval portraits in other media are thought to be iconic at the expense of facial likeness. One of the earliest known examples of an English portrait that aims to represent the likeness of a face as well as to convey symbolic information is a portrait of Chaucer that appears in a marginal illustration of a manuscript of Thomas Hoccleve's *Regement of Princes*. (Pearsall's *Life* includes a good discussion of the portraits of Chaucer in appendix 1.) That such an image would be associated with Chaucer and passed along by his disciple seems particularly apt. It is not a frontispiece; nor does it accompany a bid for patronage as many Tudor portraits will do. Nonetheless, Hoccleve's Chaucer champions the social person of the poet as an expert teacher ("maister") in the matters of interior experience as they are expressed in the face, the voice, and the character. It shows Chaucer's centrality to English practices of verbal and visual representations of the interior as they evolved toward the social person of the early modern self. Compare Chaucer's image with the effigies of poets that appear on the tomb sculpture in Westminster Abbey, with the Elizabethan miniatures that correlate so well with sonnets (see Fumerton), and with the portraits of patrons that are apt companions for epideictic poetry. For students interested in Tudor faces, good starting places are the chapter "Painting and Imagery" in the third volume of the *Cambridge Cultural History of Britain* (Ford) and the collection of Tudor and Jacobean portraiture edited by Roy Strong.

Exercises with historical dictionaries and comparisons between poems and other art forms help us reveal the social and intellectual valences of lexis and the cultural practices and institutions through which poetry acquires its meaning. With the help of its English literary heritage, Elizabethan lyric invented at least one resilient social person that still dominates concepts of the person today. In significant tension with the early analysis of interiority that had been developed by penitential theology, an analysis that in time it substantially displaced and restructured, the "selfe" paved the way for political notions of the "individual" to arise in the seventeenth century and to shape the institutions of the modern West. "Uncouthe unkiste": the unknown remains unembraced. It is good to know how the self comes to us as we choose among the cultural practices and social persons designed to produce our own experiences of interior life.

Wolves in Shepherds' Folds: Elizabethan Shorter Poetry and Reformation Culture

John N. King

It's difficult for twentieth-century readers to imagine the nationalistic moment when Philip Sidney lamented that England, "the Mother of excellent mindes," has "growne so hard a step-mother to Poets, who certainly in wit ought to passe all other" (G. Smith 1: 193). After all, Sidney was a contemporary of Marlowe, Spenser, and Shakespeare. Poor Sidney died young, however, and he was not content with poetry printed during his lifetime. His *Apology for Poetry* mentions only Tottel's *Miscellany* and the recently published, but as yet anonymous, *Shepheardes Calender*. He even complains that the archaic style of *The Shepheardes Calender* violates stylistic decorum by adopting "an old rustick language" (G. Smith 1: 196). George Puttenham concurs in his *Arte of English Poesie*, which explains that "a new company of courtly makers" led by Wyatt and Surrey, the chief contributors to Tottel's *Miscellany*, reformed the "rude & homely maner" of English poetry with the "sweete and stately measures and stile of the Italian Poesie" (G. Smith 2: 62, 63). In the 1580s, English poetry seemed to need all the help it could get.

I like to pose the question of what happened in between the era of the Henrician courtier poets and the late Elizabethan flowering because it enables students to go beyond the familiar staples of undergraduate survey courses. What happens if we pause to examine poetry of the 1540s, 1550s, and 1560s? We may have a passing familiarity with Thomas Sackville or George Gascoigne, but teachers of sixteenth-century literature generally neglect an important Protestant literary tradition. It fuses late medieval anticlerical satire, plain vernacular style, and heavily biblical language and metaphor.

Shorter poetry of the Reformation era offers much more than the crudely "Englished" Psalms of Thomas Sternhold and John Hopkins (the most popular collection of Elizabethan lyrics). Notable examples include a consolatory ballad sung by Anne Askew at Newgate Prison as she awaited being burnt alive as a Protestant heretic (Beilin, *Examinations* 149–50) and the "hymn" that concludes *Beware the Cat*, a sardonic satire by William Baldwin, editor of the *Mirror for Magistrates*. Robert Crowley, one of the earliest English Puritans, composed satirical epigrams and *Philargyry of Great Britain*, an allegory that satirizes failures of the English Reformation (King, "*Philargyrie*"). An enigmatic Londoner known as Luke Shepherd contributed poems that mock the clerical mystifications and celebrate the ability of simple men, women, and children to understand the Bible in their own language. His satires include *John Bon and Mast[er] Parson*, a dialogue in which a witty husbandman outwits an ignorant cleric, and *Doctor Double Ale*, a dramatic monologue by a tavern-haunting curate who drunkenly mumbles a laughable self-confession (Norbrook and Woudhuysen 89–90, 527–30; see King, *English Reformation Literature*, chs. 5,

7). Spenser's ecclesiastical eclogues (*Maye, July*, and *September*) feature Protestant speakers whose blunt satirical attacks mock religious formalism.

Reading poems by Crowley, Shepherd, and their contemporaries enables students to learn that a shift in Elizabethan taste obscured the literary production of an entire generation that preceded that of Shakespeare, Spenser, Sidney, and Marlowe. As members of a new generation of cultivated intellectuals, Sidney and Puttenham endorsed an enduring form of cultural amnesia when they claimed that early Tudor literature and culture are inferior to the achievements of their own age. By rejecting the popular ethos of Reformation culture, they molded the canon of early modern English literature. Their views live on in C. S. Lewis's influential opposition of the mid-Tudor "Drab Age" to the Elizabethan "Golden Age" that followed (*English Literature*, 64; for an alternative view, see Aers, "Reflections"). Nevertheless, Reformation literary culture contributed to the Ister Bank eclogue in Sidney's *Old Arcadia*. It also left its imprint on short poems that include eclogues in Spenser's *Shepheardes Calender*, Ralegh's "The Lie," and Shakespeare's sonnet 121 ("'Tis better to be vile than vile esteemed"). Recent revisionist scholarship has remarked on the vitality of the earlier tradition of Reformation literature and culture (Collinson, *Birthpangs*; Hadfield, *Literature*; King, *English Reformation Literature*, *Spenser's Poetry*; Norbrook; A. Patterson, "Still Reading").

The present moment affords an occasion to revise the literary canon in line with the efforts of feminists and socially oriented critics to recover writings by forgotten women and oppositional authors who contested authoritarian assumptions of the Elizabethan establishment. David Norbrook and H. R. Woudhuysen contribute to this enterprise in *The Penguin Book of Renaissance Verse, 1509–1659*, a text that cuts against the grain of traditional anthologies by incorporating verse by Askew, Crowley, Shepherd, and Nicholas Grimald, as well as their recusant contemporary John Heywood. I am currently compiling a complementary collection of Reformation texts from Tyndale to Spenser. It accompanies verse satires by Crowley and Shepherd with writings by William Tyndale, John Bale, Askew, Baldwin, Thomas Cranmer, John Foxe, and others. The Renaissance English Text Society will soon publish Janice Devereux's edition of Luke Shepherd's works.

The Penguin Book of Renaissance Verse and my collection, through their inclusion of Spenser's *Maye* eclogue rather than the more commonly anthologized *Aprill* or *October* eclogues, will enable students to discover how *The Shepheardes Calender* incorporates more than a domestication of newly imported French and Italian poetic modes. Piers's beast fable about the fate of the unwary kid shows how techniques and conventions of Reformation verse survived during the era of Sidney and Puttenham. E. K. glosses "the Foxe, maister of collusion" (Spenser, *Maye*, line 219) as a figure for "the false and faithlesse Papistes" (note on line 174). The allegorical tale represents a variation on fables about the depredations of ecclesiastical wolves, "ful of fraude and guile" (line 127), on sheep who lack protection from "false" pastors. Piers's warning that wolves intruded into shepherds' folds preserves the plainspoken voice of earlier Tudor poetry.

The Experimental and the Local
Roland Greene

As teachers of sixteenth-century poetry, I believe, we are drawn to devising stories about our period because the multifarious material tells no obvious story itself: this has always been a period about which the teacher, the critic, and the student have an unusual freedom in bringing one another from Skelton or Wyatt to Shakespeare and Donne. We have learned from a set of emphatic stories told by our best critics, from C. S. Lewis and Yvor Winters to Stephen Greenblatt. (And it is worth remembering that some of the most astute scholars of the period, such as Harry Berger, tend not to tell overarching stories at all.) When I teach sixteenth-century poetry, I tell a story that is centered on Petrarchism and follows the international development of the lyric. My narrative of an emergent genre and its cultural history in England is constructed with probably more than usual reference to Continental theories and practitioners, because I think that an event in early modern letters such as *Tottel's Miscellany* or *Astrophil and Stella* gains import by comparison with related events in France, Spain, and elsewhere (even New Spain)—that such an event actually brings more to a wider context than to a narrower one.

But I like multiple versions of such a plot to work together in the classroom, and I look for ways of encouraging the students to articulate stories of their own. Besides the historical and cultural backgrounds, I often give them some interlocking perspectives with which to collate their reactions, and I suggest that they tell one another and tell me fresher, more searching, perhaps more radical versions of the stories I am telling them. Two such perspectives on early modern poetry might be called the experimental and the local.

Today lyric is a ubiquitous genre that shows up in all spheres of culture, and some of the most significant theory about lyric is currently being written by poets and critics such as Charles Bernstein and Susan Stewart. For the Middle Ages and much of the Renaissance, however, lyric was merely a poorly defined catchall: the sixteenth century is probably the period in which the genre takes on its recognizably modern identity. How the genre developed makes a compelling object of study, describing a fairly strong literary-historical narrative and drawing on the vantages of gender, institutions, politics, print, and religion. In one sense, lyric culture arrives in its early modern phase through a continual process of experiment. Constitutive elements such as voice, temporality, materiality, and figuration are often reworked by poets for whom experiment or invention is a drive, and this process of adjustment produces the rich array of sixteenth-century poems we read again and again (and many we do not read enough). In my experience, this particular range of literary history and the open-ended character of lyric theory together give students the chance to participate in a description of the field that is less likely to arise in more exhaustively discussed areas. Early modern lyric poetry in English includes a certain number of landmarks about which we have established, conventional stories and a large body of work about which we do not, such as the poetry of 1550 to 1580 and the less prominent sonnet sequences after 1582.

How then to convey the qualities and issues involved in an age of experiment? Consider the lyric poetry written between the execution of Surrey and the coming of a second-generation English Petrarchism. I have sometimes introduced a key term in recent lyric theory and then encouraged the students to use it to think their way through a selection of lyrics written between 1550 and 1580, when English poetics was in flux and an extraordinary range of possibilities was in play. How might such a term be used heuristically to tell the story of the period? In the 1960s and 1970s and culminating in *Semiotics of Poetry* and *Text Production*, for instance, Michael Riffaterre conceived the terms *matrix* and *hypogram* to describe how poems mean and how readers struggle over the hurdles put up by their expectations of those meanings. For Riffaterre, we approach poems expecting them to operate mimetically, but we end up having to compromise with the periphrastic verbal protocol that we actually find there: the poem is a walled-off space where a unity has been effected, and our task as readers is to phase down our expectations so that we can mediate between what we bring to the poem and what the poem offers. The matrix is an abstract concept that cannot be actualized in the poem, but that generates the features we can see, especially the ungrammaticalities that are the matrix's variants and symptoms; the matrix is what stands in for "reality" when we discard our naive ideas about the poem's mimesis and recognize its semiosis. The hypogram, a term Riffaterre adapts from Ferdinand de Saussure, is the actualized feature of the poem that plays closest to the matrix, a text that can be extracted from the poem and laid out to give an idea of what the matrix might be.

What happens then in a body of poetry that seems not to run very hard or fast away from its matrices, where Riffaterre's multilevel process that takes place among the text of the poem, the hypogram, and the matrix is flattened and the poem seems about to break into showing forth its matrix—or even does so? Much lyric writing in the so-called plain style works in this way, dealing in aphorisms and other directly referential strategies that make Riffaterre's ungrammaticalities difficult to observe and hence make the interpretive movement—from mimesis to semiosis—hard to sustain. At the same time, this period sees some unusual productions outside the plain style that carry periphrasis to an astonishing extreme: Ann Lock's *Meditation of a Penitent Sinner* (1560), probably the earliest sonnet sequence in English, generates twenty-six sonnets from Psalm 51 in a feat of dilation. My students are fascinated when they measure a sonnet of Lock's alongside a corresponding verse from the Geneva Bible and use (for example) terms such as *matrix* and *hypogram* to account for what she might be doing.

One approach to this problem of plain-style poetry goes like this. If the poetry of George Gascoigne, George Turbervile, and their contemporaries simplifies

260   EXPERIMENTAL AND THE LOCAL

Riffaterre's relation of matrix to poem—pushes toward, without actually achieving, a one-to-one equivalence between the two so that the poem's unforgettable moments and climaxes occur when it gets closer to, not further from, its unspoken model—then Lock's *Meditation* tests and elaborates this semiotics to the other extreme, realizing its effects in the long detour that makes more than one hundred words from five or ten. The two sorts of poem, plain and periphrastic, seem intrinsically very much unlike each other, but it is more precise to say that they are equidistant from the sort of conventional lyric that Riffaterre describes well and to consider how and why they are tethered to authority in different but equally unconventional ways. The dynamic elements involved in this teaching episode are a range of poetry, an illuminating term from recent theory, and a group of students willing to put the two together. The ensuing discussion resembles a speculative literary history conceived by and for the students.

While the approach through experiment opens a poem descriptively, a complementary strategy invites students to consider how the events in the development of early modern lyric respond to historical and cultural change and how these events can be seen both in their local contexts and in what might be called multilocal or translocal perspective, as against corresponding events in other parts of the world. In some elementary way, this second approach is about demonstrating that England is a necessary but not a sufficient horizon for the literary study of English, that it is a local culture whose productions depend on the dialogic interventions of other equally local cultures.

Poetry tends to fashion new topographies out of the semantic and material commonplaces it receives from other kinds of literature and language: in doing so it reinstates literalness in the concept of topoi, positing a "here" of the poem, a verbal landscape, that corresponds in direct and oblique ways to the "here" of the society to which the poem is oriented. "We need, on the one hand," Raymond Williams writes,

> to acknowledge (and welcome) the specificity of these [poetic and affective] elements—specific feelings, specific rhythms—and yet to find ways of recognizing their specific sociality, thus preventing that extraction from social experience which is conceivable only when social experience itself has been categorically (and at root historically) reduced.   (133)

From this perspective, then, to read a lyric poem attentively is to account for the "structure of feeling" that mediates between the locality in which it is situated and the corresponding arrangement of commonplaces it makes of itself. To say that one is reconstructing the relations between these two localities is a pedagogical device, meant to give concrete form to the job of recovering the history around the poem while hewing closely to the poem's specificity and encouraging students to frame the questions that will indicate where they know too little about either history or poem; but this device also addresses

Roland Greene   261

something often overlooked about poetry, that it can be grounded in place almost as much as in time. Moreover, in poetry as in much else, the local perspective accomplishes more when it is put into relief by another local—or a multilocal or translocal—perspective, and a comparative approach in turn depends on an articulate sense of these localities. Therefore, some of my teaching is geared toward cultivating an awareness of locality (How does a local view become such? What is local about it? What are the limits of the locus it refers to? and so forth) and then setting one version of locality next to another, and another, to adjust the local toward the multilocal.

To realize this perspective, I might take a short poem and put it alongside a suggestive English or other prose text from the period, observing how the two texts elucidate each other, and then compare the same poem with a roughly similar poem from a contemporaneous Continental or American society. The purpose of this exercise is not simply to throw poems together to foreground their conventionality but also to inquire how each addresses its own locality or situatedness. If it is English, how is it English—and, for instance, how is it also European, Tudor, Elizabethan, Protestant, humanist, courtly, urban, absolutist, imperialist, Petrarchan, middle class, male gendered, heterosexual, generational, and otherwise socially and ideologically grounded? In other words, how does the poem record its own overlapping investments in the world, which amount to not only its literal place but also its locality? Having addressed such questions, it is just as important to turn the paradigm around—if for no other reason than that the poem not be seen in a tautological relation with the facts of its external history—and ask how the same specimen is not any of these things; whether and how it attempts to posit an identity for itself, its speaker, and audience that might be transnational, nonideological, beautiful, universal; and so forth. A cycle of readings would include, first, the opening sonnet of Petrarch's *Rime sparse*, then the first sonnet of Sidney's *Astrophil and Stella*, and then the first of Louise Labé's sonnets (1555), which crosses cultures by appearing in Italian:

> Non havria Ulysse o qualunqu'altro mai
> Più accorto fu, da quel divino aspetto
> Pien de gratie, d'honor et di rispetto
> Sperato qual i' sento affanni e guai.   (lines 1–4; 121)

> Not Ulysses or any other man
> However shrewd, longed for that divine face
> Full of grace, honor, and respect
> More than I feel desire for you, and woe.   (my trans.)

As critics sometimes observe, Labé's poem is not exactly successful as an Italian sonnet, but it has a great deal to say about the positioning of its persona (who will, of course, speak the rest of the sonnets in French). On the surface,

262   EXPERIMENTAL AND THE LOCAL

the poem is all about the second set of questions mentioned above: it seems to call attention extravagantly to its transcendence of specificity, its participation in a decidedly transnational current. But suppose we use these claims to empower the first set of questions. If Labé is self-consciously working in an unaccustomed language, how many of the rest of the poems likewise belong to a deliberately conventionalized procedure, a masquerade, a transculturation? What are those elements that correspond to the Italian language as "put on" here—elements of gender identity, ideology, affect, style, and so on? Questions such as these take us back to the "here" of Labé's sonnets, the locality from which this opening gesture represents a departure. Moreover, this poem authorizes us to ask of its counterpart from *Astrophil and Stella*, How in turn does Sidney's poem put on an Italianate, or a Continental, or another identity, and how is it identifiably English? Without assuming a literal change of language, how does Sidney use other "languages"—of aesthetics, class, politics, and sexuality—in the poem? In short, what is the verbal locality from which his poem is produced, and how does it relate to the social and other localities in which it is situated?

If these heuristic perspectives work in the classroom, they do so because they not only tell the story of a vital, international poetry but also invite the students' own contributions to that story. Most important, I think, the perspectives teach something about how scholarship is made, by unsettling and revising received stories, by inflecting narratives with theoretical and historical observation, by extending as well as honoring literary history.

Elizabethan Lyric Poetry and
Early Modern Print Culture

Arthur F. Marotti

The story of lyric poetry and print culture is connected to large-scale changes in the institution of "literature" and in the relationships among authors, patrons, publishers, and readers in early modern England. Lyrics changed from private and occasional verse normally circulated in manuscript to poems for restricted readerships to artifacts properly preserved in printed books available for purchase by all. Between the times of Thomas Wyatt and Andrew Marvell print culture developed alongside the older (but unusually persistent) manuscript culture, absorbing various sorts of texts, but, among the literary kinds, the lyric was one of the last genres to be naturalized in the world of the book (Marotti, *Manuscript*). Linguistic nationalism and a sense of a strong tradition of vernacular literature developed later in England than in France and Italy (Helgerson, *Self-Crowned Laureates, Forms*), where, for example, Petrarchan poetry and its imitations were well established in print culture and lyric poetry had a cultural centrality it did not have in England until well into the seventeenth century (Kennedy, "Petrarchan Audiences"; Marotti, *Manuscript* 209).

Partly because of the "stigma of print" (Saunders), many poets of the sixteenth and early seventeenth centuries feared social debasement resulting from exposure of their lyric "toys" in the commercial, democratizing environment of print. They also realized that, in exposing their love poetry to public view, they risked violating the moral and intellectual norms of a Protestant humanism suspicious of or hostile to secular lyric verse, writing viewed as the product of idleness and (possibly) illicit desire. Poets usually regarded their lyrics as ephemera, as recreational or socially occasional acts separate from their more serious endeavors: Wyatt was a diplomat and government servant under Henry VIII, Philip Sidney a political activist and soldier, John Donne (for part of his career) a secretary to Queen Elizabeth's lord keeper. Each withheld his lyrics from print.

There developed, nevertheless, a market for printed poetry, partly because it provided vicarious access to such elite social and intellectual worlds as the court, the Inns of Court, the university, and the great houses of the aristocracy. Furthermore, some writers of verse—such as George Gascoigne, Nicholas Breton, Samuel Daniel, and Michael Drayton—turned to print as a means of securing or reinforcing artistic and social patronage. So there were good reasons for many publishers and some authors to print lyrics. But as lyrics began regularly to appear in print, especially the contemporary and posthumous work of writers with high social and literary prestige, the sociocultural status of lyric composition was elevated, and the roles of author, publisher, and reader in the emerging institution of literature were given their modern definitions. In print, authors assumed both literary and cultural authority, publishers both responded

264   POETRY AND EARLY MODERN PRINT CULTURE

to and shaped public tastes, and readers changed from being the active partic-
ipants they were in the manuscript system of literary transmission (in which
they sometimes deliberately changed texts and composed answer poems or
their own independent verse [Marotti, *Manuscript* 135–208]) to being con-
noisseur consumers of fixed, printed texts in a capitalist economy.

In England, the history of the incorporation of lyric poetry into print culture
is marked by a number of moments: the publication of the first of the impor-
tant late Tudor poetical anthologies by Richard Tottel in 1557; the posthumous
editions of Sidney's work in the 1590s, culminating in the Folio of 1598; the
1616 printing of Ben Jonson's self-monumentalizing folio *Workes* (which con-
tains two collections of poems, *Epigrammes* and *The Forrest*) (Loewenstein,
"Script"; Newton, "Jonson"); and the virtually simultaneous posthumous pub-
lication of Donne's *Poems* and George Herbert's *The Temple* in 1633. There
were, of course, other landmark publications—such as Gascoigne's *An Hun-
dreth Sundrie Flowres* in 1573 (and its revision, *The Posies* [1575]), a collection
including his lyric verse; Edmund Spenser's *The Shepheardes Calender* (1579),
which Paul Alpers has discussed as a major "lyric" collection ("Pastoral"); the
bardolatrous publication of the First Folio of Shakespeare's plays in 1623 (Mar-
cus, *Puzzling* 1–50); and the outpouring of editions of lyric poetry in the 1640s
and 1650s by the publisher Humphrey Moseley, including the work of Francis
Quarles (1642), John Milton (1645), Edmund Waller (1645), Richard Crashaw
(1646 and 1648), James Shirley (1646), John Suckling (1646, 1648, and 1658),
Abraham Cowley (1647 and 1655), Thomas Carew (1651), William Cartwright
(1651), and Thomas Stanley (1651) (Marotti, *Manuscript* 259–65). All these
and the publication and republication of the works of the father of English
poetry, Chaucer, were significant (Miskimin), but Tottel's poetical miscellany,
the first editions of Sidney's individual and collected works, Jonson's mid-
career collection, and Donne's and Herbert's posthumous editions each had a
major impact on the status of lyric poetry in print, elevating the sociocultural
status of the poet and installing lyric verse securely in print culture within the
context of the establishment of the modern institution of literature.

Tottel's collection, entitled (to highlight its highest-born poet) *Songes and
Sonettes, Written by the Right Honorable Lorde Henry Haward Late Earle of
Surrey, and Other*, created the fashion for poetic anthologies in the latter part
of the sixteenth century, going through at least nine editions in thirty years and
leading to the publication (and republication) of such collections as *The Par-
adise of Dainty Devices* (1576), *A Gorgeous Gallery of Gallant Inventions*
(1578), *Brittons Bowre of Delights* (1591), *The Phoenix Nest* (1593), *The Arbor
of Amorous Devices* (1597), *England's Helicon* (1600), and *A Poetical Rhap-
sody* (1602) (Pomeroy). Tottel not only disseminated what had been the pri-
vately circulated lyrics of Wyatt, Surrey, and others from the early Tudor period
but also stimulated publishers' desire and public demand for courtly and
socially elite lyrics, which were redirected, with or without the cooperation of
their authors, from manuscript circulation into print.

It was difficult, however, for individual authors such as Barnabe Googe, George Turbervile, and Gascoigne, who were defensive about the publication of their verse, to benefit socially or economically from printing their lyrics. It was really the example of Sidney, a poet celebrated as a Protestant martyr and cultural icon (Baker-Smith), that authorized many other poets to print their verse. The posthumous publication of his *Astrophil and Stella* (1591 and 1592) inaugurated the late Elizabethan sonnet fashion, leading to the publication of sonnet sequences by Daniel, Spenser, Barnabe Barnes, Drayton, William Shakespeare, and others, including Sidney's neice, Mary Wroth, who appended *Pamphilia to Amphilanthus* to the printed edition (the first part) of her imitative prose romance *Urania* (1621). The *Astrophil and Stella* quartos, along with the 1590 and 1593 editions of the *Arcadia* and the outpouring of commemorative poetry for the deceased poet, even affected two of the important late Elizabethan poetical miscellanies: *The Phoenix Nest* (1593) memorializes Sidney by beginning with prose and poetry associated with the poet and his circle, and Francis Davison, the editor of *A Poetical Rhapsody* (1602), associates his collection with the Sidney legend and example (Marotti, *Manuscript* 234–35). The 1598 Sidney folio (coincident with Thomas Speght's new folio edition of Chaucer) encouraged the printing of (usually posthumous) collected editions of other Elizabethan and later authors—Daniel's in 1601, Spenser's in 1611, and Jonson's in 1616. Printed in the same year as the collected works of King James, Jonson's *Workes*, a testimony to the "bibliographic ego" (Loewenstein, "Script" 101), not only printed the first two of the three collections of that author's poems but also set the precedent for gathering play texts, hitherto published only in impermanent quarto pamphlets, in a prestigious, monumentalizing edition—no doubt encouraging the production of the collected Shakespeare plays of 1623.

There was something of a drop-off in the rate of publication and republication of poetic anthologies and of editions of single-author lyric collections in the Jacobean period, and the manuscript system of circulation of lyric verse took on a new vitality in the period from the 1620s through the 1640s (Hobbs; Woudhuysen; Marotti, *Manuscript*). With the publication of posthumous editions of Donne's and Herbert's poetry in 1633 (and after), however, new impetus was given to the production of printed collections of lyric verse; a new market was created for both secular and religious lyrics that the enterprising royalist publisher Humphrey Moseley readily expoited. Certainly by the middle of the seventeenth century, collections of lyric verse were naturalized in print, and the old stigma associated with exposure in that democratizing medium was largely dispelled—especially when, during the interregnum, anthologies such as *Wits Recreations* (1640), *The Harmony of the Muses* (1654), and *Parnassus Biceps* (1656), as well as individual poets' collections, could proclaim a kind of fashionable elitist style in the midst of royalist political disempowerment (Potter; Marotti, *Manuscript*). Though one must look to the period of Milton, Pope, and Samuel Johnson to perceive the completion of

266   POETRY AND EARLY MODERN PRINT CULTURE

some of the changes taking place in the literary institution between Tottel and the mid-seventeenth century (Kernan, *Printing Technology*; Lindenbaum), the association of poetry and literature in general with print culture in the early modern period inevitably produced them. Poets gradually answered less to patrons than to familiar or general readerships they envisioned for their printed works and even assumed the kind of sociocultural authority their economic or social status might earlier have made impossible.

Several bibliographical elements of print publication deserve attention as part of this historical development of lyric poetry in book culture. First, the size and length of published poetic collections dramatically affected both their survivability and their sociocultural prestige (Febvre and Martin 89; Marotti, *Manuscript* 286–90). A thirty- to forty-page poetic "pamphlet," like a play quarto, was fundamentally an ephemeral publication—sold unbound, often destroyed through repeated handling, and therefore usually lost: hence so few copies survive of works such as the 1591 Newman edition of Sidney's *Astrophil and Stella* or the 1609 quarto of Shakespeare's *Sonnets* (Birrell). A lengthy octavo or quarto book, however, would have been bound and kept in a personal library as a text to be preserved, and so the 1633 Donne or the 1645 *Poems of Mr. John Milton* had considerably higher prestige than thinner poetic texts. The most prestigious publication format, however, was the folio—the format reserved for major editions of classical authors, for collections of sermons, for encyclopedias, and so on (Chartier, *Cultural Uses* 181). The example of the sixteenth-century editions of Chaucer was emulated by publishers in producing the folio editions of Sidney, Daniel, Jonson, Shakespeare, Francis Beaumont and John Fletcher, and others.

Though poetry through most of the sixteenth century was printed in black-letter type, a font that continued to be used for popular ballads through the seventeenth century since "black letter literacy" was the most common kind on the popular level (Thomas, "Meaning"), by the 1590s printers had shifted to roman and italic fonts for their printed editions of poetry, which signaled humanist intellectual and social elitism (Marotti, *Manuscript* 282–84). Analogously, the architectural frontispieces for title pages of some books (e.g., Gascoigne's *Posies* of 1575) monumentalized and lent intellectual and social prestige to them (Corbett and Lightbown). And the portraits of authors affixed to editions of their poetry (e.g., the image of the earl of Surrey in Tottel, of Gascoigne in the 1587 posthumous collection of his works, of the youthful Donne in the 1635 edition of his poems, and of the austerely religious George Herbert found in the 1670 edition of *The Temple*) idealized authorship and portrayed authors as celebrities (Braudy 264–312; Marotti, *Manuscript* 240).

Other front matter of printed books records the actual and attempted negotiations among authors (and their social networks), publishers or printers, patrons, and readers: dedications, epistles (by authors or publishers) to readers and to patrons, and commendatory or elegiac verse. These material features of print publication chart the development of poetry from the older system of patronage and dependency within a strictly hierarchical social system to its incorporation in a self-authorizing literary institution set within the socioeconomic context of a modern capitalist economy (Marotti, *Manuscript* 291–324). In such an environment, finally, poems could be treated as art objects, and the social identity of the poet could emerge in its modern form.

NOTES ON CONTRIBUTORS

Judith H. Anderson, professor of English at Indiana University, has written numerous articles and a book, *The Growth of a Personal Voice: Piers Plowman and* The Faerie Queene (1976), on Spenser. She is also an editor of *Spenser's Life and the Subject of Biography* (1996) and of Donaldson's translation of *Piers Plowman* (1990) and the author of *Biographical Truth: The Representation of Historical Persons in Tudor-Stuart Writing* (1984) and *Words That Matter: Linguistic Perception in Renaissance English* (1996).

Georgia E. Brown is fellow and director of Studies in English at Queen's College, Cambridge University. Her forthcoming study of the cultural logic of the 1590s, *The Generation of Shame*, concentrates on three genres characteristic of the period—the epyllion, the fictional verse epistle, and the sonnet sequence. She has published on Marlowe, and has essays on Spenser and on Queen Elizabeth forthcoming.

Sheila T. Cavanagh, associate professor of English and associate faculty in Women's Studies at Emory University, is the author of *Wanton Eyes and Chaste Desires: Female Sexuality in* The Faerie Queene (1994) as well as of articles on Spenser and other early modern authors. She is now revising a book-length manuscript entitled *Cherished Torment: The Emotional Geography of Lady Mary Wroth's* Urania.

Patrick Cheney, professor of English and comparative literature at Pennsylvania State University, is an editor of *Comparative Literature Studies*, the author of *Spenser's Famous Flight: A Renaissance Idea of a Literary Career* (1993) and *Marlowe's Counterfeit Profession: Ovid, Spenser, Counter-nationhood* (1997), and coeditor of *Worldmaking Spenser: Explorations in the Early Modern Age* (1999). He is currently president of the International Spenser Society.

Mario DiGangi, assistant professor of English at Lehman College, CUNY, is the author of *The Homoerotics of Early Modern Drama* (1997) and of articles on gender and sexuality in Renaissance culture.

Heather Dubrow is Tighe-Evans Professor (and John Bascom Professor) at the University of Wisconsin, Madison. She is the author of five books on Renaissance topics, the most recent being *Shakespeare and Domestic Loss: Forms of Deprivation, Mourning, and Recuperation* (1999). Her other publications include a coedited collection of essays, a chapbook of poetry, and articles on teaching.

Susan M. Felch, associate professor of English at Calvin College, is the editor of *The Collected Works of Anne Vaughan Lock* (1999) and the author of various articles on sixteenth-century English writers.

Elizabeth Fowler is associate professor of English at the University of Virginia. Her work on the category of the person has appeared in *Representations, Speculum, Spenser Studies*, and several edited volumes. She is coeditor, with Roland Greene, of *The Project of Prose in Early Modern Europe and the New World* (1997) and the author of *The Human Figure in Words: The Arguments of Person in Chaucer, Langland, Skelton, and Spenser* (forthcoming).

270   NOTES ON CONTRIBUTORS

Patricia Fumerton, professor of English at the University of California, Santa Barbara, is the author of *Cultural Aesthetics: Renaissance Literature and the Practice of Social Ornament* (1991) and coeditor of *Renaissance Culture and the Everyday* (1999). She is working on a book-length study of spatial mobility, popular culture, and "low" subjectivity, *Spacious Voices / Vagrant Subjects in Early Modern England*.

Roland Greene, professor of comparative literature and English at the University of Oregon, is the author of *Unrequited Conquests: Love and Empire in the Colonial Americas* (1999) and *Post-Petrarchism: Origins and Innovations of the Western Lyric Sequence* (1991) and, with Elizabeth Fowler, coeditor of *The Project of Prose in Early Modern Europe and the New World* (1997). He is writing a book on early modern world making.

Margaret P. Hannay, professor of English at Siena College, has coedited, with Noel J. Kinnamon and Michael G. Brennan, *The Collected Works of Mary Sidney Herbert, Countess of Pembroke* (1998). She is the author of *Philip's Phoenix: Mary Sidney, Countess of Pembroke* (1990) and editor of *Silent but for the Word: Tudor Women as Patrons, Translators, and Writers of Religious Works* (1985). She is coeditor, with Susanne Woods, of *Teaching Tudor and Stuart Women Writers*, forthcoming from the Modern Language Association.

Jane Hedley is K. Laurence Stapleton Professor of English at Bryn Mawr College. She is the author of *Power in Verse* (1988), a study of Renaissance lyric, and has also published on Gascoigne, Sidney and Greville, and Shakespeare's *Sonnets*. Her current research and writing deal with American poetry since 1950; an article on gender and politics in Sexton, Rich, and Lowell is forthcoming in *Raritan*.

Richard Helgerson, professor of English at the University of California, Santa Barbara, is the author of *The Elizabethan Prodigals* (1976) and *Self-Crowned Laureates* (1983). His *Forms of Nationhood* (1992) was awarded the British Council Prize in the Humanities and the James Russell Lowell Prize of the Modern Language Association.

Diana E. Henderson is associate professor of literature at MIT. She is the author of *Passion Made Public: Elizabethan Lyric, Gender, and Performance* (1995) as well as of articles on works by Joyce, Spenser, and Heywood. Recent essays have appeared in *Shakespeare: The Movie* (1997), *A New History of Early English Drama* (1997), and *Dwelling in Possibility: Women Poets and Critics on Poetry* (1997). Her current book project is entitled *Uneasy Collaborations: Transforming Shakespeare across Time and Media*.

Margo Hendricks teaches at the University of California, Santa Cruz. She has published articles on Shakespeare, Aphra Behn, and Marlowe and has recently completed a book on Behn and race.

Peter C. Herman, associate professor of English at San Diego State University, is the author of *Squitter-Wits and Muse-Haters: Sidney, Spenser, Milton, and Renaissance Antipoetic Sentiment* (1996) as well as the editor of *Rethinking the Henrician Era: Essays on Early Tudor Texts and Contexts* (1994), *Opening the Borders: Inclusivity in Early Modern Studies: Essays in Honor of James V. Mirollo* (1999), and the forthcoming *Reading Monarchs Writing: The Poetry of Henry VIII, Mary Stuart, Elizabeth I, and James VI/I*. He is currently working on early modern historiography.

NOTES ON CONTRIBUTORS 271

Clark Hulse is professor of English and art history at the University of Illinois, Chicago. He is the author of *The Rule of Art: Literature and Painting in the Renaissance* (1990), *Metaphoric Verse: The Elizabethan Minor Epic* (1981), and articles about sixteenth-century literature and visual culture. He is coeditor of *Early Modern Visual Culture: Representation, Race, and Empire in Renaissance England* (2000). The recipient of NEH, Guggenheim, and British Academy fellowships, he is currently working on a study of literature and portraiture in the age of Henry VIII.

David Scott Kastan, professor of English and comparative literature at Columbia University, has published widely on Renaissance literature; his most recent book is *Shakespeare after Theory* (1999). He is general editor of the Arden Shakespeare and is editing *1 Henry IV* for that series.

William J. Kennedy, professor of comparative literature at Cornell University, is the author of *Rhetorical Norms in Renaissance Literature* (1978), *Jacopo Sannazaro and the Uses of Pastoral* (1983), and *Authorizing Petrarch* (1994). He is completing *The Site of Petrarchism*, a study of early modern national sentiment in European poetry.

John N. King, author of *English Reformation Literature: The Tudor Origins of the Protestant Tradition* (1982), *Tudor Royal Iconography: Literature and Art in an Age of Religious Crisis* (1989), *Spenser's Poetry and the Reformation Tradition* (1990), and *Milton and Religious Controversy: Satire and Polemic in* Paradise Lost (2000), is professor of English literature at Ohio State University. He serves as coeditor of *Literature and History*, literature editor of *Reformation*, and advisory board member for the British Academy project to edit John Foxe's *Acts and Monuments of These Latter and Perilous Days*.

Arthur F. Kinney, editor of the journal *English Literary Renaissance*, is Thomas W. Copeland Professor of Literary History and director of the Massachusetts Center for Renaissance Studies at the University of Massachusetts, Amherst, and adjunct professor of English at New York University. His books include *Humanist Poetics* (1986), *Continental Humanist Poetics* (1989), and *John Skelton: The Priest as Poet* (1987). He has edited the plays of Marlowe and others for Blackwell (1999) and the *Cambridge Companion to English Literature, 1500–1600* (2000).

Clare R. Kinney, associate professor of English at the University of Virginia, is the author of *Strategies of Poetic Narrative: Chaucer, Spenser, Milton, Eliot* (1992) and articles on the *Gawain* poet, Spenser, Shakespeare, Philip Sidney, Mary Wroth, Marlowe, and the Renaissance reception of Chaucer. She is working on a study of gendered representation and the metamorphoses of Petrarchism in the romances of Sidney, Shakespeare, and Wroth.

Theresa M. Krier teaches at the University of Notre Dame and writes on ancient, late Medieval, and Renaissance poetry. She is the author of *Gazing on Secret Sights: Spenser, Classical Imitation, and the Decorums of Vision* (1990) and editor of *Refiguring Chaucer in the Renaissance* (1998).

Roger Kuin, professor of English at York University, Toronto, is the editor of Robert Langham's *Letter* on the Kenilworth entertainments for Elizabeth I and the author of *Chamber Music: Elizabethan Sonnet-Sequences and the Pleasures of Criticism* (1998); his articles include studies of Spenser's *Amoretti* and Philip Sidney's New World connections.

272 NOTES ON CONTRIBUTORS

Mary Ellen Lamb, professor of English at Southern Illinois University, Carbondale, is the author of *Gender and Authorship in the Sidney Circle* (1990) and numerous essays on early modern women and on Shakespeare. Her essay for this volume is part of a book project with the working title *Engendering Narrative in Sidney, Spenser, Shakespeare*.

Julia Reinhard Lupton teaches English and comparative literature at the University of California, Irvine. She is the coauthor, with Kenneth Reinhard, of *After Oedipus: Shakespeare in Psychoanalysis* (1993) and is the author of *Afterlives of the Saints: Hagiography, Typology, and Renaissance Literature* (1996). In 1997 she founded Humanities Out There, an outreach program between the University of California at Irvine's School of Humanities and local schools that encourages students from all backgrounds to integrate the humanities into their studies for a lifetime of learning.

Arthur F. Marotti is professor of English at Wayne State University and editor of *Catholicism and Anti-Catholicism in Early Modern English Texts* (1999). He is the author of *John Donne, Coterie Poet* (1986) and *Manuscript, Print, and the English Renaissance Lyric* (1995) as well as editor of *Critical Essays on John Donne* (1994) and coeditor of *Reading with a Difference: Gender, Race, and Cultural Identity* (1993) and *Texts and Cultural Change in Early Modern England* (1997).

Steven W. May teaches English literature at Georgetown College. His research interests include the Elizabethan court, editing, and Renaissance texts in manuscript. The author of *The Elizabethan Courtier Poets* (1991), he has edited a number of Elizabethan manuscript texts and is completing work on the *Bibliography and First-Line Index of English Verse, 1559–1603*.

Caroline McManus is associate professor of English at California State University, Los Angeles. Her essay on the depiction of female courtiers in portraits of Elizabeth I appeared in the *Ben Jonson Journal*, and her essay on female piety in book 1 of *The Faerie Queene* appeared in the *Huntington Library Quarterly*. She is working on a book entitled *Spenser's* Faerie Queene *and the Fashioning of Female Readers*.

John W. Moore, Jr., prepares the annual "Spenser Bibliography Update" for *Spenser Newsletter* and is editor of the *Annotated Spenser Bibliography*, in progress.

Janel Mueller is William Rainey Harper Professor of English and Humanities and the dean of the Division of the Humanities at the University of Chicago. She has published on earlier English women authors, including Margery Kempe, Katherine Parr, Elizabeth I, and Aemilia Lanyer, and is coeditor, with Leah Marcus and Mary Beth Rose, of *Elizabeth I: Collected Works* (2000).

Anne Lake Prescott is Helen Goodhart Altschul Professor of English at Barnard College. The author of *French Poets and the English Renaissance* (1978) and *Imagining Rabelais in Renaissance England* (1998), she is coeditor, with Hugh Maclean, of the Norton edition of Spenser's poetry (1993) and, with Thomas Roche and William Oram, of *Spenser Studies*. Her current interests include giants and the figure of David in the Renaissance.

Stephen Ratcliffe, chair of the English department at Mills College, is the author of *Listening to Reading*, a study of sound, shape, and meaning in contemporary "experimental" poetry (2000), and *Campion: On Song* (1981). His current project is a study of

NOTES ON CONTRIBUTORS 273

offstage action in *Hamlet*. His recent books of poetry include *Idea's Mirror* (1999), *Mallarmé: poem in prose* (1998), *Sculpture* (1996), *Present Tense* (1995), *Selected Letters* (1992), and *spaces in the light said to be where one comes from* (1992).

Louise Schleiner teaches at Washington State University, where she has set up a Web page with the syllabus for her seventeenth-century literature class in spring 1999. Her recent books are *Tudor and Stuart Women Writers* (1994) and *Cultural Semiotics, Spenser, and the Captive Woman* (1995). Her article "Voice, Ideology, and Gendered Subjects: The Case of *As You Like It* and *Two Gentlemen*," theorizing possible future directions in the profession, is in the millennium issue of *Shakespeare Quarterly* (50.3).

Michael Schoenfeldt, professor of English at the University of Michigan, Ann Arbor, is the author of *Prayer and Power: George Herbert and Renaissance Courtship* (1991) and *Bodies and Selves in Early Modern England: Physiology and Interiority in Spenser, Shakespeare, Herbert, and Milton* (1999).

Debora Shuger, professor of English at the University of California, Los Angeles, is the author of *Sacred Rhetoric* (1988), *Habits of Thought in the English Renaissance* (1990), *The Renaissance Bible* (1994), and numerous essays.

John Webster's use of portfolios to teach literature developed from eight years of directing the University of Washington's First-Year Writing Program. Since then his research has increasingly centered on pedagogy. Now a Pew Scholar in the Teaching Academy newly inaugurated by the Carnegie Foundation for the Advancement of Teaching, Webster is at work on a project to document current classroom practice in the teaching of early modern literature.

Susanne Woods is provost of Wheaton College, MA. She is the author of *Natural Emphasis: English Versification from Chaucer to Dryden* (1985) and *Lanyer: A Renaissance Woman Poet* (1999) and coeditor, with Elizabeth H. Hageman, of the Oxford series Women Writers in English, 1350–1850. She has taught at the University of Hawaii, at Franklin and Marshall College, and at Brown University, where in 1988 she founded the Brown University Women Writers Project. She is coeditor, with Margaret Hannay, of *Teaching Tudor and Stuart Women Writers*, forthcoming from the Modern Language Association.

SURVEY PARTICIPANTS

Judith H. Anderson, *Indiana University*
Dana E. Aspinall, *University of Connecticut*
John Bernard, *University of Houston*
Bruce Boehrer, *Florida State University*
F. W. Brownlow, *Mount Holyoke College*
Jonathan W. Crewe, *Dartmouth College*
John T. Day, *St. Olaf College*
Mario DiGangi, *Lehman College, CUNY*
Heather Dubrow, *University of Wisconsin, Madison*
Susan M. Felch, *Calvin College*
Elizabeth Fowler, *University of Virginia*
Raymond J. Frontain, *University of Central Arkansas*
David Galbraith, *University of Toronto*
Sayre N. Greenfield, *University of Pittsburgh, Greensburg*
Jane Hedley, *Bryn Mawr College*
Peter C. Herman, *San Diego State University*
Peggy Huey, *University of Alabama*
Carol Kaske, *Cornell University*
Suzanne Keen, *Washington and Lee University*
Arthur F. Kinney, *University of Massachusetts*
Clare R. Kinney, *University of Virginia*
George Klawitter, *St. Edward's University*
Jeff Knapp, *University of California, Berkeley*
Theresa M. Krier, *University of Notre Dame*
Roger Kuin, *York University*
Mary Ellen Lamb, *Southern Illinois University*
Julia Reinhard Lupton, *University of California, Irvine*
Richard Mallette, *Lake Forest College*
Louis Martz, *Yale University*
Steven W. May, *Georgetown College*
Caroline McManus, *California State University, Los Angeles*
Jerry Leath Mills, *University of North Carolina, Chapel Hill*
Karen Newman, *Brown University*
Theresa di Pasquale, *Whitman College*
Lawrence F. Rhu, *University of South Carolina*
Louise Schleiner, *Washington State University*
William A. Sessions, *Georgia State University*
Anne Shaver, *Denison University*
Stanley Stewart, *University of California, Riverside*
Emily E. Stockard, *Florida Atlantic University*
Karoline Szatek, *Bentley College*
William Tate, *University of North Carolina, Chapel Hill*
Edward Tayler, *Columbia University*

276 SURVEY PARTICIPANTS

Paul J. Voss, *Georgia State University*
J. Christopher Warner, *Kent State University*
John Webster, *University of Washington*
Susanne Woods, *Wheaton College, MA*

WORKS CITED

Aers, David. "Reflections on Current Histories of the Subject." *Literature and History* 3rd ser. 2.2 (1991): 20–34.

——. "A Whisper in the Ear of Early Modernists; or, Reflections on Literary Critics Writing the 'History of the Subject.'" *Culture and History, 1350–1600: Essays on English Communities, Identities, and Writing*. Ed. Aers. Detroit: Wayne State UP, 1992. 177–202.

Alexander, Nigel, ed. *Elizabethan Narrative Verse*. Stratford-upon-Avon Lib. 3. London: Arnold, 1967.

Allen, Don Cameron. *Mysteriously Meant: The Rediscovery of Pagan Symbolism and Allegorical Interpretation in the Renaissance*. Baltimore: Johns Hopkins P, 1970.

Allen, Michael J. B. Icastes: *Marsilio Ficino's Interpretation of Plato's* Sophist *(Five Studies and a Critical Edition with Translation)*. Berkeley: U of California P, 1984.

——. *Marsilio Ficino and the Phaedran Charioteer*. Berkeley: U of California P, 1981.

——, ed. and trans. *Marsilio Ficino: The* Philebus *Commentary*. Berkeley: U of California P, 1975.

——. *The Platonism of Marsilio Ficino: A Study of His* Phaedrus *Commentary, Its Sources, and Genesis*. Berkeley: U of California P, 1984.

——. *Plato's Third Eye: Studies in Marsilio Ficino's Metaphysics and Its Sources*. Aldershot, Eng.: Variorum, 1994.

Allott, Robert. *Englands Parnassus; or, The Choysest Flowers of Our Moderne Poets, with Their Poeticall Comparisons*. 1600. Ed. Charles Crawford. Oxford: Clarendon, 1913.

Alpers, Paul J., ed. *Edmund Spenser: A Critical Anthology*. Penguin Critical Anthologies. Harmondsworth: Penguin, 1979.

——, ed. *Elizabethan Poetry: Modern Essays in Criticism*. London: Oxford UP, 1967.

——. "Pastoral and the Domain of Lyric in Spenser's *Shepheardes Calender*." *Representations* 12 (1985): 83–100.

——. "The Poet's Poet." *Spenser Encyclopedia*. 551.

——. "Spenser's Late Pastorals." *ELH* 56 (1989): 797–817.

——. *What Is Pastoral?* Chicago: U of Chicago P, 1996.

Altieri, Charles. "Rhetoric, Rhetoricity, and the Sonnet as Performance." *Tennessee Studies in Literature* 25 (1980): 1–23.

Altieri, Joanne. "*Hero and Leander*: Sensible Myth and Lyric Subjectivity." *John Donne Journal* 8 (1989): 151–66.

Alwes, Derek B. "John Lyly (between 1552 and 1554–November 1606)." *Dictionary of Literary Biography*. 167: 102–15.

Alwes, Derek B., and William L. Godshalk, eds. "Recent Studies in Sidney (1978–86)." Kinney, *Sidney* 242–63.

278 WORKS CITED

Anderson, Benedict. *Imagined Communities: Reflections on the Origins and Spread of Nationalism*. London: Verso, 1983.

Anderson, Douglas. "'Unto My Selfe Alone': Spenser's Plenary *Epithalamion*." *Spenser Studies: A Renaissance Poetry Annual* 5 (1985): 149–66.

Anderson, Judith H. *Words That Matter: Linguistic Perception in Renaissance English*. Stanford: Stanford UP, 1996.

Anderson, Judith H., Donald Cheney, and David A. Richardson, eds. *Spenser's Life and the Subject of Biography*. Mass. Studies in Early Modern Culture. Amherst: U of Massachusetts P, 1996.

Anderson, Marjorie, and Blanche Colton Williams. *Old English Handbook*. Cambridge: Riverside, 1935.

Anderson, Perry. *Lineages of the Absolutist State*. London: NLB; Atlantic Highlands: Humanities, 1974.

Appiah, Kwame Anthony. "Race." *Critical Terms for Literary Study*. Ed. Frank Lentricchia and Thomas McLaughlin. Chicago: U of Chicago P, 1990. 274–87.

Attridge, Derek. *Well-Weighed Syllables: Elizabethan Verse in Classical Metres*. Cambridge: Cambridge UP, 1974.

Auden, W. H., ed. *Selected Songs of Thomas Campion*. Boston: Godine, 1972.

Ault, Norman, ed. *Elizabethan Lyrics from the Original Texts*. London: Faber, 1925.

Bahti, Timothy. *Ends of the Lyric: Direction and Consequence in Western Poetry*. Baltimore: Johns Hopkins UP, 1996.

Bakeless, John. *The Tragicall History of Christopher Marlowe*. 1942. 2 vols. Hamden: Archon, 1964.

Baker, David J. *Between Nations: Shakespeare, Spenser, Marvell, and the Question of Britain*. Stanford: Stanford UP, 1997.

Baker-Smith, Dominic. "'Great Expectation': Sidney's Death and the Poets." van Dorsten, Kinney, and Baker-Smith 83–103.

Baldwin, William. *The Mirror for Magistrates*. Ed. Lily B. Campbell. Cambridge: Cambridge UP, 1938.

Banton, Michael. *The Idea of Race*. London: Tavistock, 1977.

Barber, C. L. "An Essay on the Sonnets." Alpers, *Elizabethan Poetry* 299–320.

Barbour, Reid. "Thomas Nashe (November 1567–1601?)." *Dictionary of Literary Biography*. 167: 142–59.

Barish, Jonas. *The Antitheatrical Prejudice*. Berkeley: U of California P, 1981.

Barkan, Leonard. *The Gods Made Flesh: Metamorphosis and the Pursuit of Paganism*. New Haven: Yale UP, 1986.

———. *Transuming Passion: Ganymede and the Erotics of Humanism*. Stanford: Stanford UP, 1991.

Barker, Francis. *The Tremulous Private Body: Essays on Subjection*. Ann Arbor: U of Michigan P, 1995.

Barnfield, Richard. *Cynthia, with Certain Sonnets, and the Legend of Cassanora*. *Richard Barnfield: The Complete Poems*. Ed. George Klawitter. Selinsgrove: Susquehanna UP, 1990. 113–47.

Bartels, Emily C., ed. *Critical Essays on Christopher Marlowe*. New York: Hall; London: Prentice, 1996.

WORKS CITED 279

Barthes, Roland. *Systeme de la mode*. Paris: Seuil, 1967.

——. *S/Z*. Paris: Seuil, 1970.

Bartlett, John, ed. *New and Complete Concordance to Shakespeare*. London, 1894.

Bate, Jonathan. *The Genius of Shakespeare*. London: Picador, 1997.

——. *Shakespeare and Ovid*. Oxford: Clarendon, 1993.

Bates, Catherine. "The Politics of Spenser's *Amoretti*." *Criticism* 33 (1991): 73–89.

——. *The Rhetoric of Courtship in Elizabethan Language and Literature*. Cambridge: Cambridge UP, 1992.

——, ed. *Sir Philip Sidney: Selected Poems*. Harmondsworth: Penguin, 1994.

Beal, Peter. "Notions in Garrison: The Seventeenth-Century Commonplace Book." *New Ways of Looking at Old Texts: Papers of the RETS, 1985–1991*. Ed. W. Speed Hill. Medieval and Renaissance Texts and Studies. Binghamton: Center for Medieval and Early Renaissance Studies. 1993. 131–47.

Beebee, Thomas O. *The Ideology of Genre: A Comparative Study of Generic Instability*. University Park: Pennsylvania State UP, 1994.

Beilin, Elaine, ed. *The Examinations of Anne Askew*. Oxford: Oxford UP, 1996.

——. *Redeeming Eve: Women Writers of the English Renaissance*. Princeton: Princeton UP, 1987.

Bellamy, Elizabeth J. *Translations of Power: Narcissus and the Unconscious in Epic History*. Ithaca: Cornell UP, 1992.

Belsey, Catherine. "Love as Trompe-l'Oeil: Taxonomies of Desire in *Venus and Adonis*." *Shakespeare Quarterly* 46 (1995): 257–76.

Bembo, Pietro. *Prose e rime*. Ed. Carlo Dionisotti. 2nd ed. Turin: UTET, 1966.

Bennett, Paula. "Recent Studies in Greville." *English Literary Renaissance* 2 (1972): 376–82.

Benson, Larry D. *A Glossarial Concordance to* The Riverside Chaucer. 2 vols. Garland Reference Lib. of the Humanities, 1699. New York: Garland, 1993.

Berger, Harry, Jr. "Pico and Neoplatonist Idealism: Philosophy as Escape." *Second World and Green World: Studies in Renaissance Fiction-Making*. Introd. John Patrick Lynch. Berkeley: U of California P, 1988. 189–228.

——. *Revisionary Play: Studies in the Spenserian Dynamics*. Berkeley: U of California P, 1988.

——, ed. *Spenser: A Collection of Critical Essays*. Twentieth Century Views. Englewood Cliffs: Prentice, 1968.

——. "Spenser's *Prothalamion*: An Interpretation." *Essays in Criticism* 15 (1965): 363–79. Rpt. in Hamilton, *Essential Articles* 509–23.

Bergeron, David M., and Geraldo U. de Sousa. *Shakespeare: A Study and Research Guide*. 3rd ed. Lawrence: UP of Kansas, 1995.

Bernard, John. *Ceremonies of Innocence: Pastoralism in the Poetry of Edmund Spenser*. Cambridge: Cambridge UP, 1989.

——. "Recent Studies in Renaissance Pastoral." *English Literary Renaissance* 26 (1996): 356–84.

Bernstein, Charles. *A Poetics*. Cambridge: Harvard UP, 1992.

Berry, Cicely. *Voice and the Actor*. New York: Collier, 1973.

280 WORKS CITED

Berry, Philippa. *Of Chastity and Power*. London: Routledge, 1989.

Bevington, David, ed. *The Complete Works of Shakespeare*. 4th ed. New York: Longman, 1997.

Beza, Theodore. *Abraham sacrifiant*. Introd. C. R. Frankish. New York: Johnson Rpts., 1969.

———. *A Booke of Christian Questions*. Trans. Arthur Golding. London, 1572.

———. *The Psalmes of David, Truly Opened and Explaned by Paraphrasis, According to the Right Sense of Everie Psalme*. Trans. Anthony Gilby. London, 1581.

Bhabha, Homi K., ed. *Nation and Narration*. New York: Routledge, 1990.

Bieman, Elizabeth. "Comic Rhyme in Marlowe's *Hero and Leander*." *English Literary Renaissance* 9 (1979): 69–77.

———. *Plato Baptized: Towards the Interpretation of Spenser's Mimetic Fictions*. Toronto: U of Toronto P, 1988.

Biester, James. *Lyric Wonder: Rhetoric and Wit in Renaissance English Poetry*. Ithaca: Cornell UP, 1997.

Birrell, T. A. "The Influence of Seventeenth-Century Publishers on the Presentation of English Literature." *Historical and Editorial Studies in Medieval and Early Modern English*. Ed. Mary-Jo Arn and Hanneke Wirtjes. Groningen: Wolters-Noordhoff, 1985. 163–73.

Bjorvand, Einar. "Spenser's Defence of Poetry: Some Structural Aspects of *Fowre Hymnes*." *Fair Forms: Essays in English Literature from Spenser to Jane Austen*. Ed. Maren-Sofie Røstvig. Totowa: Rowman, 1975. 13–53.

Black, L. G. "A Lost Poem by Queen Elizabeth I." *Times Literary Supplement* 23 May 1968: 535.

Blanchard, W. Scott. *Scholar's Bedlam: Menippean Satire in the Renaissance*. Lewisburg: Bucknell UP, 1995.

Blank, Paula. *Broken English: Dialects and the Politics of Language in Renaissance Writings*. London: Routledge, 1996.

Blessington, Francis C. "'That Undisturbed Song of Pure Concent': *Paradise Lost* and the Epic-Hymn." Lewalski, *Renaissance Genres* 468–95.

Blissett, William. "Lucan's Caesar and the Elizabethan Villain." *Studies in Philology* 53 (1956): 553–75.

Bloom, Harold, ed. *Modern Critical Views: Christopher Marlowe*. New York: Chelsea, 1986.

———, ed. *Modern Critical Views: Edmund Spenser*. New York: Chelsea, 1986.

Bloomfield, Morton W. "The Elegy and the Elegiac Mode: Praise and Alienation." Lewalski, *Renaissance Genres* 147–57.

Boas, Frederick S. *Christopher Marlowe: A Biographical and Critical Study*. Oxford: Clarendon, 1940.

Bolgar, R. R. *The Classical Heritage and Its Beneficiaries*. Cambridge: Cambridge UP, 1954.

Booth, Stephen. *An Essay on Shakespeare's Sonnets*. New Haven: Yale UP, 1969.

———, ed. *Shakespeare's Sonnets*. New Haven: Yale UP, 1977.

WORKS CITED 281

Booty, John E., ed. *The Book of Common Prayer: The Elizabethan Prayer Book*. Charlottesville: UP of Virginia, 1976.

Borris, Kenneth. "Richard Barnfield (June 1574–March 1627)." *Dictionary of Literary Biography*. 172: 10–16.

Bourdieu, Pierre. *Outline of a Theory of Practice*. Trans. Richard Nice. Cambridge Studies in Social Anthropology 16. Cambridge: Cambridge UP, 1991.

Bowers, Fredson, ed. *The Complete Works of Christopher Marlowe*. 2 vols. 2nd ed. Cambridge: Cambridge UP, 1981.

Bradbrook, Muriel C. *Shakespeare and Elizabethan Poetry*. London: Chatto, 1961.

Braden, Gordon. *The Classics and English Renaissance Poetry*. New Haven: Yale UP, 1978.

———. "Shakespeare's Petrarchism." Schiffer 163–84.

Bradner, Leicester, ed. *The Poems of Queen Elizabeth I*. Providence: Brown UP, 1964.

Brandt, Bruce E. *Christopher Marlowe in the Eighties: An Annotated Bibliography of Marlowe Criticism from 1978 through 1989*. West Cornwall: Locust, 1992.

Brathwaite, Richard. *The Schollars Medly; or, An Intermixt Discourse upon Historical and Poetical Relations*. London, 1614.

Braudy, Leo. *The Frenzy of Renown: Fame and Its History*. New York: Oxford UP, 1986.

Braunmuller, A. R. "Marlowe's Amorous Fates in *Hero and Leander*." *Review of English Studies* 29 (1978): 56–61.

Bray, Alan. *Homosexuality in Renaissance England*. London: Gay Men's, 1982.

Bredbeck, Gregory W. *Sodomy and Interpretation: Marlowe to Milton*. Ithaca: Cornell UP, 1991.

Brennan, Michael. *Literary Patronage in the English Renaissance: The Pembroke Family*. London: Routledge, 1988.

Brereton, Geoffrey, ed. *The Penguin Book of French Verse*. Vol. 2. Harmondsworth: Penguin, 1958.

Breton, Nicolas. *The Works in Verse and Prose*. Ed. Alexander B. Grosart. 2 vols. 1879. New York: AMS, 1966.

Briggs, Julia. *This Stage-Play World: Texts and Contexts, 1580–1625*. 2nd ed. Oxford: Oxford UP, 1997.

Briggs, Katherine. *The Anatomy of Puck: An Examination of Fairy Beliefs among Shakespeare's Contemporaries*. New York: Arno, 1977.

Brink, J. R. "Who Fashioned Edmund Spenser? The Textual History of *Complaints*." *Studies in Philology* 88 (1991): 153–68.

Bromley, Laura G. "Lucrece's Re-Creation." *Shakespeare Quarterly* 34 (1983): 200–11.

Brooks-Davies, Douglas, ed. *Edmund Spenser: Selected Shorter Poems*. London: Longman, 1995.

———. *The Mercurian Monarch: Magical Politics from Spenser to Pope*. Manchester: Manchester UP, 1983.

———. "Mercury." *The Spenser Encyclopedia*. 469.

———, ed. *Silver Poets of the Sixteenth Century: Sir Thomas Wyatt, Henry Howard, Sir*

282 WORKS CITED

Walter Ralegh, Sir Philip Sidney, Mary Sidney, Michael Drayton and Sir John Davies. Everyman Lib. London: Dent; Rutland: Tuttle, 1992.

Brown, Cedric C., ed. *Patronage, Politics, and Literary Traditions in England, 1558–1658.* Detroit: Wayne State UP, 1991.

Brown, Georgia. "Breaking the Canon: Marlowe's Challenge to the Status Quo in *Hero and Leander.*" P. White 59–76.

———. *The Generation of Shame: Defining Literature in the 1590s.* Cambridge: Cambridge UP, forthcoming.

Bruster, Douglas. "'Come to the Tent Again': 'The Passionate Shepherd,' Dramatic Rape, and Lyric Time." *Criticism* 33 (1991): 49–72.

Bullen, A. H., ed. *Lyrics from the Song-Books of the Elizabethan Age.* London, 1887.

Bullett, Gerald, ed. *Silver Poets of the Sixteenth Century.* 1947. London: Dent; New York, Dutton, 1975.

Bullough, Geoffrey, ed. *Narrative and Dramatic Sources of Shakespeare.* 8 vols. London: Routledge; New York: Columbia UP, 1957–75.

Burchmore, David W. "The Image of the Centre in *Colin Clouts Come Home Againe.*" *Review of English Studies* 28 (1977): 393–406.

Burckhardt, Jacob. *The Civilization of the Renaissance in Italy.* Trans. Ludwig Geiger and Walther Götz. 2 vols. 1929. New York: Harper, 1975.

Burnett, Mark Thornton. "Apprentice Literature and the 'Crisis' of the 1590s." C. Brown 47–58.

———, ed. *Christopher Marlowe: The Complete Plays.* Everyman Lib. London: Dent, 1999.

Burrow, Colin. *Edmund Spenser.* Plymouth, Eng.: Northcote, 1996.

———. *Epic Romance: Homer to Milton.* Oxford: Clarendon, 1993.

———. "Life and Work in Shakespeare's Poems." Chatterton Lecture on Poetry. *Proceedings of the British Academy* 97 (1993): 15–50.

———. "The Sixteenth Century: An Introduction." Kinney, *Cambridge Companion* 11–28.

Burt, Richard, and John Michael Archer. *Enclosure Acts: Sexuality, Property, and Culture in Early Modern England.* Ithaca: Cornell UP, 1994.

Burto, William, ed. *The Sonnets / The Narrative Poems: The Complete Non-dramatic Poetry.* By William Shakespeare. 1964. New York: Signet, 1988.

Bush, Douglas. *Mythology and the Renaissance Tradition in English Poetry.* New York: Norton, 1963.

———. *Prefaces to Renaissance Literature.* New York: Norton, 1965.

Bush, Douglas, and Alfred Harbage, eds. *The Sonnets.* By William Shakespeare. Pelican Shakespeare. 1961. Baltimore: Penguin, 1970.

Butler, Christopher. *Number Symbolism.* London: Routledge, 1970.

Buxton, John. *Sir Philip Sidney and the English Renaissance.* 3rd ed. London: Macmillan, 1987.

Cain, Thomas H. "Spenser and the Renaissance Orpheus." *University of Toronto Quarterly* 41 (1971): 24–47.

WORKS CITED 283

Caldwell, Ellen C. "Recent Studies in Henry Howard, Earl of Surrey (1970–1989)." *English Literary Renaissance* 19 (1989): 389–401.

——. "Recent Studies in Sir Thomas Wyatt (1970–1987)." *English Literary Renaissance* 19 (1989): 226–46.

——. "Sir Thomas Wyatt (circa 1503–11 Oct. 1542)." *Dictionary of Literary Biography*. 132: 346–63.

Campbell, Lily B. *Divine Poetry and Drama in Sixteenth-Century England*. Cambridge: Cambridge UP; Berkeley: U of California P, 1959.

Campbell, Marion. "'Desunt Nonnulla': The Construction of Marlowe's *Hero and Leander* as an Unfinished Poem." *ELH* 51 (1984): 241–68.

Campbell, Oscar James, and Edward G. Quinn, eds. *The Reader's Encyclopedia of Shakespeare*. New York: Crowell, 1966.

Cassirer, Ernst, Paul Oskar Kristeller, and John Herman Randall, Jr., eds. *The Renaissance Philosophy of Man*. Chicago: U of Chicago P, 1948.

Cavanaugh, Jean C. "Lady Southwell's Defense of Poetry." *Women in the Renaissance: Selections from* English Literary Renaissance. Ed. Kirby Farrell, Elizabeth H. Hageman, and Arthur F. Kinney. Amherst: U of Massachusetts P, 1990. 175–77.

Champion, Larry S. *The Essential Shakespeare: An Annotated Bibliography of Major Modern Studies*. 2nd ed. Boston: Hall, 1986.

Chan, Lois Mai, and Sarah A. Pedersen. *Marlowe Criticism: A Bibliography*. Boston: Hall, 1978.

Chapman, George. *Ovids Banquet of Sence*. Donno, *Epics* 207–43.

Chartier, Roger. *The Cultural Uses of Print in Early Modern France*. Trans. Lydia Cochrane. Princeton: Princeton UP, 1987.

——. *Forms and Meanings: Texts, Performances, and Audiences from Codex to Computer*. Philadelphia: U of Pennsylvania P, 1995.

——. "Leisure and Sociability: Reading Aloud in Early Modern Europe." Trans. Carol Mossman. *Urban Life in the Renaissance*. Ed. Susan Zimmerman and Ronald F. E. Weissman. Newark: U of Delaware P, 1989. 103–20.

Chaucer, Geoffrey. *The Riverside Chaucer*. Gen. ed. Larry D. Benson et al. 3rd ed. Boston: Houghton, 1987.

Chaudhuri, Sukanta. *Renaissance Pastoral and Its English Developments*. Oxford: Clarendon, 1989.

Cheney, Patrick. "Career Rivalry and the Writing of Counter-nationhood: Ovid, Spenser, and Philomela in Marlowe's 'The Passionate Shepherd to His Love.'" *ELH* 65 (1998): 523–55.

——. *Marlowe's Counterfeit Profession: Ovid, Spenser, Counter-nationhood*. Toronto: U of Toronto P, 1997.

——. "The Old Poet Presents Himself: *Prothalamion* as a Defense of Spenser's Career." *Spenser Studies: A Renaissance Poetry Annual* 8 (1988): 220–38.

——. "Recent Studies in Marlowe (1987–1998)." *English Literary Renaissance*, forthcoming.

——. *Spenser's Famous Flight: A Renaissance Idea of a Literary Career*. Toronto: U of Toronto P, 1993.

284 WORKS CITED

——. "Spenser's Pastorals: *The Shepheardes Calender* and *Colin Clouts Come Home Againe.*" Hadfield, *Cambridge Companion*, forthcoming.

Chinitz, David. "The Poem as Sacrament: Spenser's *Epithalamion* and the Golden Section." *Journal of Medieval and Renaissance Studies* 21 (1991): 251–68.

Cirillo, A. R. "Spenser's *Epithalamion*: The Harmonious Universe of Love." *Studies in English Literature, 1500–1900* 8 (1968): 19–34.

Clark, Sandra, ed. *Amorous Rites: Elizabethan Erotic Verse*. Everyman Lib. London: Dent, 1994.

——. "Robert Greene (July 1558–3 September 1592)." *Dictionary of Literary Biography*. 167: 61–76.

Clemen, Wolfgang. "The Uniqueness of Spenser's *Epithalamion*." Hamilton, *Essential Articles* 569–84, 655–56.

Clulee, Nicholas H. *John Dee's Natural Philosophy: Between Science and Religion*. London: Routledge, 1988.

Cohen, Walter. *Drama of a Nation*. Ithaca: Cornell UP, 1985.

Colaianne, A. J., and William L. Godshalk, eds. "Recent Studies in Sidney (1970–77)." *English Literary Renaissance* 8 (1972): 212–33. Rpt. in Kinney, *Sidney* 220–41.

Cole, A. Thomas. "Classical Greek and Latin." Wimsatt 66–88.

Cole, Howard C. *A Quest of Inquirie: Some Contexts of Tudor Literature*. Indianapolis: Pegasus, 1973.

Colie, Rosalie L. *Paradoxica Epidemica: The Renaissance Tradition of Paradox*. Princeton: Princeton UP, 1966.

——. *The Resources of Kind: Genre-Theory in the Renaissance*. Ed. Barbara K. Lewalski. Berkeley: U of California P, 1973.

——. *Shakespeare's Living Art*. Princeton: Princeton UP, 1974.

Collinson, Patrick. *The Birthpangs of Protestant England: Religious and Cultural Change in the Sixteenth and Seventeenth Centuries*. London: Macmillan, 1988.

——. "The Role of Women in the English Reformation Illustrated by the Life and Friendships of Anne Locke." *Studies in Church History* 2 (1965): 258–72. Rpt. in *Godly People: Essays on English Protestantism and Puritanism*. London: Hambledon, 1983. 273–87.

Connell, Dorothy. *Sir Philip Sidney: The Maker's Mind*. Oxford: Clarendon, 1977.

Connery, Brian A., and Kirk Combe, eds. *Theorizing Satire: Essays in Literary Criticism*. New York: St. Martin's, 1995.

Conrad, Peter. *The Everyman History of English Literature*. London: Dent, 1985.

Cook, James Wyatt, trans. *Petrarch's Songbook*. Medieval and Renaissance Texts and Studies. Binghamton: Center for Medieval and Early Renaissance Studies, 1996.

Coote, Stephen, ed. *The Penguin Book of Homosexual Verse*. Harmondsworth: Penguin, 1983.

——. *The Penguin Short History of English Literature*. Harmondsworth: Penguin, 1993.

Corbett, Margery, and R. W. Lightbown. *The Comely Frontispiece: The Emblematic Title-Page in England, 1550–1660*. London: Routledge, 1979.

WORKS CITED   285

Cousins, A. D. *The* Sonnets *and the Narrative Poems*. New York: Longman, forthcoming.

———. "Subjectivity, Exemplarity, and the Interplay of Discourse: The Establishing of Characterization in *Lucrece*." *Studies in English Literature, 1500–1900* 38 (1998): 45–60.

———. "Towards a Reconsideration of Shakespeare's Adonis: Rhetoric, Narcissus, and the Male Gaze." *Studia Neophilologica* 68 (1996): 195–204.

———. "Venus Reconsidered: The Goddess of Love in *Venus and Adonis*." *Studia Neophilologica* 66 (1994): 197–207.

Craft, William. *Labyrinth of Desire: Invention and Culture in the Work of Sir Philip Sidney*. Newark: U of Delaware P, 1994.

Craig, Hardin. *The Enchanted Glass: The Elizabethan Mind in Literature*. New York: Oxford UP, 1950.

———. *The Literature of the English Renaissance (1485–1600)*. Vol. 2 of *A History of English Literature*. Craig, gen. ed. New York: Oxford UP, 1950. 4 vols. New York: Collier; London: Collier–Macmillan, 1962.

Crane, Mary Thomas. "Elizabeth I (1553—1603)." *Dictionary of Literary Biography*. 136: 85–93.

———. *Framing Authority: Sayings, Self, and Society in Sixteenth-Century England*. Princeton: Princeton UP, 1993.

Crewe, Jonathan. *Hidden Designs: The Critical Profession and Renaissance Literature*. New York: Methuen, 1986.

Croft, P. J. *Autograph Poetry in the English Language*. 2 vols. London: Cassell, 1973.

Cropper, Elizabeth. "The Beauty of Woman: Problems in the Rhetoric of Renaissance Portraiture." Ferguson, Quilligan, and Vickers 175–90.

Cullen, Patrick. *Spenser, Marvell, and Renaissance Pastoral*. Cambridge: Harvard UP, 1970.

Cummings, R. M., ed. *Spenser: The Critical Heritage*. London: Barnes, 1971.

Cunnar, Eugene R. "Donne's Witty Theory of Atonement in 'The Baite.'" *Studies in English Literature, 1500–1900* 29 (1989): 77–98.

Curtius, Ernst Robert. *European Literature and the Latin Middle Ages*. Trans. Willard R. Trask. Bollingen Series 36. Princeton: Princeton UP, 1953.

Daniel, Samuel. Delia. *Contayning Certayne Sonnets: With The Complaint of Rosamond*. London, 1592.

———. *Poems and a Defence of Ryme*. Ed. Arthur C. Sprague. Cambridge: Harvard UP, 1930.

Darnton, Robert. "First Steps toward a History of Reading." *The Kiss of Lamourette: Reflections in Cultural History*. New York: Norton, 1990. 154–87.

Dasenbrock, Reed Way. "The Petrarchan Context of Spenser's *Amoretti*." *PMLA* 100 (1985): 38–49.

Davis, Walter R., ed. *The Works of Thomas Campion*. New York: Norton, 1970.

Day, Angel. *The English Secretary, or Methods of Writing Epistles and Letters with a Declaration of Such Tropes, Figures, and Schemes, As Either Usually or for Ornament Sake Are Therein Required*. 1599. Ed. Robert O. Evans. Facsim. ed. Gainesville: Scholars', 1967.

286 WORKS CITED

Dean, Leonard F., ed. *Shakespeare: Modern Essays in Criticism.* Rev. ed. London: Oxford UP, 1967.

de Grazia, Margreta. "Fin de Siècle Renaissance England." *Fins de Siècle: English Poetry in 1590, 1690, 1790, 1890, 1990.* Ed. Elaine Scarry. Parallax: Re-visions of Culture and Society. Baltimore: Johns Hopkins UP, 1995. 37–63.

———. "The Ideology of Superfluous Things: *King Lear* as a Period Piece." de Grazia, Quilligan, and Stallybrass 17–42.

———. "Lost Potential in Grammar and Nature: Sidney's *Astrophil and Stella.*" *Studies in English Literature, 1500–1900* 21 (1981): 21–35.

———. "The Motive for Interiority: Shakespeare's *Sonnets* and *Hamlet.*" *Style* 23 (1989): 430–44.

———. "The Scandal of Shakespeare's *Sonnets.*" *Shakespeare Survey* 47 (1994): 35–49. Rpt. in Schiffer 89–112.

———. *Shakespeare Verbatim: The Reproduction of Authenticity and the 1790 Apparatus.* Oxford: Clarendon, 1991.

de Grazia, Margreta, Maureen Quilligan, and Peter Stallybrass, eds. *Subject and Object in Renaissance Culture.* Cambridge Studies in Renaissance Lit. and Culture. Cambridge: Cambridge UP, 1996.

de Grazia, Margreta, and Peter Stallybrass. "The Materiality of the Shakespearean Text." *Shakespeare Quarterly* 44 (1993): 255–83.

Deloney, Thomas. *Works.* Ed. Francis Oscar Mann. Oxford: Oxford UP, 1912.

DeNeef, A. Leigh. *Spenser and the Motives of Metaphor.* Durham: Duke UP, 1982.

Dent, R. W., ed. *Shakespeare's Proverbial Language: An Index.* Berkeley: U of California P, 1981.

Derrida, Jacques. *Glas.* Trans. John P. Leavey, Jr., and Richard Rand. Lincoln: U of Nebraska P, 1987.

Desportes, Philippe. *Diverses amours et autres œuvres meslées.* Ed. Victor E. Graham. Paris: Minard, 1963.

Dictionary of Literary Biography. Ed. David A. Richardson. Detroit: Gale, 1993–96. Vols. 132, 136, 167, and 172.

DiGangi, Mario. *The Homoerotics of Early Modern Drama.* Cambridge: Cambridge UP, 1997.

Doherty, M. J. *The Mistress-Knowledge: Sir Philip Sidney's Defence of Poesie and Literary Architectonics in the English Renaissance.* Nashville: Vanderbilt UP, 1991.

Dollimore, Jonathan. "Desire Is Death." de Grazia, Quilligan, and Stallybrass 369–86.

Donaldson, Ian. *The Rapes of Lucretia: A Myth and Its Transformations.* Oxford: Clarendon, 1982.

Donawerth, Jane. "Women's Poetry and the Tudor-Stuart System of Gift Exchange." *Women, Writing, and the Reproduction of Culture in Tudor and Stuart Britain.* Ed. Mary E. Burke, Donawerth, Linda Dove, and Karen Nelson. Syracuse: Syracuse UP, 1998.

Donington, Robert. *The Interpretation of Early Music.* Rev. ed. New York: Norton, 1992.

WORKS CITED 287

Donker, Marjorie, and George M. Muldrow. *Dictionary of Literary-Rhetorical Conventions of the English Renaissance*. Westport: Greenwood, 1982.

Donne, John. *The* Elegies *and the* Songs and Sonnets. Ed. Helen Gardner. Oxford: Clarendon, 1965.

——. *The Poems of John Donne*. Ed. J. C. Grierson. Oxford: Oxford UP, 1963.

——. Satire 1. Hiller 175–80.

Donno, Elizabeth Story, ed. *Elizabethan Minor Epics*. New York: Columbia UP; London: Routledge, 1963.

——. "The Epyllion." *English Poetry and Prose, 1540–1674*. Ed. Christopher Ricks. London: Sphere, 1970. 82–95.

Donovan, Kevin J. "Recent Studies in George Peele (1969–1990)." *English Literary Renaissance* 23 (1993): 212–20.

——. "Recent Studies in Robert Greene (1968–1988)." *English Literary Renaissance* 20 (1990): 163–75.

——. "Recent Studies in Thomas Lodge (1969–1990)." *English Literary Renaissance* 23 (1993): 201–11.

Donow, Herbert S. *Concordance to the Poems of Sir Philip Sidney*. Ithaca: Cornell UP, 1975.

Doughtie, Edward, ed. *Liber Lilliati, Elizabethan Verse and Song (Bodleian MS Ralinson Poetry 148)*. Newark: U of Delaware P, 1985.

——, ed. *Lyrics from English Airs, 1596–1622*. Cambridge: Harvard UP, 1970.

Dove, Linda. "Women at Variance: Sonnet Sequences and Social Commentary in Early Modern England." Diss. U of Maryland, 1997.

Dowland, John. *Ayres for Four Voices*. Perf. Julian Bream. Golden Age Singers. LP. ABC Records, 1973.

——. *The First Booke of Songes or Ayres*. London, 1597.

——. "In Darkness Let Me Dwell." *Elizabethan Verse and Its Music*. New York Pro Musica Antiqua. Cond. Noah Greenberg. LP. Odyssey, n.d.

Drayton, Michael. *The Works of Michael Drayton*. Ed. J. William Hebel. 5 vols. Oxford: Blackwell, 1931–41.

Dubrow, Heather. *Captive Victors: Shakespeare's Narrative Poems and Sonnets*. Ithaca: Cornell UP, 1987.

——. *Echoes of Desire: English Petrarchism and Its Counterdiscourses*. Ithaca: Cornell UP, 1995.

——. *Genre*. Critical Idiom 42. London: Methuen, 1982.

——. *A Happier Eden: The Politics of Marriage in the Stuart Epithalamium*. Ithaca: Cornell UP, 1990.

——. "Lyric." Kinney, *Cambridge Companion* 178–99.

Dubrow, Heather, and Richard Strier, eds. *The Historical Renaissance: New Essays on Tudor and Stuart Literature and Culture*. Chicago: U of Chicago P, 1988.

Duncan-Jones, Katherine. "The Non-dramatic Poems." S. Wells, *Shakespeare: A Bibliographical Guide* 69–82.

——, ed. *Shakespeare's Sonnets*. Arden Shakespeare. 3rd ser. London: Nelson, 1997.

288 WORKS CITED

———, ed. *Sir Philip Sidney*. Oxford: Oxford UP, 1989.

———. *Sir Philip Sidney: Courtier Poet*. New Haven: Yale UP, 1991.

Dunlop, Alexander. "The Drama of *Amoretti*." *Spenser Studies: A Renaissance Poetry Annual* 1 (1980): 107–20.

———. "The Unity of Spenser's *Amoretti*." *Silent Poetry: Essays in Numerological Analysis*. Ed. Alastair Fowler. London: Barnes, 1970. 153–69.

Durling, Robert M. *The Figure of the Poet in Renaissance Epic*. Cambridge: Harvard UP, 1965.

———, trans. *Petrarch's Lyric Poems: The Rime Sparse and Other Lyrics*. Cambridge: Harvard UP, 1976.

Easthope, Anthony. *Poetry as Discourse*. London: Methuen, 1983.

Eaves, Morris. "Lamb, Charles." *Spenser Encyclopedia*. 423–25.

Edwards, Philip. *Threshold of a Nation: A Study in English and Irish Drama*. Cambridge: Cambridge UP, 1979.

Eliot, T. S. "Christopher Marlowe." *Elizabethan Dramatists*. London: Faber, 1963. 58–66.

———. "Sir John Davies." Alpers, *Elizabethan Poetry* 321–26.

———. "Tradition and the Individual Talent." *Selected Prose of T. S. Eliot*. 1919. Ed. Frank Kermode. London: Faber, 1975. 37–44.

———. *The Waste Land*. New York: Boni, 1922. 22 Mar. 2000 <http://www.bartleby.com/201/1.html>.

Elizabeth I. *Autograph Quatrain Entered on the Last Leaf of Elizabeth's French Psalter* [. . .]. Ms. Royal Lib., Windsor Castle.

———. "Verses Made by the Queen's Majesty." MS. V.b.317, fol. 20v. Folger Shakespeare Lib., Washington.

Elliot, Robert C. *The Power of Satire: Magic, Ritual, Art*. Princeton: Princeton UP, 1960.

Elliott, John R., Jr., ed. *The Prince of Poets: Essays on Edmund Spenser*. New York: New York UP; London: U of London P, 1968.

Ellis-Fermor, Una M. *Christopher Marlowe*. Hamden: Archon, 1967.

Ellrodt, Robert. *Neoplatonism in the Poetry of Spenser*. Geneva: Droz, 1960.

———. "Shakespeare the Non-dramatic Poet." S. Wells, *Cambridge Companion* 35–48.

Elsky, Martin. *Authorizing Words: Speech, Writing, and Print in the English Renaissance*. Ithaca: Cornell UP, 1989.

Empson, William. *Some Versions of Pastoral*. 1935. New York: New Directions, 1974.

Enterline, Lynn. "Embodied Voices: Petrarch Reading (Himself Reading) Ovid." Finucci and Schwartz 120–45.

Erasmus, Desiderius. *On the Writing of Letters [De conscribendis epistolis]*. Trans. Charles Fantazzi. Ed. J. K. Sowards. Toronto: U of Toronto P, 1985. 1–254. Vol. 25 of *Collected Works of Erasmus: Literary and Educational Writings* 3.

Eriksen, Roy. "Spenser's Mannerist Manoeuvres: *Prothalamion* (1596)." *Studies in Philology* 90 (1993): 143–75.

Estrin, Barbara L. *Laura: Uncovering Gender and Genre in Wyatt, Donne, and Marvell*. Durham: Duke UP, 1994.

WORKS CITED   289

Ettin, Andrew V. *Literature and the Pastoral*. New Haven: Yale UP, 1984.

Evans, G. Blakemore, ed. *The Sonnets*. By William Shakespeare. New Cambridge Shakespeare. Cambridge: Cambridge UP, 1996.

Evans, Maurice, ed. *Elizabethan Sonnets*. Rev. Roy J. Booth. 2nd ed. Everyman Lib. London: Dent; Rutland: Tuttle, 1994.

———. *English Poetry in the Sixteenth Century*. London: Hutchinson, 1955.

Falco, Raphael. *Conceived Presences: Literary Genealogy in Renaissance England*. Amherst: U of Massachusetts P, 1994.

Febvre, Lucien, and Henri-Jean Martin. *The Coming of the Book: The Impact of Printing 1450–1800*. Trans. David Gerard. Ed. Geoffrey Nowell-Smith and David Wooton. London: NLB, 1976.

Fehrenbach, Robert J. "Recent Studies in Nashe." *English Literary Renaissance* 11 (1981): 344–50.

Fehrenbach, Robert J., Lea Ann Boone, and Mario A. Di Cesare, eds. *A Concordance to the Plays, Poems, and Translations of Christopher Marlowe*. Ithaca: Cornell UP, 1982.

Feinberg, Nona. "The Emergence of Stella in *Astrophil and Stella*." *Studies in English Literature, 1500–1900* 25 (1985): 5–19.

Felch, Susan M., ed. *The Collected Works of Anne Vaughan Lock*. Medieval and Renaissance Texts and Studies 185. Tempe: Arizona Center for Medieval and Renaissance Studies, 1999.

Feldman, Martha. *City Culture and the Madrigal at Venice*. Berkeley: U of California P, 1995.

Fellowes, E. H., ed. *English Madrigal Verse, 1588–1632*. 3rd ed. Oxford: Oxford UP, 1967.

Felperin, Howard. *The Uses of the Canon: Elizabethan Literature and Contemporary Theory*. Oxford: Clarendon, 1990.

Ferguson, A. B. *Clio Unbound: Perception of the Social and Cultural Past in Renaissance England*. Durham: Duke UP, 1979.

Ferguson, Margaret W. *Trials of Desire: Renaissance Defenses of Poetry*. New Haven: Yale UP, 1983.

Ferguson, Margaret W., Maureen Quilligan, and Nancy J. Vickers, eds. *Rewriting the Renaissance: The Discourses of Sexual Difference in Early Modern Europe*. Chicago: U of Chicago P, 1986.

Ferry, Anne. *The Art of Naming*. Chicago: U of Chicago P, 1988.

———. *The "Inward" Language: Sonnets of Wyatt, Sidney, Shakespeare, Donne*. Chicago: U of Chicago P, 1983.

Fichter, Andrew. *Poets Historical: Dynastic Epic in the Renaissance*. New Haven: Yale UP, 1982.

Field, John. *A Notable and Comfortable Exposition of M. John Knoxes, upon the Fourth of Mathew, [. . .]*. London, 1583.

Fineman, Joel. *Shakespeare's Perjured Eye: The Invention of Poetic Subjectivity in the Sonnets*. Berkeley: U of California P, 1986.

———. "Shakespeare's *Sonnets'* Perjured Eye." Hošek and Parker 116–31.

290 WORKS CITED

———. "Shakespeare's Will: The Temporality of Rape." *Representations* 20 (1987): 25–76.

Finucci, Valerie, and Regina Schwartz, eds. *Desire in the Renaissance: Psychoanalysis and Literature*. Princeton: Princeton UP, 1994.

Fischlin, Daniel. *In Small Proportions: A Poetics of the English Ayre, 1596–1622*. Detroit: Wayne State UP, 1998.

Flescher, Jacqueline. "French." Wimsatt 177–90.

Fletcher, Angus. *Allegory: The Theory of a Symbolic Mode*. Ithaca: Cornell UP, 1964.

Fónagy, I. "The Voice of the Poet." *Toward a Theory of Context in Linguistics and Literature*. Ed. Adam Makkai. The Hague: Mouton, 1976. 81–143.

Ford, Boris, ed. *Sixteenth-Century Britain*. Cambridge: Cambridge UP, 1989. Vol. 3 of *The Cambridge Cultural History of Britain*.

Forster, Leonard. *The Icy Fire: Five Studies in European Petrarchism*. Cambridge: Cambridge UP, 1969.

Forsythe, R. S. "'The Passionate Shepherd' and English Poetry." *PMLA* 40 (1925): 692–742.

Foucault, Michel. "Body/Power." *Power/Knowledge: Selected Interviews and Other Writings, 1972–1977*. Ed. Colin Gordon. Hassocks: Harvester, 1980. 55–62.

Fowler, Alastair. *A History of English Literature: Forms and Kinds from the Middle Ages to the Present*. Oxford: Blackwell, 1987.

———. *Kinds of Literature: An Introduction to the Theory of Genres and Modes*. Cambridge: Harvard UP, 1982.

———. *Spenser and the Numbers of Time*. New York: Barnes, 1964.

———. "Spenser's *Prothalamion*." *Conceitful Thought: The Interpretation of English Renaissance Poems*. Edinburgh: Edinburgh UP, 1975. 59–86.

———. *Time's Purpled Masquers: Stars and the Afterlife in Renaissance Literature*. Oxford: Clarendon, 1996.

———. *Triumphal Forms: Structural Patterns in Elizabethan Poetry*. Cambridge: Cambridge UP, 1970.

Fowler, Elizabeth. "The Afterlife of the Civil Dead: Conquest in The Knight's Tale." *Critical Essays on Geoffrey Chaucer*. Ed. Thomas C. Stillinger. New York: Hall, 1998. 59–79.

———. "The Rhetoric of Political Forms: Social Persons and the Criterion of Fit in Colonial Law, *Macbeth*, and *The Irish Masque at Court*." *Form and Reform in Renaissance England: Essays in Honor of Barbara Kiefer Lewalski*. Ed. Amy Boesky and Mary Thomas Crane. Newark: U of Delaware P, 1999. 68–101.

Foxe, John. *Actes and Monuments of These Latter and Perillous Dayes*. London, 1563.

Fraser, Russell. *Shakespeare: The Later Years*. New York: Columbia UP, 1992.

———. *The War against Poetry*. Princeton: Princeton UP, 1970.

———. *Young Shakespeare*. New York: Columbia UP, 1988.

Fraunce, Abraham. *The Third Part of the Countesse of Pembroke's Yvychurch, entitled Amintas Dale*. Ed. Gerald Snare. Northridge: California State UP, 1975.

WORKS CITED   291

Freccero, John. "The Fig Tree and the Laurel: Petrarch's Poetics." *Diacritics* 5.1 (1975): 34–40. Rpt. in Parker and Quint 20–32.

Freer, Coburn. "The Style of Sidney's *Psalms*." Kinney, *Essential Articles* 425–42.

French, Peter J. *John Dee: The World of an Elizabethan Magus*. London: Routledge, 1972.

Friedenreich, Kenneth. *Christopher Marlowe: An Annotated Bibliography of Criticism since 1950*. Metuchen: Scarecrow, 1979.

Friedenreich, Kenneth, Roma Gill, and Constance B. Kuriyama, eds. "*A Poet and a Filthy Play-maker*": *New Essays on Christopher Marlowe*. New York: AMS, 1988.

Fritze, Ronald H., ed. *Historical Dictionary of Tudor England, 1485–1603*. Westport: Greenwood, 1991.

Frye, Northrop. *Anatomy of Criticism: Four Essays*. Princeton: Princeton UP, 1957.

———. "Approaching the Lyric." Hošek and Parker 31–37.

Fukuda, Shohachi. "The Numerological Patterning of *Amoretti* and *Epithalamion*." *Spenser Studies: A Renaissance Poetry Annual* 9 (1991): 33–48.

Fuller, John. *The Sonnet*. Critical Idiom 26. London: Methuen, 1972.

Fumerton, Patricia. *Cultural Aesthetics: Renaissance Literature and the Practice of Social Ornament*. Chicago: U of Chicago P, 1991.

Garrett, Messrs. *Mrs. Locke's Little Book: A Lupton Reprint*. London: Olive Tree, 1973.

Gascoigne, George. *Adventures of Master F. J. A Hundreth Sundrie Flowres*. Ed. C. T. Prouty. U of Missouri Studies 17.2. Columbia: U of Missouri P, 1942. 49–106.

The Geneva Bible: A Facsimile Edition. Ed. Lloyd E. Berry. Madison: U of Wisconsin P, 1969.

Giamatti, A. Bartlett. *The Earthly Paradise and the Renaissance Epic*. Princeton: Princeton UP, 1966.

Gibbs, Donna. *Spenser's* Amoretti: *A Critical Study*. Hampshire, Eng.: Scolar; Brookfield: Gower, 1990.

Giddens, Anthony. *The Nation-State and Violence*. Berkeley: U of California P, 1985. Vol. 2 of *A Contemporary Critique of Historical Materialism*.

Gill, Roma. "Marlowe and the Art of Translation." Friedenreich, Gill, and Kuriyama 327–41.

———. "Marlowe, Lucan, and Sulpitius." *Review of English Studies* 24 (1973): 401–13.

———. "Snakes Leape by Verse." Morris, *Christopher Marlowe* 135–50.

Gill, Roma, and Robert Krueger. "The Early Editions of Marlowe's Elegies and Davies's Epigrams: Sequence and Authority." *Library* 5th ser. 26 (1971): 243–49.

Gilman, Ernest B. *Iconoclasm and Poetry in the English Reformation: Down Went Dagon*. Chicago: U of Chicago P, 1986.

Gleason, John B. "Opening Spenser's Wedding Present: The 'Marriage Numbers' of Plato in the *Epithalamion*." *English Literary Renaissance* 24 (1994): 620–37.

Gleckner, Robert F. *Blake and Spenser*. Baltimore: Johns Hopkins UP, 1985.

———. *Blake's Prelude: "Poetical Sketches"*. Baltimore: Johns Hopkins UP, 1982.

Godshalk, William L. "*Hero and Leander*: The Sense of an Ending." Friedenreich, Gill, and Kuriyama 293–314.

292 WORKS CITED

———. "Recent Studies in Samuel Daniel (1975–1990)." *English Literary Renaissance* 24 (1994): 489–502.

———. "Recent Studies in Sidney (1940–69)." *English Literary Renaissance* 2 (1972): 148–64. Rpt. in Kinney, *Sidney* 203–19.

Goldberg, Jonathan. "The Countess of Pembroke's Literal Translation." de Grazia, Quilligan, and Stallybrass 321–36.

———. *Sodometries: Renaissance Texts, Modern Sexualities.* Stanford: Stanford UP, 1992.

———. "Sodomy and Society: The Case of Christopher Marlowe." *Staging the Renaissance: Reinterpretations of Elizabethan and Jacobean Drama.* Ed. David Scott Kastan and Peter Stallybrass. London: Routledge, 1991. 75–82.

———. *Voice Terminal Echo: Postmodernism and English Renaissance Texts.* New York: Methuen, 1986.

Gosson, Stephen. *The School of Abuse. Markets of Bawdrie: The Dramatic Criticism of Stephen Gosson.* Ed. Arthur F. Kinney. Salzburg: Salzburg Studies in Eng. Lit., 1974. 69–118.

Gottlieb, Sidney, ed. *Approaches to Teaching the Metaphysical Poets.* Approaches to Teaching World Lit. New York: MLA, 1990.

Gouws, John. "Fulke Greville, First Lord Brooke (30 October 1554–30 September 1628)." *Dictionary of Literary Biography.* 172: 105–15.

Grafton, Anthony. *Defenders of the Text: The Traditions of Scholarship in an Age of Science, 1450–1800.* Cambridge: Harvard UP, 1991.

———. *Forgers and Critics: Creativity and Duplicity in Western Scholarship.* Princeton: Princeton UP, 1990.

———. "Renaissance Readers and Ancient Texts: Comments on Some Commentaries." *Renaissance Quarterly* 38 (1985): 615–49.

———. *The Transmission of Culture in Early Modern Europe.* Philadelphia: U of Pennsylvania P, 1990.

Grafton, Anthony, and Lisa Jardine. *From Humanism to the Humanities: Education and the Liberal Arts in Fifteenth- and Sixteenth-Century Europe.* Cambridge: Harvard UP, 1986.

Grafton, Anthony, April Shelford, and Nancy Siraisi. *New Worlds, Ancient Texts: The Power of Tradition and the Shock of Discovery.* Cambridge: Belknap–Harvard UP, 1992.

Graham, Kenneth J. E. *The Performance of Conviction: Plainness and Rhetoric in the Early English Renaissance.* Ithaca: Cornell UP, 1994.

Grantley, Darryll, and Peter Roberts, eds. *Christopher Marlowe and English Renaissance Culture.* Aldershot, Eng.: Scolar, 1996.

Greenblatt, Stephen J. "Psychoanalytic and Renaissance Culture." Parker and Quint 210–24.

———. "Remnants of the Sacred in Early Modern England." de Grazia, Quilligan, and Stallybrass 337–45.

———. *Renaissance Self-Fashioning: From More to Shakespeare.* Chicago: U of Chicago P, 1980.

WORKS CITED   293

———. *Shakespearean Negotiations: The Circulation of Social Energy in Renaissance England*. The New Historicism: Studies in Cultural Poetics 4. Berkeley: U of California P, 1988.

———. *Sir Walter Ralegh: The Renaissance Man and His Roles*. New Haven: Yale UP, 1973.

Greenblatt, Stephen, et al., eds. *The Norton Shakespeare*. New York: Norton, 1997.

Greenblatt, Stephen, and Giles Gunn, eds. *Redrawing the Boundaries: The Transformation of English and American Literary Studies*. New York: MLA, 1992.

Greene, Roland. "The Colonial Wyatt: Contexts and Openings." *Rethinking the Henrician Era: Essays on Early Tudor Texts and Contexts*. Ed. Peter C. Herman. Urbana: U of Illinois P, 1994. 240–66.

———. "The Lyric." *The Renaissance*. Ed. Glyn P. Norton. Cambridge: U of Cambridge P, forthcoming. Vol. 3 of *Cambridge History of Literary Criticism*.

———. *Post-Petrarchism: Origins and Innovations of the Western Lyric Sequence*. Princeton: Princeton UP, 1991.

———. "Sir Philip Sidney's *Psalms*, the Sixteenth-Century Psalter, and the Nature of Lyric." *Studies in English Literature, 1500–1900* 30 (1990): 19–40.

Greene, Thomas M. *The Descent from Heaven: A Study in Epic Continuity*. New Haven: Yale UP, 1963.

———. *The Light in Troy: Imitation and Discovery in Renaissance Poetry*. New Haven: Yale UP, 1982.

———. "The Renaissance." *Spenser Encyclopedia*. 597–98.

———. "Spenser and the Epithalamic Convention." *Comparative Literature* 9 (1957): 215–28. Rpt. in Elliott 152–69.

Greenfield, Matthew. "The Cultural Functions of English Renaissance Elegy." *English Literary Renaissance* 28 (1998): 75–94.

Gregerson, Linda. *The Reformation of the Subject: Spenser, Milton and the English Protestant Epic*. Cambridge: Cambridge UP, 1996.

Greville, Fulke. *Caelica. Poems and Dramas of Fulke Greville, First Lord Brooke*. Ed. Geoffrey Bullough. Vol. 1. New York: Oxford UP, 1945. 73–151. 2 vols.

Griffin, Dustin. *Satire: A Critical Reintroduction*. Lexington: UP of Kentucky, 1994.

Groos, G. W., ed. and trans. *The Diary of Baron Waldstein: A Traveller in Elizabethan England*. By Zdenek Brtnicky z Valdstejna. London: Thames, 1981.

Gross, Kenneth. "'Each Heav'nly Close': Mythologies and Metrics in Spenser and the Early Poetry of Milton." *PMLA* 98 (1983): 21–36.

Guillén, Claudio. *Literature as System*. Princeton: Princeton UP, 1971.

Guilpin, Everard. *Skialetheia; or, A Shadowe of Truth, in Certaine Epigrams and Satyres*. Ed. D. Allen Carroll. Chapel Hill: U of North Carolina P, 1974.

Guy, John. *Tudor England*. Oxford: Oxford UP, 1988.

Haber, Judith. *Pastoral and the Poetics of Self-Contradiction: Theocritus to Marvell*. Cambridge: Cambridge UP, 1994.

Habermas, Jürgen. "The Public Sphere: An Encyclopedia Article (1964)." *New German Critique* 1.3 (1974): 49–55.

294 WORKS CITED

Hadfield, Andrew, ed. *The Cambridge Companion to Spenser*. Cambridge: Cambridge UP, forthcoming.

———, ed. *Edmund Spenser*. Longman Critical Readings. Stanley Smith, gen. ed. London: Longman, 1996.

———. *Edmund Spenser's Irish Experience: Wilde Fruit and Salvage Soyl*. Oxford: Clarendon, 1997.

———. *Literature, Politics and National Identity: Reformation to Renaissance*. Cambridge: Cambridge UP, 1994.

Hager, Alan. *Dazzling Images: The Masks of Sir Philip Sidney*. Newark: U of Delaware P, 1991.

Hainsworth, Peter. *Petrarch the Poet*. London: Routledge, 1988.

Hall, Kim F. "*Astrophil and Stella*: 'New Found Tropes with Problems Old.'" Hall, *Things* 73–84.

———. *Things of Darkness: Economies of Race and Gender in Early Modern England*. Ithaca: Cornell UP, 1995.

Halperin, David M. *Before Pastoral: Theocritus and the Ancient Tradition of Bucolic Poetry*. New Haven: Yale UP, 1983.

Hamilton, A. C. *The Early Shakespeare*. San Marino: Huntington, 1967.

———, ed. *Essential Articles for the Study of Edmund Spenser*. Hamden: Archon, 1972.

———. *Sir Philip Sidney: A Study of His Life and Works*. Cambridge: Cambridge UP, 1977.

Hammond, Gerald, ed. *Elizabethan Poetry: Lyrical and Narrative: A Casebook*. London: Macmillan, 1984.

Hannay, Margaret P. "Mary Sidney Herbert, Countess of Pembroke (27 October 1561–25 September 1621)." *Dictionary of Literary Biography*. 167: 184–93.

———. *Philip's Phoenix: Mary Sidney, Countess of Pembroke*. New York: Oxford UP, 1990.

———. "'Unlock my lipps': The *Miserere mei Deus* of Anne Vaughan Lok and Mary Sidney Herbert, Countess of Pembroke." *Sixteenth-Century Essays and Studies* 23 (1993): 19–36.

Harbage, Alfred, and Richard Wilbur, eds. *The Narrative Poems and Poems of Doubtful Authenticity*. By William Shakespeare. Pelican Ser. New York: Penguin, 1966.

Hardison, O. B., Jr. *The Enduring Monument: A Study of the Idea of Praise in Renaissance Literary Theory and Practice*. Westport: Greenwood, 1973.

———. "Humanism." *Spenser Encyclopedia*. 379–81.

———. *Prosody and Purpose in the English Renaissance*. Baltimore: Johns Hopkins UP, 1989.

———. "The Two Voices of Sidney's *Apology for Poetry*." *English Literary Renaissance* 2 (1972): 83–99. Rpt. in Kinney, *Sidney* 45–61.

Harington, John. *Letters and Epigrams of Sir John Harington*. Ed. Norman Egbert MacClure. Philadelphia: U of Pennsylvania P, 1930.

———. *Nugae Antiquae*. 2 vols. London, 1769.

WORKS CITED 295

Harris, Barbara J. "Women and Politics in Early Tudor England." *Historical Journal* 33 (1990): 259–81.

Harrison, G. B., ed. *Willobie His Avisa, 1594, with an Essay on Willobie His Avisa.* New York: Barnes, 1966.

Harsdörfer, Georg Phillip. *Frauenzimmer Gesprächspiele.* Nürnberg, 1641.

Hartley, L. P. *The Go-Between.* London: Hamilton, 1953.

Hartman, Geoffrey H. *Wordsworth's Poetry, 1787–1814.* New Haven: Yale UP, 1964.

Haskell, Ann S., ed. *A Middle English Anthology.* New York: Doubleday, 1969.

Hattaway, Michael. "Christopher Marlowe: Ideology and Subversion." Grantley and Roberts 198–223.

Haydn, Hiram. *The Counter-Renaissance.* New York: Harcourt, 1950.

———, ed. *The Portable Elizabethan Reader.* New York: Viking, 1955.

Healy, Thomas. *Christopher Marlowe.* Plymouth, Eng.: Northcote with the British Council, 1994.

———. *New Latitudes: Theory and English Renaissance Literature.* London: Arnold, 1992.

Hedley, Jane. *Power in Verse: Metaphor and Metonymy in the Renaissance Lyric.* University Park: Pennsylvania State UP, 1988.

Helgerson, Richard. "Barbarous Tongues: The Ideology of Poetic Form in Renaissance England." Dubrow and Strier 273–92.

———. *The Elizabethan Prodigals.* Berkeley: U of California P, 1976.

———. *Forms of Nationhood: The Elizabethan Writing of England.* Chicago: U of Chicago P, 1992.

———. *Self-Crowned Laureates: Spenser, Jonson, Milton, and the Literary System.* Berkeley: U of California P, 1983.

Henderson, Diana E. "Female Power and the Devaluation of Renaissance Love Lyric." *Dwelling in Possibility: Women Poets and Critics on Poetry.* Ed. Yopie Prins and Maeera Shreiber. Ithaca: Cornell UP, 1997. 38–59.

———. *Passion Made Public: Elizabethan Lyric, Gender, and Performance.* Urbana: U of Illinois P, 1995.

Heninger, S. K., Jr. *The Cosmographical Glass: Renaissance Diagrams of the Universe.* San Marino: Huntington, 1977.

———. "The Passionate Shepherd and the Philosophical Nymph." *Renaissance Papers* (1962): 63–70.

———. *Sidney and Spenser: The Poet as Maker.* University Park: Pennsylvania State UP, 1989.

———. *The Subtext of Form in the English Renaissance: Proportion Poetical.* University Park: Pennsylvania State UP, 1994.

———. *Touches of Sweet Harmony: Pythagorean Cosmology and Renaissance Poetics.* San Marino: Huntington, 1974.

Hentzner, Paul. *Itinerarium.* Nuremberg, 1612.

Herendeen, Wyman H. "Spenserian Specifics: Spenser's Appropriation of a Renaissance Topos." *Medievalia et Humanistica* 10 (1981): 159–88.

296   WORKS CITED

Herman, Peter C. *Squitter-Wits and Muse-Haters: Sidney, Spenser, Milton, and Renaissance Antipoetic Sentiment*. Detroit: Wayne State UP, 1996.

Hieatt, A. Kent. "The Passing of Arthur in Malory, Spenser, and Shakespeare: The Avoidance of Closure." *The Passing of Arthur: New Essays in Arthurian Tradition*. Ed. Christopher Baswell and William Sharpe. New York: Garland, 1988. 173–92.

——. "The Projected Continuation of *The Faerie Queene*: Rome Delivered?" *Spenser Studies: A Renaissance Poetry Annual* 8 (1990): 335–42.

——. *Short Time's Endless Monument: The Symbolism of the Numbers in Edmund Spenser's* Epithalamion. New York: Columbia UP, 1960.

Highley, Cristopher. *Shakespeare, Spenser, and the Elizabethan Crisis in Ireland*. Cambridge: Cambridge UP, 1997.

Hill, W. Speed. "Order and Joy in Spenser's *Epithalamion*." *Southern Humanities Review* 6 (1972): 81–90.

Hiller, Geoffrey G., ed. *Poems of the Elizabethan Age: An Anthology*. 2nd ed. New York: Routledge, 1990.

Hilliard, Nicholas. *A Treatise concerning the Arte of Limning*. Ashington, Eng.: Mid Northumberland Arts Group with Carcanet, 1981. Bound with Edward Norgate, *A More Compendious Discourse concerning ye Art of Liming*. Vol. ed. R. K. R. Thornton and T. G. S. Cain.

Hillman, David, and Carla Mazzio, eds. *The Body in Parts: Fantasies of Corporeality in Early Modern Europe*. New York: Routledge, 1997.

Hobbs, Mary. *Early Seventeenth-Century Verse Miscellany Manuscripts*. Aldershot, Eng.: Scolar, 1992.

Hobsbawm, E. J. *Nations and Nationalism since 1780: Programme, Myth, Reality*. Cambridge: Cambridge UP, 1990.

Holinshed, Raphael. *The Third Volume of* Chronicles. London, 1587.

Hollander, John. *In Time of Place*. Baltimore: Johns Hopkins UP, 1986.

——. *Powers of Thirteen: Poems*. London: Secker, 1984.

——. "Spenser's Undersong." *Melodious Guile: Fictive Pattern in Poetic Language*. New Haven: Yale UP, 1988. 148–63.

——. *Vision and Resonance: Two Senses of Poetic Form*. New York: Oxford UP, 1975.

——. *Visions from the Ramble*. 1st ed. New York: Atheneum, 1965.

Hollander, John, and Frank Kermode, eds. *The Literature of Renaissance England*. New York: Oxford UP, 1973. Vol. 2 of *The Oxford Anthology of English Literature*. Ed. Kermode and Hollander. 6 vols.

Hošek, Chaviva, and Patricia Parker, eds. *Lyric Poetry: Beyond New Criticism*. Ithaca: Cornell UP, 1985.

Howard, Henry. *Poems*. Ed. Emrys Jones. Oxford: Clarendon, 1964.

Howard, Jean, and Marion F. O'Conner, eds. *Shakespeare Reproduced: The Text in History and Ideology*. New York: Methuen, 1987.

Howard, Skiles. *The Politics of Courtly Dancing in Early Modern England*. Amherst: U of Massachusetts P, 1998.

Hubler, Edward. *The Sense of Shakespeare's Sonnets*. Princeton: Princeton UP, 1952.

———, ed. *Shakespeare's Songs and Poems*. New York: McGraw, 1964.

Huelgas Ensemble. *Italia Mia*. SONY Classical Records, 1992.

Hughes, Joan, and W. S. Ramson, eds. *Poetry of the Stewart Court*. Canberra: Australian National UP, 1982.

Hughes, Ted. "Conception and Gestation of the Equation's Tragic Myth: The *Sonnets, Venus and Adonis, Lucrece.*" *Shakespeare and the Goddess of Complete Being*. New York: Farrar; and London: Faber, 1992. 49–92.

Hughey, Ruth, ed. *The Arundel Harington Manuscript of Tudor Poetry*. 2 vols. Columbus: Ohio State UP, 1960.

Hulse, Clark. "Marlowe: The Primeval Poet." Hulse, *Verse* 93–140.

———. *Metamorphic Verse: The Elizabethan Minor Epic*. Princeton: Princeton UP, 1981.

———. "Stella's Wit: Penelope Rich as Reader of Sidney's Sonnets." Ferguson, Quilligan, and Vickers 272–86.

Hume, Anthea. *Edmund Spenser: Protestant Poet*. Cambridge: Cambridge UP, 1984.

Hume, Robert D. "Texts within Contexts: Notes toward a Historical Method." *Philological Quarterly* 71 (1992): 69–100.

Hunt, Marvin. "Sir Philip Sidney (30 November 1554–17 October 1586)." *Dictionary of Literary Biography*. 167: 194–219.

Hunt, Maurice, ed. *Approaches to Teaching Shakespeare's* Tempest *and Other Late Romances*. Approaches to Teaching World Lit. New York: MLA, 1992.

Hurstfield, Joel. *The Elizabethan Nation*. New York: Harper, 1964.

Inglis, Fred. *The Elizabethan Poets: The Making of English Poetry from Wyatt to Ben Jonson*. Lit. in Perspective. London: Evans, 1969.

Innes, Paul. *Shakespeare and the English Renaissance Sonnet: Verses of Feigning Love*. Houndmills, Eng.: Macmillan; New York: St. Martin's, 1997.

Irigaray, Luce. "Divine Women." *Sexes and Genealogies*. Trans. Gillian C. Gill. New York: Columbia UP, 1993. 55–72.

Jackson, M. P. "Echoes of Spenser's *Prothalamion* as Evidence against an Early Date for Shakespeare's *A Lover's Complaint.*" *Notes and Queries* ns 37 (1990): 180–82.

Jacobsen, Eric. *Translation: A Traditional Craft*. Copenhagen: Gyldendanske Boghandel-Nordisk, 1958.

James, Heather. *Shakespeare's Troy: Drama, Politics, and the Translation of Empire*. Cambridge Studies in Renaissance Lit. and Culture 22. Cambridge: Cambridge UP, 1997.

Jameson, Fredric. "Magical Narratives: On the Dialectical Use of Genre Criticism." *The Political Unconscious: Narrative as Socially Symbolic Act*. Ithaca: Cornell UP, 1981. 103–50.

Jardine, Lisa. *Worldly Goods: A New History of the Renaissance*. New York: Doubleday, 1996.

Jardine, Lisa, and Anthony Grafton. "'Studied for Action': How Gabriel Harvey Read His Livy." *Past and Present* 129 (1990): 30–78.

Javitch, Daniel. *Poetry and Courtliness in Renaissance England*. Princeton: Princeton UP, 1978.

298   WORKS CITED

Jayne, Sears Reynolds, trans. *Marsilio Ficino's Commentary on Plato's* Symposium: *The Text and a Translation, with an Introduction*. Columbia: U of Missouri P, 1944.

———. *Plato in Renaissance England*. International Archives of the History of Ideas 141. Dordrecht, Neth.: Kluwer, 1995.

Jed, Stephanie H. *Chaste Thinking: The Rape of Lucretia and the Birth of Humanism*. Bloomington: U of Indiana P, 1989.

Johnson, Lynn Staley. The Shepheardes Calender: *An Introduction*. University Park: Pennsylvania State UP, 1990.

Johnson, William C. "'Sacred Rites' and Prayer-Book Echoes in Spenser's *Epithalamion*." *Renaissance and Reformation* 12 (1976): 49–54.

———. *Spenser's* Amoretti: *Analogies of Love*. Lewisburg: Bucknell UP; London: Associated UP, 1990.

Johnson, W. R. *The Idea of Lyric: Lyric Modes in Ancient and Modern Poetry*. Berkeley: U of California P, 1982.

Jones, Ann Rosalind. *The Currency of Eros: Women's Love Lyric in Europe, 1540–1620*. Bloomington: Indiana UP, 1990.

———. "Dematerializations: Textile and Textual Properties in Ovid, Sandys, and Spenser." de Grazia, Quilligan, and Stallybrass 189–209.

Jones, Ann Rosalind, and Peter Stallybrass. "The Politics of *Astrophil and Stella*." *Studies in English Literature, 1500–1900* 24 (1984): 53–68.

Jones, Emrys, ed. *The New Oxford Book of Sixteenth Century Verse*. Oxford: Oxford UP, 1991.

Jorgens, Elise Bickford. "Thomas Campion (12 February 1567–1 March 1620)." *Dictionary of Literary Biography*. 172: 38–47.

Judson, Alexander C. *The Life of Edmund Spenser*. Baltimore: Johns Hopkins P, 1945. Vol. 11 of *The Works of Edmund Spenser: A Variorum Edition*.

Kahn, Coppélia. *Man's Estate: Masculine Identity in Shakespeare*. Berkeley: U of California P, 1981.

———. "The Rape in Shakespeare's *Lucrece*." *Shakespeare Studies* 9 (1976): 45–72.

Kalstone, David. *Sidney's Poetry: Contexts and Interpretations*. New York: Norton, 1965.

———. "Sir Philip Sidney: The Petrarchan Vision." Alpers, *Elizabethan Poetry* 187–209.

Kaske, Carol V. "Spenser's *Amoretti* and *Epithalamion* of 1595: Structure, Genre, and Numerology." *English Literary Renaissance* 8 (1978): 271–95.

Kay, Dennis. *Melodious Tears: The English Funeral Elegy from Spenser to Milton*. Oxford: Clarendon, 1990.

———, ed. *Sir Philip Sidney: An Anthology of Modern Criticism*. Oxford: Clarendon, 1987.

———. "William Shakespeare (circa 23 April 1564–23 April 1616)." *Dictionary of Literary Biography*. 172: 217–37.

———. *William Shakespeare: His Life and Times*. Twayne's English Author Ser. New York: Twayne, 1995.

———. *William Shakespeare: Sonnets and Poems*. Twayne's English Author Ser. New York: Twayne; London: Prentice, 1998.

WORKS CITED 299

Keach, William. *Elizabethan Erotic Narratives: Irony and Pathos in the Ovidian Poetry of Shakespeare, Marlowe, and Their Contemporaries.* New Brunswick: Rutgers UP, 1977.

———. "Hero and Leander." Bloom, *Modern Critical Views: Christopher Marlowe* 147–70.

Kedouri, Elie. *Nationalism.* 4th ed. Oxford: Blackwell, 1993.

Kellogg, Robert, and Oliver Steele, eds. *Books 1 and 2 of* The Faerie Queene, The Mutability Cantos *and Selections from the Minor Poetry.* By Edmund Spenser. New York: Odyssey, 1965.

Kelsall, Malcolm. *Christopher Marlowe.* Leiden: Brill, 1981.

Kennedy, William J. *Authorizing Petrarch.* Ithaca: Cornell UP, 1994.

———. "Petrarchan Audiences and Print Technology." *Journal of Medieval and Renaissance Studies* 14 (1984): 1–20.

Kernan, Alvin B. *The Cankered Muse: Satire of the English Renaissance.* New Haven: Yale UP, 1959.

———, ed. *Modern Shakespearean Criticism: Essays on Style, Dramaturgy, and the Major Plays.* New York: Harcourt, 1970.

———. *Printing Technology, Letters, and Samuel Johnson.* Princeton: Princeton UP, 1987.

———. "A Theory of Satire." Kernan, *Cankered Muse* 1–36. Rpt. in Paulson 249–77.

Kerrigan, John. "The Editor as Reader: Constructing Renaissance Texts." *The Practice and Representation of Reading in England.* Ed. James Raven, Helen Small, and Naomi Tadmor. Cambridge: Cambridge UP, 1996. 102–24.

———, ed. *Motives of Woe: Shakespeare and "Female Complaint": A Critical Anthology.* Oxford: Clarendon, 1991.

———, ed. *The Sonnets and* A Lover's Complaint. By William Shakespeare. New York: Viking, 1995.

Kerrigan, William, and Gorden Braden. *The Idea of the Renaissance.* Baltimore: Johns Hopkins UP, 1989.

Kiefer, Frederick. "*Mirror for Magistrates.*" *Dictionary of Literary Biography.* 167: 116–27.

Kimbrough, Robert, ed. *Sir Philip Sidney.* Twayne's English Author Ser. New York: Twayne, 1971.

———, ed. *Sir Philip Sidney: Selected Prose and Poetry.* 2nd ed. Madison: U of Wisconsin P, 1983.

King, John N. *English Reformation Literature: The Tudor Origins of the Protestant Tradition.* Princeton: Princeton UP, 1982.

———. "*Philargyrie of Great Britayne* by Robert Crowley." *English Literary Renaissance* 10 (1980): 46–75.

———. "Recent Studies in Southwell." *English Literary Renaissance* 13 (1983): 221–27.

———. "The Reformation." *Spenser Encyclopedia.* 593–95.

———. *Spenser's Poetry and the Reformation Tradition.* Princeton: Princeton UP, 1990.

King, John N., and Robin Smith. "Recent Studies in Protestant Poetics." *English Literary Renaissance* 21 (1991): 283–307.

300 WORKS CITED

King's Singers. *All at Once Well Met*. EMI Records, 1987.

Kinney, Arthur F., ed. *The Cambridge Companion to English Literature, 1500–1600*. Cambridge: Cambridge UP, 2000.

———. *Continental Humanist Poetics: Studies in Erasmus, Castiglione, Marguerite de Navarre, Rabelais, and Cervantes*. Amherst: U of Massachusetts P, 1989.

———, ed. *Elizabethan Backgrounds: Historical Documents of the Age of Elizabeth I*. Hamden: Archon, 1990.

———, ed. *Essential Articles for the Study of Sir Philip Sidney*. Hamden: Archon, 1986.

———. *Humanist Poetics: Thought, Rhetoric, and Fiction in Sixteenth-Century England*. Amherst: U of Massachusetts P, 1986.

———, ed. *Sidney in Retrospect: Selections from* English Literary Renaissance. Amherst: U of Massachusetts P, 1988.

———, ed. *The State of Renaissance Studies*. Spec. issue of *English Literary Renaissance* 25.3 (1995): 285–471.

Kintgen, Eugene R. *Reading in Tudor England*. Pittsburgh: U of Pittsburgh P, 1996.

Kirkpatrick, Robin. *English and Italian Literature from Dante to Shakespeare: A Study of Source, Analogue and Divergence*. London: Longman, 1995.

Klawitter, George. *The Enigmatic Narrator: The Voicing of Same-Sex Love in the Poetry of John Donne*. New York: Lang, 1994.

Klein, Lisa A. "'Let Us Love, Dear Love, Lyke As We Ought': Protestant Marriage and the Revision of Petrarchan Loving in Spenser's *Amoretti*." *Spenser Studies: A Renaissance Poetry Annual* 10 (1992): 109–37.

Knight, G. Wilson. *The Mutual Flame: On Shakespeare's* Sonnets *and* The Phoenix and the Turtle. London: Methuen, 1955.

Knights, L. C. "Shakespeare's *Sonnets*." Alpers, *Elizabethan Poetry* 274–98.

Knoll, Robert E. *Christopher Marlowe*. Twayne's English Author Ser. New York: Twayne, 1969.

Kolin, Philip C., ed. Venus and Adonis: *Critical Essays*. Shakespeare Criticism 16. New York: Garland, 1997.

Kramer, Jerome A., and Judith Kaminsky. "'These Contraries Such Unity Do Hold': Structure in *The Rape of Lucrece*." *Mosaic* 10.4 (1977): 143–55.

Krier, Theresa M. *Gazing on Secret Sights: Spenser, Classical Imitation, and the Decorums of Vision*. Ithaca: Cornell UP, 1990.

Kristeller, Paul Oskar. *Renaissance Thought and Its Sources*. New York: Columbia UP, 1979.

Kuin, Roger. *Chamber Music: Elizabethan Sonnet-Sequences and the Pleasure of Criticism*. Toronto: U of Toronto P, 1998.

Labé, Louise. *Œuvres complètes: Sonnets-élégies-débat de folie et d'amour*. Ed. Francois Rigolot. Paris: Flammarion, 1986.

Lamb, Mary Ellen. *Gender and Authorship in the Sidney Circle*. Madison: U of Wisconsin P, 1990.

———. "'Nett Which Paultrye Prayes Disdaines': Sidney's Influence on Two Unattributed Poems in the Bright Manuscript." *Sidney Newsletter* 5 (1984): 3–14.

WORKS CITED   301

Lamson, Roy, and Hallett Smith, eds. *The Golden Hind: An Anthology of Elizabethan Prose and Poetry*. New York: Norton, 1942.

Lane, Robert Craig. *Shepherds Devises: Edmund Spenser's* Shepheardes Calender *and the Institutions of Elizabethan Society*. Athens: U of Georgia P, 1993.

Lanham, Richard A. *A Handlist of Rhetorical Terms: A Guide for Students of English Literature*. Berkeley: U of California P, 1968.

——. *The Motives of Eloquence: Literary Rhetoric in the Renaissance*. New Haven: Yale UP, 1976.

Lanyer, Aemylia. *The Poems of Aemylia Lanyer: "Salve Deus Rex Judaeorum."* Ed. Susanne Woods. New York: Oxford UP, 1993.

Larkin, Philip. *Collected Poems*. Ed. Anthony Thwaite. London: Marvell; Faber, 1988.

Lee, John, ed. *Edmund Spenser, Shorter Poems: A Selection*. Everyman Lib. London: Dent, 1998.

Leech, Clifford. *Christopher Marlowe: Poet for the Stage*. Ed. Anne Lancashire. New York: AMS, 1986.

Leishman, J. B. *Themes and Variations in Shakespeare's Sonnets*. 2nd. ed. New York: Harper, 1963.

Leiter, Louis H. "Deification through Love: Marlowe's 'The Passionate Shepherd to His Love.'" *College English* 27 (1966): 444–49.

Levao, Ronald. "Recent Studies in Marlowe (1977–1986)." *English Literary Renaissance* 18 (1988): 329–42.

——. *Renaissance Minds and Their Fictions: Cusanus, Sidney, Shakespeare*. Berkeley: U of California P, 1985.

Lever, J. W. *The Elizabethan Love Sonnet*. University Paperbacks 176. 1956. London: Methuen, 1966.

——. "Shakespeare's Narrative Poems." Muir and Schoenbaum 116–26.

Levin, Harry. *The Myth of the Golden Age in the Renaissance*. New York: Oxford UP, 1969.

——. *The Overreacher: A Study of Christopher Marlowe*. Cambridge: Harvard UP, 1952.

Levin, Richard. "The Ironic Reading of *The Rape of Lucrece* and the Problem of External Evidence." *Shakespeare Survey* 34 (1981): 85–92.

Lewalski, Barbara Kiefer. Paradise Lost *and the Rhetoric of Literary Forms*. Princeton: Princeton UP, 1985.

——. *Protestant Poetics and the Seventeenth-Century Religious Lyric*. Princeton: Princeton UP, 1979.

——, ed. *Renaissance Genres: Essays on Theory, History, and Interpretation*. Harvard Eng. Studies 14. Cambridge: Harvard UP, 1986.

——. "Re-writing Patriarchy and Patronage: Margaret Clifford, Anne Clifford, and Aemilia Lanyer." C. Brown 59–78.

Lewis, C. S. *The Discarded Image: An Introduction to Medieval and Renaissance Literature*. Cambridge: Cambridge UP, 1971.

——. *English Literature in the Sixteenth Century, Excluding Drama*. 1954. London: Oxford UP, 1973.

302   WORKS CITED

———. "*Hero and Leander.*" *Proceedings of the British Academy* 38 (1952): 23–37. Rpt. in Alpers, *Elizabethan Poetry* 235–50.

Lievsay, John Leon, ed. *The Sixteenth Century: Skelton through Hooker.* Goldentree Bibliographies in Lang. and Lit. Ed. O. B. Hardison, Jr. New York: Appleton, 1968.

Linden, Stanton J. *Darke Hierogliphicks: Alchemy in English Literature from Chaucer to the Restoration.* Lexington: UP of Kentucky, 1996.

Lindenbaum, Peter. "Milton's Contract." *The Construction of Authorship: Textual Appropriation in Law and Literature.* Ed. Martha Woodmansee and Peter Jaszi. Durham: Duke UP, 1994. 175–90.

Lindley, David. *Lyric.* Critical Idiom 44. London: Methuen, 1985.

Linklater, Kristin. *Freeing Shakespeare's Voice: The Actor's Guide to Talking the Text.* New York: Theatre Communications Group, 1992.

Lock, Anne. *A Meditation of a Penitent Sinner: Anne Locke's Sonnet Sequence.* Ed. Kel Morin-Parsons. Waterloo, ON: North Waterloo Academic, 1998.

Loewenstein, Joseph. "Echo's Ring: Orpheus and Spenser's Career." *English Literary Renaissance* 16 (1986): 287–302.

———. "The Script in the Marketplace." *Representations* 12 (1985): 101–14.

Logan, Robert A. "Perspective in Marlowe's *Hero and Leander*: Engaging Our Detachment." Friedenreich, Gill, and Kuriyama 279–91.

Lotspeich, Henry Gibbons. *Classical Mythology in the Poetry of Edmund Spenser.* Princeton Studies in Eng. 9. Princeton: Princeton UP, 1932.

Love, Harold. *Scribal Publication in Seventeenth-Century England.* Oxford: Clarendon, 1993.

Lovejoy, Arthur O. *The Great Chain of Being: A Study of the History of an Idea.* Cambridge: Harvard UP, 1936.

Low, Anthony. "The Compleat Angler's 'Baite'; or, The Subverter Subverted." *John Donne Journal* 4 (1985): 1–12.

———. *The Reinvention of Love: Poetry, Politics and Culture from Sidney to Milton.* Cambridge: Cambridge UP, 1993. 12–30.

———. "Sir Philip Sidney: 'Huge Desyre.'" Low, *Reinvention* 12–30.

Lupton, Julia Reinhard. "Sphinx with Bouquet." *Excavations and Their Objects: Freud's Collection of Antiquity.* Ed. Stephen Barker. Albany: State U of New York P, 1996. 107–26.

Lytle, Guy Fitch, and Stephen Orgel, eds. *Patronage in the Renaissance.* Princeton: Princeton UP, 1981.

Maclean, Hugh. "Complaints." *Spenser Encyclopedia.* 177–81.

———. "'Restlesse Anguish and Unquiet Paine': Spenser and the Complaint, 1579–90." *The Practical Vision: Essays in English Literature in Honour of Flora Roy.* Ed. Jane Campbell and James Doyle. Waterloo, ON: Wilfrid Laurier UP, 1978. 29–47.

Maclean, Hugh, and Anne Lake Prescott, eds. *Edmund Spenser's Poetry: Authoritative Texts and Criticism.* 3rd ed. New York: Norton, 1993.

MacLure, Millar, ed. *Marlowe: The Critical Heritage, 1588–1896.* London: Routledge, 1979.

WORKS CITED 303

————, ed. *The Poems: Christopher Marlowe*. London: Methuen, 1968.

Maley, Willy. *Salvaging Spenser: Colonialism, Culture and Identity*. Houndmills, Eng.: Macmillan; New York: St. Martin's, 1997.

————. *A Spenser Chronology*. London: Macmillan; Lanham: Barnes, 1994.

Mallette, Richard. *Spenser, Milton, and Renaissance Pastoral*. Lewisburg: Bucknell UP, 1979.

Malone, Edmund. *The Plays and Poems of William Shakespeare*. 10 vols. London, 1790.

Manley, Lawrence. *Convention, 1500–1750*. Cambridge: Harvard UP, 1980.

————. "Spenser and the City: The Minor Poems." *Modern Language Quarterly* 43 (1982): 203–27.

Mann, Nicholas. *Petrarch*. Oxford: Oxford UP, 1984.

Marcus, Leah S. *Puzzling Shakespeare: Local Reading and Its Discontents*. Berkeley: U of California P, 1988.

————. "Renaissance / Early Modern Studies." Greenblatt and Gunn 41–63.

Marcus, Leah S., Janel Mueller, and Mary Beth Rose, eds. *Elizabeth I: Collected Works*. 2 vols. Chicago: U of Chicago P, 2000.

Marinelli, Peter V. *Pastoral*. Critical Idiom 15. London: Methuen, 1971.

Marlowe, Christopher. *Poems and Translations and* Dido, Queen of Carthage. Ed. Roma Gill. Oxford: Clarendon, 1987. Vol. 1 of *The Complete Works of Christopher Marlowe*. 5 vols. 1987–98.

Marotti, Arthur F. "'Love Is Not Love': Elizabethan Sonnet Sequences and the Social Order." *ELH* 49 (1982): 369–428.

————. *Manuscript, Print, and the English Renaissance Lyric*. Ithaca: Cornell UP, 1995.

————. "Patronage, Poetry, and Print." C. Brown 21–46.

Martin, Christopher. *Policy in Love: Lyric and Public in Ovid, Petrarch, and Shakespeare*. Pittsburgh: Duquesne UP, 1994.

Martin, Randall, ed. *Women Writers in Renaissance England*. London: Longman, 1997.

Martindale, Charles. *Redeeming the Text: Latin Poetry and the Hermeneutics of Reception*. Cambridge: Cambridge UP, 1993.

Martz, Louis L., ed. Hero and Leander *by Christopher Marlowe: A Facsimile of the First Edition, London 1598*. New York: Johnson Rpts., 1972.

————. *The Poetry of Meditation: A Study in English Religious Literature*. New Haven: Yale UP, 1962.

Maus, Katharine Eisaman. *Inwardness and Theater in the English Renaissance*. Chicago: U of Chicago P, 1995.

————. "Taking Tropes Seriously: Language and Violence in Shakespeare's *Rape of Lucrece*." *Shakespeare Quarterly* 37 (1986): 66–82.

Mauss, Marcel. *The Gift: Forms and Functions of Exchange in Archaic Societies*. Trans. Ian Cunnison. Introd. E. E. Evans-Pritchard. 1925. London: Routledge, 1974.

May, Steven W. *Bibliography and First-Line Index of English Verse, 1559–1603*. Forthcoming.

————. *The Elizabethan Courtier Poets: The Poems and Their Contexts*. Columbia: U of Missouri P, 1991.

304   WORKS CITED

———. *Henry Stanford's Anthology: An Edition of Cambridge University MS Dd.5.75.* New York: Garland, 1988.

———. "Recent Studies in Elizabeth I." *English Literary Renaissance* 23 (1993): 345–54.

———. "Tudor Aristocrats and the Mythical Stigma of Print." *Renaissance Papers* (1980): 11–18.

May, Steven W., and Anne Lake Prescott. "The Stanzaic French Verses of Elizabeth I." *English Literary Renaissance* 24 (1994): 9–43.

Mazarro, Jerome. *Transformations in the Renaissance English Lyric.* Ithaca: Cornell UP, 1970.

Mazzola, Elizabeth. "Marrying Medusa: Spenser's *Epithalamion* and Renaissance Reconstructions of Female Privacy." *Genre* 25 (1992): 193–210.

Mazzotta, Giuseppe. *The Worlds of Petrarch.* Durham: Duke UP, 1993.

McCabe, Richard. "Edmund Spenser, Poet of Exile." Chatterton Lecture on Poetry. *Proceedings of the British Academy* 80 (1993): 73–103.

———, ed. *Edmund Spenser: The Shorter Poems.* Harmondsworth: Penguin, 1999.

———. "'Little Booke: Thy Selfe Present': The Politics of Presentation in *The Shepheardes Calender.*" *Presenting Poetry: Composition, Publication, Reception.* Ed. Howard Erskine-Hill and McCabe. Cambridge: Cambridge UP, 1995. 15–40.

McColley, Diane Kelsey. *A Gust for Paradise: Milton's Eden and the Visual Arts.* Urbana: U of Illinois P, 1993.

McCoy, Richard C. *The Rites of Knighthood: The Literature and Politics of Elizabethan Chivalry.* New Historicism: Studies in Cultural Poetics 7. Berkeley: U of California P, 1989.

———. *Sir Philip Sidney: Rebellion in Arcadia.* New Brunswick: Rutgers UP, 1979.

McDonald, Russ. *The Bedford Companion to Shakespeare: An Introduction with Documents.* Boston: Bedford–St. Martin's, 1996.

———, ed. *Shakespeare Reread: The Texts in New Contexts.* Ithaca: Cornell UP, 1994.

McEachern, Claire. *The Poetics of English Nationhood, 1590–1612.* Cambridge: Cambridge UP, 1996.

McKellan, Ian, perf. *Richard III.* By William Shakespeare. Dir. Richard Loncraine. 1995. Videocassette. MGM/UA Home Video, 1996.

McNeir, Waldo F., and Foster Provost. *Annotated Bibliography of Edmund Spenser: 1937–1960.* New York: AMS, 1967.

Mebane, John S. *Renaissance Magic and the Return of the Golden Age: The Occult Tradition and Marlowe, Jonson, and Shakespeare.* Lincoln: U of Nebraska P, 1989.

Mercer, Eric. "Miniatures." *English Art, 1553–1625.* Ed. Mercer. Oxford: Oxford UP, 1962. 190–216. Vol. 8 of *The Oxford History of English Art.* 11 vols.

Meyer, Sam. *An Interpretation of Edmund Spenser's* Colin Clout. Notre Dame: U of Notre Dame P, 1969.

Miller, David Lee. "Authorship, Anonymity, and *The Shepheardes Calender.*" *Modern Language Quarterly* 40 (1979): 219–36.

———. "The Death of the Modern: Gender and Desire in Marlowe's *Hero and Leander.*" *South Atlantic Quarterly* 88 (1989): 757–87.

WORKS CITED   305

———. "The Earl of Cork's Lute." Anderson, Cheney, and Richardson 146–71.

———. *The Poem's Two Bodies: The Poetics of the 1590* Faerie Queene. Princeton: Princeton UP, 1988.

———. "Spenser's Vocation, Spenser's Career." *ELH* 50 (1983): 197–231.

Miller, David Lee, and Alexander Dunlop, eds. *Approaches to Teaching Spenser's* Faerie Queene. Approaches to Teaching World Lit. New York: MLA, 1994.

Miller, Jacqueline T. "'Love Doth Hold My Hand': Writing and Wooing in the Sonnets of Sidney and Spenser." *ELH* 46 (1979): 541–58.

Miller, Paul W. "The Decline of the English Epithalamion." *Texas Studies in Literature and Language* 12 (1970): 405–16.

Mills, Jerry Leath. "Recent Studies in *A Mirror for Magistrates.*" *English Literary Renaissance* 9 (1979): 343–52.

———. "Recent Studies in Gascoigne." *English Literary Renaissance* 3 (1973): 322–27.

———. "Recent Studies in Ralegh." *English Literary Renaissance* 15 (1985): 225–44.

———. "Sir Walter Ralegh." *Dictionary of Literary Biography*. 172: 200–16.

Minnis, Alastair. *Medieval Theory of Authorship*. London: Scolar, 1984.

Minsheu, John. *A Dictionarie in Spanish and English* [. . .]. London, 1623.

Mirollo, James V. *Mannerism and Renaissance Poetry: Concept, Mode, Inner Design*. New Haven: Yale UP, 1984.

———. "Postlude: Three Versions of the Pastoral Invitation to Love." Mirollo, *Mannerism* 160–78.

Miskimin, Alice S. *The Renaissance Chaucer*. New Haven: Yale UP, 1975.

Mohl, Ruth. "Spenser, Edmund." *Spenser Encyclopedia*. 668–71.

Montrose, Louis Adrian. "Celebration and Insinuation: Sir Philip Sidney and the Motives of Elizabethan Courtship." *Renaissance Drama* 8 (1977): 3–35.

———. "The Elizabethan Subject and the Spenserian Text." Parker and Quint 303–40.

———. "'Eliza, Queene of Shepheardes,' and the Pastoral of Power." *English Literary Renaissance* 10 (1980): 153–82.

———. "Of Gentlemen and Shepherds: The Politics of Elizabethan Pastoral Form." *ELH* 50 (1983): 415–59.

———. "'The Perfecte Paterne of a Poete': The Poetics of Courtship in *The Shepheardes Calender.*" *Texas Studies in Literature and Language* 21 (1979): 34–67.

———. "Spenser's Domestic Domain: Poetry, Property, and the Early Modern Subject." de Grazia, Quilligan, and Stallybrass 83–130.

Moore, John W., Jr. "Spenser Bibliography Update." *Spenser Newsletter* [published annually].

Morley, Thomas. *Airs*. 1602. *The English Madrigal School*. Ed. Edmund H. Fellowes. London: Stainer, 1913– .

Morris, Brian, ed. *Christopher Marlowe*. New York: Hill, 1968.

———. "Comic Method in Marlowe's *Hero and Leander.*" Morris, *Christopher Marlowe* 115–31.

Moss, Ann. *Printed Commonplace-Books and the Structuring of Renaissance Thought*. Oxford: Clarendon, 1996.

306　WORKS CITED

Moulton, Ian Frederick. "'Printed Abroad and Uncastrated': Marlowe's *Elegies* with Davies' *Epigrams*." P. White 77–90.

Muir, Kenneth, and S. Schoenbaum, eds. *A New Companion to Shakespeare Studies*. Cambridge: Cambridge UP, 1971.

Murdoch, John, Jim Murrell, Patrick J. Noon, and Roy Strong, eds. *The English Miniature*. New Haven: Yale UP, 1981.

Murrin, Michael. *The Allegorical Epic: Essays in Its Rise and Decline*. Chicago: U of Chicago P, 1980.

———. *History and Warfare in Renaissance Epic*. Chicago: U of Chicago P, 1994.

Musa, Mark, trans. *"The Canzoniere" or "Rerum Vulgarium Fragmenta."* By Petrarch. Bloomington: Indiana UP, 1996.

Nelson, William. *The Poetry of Edmund Spenser*. New York: Columbia UP, 1963.

Neuse, Richard. "Atheism and Some Functions of Myth in Marlowe's *Hero and Leander*." *Modern Language Quarterly* 31 (1970): 424–39.

———. "The Triumph over Hasty Accidents: A Note on the Symbolic Mode of the *Epithalamion*." *Modern Language Review* 61 (1966): 161–74. Rpt. in Hamilton, *Essential Articles* 534–48.

Newton, Richard. "Jonson and the (Re)Invention of the Book." *Classic and Cavalier: Essays on Jonson and the Sons of Ben*. Ed. Claude J. Summers and Ted-Larry Pebworth. Pittsburgh: U of Pittsburgh P, 1982. 31–55.

———. "Making Books from Leaves: Poets Become Editors." *Print and Culture in the Renaissance: Essays on the Advent of Printing in Europe*. Ed. Gerald P. Tyson and Sylvia S. Wagonheim. Newark: U of Delaware P, 1986. 246–64.

Nicholl, Charles. "'At Middleborough': Some Reflections on Marlowe's Visit to the Low Countries in 1592." Grantley and Roberts 38–50.

———. *The Chemical Theatre*. London: Routledge, 1980.

———. *The Reckoning: The Murder of Christopher Marlowe*. New York: Harcourt, 1992.

Nichols, J. G. *The Poetry of Sir Philip Sidney*. Liverpool: U of Liverpool P, 1974.

Nichols, John. *Progresses and Public Processions of Queen Elizabeth*. 3 vols. London, 1823. New York: Franklin, n.d.

Norbrook, David G. *Poetry and Politics in the English Renaissance*. London: Routledge, 1984.

Norbrook, David G., and H. R. Woudhuysen, eds. *The Penguin Book of Renaissance Verse, 1509–1659*. Harmondsworth: Penguin, 1992.

Norton, Dan S. "The Tradition of Prothalamia." *English Studies in Honor of James Southall Wilson*. U of Virginia Studies 4. Charlottesville: UP of Virginia, 1951. 223–41.

The Norton Anthology of English Literature. 6th ed. M. H. Abrams et al., gen. eds. Vol. 1. Ed. E. Talbot Donaldson and Alfred David (medieval); Hallett Smith and Barbara Lewalski (sixteenth century). New York: Norton, 1993.

Nosworthy, J. M. "Marlowe's Ovid and Davies's Epigrams: A Postscript." *Review of English Studies* 15 (1964): 397–98.

———. "The Publication of Marlowe's Elegies and Davies's Epigrams." *Review of English Studies* 4 (1953): 260–61.

Oakeshott, Walter. "Carew Ralegh's Copy of Spenser." *Library* 5th ser. 26 (1971): 1–21.

Oates, Mary I. "*Fowre Hymnes*: Spenser's Retractations of Paradise." *Spenser Studies: A Renaissance Poetry Annual* 4 (1984): 143–69.

O'Donnell, Brennan. "D. G. Rossetti's 'The Stream's Secret' and the *Epithalamion*." *Victorian Poetry* 25 (1987): 187–92.

Oliver, Douglas. *Poetry and Narrative in Performance*. New York: St. Martin's, 1989.

Oram, William Allan. *Edmund Spenser*. Twayne's English Author Ser. New York: Twayne, 1997.

Orgel, Stephen, ed. *Christopher Marlowe: The Complete Poems and Translations*. Harmondsworth: Penguin, 1971.

———. "Gendering the Crown." de Grazia, Quilligan, and Stallybrass 133–65.

———. *Impersonations: The Performance of Gender in Shakespeare's England*. Cambridge: Cambridge UP, 1996.

———. "Sidney's Experiment in Pastoral: *The Lady of May*." Kinney, *Essential Articles* 61–71.

Ortuñez de Calahorra, Diego. *The Mirrour of Princely Deeds and Knighthood*. Trans. Margaret Tyler. Facs. Introd. Kathryn Coad. Aldershot, Eng.: Scolar, 1996. Vol. 8 of *The Early Modern Englishwoman: Part 1: Printed Writings, 1500–1640*.

Osborn, James M. *Young Philip Sidney, 1572–1577*. New Haven: Yale UP, 1972.

Osgood, Charles Grosvenor, ed. *A Concordance to the Poems of Edmund Spenser*. Philadelphia: Lippincott, 1915. Gloucester: Smith, 1963.

Ovid. *Metamorphoses*. Trans. Frank Justus Miller. 3rd ed. Rev. G. P. Goold. 2 vols. Loeb Classical Lib. Cambridge: Harvard UP, 1984.

———. *Ovid's* Metamorphoses: *The Arthur Golding Translation 1567*. Ed. John Frederick Nims. Classics of Greece and Rome. New York: Macmillan, 1965.

The Oxford English Dictionary. 2nd ed. 1989.

Paglia, Camille. "Spenser and Apollo: *The Faerie Queene*." *Sexual Personae: Art and Decadence from Nefertiti to Emily Dickinson*. New Haven: Yale UP, 1992. 170–93.

Parker, Patricia, and Geoffrey Hartman, eds. *Shakespeare and the Question of Theory*. New York: Methuen, 1985.

Parker, Patricia, and David Quint, eds. *Literary Theory / Renaissance Texts*. Baltimore: Johns Hopkins UP, 1986.

Pask, Kevin. *The Emergence of the English Author: Scripting the Life of the Poet in Early Modern England*. Cambridge Studies in Renaissance Lit. and Culture. Cambridge: Cambridge UP, 1996.

Patterson, Annabel. *Censorship and Interpretation: The Conditions of Writing and Reading in Early Modern England*. Rev. ed. Madison: U of Wisconsin P, 1984.

———. *Pastoral and Ideology: Virgil to Valéry*. Berkeley: U of California P, 1987.

———. "Still Reading Spenser after All These Years?" *English Literary Renaissance* 25 (1995): 432–44.

Paulson, Ronald, ed. *Satire: Modern Essays in Criticism*. Englewood Cliffs: Prentice, 1971.

Pearcy, Lee T. *The Mediated Muse: English Translations of Ovid, 1560–1700*. Hamden: Archon, 1984.

308　WORKS CITED

Pears, Steuart A., ed. and trans. *The Correspondence of Sir Philip Sidney and Hubert Languet*. London, 1845.

Pearsall, Derek. *The Life of Geoffrey Chaucer: A Critical Biography*. Oxford: Blackwell, 1992.

Pendry, E. D., and J. C. Maxwell, eds. *Christopher Marlowe: Complete Plays and Poems*. Everyman Lib. London: Dent, 1976.

Pequigney, Joseph. *Such Is My Love: A Study of Shakespeare's Sonnets*. Chicago: U of Chicago P, 1985.

Percyvale, Richard. *Bibliotheca Hispanica* [. . .]. London, 1591.

Peterson, Douglas L. *The English Lyric from Wyatt to Donne: A History of the Plain and Eloquent Styles*. Princeton: Princeton UP, 1967.

Peterson, Richard S. "Laurel Crown and Ape's Tail: New Light on Spenser's Career from Sir Thomas Tresham." *Spenser Studies* 12 (1998): 1–35.

Petrarch. *Canzoniere*. Ed. Gianfranco Contini. 3rd ed. Turin: Einaudi, 1964.

Petti, Anthony G. *English Literary Hands from Chaucer to Dryden*. Cambridge: Harvard UP, 1977.

Pico della Mirandola, Giovanni. *On the Dignity of Man*. Trans. Charles Glenwallis. Indianapolis: Bobbs, 1965.

Pigman, G. W., III. *Grief and English Renaissance Elegy*. Cambridge: Cambridge UP, 1985.

Platter, Thomas. *Thomas Platter's Travels in England, 1599*. Ed. and trans. Clare Williams. London: Cape, 1937.

Poggioli, Renato. *The Oaten Flute: Essays on Pastoral Poetry and the Pastoral Ideal*. Cambridge: Harvard UP, 1975.

Pomeroy, Elizabeth. *The Elizabethan Miscellanies: Their Development and Conventions*. Berkeley: U of California P, 1973.

Porter, Roy, ed. *Rewriting the Self: Histories from the Renaissance to the Present*. New York: Routledge, 1997.

Post, Jonathan F. S. "Recent Studies in Marlowe (1968–1976)." *English Literary Renaissance* 7 (1977): 382–99.

Potter, Lois. *Secret Rites and Secret Writing: Royalist Literature, 1641–1660*. Cambridge: Cambridge UP, 1989.

Prescott, Anne Lake. "Du Bellay in Renaissance England: Recent Work on Translation and Response." *Œuvres et critiques* 20 (1995): 121–28.

———. "The Evolution of Tudor Satire." Kinney, *Cambridge Companion* 220–40.

———. *French Poets and the English Renaissance: Studies in Fame and Transformation*. New Haven: Yale UP, 1978.

———. "King David as a 'Right Poet': Sidney and the Psalmist." *English Literary Renaissance* 19 (1989): 131–51.

———. "The Shorter Poems." Hadfield, *Cambridge Companion*, forthcoming.

———. "Spenser (Re)Reading du Bellay: Chronology and Literary Response." Anderson, Cheney, and Richardson 131–45.

———. "The Thirsty Deer and the Lord of Life: Some Contexts for *Amoretti* 67–70." *Spenser Studies: A Renaissance Poetry Annual* 6 (1986): 33–76.

WORKS CITED 309

————. "*Translatio Lupae*: Du Bellay's Roman Whore Goes North." *Renaissance Quarterly* 42 (1989): 397–419.

Prince, F. T., ed. *The Poems*. By William Shakespeare. Arden Ser. London: Methuen, 1969.

Puttenham, George. *The Arte of English Poesie*. 1589. Ed. Edward Arber. Kent: Kent State UP, 1970.

————. *The Arte of English Poesie*. Ed. Gladys Doidge Willcock and Alice Walker. Cambridge: Cambridge UP, 1936.

————. *The Art of English Poesy*. G. Smith 2: 52–55.

Quilligan, Maureen. "Sidney and His Queen." Dubrow and Strier 171–96.

Quint, David. *Epic and Empire: Politics and Generic Form from Virgil to Milton*. Princeton: Princeton UP, 1993.

————. *Origin and Originality in Renaissance Literature: Versions of the Source*. New Haven: Yale UP, 1983.

Quitslund, Jon A. "Platonism." *Spenser Encyclopedia*. 546–48.

————. "Spenser and the Patronesses of the *Fowre Hymnes*: 'Ornaments of All True Love and Beautie.'" *Silent but for the Word: Tudor Women as Patrons, Translators, and Writers of Religious Works*. Ed. Margaret Patterson Hannay. Kent: Kent State UP, 1985. 184–202.

Radcliffe, David Hill. *Edmund Spenser: A Reception History*. Columbia: Camden, 1996.

Ralegh, Walter. *The Poems of Sir Walter Ralegh*. Ed. Agnes M. C. Latham. Boston: Houghton, 1929.

Rambuss, Richard. "Pleasure and Devotion: The Body of Jesus in Seventeenth-Century Religious Lyric." *Queering the Renaissance*. Ed. Jonathan Goldberg. Durham: Duke UP, 1994. 253–79.

————. "The Secretary's Study: The Secret Design of *The Shepheardes Calender*." *ELH* 59 (1992): 313–35.

————. "Spenser's Lives, Spenser's Careers." Anderson, Cheney, and Richardson 1–17.

————. *Spenser's Secret Career*. Cambridge Studies in Renaissance Lit. and Culture. Cambridge: Cambridge UP, 1993.

Ratcliffe, Stephen. *Campion: On Song*. Boston: Routledge, 1981.

Ray, Robert H., ed. *Approaches to Teaching Shakespeare's* King Lear. Approaches to Teaching World Lit. New York: MLA, 1986.

Regan, Mariann Sanders. *Love Words: The Self and the Text in Medieval and Renaissance Poetry*. Ithaca: Cornell UP, 1982.

Reiss, Timothy. *Tragedy and Truth*. New Haven: Yale UP, 1980.

Relihan, Joel C. *Ancient Menippean Satire*. Baltimore: Johns Hopkins UP, 1993.

Richardson, Brian. *Print Culture in Renaissance Italy*. Cambridge: Cambridge UP, 1994.

Ricoeur, Paul. "Time and Narrative: Three-fold Mimesis." *Time and Narrative*. Vol. 1. Trans. Kathleen McLaughlin and David Pellauer. Chicago: U of Chicago P, 1984. 52–87.

Riffaterre, Michael. *Semiotics of Poetry*. Bloomington: Indiana UP, 1978.

310   WORKS CITED

———. *Text Production*. Trans. Terese Lyons. New York: Columbia UP, 1983.

Ringler, William A., Jr., ed. *Bibliography and Index of English Verse Printed 1476–1558*. London: Mansell, 1988.

Rivers, Elias L. *Renaissance and Baroque Poetry of Spain*. Prospect Heights: Waveland, 1988.

Rivers, Isabel. *Classical and Christian Ideas in English Renaissance Poetry: A Student's Guide*. 2nd ed. London: Routledge, 1994.

Roberts, Gareth. *The Mirror of Alchemy: Alchemical Ideas and Images in Manuscripts and Books from Antiquity to the Seventeenth Century*. Toronto: U of Toronto P, 1994.

Roberts, Josephine A. "Recent Studies in Women Writers of the English Renaissance: Mary Sidney, Countess of Pembroke." *Women in the Renaissance: Selections from English Literary Renaissance*. Ed. Kirby Farrell, Elizabeth H. Hageman, and Arthur F. Kinney. Amherst: U of Massachusetts P, 1990. 245–58.

———. "Recent Studies in Women Writers of Tudor England, Part II: Mary Sidney, Countess of Pembroke." *English Literary Renaissance* 14 (1984): 426–39.

Robertson, Jean, ed. *Sidney, Sir Philip:* The Countess of Pembroke's Arcadia *(The Old Arcadia)*. Oxford: Clarendon, 1973.

Roche, Thomas P., Jr. "*Astrophil and Stella*: A Radical Reading." *Spenser Studies: A Renaissance Poetry Annual* 3 (1982): 139–91. Rpt. in Kay, *Sir Philip Sidney* 185–226.

———. *Petrarch and the English Sonnet Sequences*. New York: AMS, 1989.

Rodenburg, Patsy. *The Right to Speak: Working with the Voice*. New York: Routledge, 1992.

Roe, John, ed. *The Poems:* Venus and Adonis, The Rape of Lucrece, The Phoenix and the Turtle, The Passionate Pilgrim, A Lover's Complaint. By William Shakespeare. New Cambridge Shakespeare. Cambridge: Cambridge UP, 1992.

Rogers, William Elford. "The Carmina of Horace in Prothalamion." *American Notes and Queries* 15 (1977): 148–53.

———. "Proserpina in the *Prothalamion*." *American Notes and Queries* 15 (1977): 131–35.

Rollins, H. E., and Herschel Baker, eds. *The Renaissance in England: Non-dramatic Prose and Verse of the Sixteenth Century*. Lexington: Heath, 1954.

Rollinson, Philip B. "A Generic View of Spenser's *Four Hymns*." *Studies in Philology* 68 (1971): 292–304.

———. "Hymn." *Spenser Encyclopedia*. 385.

———. "The Renaissance of the Literary Hymn." *Renaissance Papers* (1968): 11–20.

Ronan, Clifford J. "*Pharsalia* 1.373–378: Roman Parricide and Marlowe's Editors." *Classical and Modern Literature* 6 (1986): 305–09.

Rooley, Anthony. *Performance: Revealing the Orpheus Within*. Longmead: Element, 1990.

Roston, Murray. *Sixteenth-Century English Literature*. History of Lit. New York: Schocken, 1982.

Rowse, A. L. *The Elizabethan Renaissance: The Cultural Achievement*. 2 vols. New York: Scribner's, 1971–72.

WORKS CITED   311

Royston, Pamela. *"Hero and Leander* and the Eavesdropping Reader." *John Donne Journal* 2 (1983): 31–53.

Rudenstine, Neil L. "Sidney and Energia." Alpers, *Elizabethan Poetry* 210–34.

———. *Sidney's Poetic Development*. Cambridge: Harvard UP, 1967.

Ryskamp, Charles, introd. *British Literary Manuscripts, Series I from 800 to 1800*. New York: Dover, 1981.

Sacks, Peter M. *The English Elegy: Studies in the Genre from Spenser to Yeats*. Baltimore: Johns Hopkins UP, 1985.

Sams, Eric. *The Real Shakespeare: Retrieving the Early Years, 1564–1594*. New Haven: Yale UP, 1995.

Sanders, Andrew. *The Short Oxford History of English Literature*. Rev. ed. Oxford: Clarendon, 1996.

Sanderson, James L. "Recent Studies in Sir John Davies." *English Literary Renaissance* 4 (1974): 411–17.

Saslow, James M. *Ganymede in the Renaissance: Homosexuality in Art and Society*. New Haven: Yale UP, 1986.

Saunders, J. R. "The Stigma of Print: A Note on the Social Bases of Tudor Poetry." *Essays in Criticism* 1 (1951): 139–64.

Schenck, Celeste Marguerite. *Mourning and Panegyric: The Poetics of Pastoral Ceremony*. University Park: Pennsylvania State UP, 1988.

Schiffer, James, ed. *Shakespeare's* Sonnets: *Critical Essays*. New York: Garland, 1999.

Schleiner, Louise. *Cultural Semiotics, Spenser, and the Captive Woman*. Bethlehem: Lehigh UP; London: Associated UP, 1995.

———. "Recent Studies in Poetry and Music of the English Renaissance." *English Literary Renaissance* 16 (1986): 253–68.

———. *Tudor and Stuart Women Writers*. Bloomington: Indiana UP, 1994.

Schmidgall, Gary. *Shakespeare and the Poet's Life*. Lexington: UP of Kentucky, 1990.

Schoenbaum, Samuel. *Shakespeare's Lives*. Rev. ed. Oxford: Clarendon, 1991.

———. *William Shakespeare: A Compact Documentary Life*. Oxford: Clarendon, 1987.

———. *William Shakespeare: A Documentary Life*. New York: Oxford UP, 1975.

Schoenfeldt, Michael. "The Matter of Inwardness: Shakespeare's *Sonnets*." Schiffer 305–24.

Schuler, Robert M. *Alchemical Poetry, 1575–1700: From Previously Unpublished Manuscripts*. New York: Garland, 1995.

Schulman, Samuel E. "The Spenser of the Intimations Ode." *Wordsworth Circle* 12 (1981): 31–35.

Schwartz, Murray M., and Coppélia Kahn, eds. *Representing Shakespeare: New Psychoanalytic Essays*. Baltimore: Johns Hopkins UP, 1980.

Sedgwick, Eve Kosofsky. *Between Men: English Literature and Male Homosocial Desire*. New York: Columbia UP, 1985.

Selden, John. *The Table Talk of John Selden*. Ed. Samuel Harvey Reynolds. Oxford, 1892.

Selden, Raman. *English Verse Satire, 1590–1765*. London: Allen, 1978.

312 WORKS CITED

Selleck, Nancy. "Coining the Self: Language, Gender, and Exchange in Early Modern English Literature." Diss. Princeton U, 1997.

Sessions, William A., ed. *New Readings of Sidney: Experiment and Tradition*. Spec. issue of *Studies in the Literary Imagination* 15.1 (1982): 1–128.

Seznec, Jean. *The Survival of the Pagan Gods: The Mythological Tradition and Its Place in Renaissance Humanism and Art*. Trans. Barbara F. Sessions. Bollingen Ser. 38. Princeton: Princeton UP, 1972.

Shaheen, Naseeb. *Biblical References in* The Fairie Queene. Memphis: Memphis State UP, 1976.

Shakespeare, William. *The Riverside Shakespeare*. Ed. G. Blakemore Evans et al. 1974. 2nd ed. Boston: Houghton, 1997.

Shapiro, James. "'Metre Meete to Furnish Lucans Style': Reconsidering Marlowe's *Lucan*." Friedenreich, Gill, and Kuriyama 315–25.

———. *Shakespeare and the Jews*. New York: Columbia UP, 1995.

Shepherd, Simon. *Spenser*. New York: Harvester, 1989.

Sherman, William H. *John Dee: The Politics of Reading and Writing in the English Renaissance*. Amherst: U of Massachusetts P, 1995.

Shire, Helena. *A Preface to Spenser*. London: Longman, 1978.

Shore, David R. *Spenser and the Poetics of Pastoral: A Study of the World of Colin Clout*. Kingston: McGill–Queen's UP, 1985.

Shuger, Debora Kuller. "'Gums of Glutinous Heat' and the Stream of Consciousness: The Theology of Milton's *Maske*." *Representations* 60 (1997): 1–21.

———. *Habits of Thought in the English Renaissance: Religion, Politics, and the Dominant Culture*. Berkeley: U of California P, 1990.

———. *The Renaissance Bible: Scholarship, Sacrifice, and Subjectivity*. Berkeley: U of California P, 1994.

———. *Sacred Rhetoric: The Christian Grand Style in the English Renaissance*. Princeton: Princeton UP, 1988.

Shumaker, Wayne, ed. *John Dee on Astronomy: Propaedeumata Aphoristica (1558–1568)*. Berkeley: U of California P, 1978.

Sidney, Henry. *A Very Godly Letter*. London, 1591.

Sidney, Mary. *The Collected Works of Mary Sidney Herbert, Countess of Pembroke*. Ed. Margaret P. Hannay, Noel J. Kinnamon, and Michael G. Brennan. 2 vols. Oxford: Clarendon, 1998.

———. *The* Psalms *of Sir Philip Sidney and the Countess of Pembroke*. Ed. J. C. A. Rathmell. New York: New York UP, 1963.

———. The Triumph of Death *and Other Unpublished and Uncollected Poems*. Ed. Gary F. Waller. Salzburg: Institut für Englische Sprache, 1977.

Sidney, Philip. *An Apology for Poetry*. Ed. Forrest G. Robinson. New York: Macmillan, 1970.

———. *A Defense of Poetry*. Ed. J. A. Van Dorsten. Oxford: Oxford UP, 1966.

———. *Miscellaneous Prose of Sir Philip Sidney*. Ed. Katherine Duncan-Jones and Jan van Dorsten. Oxford: Clarendon, 1973.

WORKS CITED 313

———. *The Poems of Sir Philip Sidney*. Ed. William A. Ringler, Jr. Oxford: Clarendon, 1962.

Sinfield, Alan. "Double Meanings: II: Sexual Puns in *Astrophil and Stella*." *Essays in Criticism* 24 (1974): 341–55.

———. *Literature in Protestant England, 1560–1660*. London: Croom, 1983.

———. "Sidney and Astrophil." *Studies in English Literature, 1500–1900* 20 (1980): 25–41.

Singman, Jeffrey L. *Daily Life in Elizabethan England*. Daily Life through History. Westport: Greenwood, 1995.

Sloane, Thomas O. *Donne, Milton, and the End of Humanist Rhetoric*. Berkeley: U of California P, 1985.

Smith, Anthony D. *Theories of Nationalism*. 2nd ed. New York: Holmes, 1983.

Smith, Barbara Herrnstein, ed. *Discussions of Shakespeare's* Sonnets. Boston: Heath, 1964.

———. *Poetic Closure: A Study of How Poems End*. Chicago: U of Chicago P, 1968.

Smith, Bruce R. *Homosexual Desire in Shakespeare's England: A Cultural Poetics*. Chicago: U of Chicago P, 1991.

———. "I, You, He, She, and We: On the Sexual Politics of Shakespeare's *Sonnets*." Schiffer 411–30.

Smith, Charles G. *Spenser's Proverb Lore*. Cambridge: Harvard UP, 1970.

Smith, G. Gregory, ed. *Elizabethan Critical Essays*. 2 vols. London: Oxford UP, 1904.

Smith, Hallett Darius. *Elizabethan Poetry: A Study in Conventions, Meaning, and Expression*. Cambridge: Harvard UP, 1952.

———. "*The Shepheardes Calender* and Pastoral Poetry." Alpers, *Elizabethan Poetry* 169–86.

———. *The Tension of the Lyre: Poetry in Shakespeare's* Sonnets. San Marino: Huntington, 1981.

Snyder, Susan. *Pastoral Process: Spenser, Marvell, Milton*. Stanford: Stanford UP, 1998.

Sontag, Susan. "The Pornographic Imagination." *Styles of Radical Will*. London: Secker, 1969. 35–73.

Southall, Raymond. *The Courtly Maker: An Essay on the Poetry of Wyatt and His Contemporaries*. Oxford: Blackwell, 1964.

Sowerby, Robin. *The Classical Legacy in Renaissance Poetry*. London: Longman, 1994.

Spearing, A. C. *Medieval to Renaissance in English Poetry*. Cambridge: Cambridge UP, 1985.

Spenser, Edmund. *The Faerie Queene*. Ed. A. C. Hamilton. Longman Annotated English Poets. London: Longman, 1977.

———. *The Poetical Works of Edmund Spenser*. Ed. J. C. Smith and Ernest de Selincourt. 3 vols. 1909–10. Oxford: Clarendon, 1970.

———. *Spenser's Minor Poems*. Ed. Ernest de Selincourt. Oxford: Clarendon, 1910.

———. *The Works of Edmund Spenser: A Variorum Edition*. Ed. Edwin Greenlaw et al. 11 vols. Baltimore: Johns Hopkins P, 1932–57.

———. *The Yale Edition of the Shorter Poems of Edmund Spenser*. Ed. William A. Oram et al. New Haven: Yale, 1989.

314   WORKS CITED

The Spenser Encyclopedia. Ed. A. C. Hamilton et al. Toronto: U of Toronto P, 1990.

Spevack, Marvin, ed. *Complete and Systematic Concordance to the Works of Shakespeare*. 9 vols. Hildesheim, Ger.: Olms, 1968–80.

——, ed. *Harvard Concordance to Shakespeare*. Cambridge: Belknap–Harvard UP, 1969.

Spiller, Michael R. G. *The Development of the Sonnet: An Introduction*. London: Routledge, 1992.

Stallybrass, Peter. "Editing as Cultural Formation: The Sexing of Shakespeare's Sonnets." *Modern Language Quarterly* 54 (1993): 91–103. Rpt. in Schiffer 75–88.

Stapleton, M. L. *Harmful Eloquence: Ovid's* Amores *from Antiquity to Shakespeare*. Ann Arbor: U of Michigan P, 1996.

Staub, Susan C. "George Gascoigne (1539?–7 October 1577)." *Dictionary of Literary Biography*. 136: 127–39.

Steane, J. B. *Christopher Marlowe: A Critical Study*. Cambridge: Cambridge UP, 1964.

Stein, Arnold. *The House of Death: Messages from the English Renaissance*. Baltimore: Johns Hopkins UP, 1986.

Steinberg, Theodore L. "The Sidneys and the Psalms." *Studies in Philology* 92 (1995): 1–17.

Stillinger, Jack. "The Biographical Problem of *Astrophil and Stella*." Kinney, *Essential Articles* 167–91.

Stillman, Robert E. "Justice and the 'Good Word' in Sidney's *The Lady in May*." *Studies in English Literature, 1500–1900* 24 (1984): 23–38.

——. *Sidney's Poetic Justice: The* Old Arcadia, *Its Eclogues, and Renaissance Pastoral Traditions*. Lewisburg: Bucknell UP, 1986.

Stimpson, Catharine R. "Shakespeare and the Soil of Rape." *The Woman's Part: Feminist Criticism of Shakespeare*. Ed. Carolyn Ruth Swift Lenz et al. Urbana: U of Illinois P, 1980. 56–64.

Stone, Lawrence. *The Crisis of the Aristocracy, 1558–1641*. Oxford: Clarendon, 1965.

——. *The Family, Sex, and Marriage in England, 1500–1800*. New York: Harper, 1977.

Striar, Brian Jay. "Theories and Practices of Renaissance Verse Translation." Diss. Claremont Graduate School, 1984.

Stringer, Gary A., ed. *The Variorum Edition of the Poetry of John Donne*. 8 vols. Bloomington: Indiana UP, 1995– .

Strong, Roy. *The English Renaissance Miniature*. New York: Thames, 1983.

——. *Gloriana: The Portraits of Queen Elizabeth I*. New York: Thames, 1987.

——. *Tudor and Jacobean Portraits*. 2 vols. London: HMSO, 1969.

Stump, Donald V. "Edmund Spenser (circa 1552–13 January 1599)." *Dictionary of Literary Biography*. 167: 228–63.

Stump, Donald V., Jerome S. Dees, and C. Stuart Hunter. *Sir Philip Sidney: An Annotated Bibliography of Texts and Criticisms (1554–1984)*. New York: Hall; Toronto: Macmillan, 1994.

Sullivan, Ernest W., ed. *The First and Second Dalhousie Manuscripts*. 2 vols. Columbia: U of Missouri P, 1988.

WORKS CITED 315

Surrey, earl of. *See* Henry Howard.

Suster, Gerald, ed. *John Dee: Essential Readings*. Wellingborough, Eng.: Crucible, 1986.

Suzuki, Mihoko, ed. *Critical Essays on Edmund Spenser*. New York: Hall; London: Prentice, 1996.

———. *Metamorphoses of Helen: Authority and Difference in Homer, Virgil, Spenser, and Shakespeare*. Ithaca: Cornell UP, 1989.

Sylvester, Richard S., ed. *The Anchor Anthology of English Sixteenth-Century Verse*. New York: Anchor, 1974.

Thomas, Keith. "The Meaning of Literacy in Early Modern England." *The Written Word: Literacy in Transition*. Ed. Gerd Baumann. Oxford: Clarendon, 1986. 97–131.

———. *Religion and the Decline of Magic*. New York: Scribner's, 1971.

Thompson, Charlotte. "Love in an Orderly Universe: A Unification of Spenser's *Amoretti*, 'Anacreontics,' and *Epithalamion*." *Viator* 16 (1985): 277–335.

Tillyard, E. M. W. *The Elizabethan World Picture*. New York: Vintage, n.d.

Tolliver, Harold. *Lyric Provinces in the English Renaissance*. Columbus: Ohio State UP, 1985.

Tottel, Richard. *Tottel's Miscellany (1557–1587)*. Ed. Hyder Rollins. 2nd ed. 2 vols. Cambridge: Harvard UP, 1965.

Trager, H. L., and G. H. Smith. *An Outline of English Structure*. Norman: U of Oklahoma P, 1951.

Traub, Valerie. *Desire and Anxiety: Circulations of Sexuality in Shakespearean Drama*. London: Routledge, 1992.

Travitsky, Betty S., ed. *The Paradise of Women: Writings by Englishwomen of the Renaissance*. New York: Columbia UP, 1989.

Tromly, Fred B. *Playing with Desire: Christopher Marlowe and the Art of Tantalization*. Toronto: U of Toronto P, 1998.

Tufte, Virginia J. "Gertrude Stein's Prothalamion: A Unique Poem in a Classical Mode." *Yale University Library Gazette* 43 (1968): 17–23.

———, ed. *High Wedlock Then Be Honoured: Wedding Poems from Nineteen Countries and Twenty-Five Centuries*. New York: Viking, 1970.

———. *The Poetry of Marriage: The Epithalamium in Europe and Its Development in England*. U of Southern California Studies in Compar. Lit. 2. Los Angeles: Tinnon–Brown, 1970.

Turner, James Grantham, ed. *Sexuality and Gender in Early Modern Europe: Institutions, Texts, Images*. Cambridge: Cambridge UP, 1993.

Turner, Myron. "Pastoral and Hermaphrodite: A Study in the Naturalism of Marlowe's *Hero and Leander*." *Texas Studies in Literature and Language* 17 (1975): 397–414.

Tuve, Rosemond. *Elizabethan and Metaphysical Imagery: Renaissance Poetic and Twentieth-Century Critics*. Chicago: U of Chicago P, 1947.

Ule, Louis, ed. *Concordance to the Works of Christopher Marlowe*. Elizabethan Concordance Ser. 1. Hildesheim, Ger.: Olms, 1979.

Urry, William. *Christopher Marlowe and Canterbury*. Ed. Andrew Butcher. London: Faber, 1988.

316 WORKS CITED

Vance, Eugene. "Love's Concordance: The Poetics of Desire and the Joy of the Text." *Diacritics* 5.1 (1975): 40–52.

Van der Noot, John. *Theatre for Worldlings*. Facsim. ed. Ed. William A. Jackson and Louis S. Friedland. New York: Scholars' Facsims. and Rpts., 1939.

van Dorsten, Jan, Arthur F. Kinney, and Dominic Baker-Smith, eds. *Sir Philip Sidney: 1586 and the Creation of a Legend*. Leiden: Leiden UP, 1986.

Vendler, Helen. *The Art of Shakespeare's Sonnets*. Cambridge: Belknap–Harvard UP, 1997.

———. *Poems, Poets, Poetry: An Introduction and Anthology*. Boston: Bedford, 1997.

Vickers, Brian, ed. *Occult and Scientific Mentalities in the Renaissance*. Cambridge: Cambridge UP, 1984.

———, ed. *Shakespeare: The Critical Heritage*. 6 vols. London: Routledge, 1974–81.

Vickers, Nancy. "'The Blazon of Sweet Beauty's Best': Shakespeare's *Lucrece*." Parker and Hartman 95–115.

———. "Diana Described: Scattered Woman and Scattered Rhyme." *Critical Inquiry* 8 (1981): 265–80. Rpt. in *Writing and Sexual Difference*. Ed. Elizabeth Abel. Chicago: U of Chicago P, 1982. 95–110.

———. "The Mistress in the Masterpiece." *The Poetics of Gender*. Ed. Nancy K. Miller. New York: Columbia UP, 1986. 19–41.

Vivian, Percival, ed. *Campion's Works*. Oxford: Oxford UP, 1909.

Walker, D. P. *Spiritual and Demonic Magic: From Ficino to Campanella*. 1958. Notre Dame: U of Notre Dame P, 1975.

Wall, Wendy. *The Imprint of Gender: Authorship and Publication in the English Renaissance*. Ithaca: Cornell UP, 1993.

Wallace, John M. "'Examples Are Best Precepts': Readers and Meanings in Seventeenth-Century Poetry." *Critical Inquiry* 1 (1974): 273–90.

Wallace, Malcolm William. *The Life of Sir Philip Sidney*. Cambridge: Cambridge UP, 1915.

Waller, Gary. "Acts of Reading: The Production of Meaning in *Astrophil and Stella*." Sessions 23–36.

———. "The Countess of Pembroke and Gendered Reading." *The Renaissance Englishwoman in Print: Counterbalancing the Canon*. Ed. Anne M. Haselkorn and Betty S. Travitsky. Amherst: U of Massachusetts P, 1990. 327–45.

———. *Edmund Spenser: A Literary Life*. New York: St. Martin's, 1994.

———. *English Poetry of the Sixteenth Century*. 2nd ed. London: Longman, 1993.

Waller, Gary, and Michael D. Moore, eds. *Sir Philip Sidney and the Interpretation of Renaissance Culture: The Poet in His Time and in Ours: A Collection of Critical and Scholarly Essays*. London: Croom, 1984.

Walsh, William P. "Sexual Discovery and Renaissance Morality in Marlowe's *Hero and Leander*." *Studies in English Literature, 1500–1900* 12 (1972): 33–54.

Walton, Izzak. *The Compleat Angler; or, The Contemplative Man's Recreation*. London, 1655.

Warkentin, Germaine. "*Amoretti, Epithalamion*." *Spenser Encyclopedia*. 30–38.

WORKS CITED 317

———. "The Meeting of the Muses: Sidney and the Mid-Tudor Poets." Waller and Moore 17–33.

———. "Robert Sidney's 'Darcke Offerings': The Making of a Late Tudor Manuscript *Canzoniere.*" *Spenser Studies* 12 (1998): 37–73.

———. "Sidney and the Supple Muse: Compositional Procedures in Some Sonnets of *Astrophil and Stella.*" Sessions 37–48. Rpt. in Kay, *Sir Philip Sidney* 171–84.

———. "Sidney's *Certain Sonnets*: Speculations on the Evolution of the Text." *Library* 2 (1980): 430–44.

———. "Sonnet, Sonnet Sequence." *Spenser Encyclopedia.* 662–65.

Warner, J. Christopher. "Poetry and Praise in *Colin Clouts Come Home Againe.*" *Studies in Philology* 94.3 (1997): 368–81.

Warnke, Frank J. "Epigram." *The New Princeton Encyclopedia of Poetry and Poetics.* Ed. Alex Preminger and T. V. F. Brogan. Princeton: Princeton UP, 1993.

Watkins, W. B. C. *Shakespeare and Spenser.* Princeton: Princeton UP, 1950.

———. "Shakespeare's Banquet of Sense." Alpers, *Elizabethan Poetry* 251–73.

Watson, Elizabeth Porges, ed. Defence of Poesie, Astrophil and Stella, *and Other Writings.* By Philip Sidney. Everyman Lib. London: Dent; Rutland: Tuttle, 1997.

———, ed. *Spenser: Selected Writings.* London: Routledge, 1992.

Weiner, Andrew D. "Structure and 'Fore Conceit' in *Astrophil and Stella.*" *Texas Studies in Literature and Language* 16 (1974): 1–25.

Wells, Stanley, ed. *The Cambridge Companion to Shakespeare Studies.* Cambridge: Cambridge UP, 1986.

———, ed. *Shakespeare: A Bibliographical Guide.* New ed. Oxford: Clarendon, 1990.

———. *Shakespeare: A Life in Drama.* New York: Norton, 1995.

———. *Shakespeare: An Illustrated Dictionary.* London: Kaye; New York: Oxford UP, 1978.

Wells, William, ed. *Spenser Allusions in the Sixteenth and Seventeenth Centuries.* Spec. issue of *Studies in Philology* 68.5 (1971): 1–172.

Welsh, Andrew. *The Roots of Lyric: Primitive Poetry and Modern Poetics.* Princeton: Princeton UP, 1978.

Whigham, Frank. *Ambition and Privilege: The Social Tropes of Elizabethan Courtesy Theory.* Berkeley: U of California P, 1984.

White, Micheline. "Recent Studies in Women Writers of Tudor England, 1485–1603 (Mid-1993 to 1999)." *English Literary Renaissance* 20 (2000): forthcoming.

White, Paul Whitfield, ed. *Marlowe, History, and Sexuality: New Critical Essays on Christopher Marlowe.* New York: AMS, 1998.

Whitman, Charles Huntington. *A Subject-Index to the Poems of Edmund Spenser.* 1919. New York: Russell, 1966.

Whitney, Geffrey. *A Choice of Emblems.* 1586. Ed. John Manning. Aldershot, Eng.: Scolar, 1989.

Whitworth, Charles. "George Peele (circa 25 July 1556–9 November 1596)." *Dictionary of Literary Biography.* 167: 165–70.

318 WORKS CITED

———. "Thomas Lodge (1558–September 1625)." *Dictionary of Literary Biography.* 172: 136–49.

Wickert, Max A. "Structure and Ceremony in Spenser's *Epithalamion.*" *ELH* 35 (1968): 135–57.

Wiesner, Merry. *Women and Gender in Early Modern Europe.* Cambridge: Cambridge UP, 1993.

Willen, Gerald, and Victor B. Reed, eds. *A Casebook on Shakespeare's Sonnets.* New York: Cromwell, 1964.

Williams, Gordon. "The Coming of Age of Shakespeare's Adonis." *Modern Language Review* 78 (1983): 769–76.

Williams, John, ed. *English Renaissance Poetry: A Collection of Shorter Poems from Skelton to Jonson.* Fayetteville: U of Arkansas P, 1990.

Williams, Raymond. *Marxism and Literature.* Oxford: Oxford UP, 1977.

Williamson, Colin. "Structure and Syntax in *Astrophil and Stella.*" Kay, *Sir Philip Sidney* 227–42.

Wiltenburg, Robert. "Sir John Davies (April? 1569–8 December 1626)." *Dictionary of Literary Biography.* 172: 53–61.

Wimsatt, W. K., ed. *Versification: Major Language Types.* New York: MLA, New York UP, 1972.

Wind, Edgar. *Pagan Mysteries in the Renaissance.* New York: Norton, 1958.

Wine, M. L. "Spenser's 'Sweete Themmes': Of Time and the River." *Studies in English Literature, 1500–1900* 2 (1962): 111–17. Rpt. in Berger, *Spenser* 40–46.

Winters, Yvor. "The Sixteenth Century Lyric in England: A Critical and Historical Reinterpretation." Alpers, *Elizabethan Poetry* 93–125.

Wood, Allen G. *Literary Satire and Theory: A Study of Horace, Boileau, and Pope.* New York: Garland, 1985.

Woodbridge, Linda, ed. *Shakespeare: A Selective Bibliography of Modern Criticism.* West Cornwall: Locust, 1988.

Woods, Susanne. "The Body Penitent: A 1560 Calvinist Sonnet Sequence." *American Notes and Queries* 5 (1992): 137–40.

———. *Natural Emphasis: English Versification from Chaucer to Dryden.* San Marino: Huntington, 1985.

Woods, Susanne, and Margaret P. Hannay, eds. *Teaching Tudor and Stuart Women Writers.* Options for Teaching. New York: MLA, forthcoming 2000.

Woodward, Daniel H. "Some Themes in Spenser's 'Prothalamion.'" *ELH* 29 (1962): 34–46.

Woudhuysen, H. R. *Sir Philip Sidney and the Circulation of Manuscripts, 1558–1640.* Oxford: Clarendon, 1996.

Wraight, A. D., and Virginia F. Stern. *In Search of Christopher Marlowe: A Pictorial Biography.* 1965. Chichester, Eng.: Hart, 1993.

Wroth, Mary. *The Poems of Lady Mary Wroth.* Ed. Josephine Roberts. Baton Rouge: Louisiana State UP, 1983.

Wyatt, Thomas. *The Complete Poems.* Ed. R. A. Rebholz. New Haven: Yale UP, 1978.

Yates, Frances A. *Giordano Bruno and the Hermetic Tradition*. New York: Random-Vintage, 1969.

———. *The Occult Philosophy in the Elizabethan Age*. London: Routledge, 1979.

Young, Frank B. "Medusa and the *Epithalamion*: A Problem in Spenserian Imagery." *English Language Notes* 11.1 (1973): 21–29.

Zagorin, Perez. *The Court and the Country: The Beginnings of the English Revolution*. New York: Atheneum, 1970.

Ziegler, Georgianna M. "Recent Studies in Women Writers of Tudor England, 1485–1603 (1990 to mid-1993)." *English Literary Renaissance* 24 (1994): 229–42.

Zim, Rivkah. *English Metrical Psalms: Poetry as Praise and Prayer, 1535–1601*. Cambridge: Cambridge UP, 1987.

Zitner, Sheldon. "Surrey's 'Epitaph on Thomas Clere': Lyric and History." Hošek and Parker 106–15.

Zunder, William. *Elizabethan Marlowe: Writing and Culture in the English Renaissance*. Cottingham, Eng.: Unity, 1994.

Zunder, William, and Suzanne Trill, eds. *Writing and the English Renaissance*. London: Longman, 1996.

INDEX OF SELECTED WORKS

"The Battle of Brunanburh," 76
Bible, 14, 22, 29, 113, 168, 194, 213–14,
    230, 249, 253, 256, 259
Campion, Thomas
    "There is a garden in her face," 103–06
Chapman, George
    Ovids Banquet of Sence, 96–97
Chaucer, Geoffrey
    Canterbury Tales, 14, 68, 82, 250–51
Daniel, Samuel
    Delia, 69, 126, 157
Donne, John
    "The Bait," 48, 71, 154, 223
    "The Broken Heart," 207
    Elegy 19, 181–83
    Satire 1, 177
Drayton, Michael
    Endymion and Phoebe, 12, 97
    Ideas Mirrour, 157
    "Since there's no help," 132
Elizabeth I
    "The doubt of future foes," 206–07
    Epigrams, 203–05
    "Speech to her Last Parliament," 19
Englands Helicon, 13, 70, 221, 264
Gascoigne, George
    Adventures of Master F. J., 123, 186, 189
    "Certayne Notes of Instruction on the
        Making of Verse or Rime in English,"
        75, 78
    "Gascoignes Woodmanship," 185–87, 204
    An Hundreth Sundrie Flowres, 264
    "Lullabie," 185, 187
Greville, Fulke
    Caelica, 90
    "An epitaph upon the Right Honorable
        Sir Philip Sidney," 199
Herbert, George
    "The Collar," 191
Howard, Henry, earl of Surrey
    "Epitaph on Sir Thomas Wyatt," 249
    "Love that doth raine and live within my
        thought," 86
    "So cruel prison, how could betide, alas,"
        204
    "The soote season," 87
Jonson, Ben
    "To Penshurst," 192
Lanyer, Aemilia
    Salve Deus Rex Judaeorum, 143
Lock, Anne Vaughan
    "The haynous gylt of my forsaken ghost,"
        212
Lodge, Thomas
    Glaucus and Scylla, 34
    Phillis, 157

Scylla's Metamorphosis, 12, 93, 97
Marlowe, Christopher
    Hero and Leander, 4, 7, 9, 10–14, 23, 34,
        46, 47–50, 57, 61, 71, 72, 94, 95, 97,
        120, 177, 220–21, 223
    Lucan's First Book, 7, 46, 48, 50
    "On the Death of Sir Roger Manwood,"
        7, 47
    Ovid's Elegies, 7, 9, 47
    "The Passionate Shepherd to His Love,"
        7, 9, 46–48, 56, 154, 220–25
Milton, John
    Lycidas, 236
    "On the Morning of Christ's Nativity," 236
    Paradise Lost, 254
The Mirror for Magistrates, 3, 13, 18, 21,
    214, 256
Ovid
    Amores, 14, 29, 47
    Metamorphoses, 14, 29, 93, 95–97,
        104–05, 108, 116
Petrarch, Francesco
    Rime sparse, 14, 33, 85–86, 89–92,
        128–29, 131, 261
Puttenham, George
    The Arte of English Poesie, 14, 32, 121,
        167, 184–85, 205, 229
Ralegh, Walter
    "The Lie," 185, 189, 257
    "The Nymph's Reply," 71, 223–24
    The Ocean to Cynthia, 185, 251
    "The Passionate Mans Pilgrimage,"
        188–89
Shakespeare, William
    A Lover's Complaint, 7, 8, 51
    The Rape of Lucrece, 51, 52, 53, 57, 92,
        121, 180
    The Sonnets, 4, 7, 8, 9, 15, 27, 51, 52, 53,
        54, 55, 57, 91, 164, 170, 173–76,
        239–44
    Venus and Adonis, 12, 34, 46, 51–54, 57,
        93, 94, 95, 97, 120
Sidney, Mary, countess of Pembroke
    "A Dialogue between Two Shepherds," 10
    "The Dolefull Lay of Clorinda," 199
    "Even now that Care which on thy
        Crowne attends," 120
    Psalms of David, 10, 124–25, 133–38
Sidney, Philip
    Astrophil and Stella, 3, 6, 7, 9–11, 23,
        44–46, 56, 63, 64, 70, 72, 75, 84,
        88–90, 92, 93, 99, 100, 112, 120, 126,
        129, 130, 133–37, 143, 157, 164,
        174–75, 196–201, 228, 246, 258,
        261–62, 265–66
    Certain Sonnets, 6, 23, 45, 78, 115, 117

322 INDEX OF SELECTED WORKS

Defence of Poesy, 6, 7, 14, 44, 45, 88, 98, 248
Old Arcadia, 6, 45, 246, 257
New Arcadia, 6, 15, 137
Skelton, John
"Garlande or Chapelet of Laurell," 251–52
Spenser, Edmund
Amoretti, 5, 6, 9, 10, 12, 33, 40, 41, 43, 62, 63, 90, 91, 112, 129, 130, 157, 167, 168, 170–72, 226–27, 229, 233, 252, 254
Colin Clouts Come Home Againe, 5, 6, 41–44, 185, 191, 252
Daphnaida, 41
Epithalamion, 5, 6, 9, 10, 11, 12, 34, 35, 39–41, 43, 61, 63, 89, 91, 106, 108, 130, 157, 167, 168, 170, 172, 180, 226–30, 233–34, 237, 254
The Faerie Queene, 5, 6, 10, 15, 16, 19, 23, 39, 40, 41, 56, 62, 93, 120, 150, 168, 187, 199, 215, 227, 234–36, 246, 251–52, 254
Fowre Hymnes, 5, 36, 40, 41, 43, 44, 89, 143, 170
Muiopotmos, 5, 6, 41, 43
Mutabilitie Cantos, 5, 40, 41
Prothalamion, 5, 6, 10, 11, 34, 40, 41, 44, 63, 154, 208, 226, 234–38
The Shepheardes Calender, 3, 5, 6, 11, 12, 23, 32, 34, 40–42, 44, 56, 63, 67, 69, 70, 88, 100, 115, 120, 155, 157, 190–95, 234, 245, 246, 248–49, 252, 256–57, 264
   Januarye, 5, 69
   Februarie, 5, 192, 246
   Aprill, 5, 9, 41, 100, 191–92
   Maye, 257
   October, 5, 6, 9, 191, 192–93, 246, 257
   November, 5, 191, 193–94
   December, 5, 42, 191, 193, 194
The Ruines of Rome, 12
The Ruines of Time, 41, 234
"To His Booke," 9
A Theatre for Worldlings, 6
Visions of the Worlds Vanitie, 6
Tottel's Miscellany, 3, 8, 13, 70, 87, 157, 249, 256, 258, 264
Vergil
Aeneid, 104
Wroth, Mary
Pamphilia to Amphilanthus, 129–30, 197, 265
Wyatt, Thomas
"Blame Not My Lute," 83
"My galley charged with forgetfulness," 82–84
"The long love that in my thought doth harbour," 174
"They flee from me," 14, 162–63, 166
"Whoso list to hunt," 87, 131, 174

INDEX OF NAMES

Adán, Martín, 33
Aers, David, 92, 257
Alexander, Nigel, 13, 97
Allen, Don Cameron, 29
Allen, Michael J. B., 38
Allott, Robert, 121
Alpers, Paul J., 19, 23, 31, 32, 42, 43, 154, 234, 264
Altieri, Charles, 33
Altieri, Joanne, 49
Alwes, Derek, 17, 21
Anderson, Benedict, 39, 180
Anderson, Douglas, 43, 229
Anderson, Judith, 20, 22, 37, 44, 62
Anderson, Perry, 39
Appiah, Kwame, 180
Ariosto, Lodovico, 88
Ascham, Roger, 13, 14, 19, 71
Askew, Anne, 11, 12, 134, 214, 256–57
Attridge, Derek, 78
Auden, W. H., 216
Augustine, 14, 53, 166, 244
Ault, Norman, 3, 8, 13

Bacon, Francis, 26
Bahti, Timothy, 31
Baird, Julianne, 113
Bakeless, John, 20, 48, 55
Baker, David J., 39
Baker, Herschel, 9, 10, 11
Baker-Smith, Dominic, 46, 265
Baldwin, William, 256–57
Bale, John, 257
Banton, Michael, 180
Barber, C. L., 23
Barbour, Reid, 21
Barish, Jonas, 98
Barkan, Leonard, 29, 177
Barker, Francis, 198, 232
Barnes, Barnabe, 10, 12, 157
Barnfield, Richard, 10, 12, 13, 21, 157, 173, 177
Bartas, Guillaume de Saluste, sieur du, 29
Bartels, Emily C., 50, 56
Barthes, Roland, 168
Bartlett, John, 21
Bashe, Edward, 140
Bate, Jonathan, 20, 29, 53, 57
Bates, Catherine, 6, 37, 43, 229
Beal, Peter, 121
Beaumont, Francis, 12, 266
Beebee, Thomas O., 151
Beilin, Elaine, 134
Bellamy, Elizabeth, 30
Bellay, Joachim du, 29, 64
Belsey, Catherine, 52, 232

Bembo, Peter, 69, 86
Bennett, Paula, 18
Benson, John, 239
Berger, Harry, Jr., 32, 38, 42, 44, 56, 208, 235, 258
Bergeron, David M., 17
Bernard, John, 18, 42, 232
Bernstein, Charles, 258
Berry, Cicely, 112
Berry, Philippa, 95
Berryman, John, 201
Bertie, Catherine Brandon, 211
Bevington, David, 8, 15, 22
Beza, Theodore, 100–01, 133, 135
Bhabha, Homi K., 40
Bieman, Elizabeth, 38, 49
Biester, James, 31
Birrell, T. A., 266
Bjorvand, Einar, 43
Black, L. G., 208
Blanchard, W. Scott, 36
Blessington, Francis C., 35
Blissett, William, 48
Bloom, Harold, 50
Bloomfield, Morton W., 35
Blunt, Edward, 72
Boas, Frederick S., 20, 48, 49
Boleyn, Anne, 211
Bolgar, R. R., 47
Bongo, Pietro, 229
Boone, Lea Ann, 20
Boose, Lynda, 22
Booth, Roy J., 12
Booth, Stephen, 7, 8, 15, 16, 54, 240, 243
Borges, Jorge Luis, 171
Bourdieu, Pierre, 94
Bowers, Fredson, 16
Boyd, Mark Alexander, 12
Boyle, Elizabeth, 226, 233
Bradbrook, Muriel, 49, 51
Braden, Gordon, 23, 25, 49, 54, 55
Bradner, Leicester, 202
Brandt, Bruce E., 17, 20
Brathwaite, Richard, 98
Braudy, Leo, 266
Braunmuller, A. R., 49
Bray, Alan, 173
Bredbeck, Gregory W., 95, 177–78
Brennan, Michael, 40
Brereton, Geoffrey, 86
Breton, Nicolas, 123, 126, 263
Briggs, Julia, 26, 55
Briggs, Katherine, 62
Brink, J. R., 43
Brinkelow, Margaret, 211
Bromley, Laura G., 53

324 INDEX OF NAMES

Brooks-Davies, Douglas, 5, 12, 38, 88, 234
Brown, Cedric C., 40
Brown, Georgia, 34, 50, 63
Brucioli, Antonio, 85
Bruster, Douglas, 48, 56
Bullen, A. H., 216
Bullett, Gerald, 13
Bullough, Geoffrey, 21
Burckhardt, Jacob, 23, 25
Burnett, Mark Thornton, 7, 40
Burrow, Colin, 25, 30, 41, 43, 51, 55–57
Burto, William, 8
Bush, Douglas, 8, 25, 29
Bushnell, Rebecca, 68
Butler, Christopher, 229
Buxton, John, 20
Byrd, William, 13, 86

Cain, Thomas H., 234–35
Caldwell, Ellen, 18, 21
Calvin, John, 91, 211
Camden, William, 5
Campbell, Lily B., 35
Campbell, Marion, 49, 54
Campbell, Oscar James, 21
Campion, Thomas, 9, 10, 13, 21, 61, 77, 103, 109, 216–19
Carew, Thomas, 264
Cartwright, William, 264
Cassirer, Ernst, 38
Castelvetro, Ludovico, 85
Castiglione, Baldassara 14, 174
Cavanagh, Sheila T., 63
Cavanaugh, Jean C., 120
Cecil, William, 13, 120, 246
Champion, Larry S., 17
Chan, Lois Mai, 17
Chapman, George, 7, 13, 21, 38, 49, 71, 72, 120, 223
Chartier, Roger, 121, 158, 266
Chaucer, Geoffrey, 10, 14, 26, 39, 64, 77, 249–56
Chaudhuri, Sukanta, 32
Cheke, Mary, 13
Cheney, Donald, 20, 44
Cheney, Patrick, 3, 17, 36, 39, 41, 44, 47, 48, 54, 56, 62, 63, 89, 117, 120, 208, 226, 234
Chinitz, David, 229
Christine de Pisan, 68
Cirillo, A. R., 229
Clark, Sandra, 12, 21
Clemen, Wolfgang, 228
Clulee, Nicholas, 38
Cohen, Joel, 113
Cohen, Walter, 39, 51
Colaianne, A. J., 17
Cole, A. Thomas, 76
Cole, Howard C., 26

Coleridge, Samuel Taylor, 5, 237
Colie, Rosalie, 28, 30, 94, 150
Collinson, Patrick, 211, 257
Combe, Kirk, 36
Connell, Dorothy, 44
Connery, Brian A., 36
Conrad, Peter, 26
Constable, Henry, 10, 12, 13, 157
Cook, James Wyatt, 87
Coote, Stephen, 13, 26
Corbett, Margery, 71, 266
Cousins, A. D., 52
Cowley, Abraham, 264
Cradock, Edward, 39
Craft, William, 45, 56
Craig, Hardin, 26, 28
Crane, Mary Thomas, 21, 37, 88, 121
Cranmer, Thomas, 257
Crashaw, Richard, 264
Crewe, Jonathan, 22, 23
Cromwell, Thomas, 211
Cropper, Elizabeth, 24
Crowley, Robert, 256
Cullen, Patrick, 20, 42
Cummings, R. M., 19
Cunnar, Eugene, 48
Curtius, E. R., 27

Daniel, Samuel, 9, 10, 12, 13, 18, 21, 22, 120, 123, 158, 263, 265
Daniello, Bernardino, 85
Dankworth, John, 113
Dante, 14, 68, 85
Darnton, Robert, 122
Dasenbrock, Reed Way, 43
Davies, John, 9, 12, 13, 18, 21, 23
Davis, Walter R., 216
Day, Richard, 202
Dean, Leonard F., 54
Dee, John, 38, 120
Dees, Jerome S., 17, 20
de Grazia, Margreta, 23, 45, 52–55, 57, 239
Dekker, Thomas, 123, 155
Deller, Alfred, 113, 217
Deloney, Thomas, 123
DeNeef, A. Leigh, 41, 43, 56, 229
Dent, R. W., 21
Dering, Edward, 211
Derrida, Jacques, 150, 167, 168
de Selincourt, Ernest, 4, 15
Desportes, Philippe, 29, 64, 228
Devereux, Janice, 257
Devereux, Robert, earl of Essex, 37, 226, 237
Di Cesare, Mario A., 20
DiGangi, Mario, 22, 62, 178
Doherty, M. J., 45
Dollimore, Jonathan, 24

INDEX OF NAMES 325

Donaldson, Ian, 53, 57
Donawerth, Jane, 214
Donington, Robert, 111
Donker, Marjorie, 18, 30, 55
Donne, John, 9, 13, 14, 23, 26, 30, 31, 34, 65, 95, 110, 115, 128–29, 138–39, 173, 179, 228, 258, 263–66
Donno, Elizabeth Story, 34, 94, 96, 97
Donovan, Kevin, 18
Donow, Herbert S., 20
Doughtie, Edward, 140, 218
Dowland, John, 13, 109–13, 158, 218
Dowriche, Anne, 12, 14
Drake, Francis, 11, 13
Drayton, Michael, 9, 10, 13, 21, 22, 32, 39, 55, 70, 71, 158, 236–37, 263, 265
Dryden, John, 94
Dubrow, Heather, 24, 25, 30, 33, 35, 37, 43, 52, 57, 63, 88, 94, 95, 151, 198, 230, 231
Dudley, Anne Russell, 212
Dudley, Robert, earl of Leicester, 37, 205
Duncan-Jones, Katherine, 6, 8, 15, 18, 20, 53–55, 159, 240, 248
Dunlop, Alexander, 16, 226
Durling, Robert, 30, 87, 128
Dyer, Edward, 13, 139

Easthope, Anthony, 31
Eaves, Morris, 237
Edwards, Philip, 39
Edwards, Thomas, 97
Eliot, T. S., 23, 24, 47, 93, 97, 237
Elliott, John R., 19
Elliott, Robert C., 36
Ellis-Fermor, Una M., 47, 48
Elizabeth I, 9, 11, 13, 18, 21, 35–37, 62, 120, 125, 126, 133, 134, 140, 147, 192, 202–09, 226, 246, 263
Ellrodt, Robert, 38, 43, 53
Elsky, Martin, 37
Elyot, Thomas, 14, 19, 96, 98
Empson, William, 24, 32, 63, 243
Enterline, Lynn, 24
Erasmus, Desiderius, 120
Estrin, Barbara L., 33
Ettin, Andrew V., 32
Evans, G. Blakemore, 8, 55
Evans, Maurice, 12, 27

Falco, Raphael, 45
Fane, Elizabeth, 134
Febvre, Lucien, 266
Fehrenback, Robert J., 18, 20
Feinberg, Nona, 45
Felch, Susan M., 21, 22, 62, 211
Fellowes, E. H., 217
Felperin, Howard, 23

Ferguson, A. B., 27
Ferguson, Margaret W., 99
Ferry, Anne, 33, 37
Fichter, Andrew, 30
Ficino, Marsilio, 38
Field, John, 211
Field, Richard, 120
Filelfo, Francesco, 85
Fineman, Joel, 24, 53, 57, 198, 242
Finucci, Valerie, 24
Finzi, Gerald, 113
Fischlin, Daniel, 112
Fish, Stanley, 22
Fletcher, Angus, 189
Fletcher, Giles, 10, 12, 157, 266
Fónagy, I., 111
Forman, Simon, 39
Forster, Leonard, 32
Forsythe, R. S., 46
Foucault, Michel, 24, 71, 96, 167
Fowler, Alastair, 24, 26, 30, 39, 44, 55, 151, 229, 234, 236
Fowler, Elizabeth, 22, 62, 63, 250–51
Foxe, John, 14, 204, 257
Fraser, Russell, 21, 96, 100
Fraunce, Abraham, 64, 70, 123–24
Freccero, John, 24
Freer, Coburn, 46
French, Peter, 38
Friedenreich, Kenneth, 17, 50
Fritze, Ronald L., 18, 55
Frye, Northrop, 24, 36
Fukuda, Shohachi, 229
Fuller, John, 32
Fumerton, Patricia, 62, 63, 249

Garnier, Robert, 133
Gascoigne, George, 9, 10, 13, 18, 21, 22, 55, 63, 117, 184, 204, 256, 259, 263–66
Gesualdo, Giovanni, 85
Giamatti, A. Bartlett, 5, 30
Gibbons, Orlando, 86
Gibbs, Donna, 43
Giddens, Anthony, 39
Gill, Roma, 7, 15, 47–50
Gilman, Ernest B., 98
Gleason, John B., 229
Gleckner, Robert F., 237
Godshalk, William L., 17, 18, 49, 50
Goldberg, Jonathan, 23, 24, 95, 178
Golding, Arthur, 13, 93, 97
Googe, Barnabe, 13, 265
Gosson, Stephen, 98–102
Gouws, John, 21
Gower, John, 252
Grafton, Anthony, 27, 119, 120
Graham, Kenneth J. E., 110
Grantley, Darryll, 50

326 INDEX OF NAMES

Greenblatt, Stephen, 8, 15, 17, 20, 22–24, 28, 55, 134, 185, 258
Greene, Robert, 10, 18, 21, 22, 55, 119, 247
Greene, Roland, 30, 33, 46, 62, 63, 88, 134, 251
Greene, Thomas M., 18, 23, 28, 29, 30–31, 33, 35, 43, 55, 86, 97, 229
Greenfield, Matthew, 35
Gregerson, Linda, 30, 249
Gresley, Thomas, 165
Greville, Fulke, 9, 10, 13, 18, 21, 120, 158
Grey, Jane, 133
Griffin, Bartholomew, 10, 12
Griffin, Dustin, 36
Grindal, Edmund, 120
Groos, G. W., 203
Gross, Kenneth, 237
Guillén, Claudio, 94
Guilpin, Everard, 179, 181–83
Gunn, Giles, 23
Guy, John, 27
Gwynnethe, Margaret, 211

Haber, Judith, 32
Habermas, Jurgen, 39
Hadfield, Andrew, 39, 43, 44, 55, 56, 235, 257
Hager, Alan, 45
Hainsworth, Peter, 86
Hall, Kim F., 45, 179, 180, 183
Halperin, David M., 32
Hamilton, A. C., 5, 17, 22, 44, 51, 55, 56
Hammond, Gerald, 24
Hannay, Margaret P., 21, 22, 37, 62, 133–34
Harbage, Alfred, 8
Hardison, O. B., Jr., 18, 31, 35, 99
Harington, John, 13, 88, 121, 139, 157, 208–09
Harner, James L., 17
Harsdörfer, Georg Phillip, 126
Hartley, L. P., 152
Hartman, Geoffrey H., 54, 237
Harvey, Gabriel, 6, 77, 100, 120, 157, 245
Haskell, Ann, 77
Hattaway, Michael, 50, 56
Haydn, Hiram, 3, 13, 26
Healy, Thomas, 23, 47, 57
Hedley, Jane, 21, 30, 62, 63
Helgerson, Richard, 5, 22, 24, 39, 45, 55, 63, 71, 96, 235–36, 263
Henderson, Diana E., 30, 48, 63, 198, 199
Hendricks, Margo, 22, 62
Heneage, Thomas, 13
Heninger, S. K., Jr., 38, 41, 48, 62
Hentzner, Paul, 203
Herbert, George, 138, 264–66
Herendeen, Wyman H., 44, 234
Herman, Peter C., 63, 99

Hesiod, 190
Heywood, John, 257
Heywood, Thomas, 97
Hieatt, A. Kent, 39, 43, 61, 229, 236
Highley, Christopher, 39
Hill, W. Speed, 229
Hiller, Geoffrey G., 13, 177
Hilliard, Nicholas, 165
Hobbs, Mary, 265
Hobsbawm, E. J., 39
Hoby, Edward, earl of Arundel, 13
Hoccleve, Thomas, 254
Holinshed, Rafael, 14, 204
Hollander, John, 13, 24, 75, 234, 237
Hopkins, John, 256
Horace, 190
Hošek, Chaviva, 24
Howard, Henry, 8–10, 12, 13, 18, 24, 34, 81, 86, 129, 139, 199, 210, 256, 259, 264, 266
Howard, Jean, 54
Howard, Skiles, 98
Hubler, Edward, 4, 15, 243
Hughes, Joan, 13
Hughes, John, 5, 235
Hughes, Ted, 52, 57
Hughey, Ruth, 140
Hulse, Clark, 22, 24, 34, 35, 43, 45, 48, 52, 53, 56, 63, 95
Hume, Anthea, 42
Hume, Robert, 119
Hunt, Marvin, 44, 56
Hunt, Maurice, 50
Hunter, C. Stuart, 17
Hurstfield, Joel, 39

Inglis, Fred, 31
Innes, Paul, 33

Jackson, M. P., 236
Jacobsen, Eric, 47
Jakobson, Roman, 30
James, Heather, 39
Jameson, Frederic, 151
Jardine, Lisa, 22, 27, 120
Javitch, Daniel, 37, 184
Jayne, Sears Reynolds, 38
Jed, Stephanie, 53
Johnson, Lynn Staley, 42
Johnson, William C., 43, 226, 229
Johnson, W. R., 31
Jones, Ann Rosalind, 24, 33, 45, 167
Jones, Emrys, 9, 11, 12, 16
Jonson, Ben, 9, 13, 26, 139, 158, 173, 264–66
Judson, Alexander C., 19

Kahn, Coppélia, 52–54
Kalstone, David, 23, 33, 44

INDEX OF NAMES 327

Kaminsky, Judith, 53
Kaske, Carol V., 43, 229, 232
Kastan, David Scott, 22, 36, 63
Kay, Dennis, 21, 34, 46, 50
Keach, William, 34, 49, 50, 52, 53, 94, 95
Kedouri, Elie, 40
Kellogg, Robert, 5, 6
Kelsall, Malcom, 47
Kennedy, William J., 33, 62, 85, 87, 263
Kermode, Frank, 13
Kernan, Alvin B., 36, 54, 266
Kerrigan, John, 7, 8, 15, 16, 35, 119, 170, 240
Kerrigan, William, 23, 25, 55
Kiefer, Frederick, 21
Kimbrough, Robert, 6, 44
King, John N., 18, 22, 42, 63, 229, 256–57
Kinney, Arthur F., 17, 19, 22, 25, 29, 40, 46, 55, 56, 63, 96
Kinney, Clare, 62, 63
Kintgen, Eugene, 121–22
Kirkby, Emma, 113
Kirkpatrick, Robin, 29
Klawitter, George, 177–78
Klein, Lisa M., 43
Knight, G. Wilson, 51
Knights, L. C., 23
Knox, John, 211
Kolin, Philip C., 53, 54, 57
Kramer, Jerome, 53
Krier, Theresa, 22, 63, 233
Kristeller, Paul O., 26, 28, 38
Kuin, Roger, 33, 63, 167, 227
Kuriyama, Constance B., 50

Labé, Louis, 228, 261–62
Laine, Cleo, 113
Lamb, Charles, 237
Lamb, Mary Ellen, 37, 46, 62, 115, 118
Lamson, Roy, 9, 11
Lane, Robert, 42
Languet, Herbert, 247
Lanham, Richard, 18, 37
Lanyer, Aemilia, 9, 12, 13, 40, 115, 120, 138
Larkin, Philip, 201
Latham, Agnes, 223
Lawes, Henry, 109, 114
Lawes, William, 110
Lee, Henry, 13, 126
Lee, John, 6
Leech, Clifford, 47, 48, 57
Leishman, J. B., 90
Leiter, Louis H., 48
Levao, Ronald, 17, 99
Lever, J. W., 32, 53
Levin, Harry, 29, 48, 57
Levin, Richard, 53
Lewalski, Barbara, 9, 30, 35, 40, 134, 253

Lewis, C[live] S[taples], 16, 23, 25, 28, 46, 54, 55, 91, 235, 257–58
Lievsay, John L., 16
Lightbown, R. W., 71, 266
Linden, Stanton J., 38
Lindenbaum, Peter, 266
Lindley, David, 31
Linklater, Kristin, 112
Liu, Alan, 70
Lock, Anne Vaughan, 13, 21, 62, 134, 210–15, 259, 260
Lodge, Thomas, 10 13, 18, 21, 22, 55, 94, 247
Loewenstein, Joseph, 43, 227, 229, 233, 264–65
Logan, Robert A., 49
Longiano, Fausto da, 85
Lotspeich, Henry Gibbons, 19
Love, Harold, 140
Lovejoy, Arthur O., 28
Low, Anthony, 45, 48
Lupton, Julia Reinhard, 62
Luther, Martin, 133
Lydgate, John, 249, 252
Lyly, John, 21, 22, 55, 247
Lynche, Richard, 10, 11
Lytle, Guy Fitch, 40

Machiavelli, Niccolò, 14, 26
Maclean, Hugh, 5, 6, 35, 43
MacLure, Millar, 16, 20
Maley, Willy, 19, 39, 42, 235
Mallette, Richard, 42, 43
Malone, Edmund, 240
Manley, Lawrence, 26, 44
Manningham, John, 120
Mantuan (Baptista Spagnuoli), 190
Marcus, Leah S., 22, 264
Marinelli, Peter V., 32
Marlowe, Christopher, 4, 7, 9, 10, 12–14, 18–23, 26, 30, 38, 40, 54–57, 61, 63, 71, 72, 93–95, 97, 120, 154, 173, 177, 220–25, 256–57
Marot, Clément, 29, 64, 133, 190
Marotti, Arthur F., 22, 33, 36, 40, 45, 54, 56, 63, 64, 69, 120, 140, 156, 158, 167, 174, 263–67
Marston, John, 12, 97
Martin, Christopher, 31
Martin, Henri-Jean, 266
Martin, Randall, 13
Martindale, Charles, 28, 46
Martz, Louis L., 49, 94, 95, 97, 135
Marvell, Andrew, 32, 42, 115, 216, 263
Mary Stuart, 13, 134, 206
Mary Tudor, 121, 203, 211
Maus, Katharine Eisaman, 22, 53, 232, 249
Maxwell, J. C., 7

328 INDEX OF NAMES

May, Steven W., 13, 18, 19, 22, 31, 36, 63, 64, 140, 156, 202, 207, 208
Mazzaro, Jerome, 31
Mazzio, Carla, 65
Mazzola, Elizabeth, 43, 229
McCabe, Richard, 4–6, 15, 41, 42, 56, 235
McColley, Diane Kelsey, 113
McCoy, Richard C., 37, 44, 56, 199
McDonald, Russ, 21, 54, 57
McLuskie, Kathleen E., 22
McManus, Caroline, 62, 63
McNeir, Waldo F., 16
Mebane, John S., 38
Melbancke, Brian, 247
Melton, John, 100
Mercer, Eric, 165
Meserole, Harrison T., 17
Meyer, Sam, 43
Miller, David Lee, 5, 16, 41, 44, 48, 49, 56, 57, 100, 235
Miller, Jacqueline T., 45
Miller, Paul, 229
Mills, Jerry Leath, 18, 21
Milton, John, 173, 264
Minnis, Alastair, 250
Minsheu, John, 180
Mirollo, James M., 37, 48
Miskimin, Alice S., 264
Mohl, Ruth, 20
Montrose, Louis A., 5, 24, 32, 33, 42, 43, 45, 56, 71, 101, 151, 154, 155, 236
Moore, John W., Jr., 16
Morley, Thomas, 13, 86, 123, 126, 216–18
Morris, Brian, 49
Moschus, 14
Moseley, Humphrey, 264
Moss, Ann, 121
Moulton, Ian F., 50
Mueller, Janel, 21, 22, 36, 62
Muir, Kenneth, 53
Muldrow, George M., 18, 30, 55
Murdoch, John, 165
Murrell, Jim, 165
Murrin, Michael, 30
Musa, Mark, 87

Nashe, Thomas, 9, 13, 18, 21, 26, 65, 70
Nelson, William, 5, 41
Neruda, Pablo, 33
Neuse, Richard, 43, 49, 229
Newman, Thomas, 157
Newton, Richard, 159, 264
Nicholl, Charles, 20, 38, 50
Nichols, J. G., 44
Nichols, John, 19, 205
Noel, Henry, 13
Noon, Patrick J., 165

Norbrook, David G., 9, 11, 12, 14, 16, 23, 27, 55, 257
Norton, Dan S., 234
Nosworthy, J. M., 47

Oates, Mary I., 43
Oliver, Douglas, 111
Oliver, Isaac, 165
Oram, William A., 5, 15, 40, 41, 43, 55, 56, 229, 235, 245–46, 248
Orgel, Stephen, 7, 16, 24, 40, 45, 55, 94, 97, 176, 178, 220
Osborn, James M., 20, 247
Osgood, Charles Grosvenor, 19
Ovid, 14, 28, 34, 47, 50, 93–97, 104, 106, 108, 116, 124, 228

Paglia, Camille, 41, 56
Parker, Matthew, 133
Parker, Patricia, 24, 54
Parr, Catherine, 211
Pask, Kevin, 26
Patterson, Annabel, 22, 26, 32, 122, 151, 154, 155, 257
Paulson, Ronald, 36
Pearcy, Lee T., 47
Pears, Steuart, 247
Pedersen, Sarah A., 17
Peele, George, 18, 21, 30
Pendry, E. D., 7
Pequigney, Joseph, 54
Percivale, Richard, 180
Percy, W., 10
Peterson, Douglas L., 31
Peterson, Richard S., 43
Petowe, Henry, 7, 97
Petrarch, Francesco, 14, 24, 25, 29, 33, 64, 85–92, 128–29, 133, 162, 166–68, 210, 227, 228, 240, 249, 261
Pettie, George, 247
Pico della Mirandola, Giovanni, 14, 26, 38, 129
Pigman, G. W., III, 34
Pilkington, Francis, 114
Plato, 38, 149
Platter, Thomas, 203
Poggioli, Renato, 32
Porter, Roy, 249
Post, Jonathan F. S., 17
Potter, Lois, 265
Prescott, Anne Lake, 5, 6, 20, 22, 25, 29, 36, 43, 44, 46, 55, 61, 63, 134, 202, 208, 226–27
Prince, F. T., 8
Provost, Foster, 16
Prowse, Richard, 211
Puttenham, George, 120, 154, 188, 206, 256–57

INDEX OF NAMES   329

Quarles, Francis, 264
Quilligan, Maureen, 23, 24, 45, 55, 56
Quinn, Edward G., 21
Quint, David, 24, 29, 30
Quitslund, Jon A., 38, 44

Radcliffe, David H., 19
Ralegh, Walter, 9, 10, 12, 13, 18, 21, 34, 48,
    63, 120, 139, 184–89, 199, 208
Rambuss, Richard, 42, 43, 100, 177, 234
Ramson, W. S., 13
Randall, John Herman, Jr., 38
Rasmussen, Mark, 42
Ratcliffe, Stephen, 21, 22, 63, 219
Ravenscroft, Thomas, 113
Ray, Robert H., 50
Reeds, Victor B., 54
Regan, Mariann Sanders, 167
Reiss, Timothy, 198
Rich, Barnabe, 247
Rich, Penelope, 120, 126
Richardson, Brian, 85
Richardson, David A., 20, 21, 44
Ricoeur, Paul, 169
Riffaterre, Michael, 168, 259–60
Ringler, William A., Jr., 15, 19, 78, 125, 139
Rivers, Elias, 86
Rivers, Isabel, 18, 55
Roberts, Gareth, 38
Roberts, J. A., 18
Roberts, Josephine, 138
Roberts, Peter, 50
Robertson, Jean, 246
Roche, Thomas P., Jr., 20, 33, 45, 46, 87, 90
Rodenburg, Patsy, 112
Roe, John, 8, 55
Rogers, William Elford, 234
Rollins, H. E., 9, 10, 11
Rollinson, Philip B., 35
Ronan, Clifford, 48
Ronsard, Pierre de, 14, 29, 64, 86, 227
Rooley, Anthony, 111
Rore, Cipriano de, 86
Rosetti, Dante Gabriel, 237
Rowse, A. L., 27
Royston, Pamela, 49
Rubio, Gerald, 20
Rudenstine, Neil, 23, 44
Russell, Elizabeth, 13

Sacks, Peter M., 34
Sackville, Thomas, 256
Saker, Austin, 247
Sams, Eric, 21
Sanders, Andrew, 26
Sanderson, James L., 18
Sannazaro, Jacopo, 14, 190
Sarton, Mary, 237

Saslow, James, 177
Saunders, J. R., 156, 263
Saussure, Ferdinand de, 259
Scaliger, Julius Caesar, 14
Schenck, Celeste Marguerite, 34, 233
Schiffer, James, 54, 57
Schleiner, Louise, 18, 42, 62, 63, 118, 134,
    136
Schmidgall, Gary, 51
Schoenbaum, Samuel, 20, 53, 55
Schoenfeldt, Michael, 54, 63
Schuler, Robert M., 39
Schulman, Samuel E., 237
Schwartz, Murray M., 54
Schwartz, Regina, 24
Selden, John, 156
Seldon, Raman, 36
Selleck, Nancy, 249, 252
Seznec, Jean, 29
Shaheen, Naseeb, 19
Shakespeare, William, 3–5, 7–13, 15–18,
    20–24, 26, 29–31, 33, 38–40, 46, 47,
    49–55, 57, 63, 78, 79, 89–91, 93–95, 97,
    109, 110, 112–13, 115, 120, 123, 126, 129,
    130, 150, 159, 164, 173, 176–77, 180, 188,
    197, 199, 215, 223, 233, 236, 239–44,
    256–58, 264–66
Shapiro, James, 48, 65
Shelford, April, 27
Shepherd, Luke, 256–57
Shepherd, Simon, 41
Sherman, William H., 38, 121
Shire, Helena, 41
Shirley, James, 264
Shore, David R., 42, 43
Shuger, Debora, 22, 28, 37, 55, 62, 64, 89,
    92, 249, 253
Shumaker, Wayne, 38
Sidney, Henry, 246, 247
Sidney, Mary, countess of Pembroke, 4, 7,
    11, 18, 21, 24, 62, 72, 115, 123, 133–39,
    251
Sidney, Philip, 4, 9, 11–14, 18–19, 21–24, 26,
    29, 33, 35, 37, 40, 41, 54–56, 61, 64,
    70–72, 75, 76, 78, 80, 84, 88–90, 91–93,
    99, 100, 110, 112, 115, 117–18, 120,
    124–26, 129, 132–39, 143, 147, 154–55,
    157–58, 164, 166–68, 174–75, 179, 190,
    196–201, 208, 215, 227, 245–48, 251,
    256–57, 261–66
Sidney, Robert, 12, 13, 33
Sinfield, Alan, 45, 251
Singman, Jeffrey L., 18, 55
Siraisi, Nancy, 27
Sitwell, Edith, 237
Skelton, John, 8, 10, 13, 16, 157, 249, 258
Sloan, Thomas O., 37
Smith, Anthony D., 39

330 INDEX OF NAMES

Smith, Barbara Herrnstein, 24, 54
Smith, Bruce R., 33, 54, 75, 173, 178
Smith, Charles G., 19
Smith, G. Gregory, 19, 78, 96, 98, 100, 157, 229, 256
Smith, G. H., 79
Smith, Hallett, 4, 9, 11, 15, 23, 27, 32, 34–36, 46, 54, 55
Smith, J. C., 245
Smith, Robin, 18
Smith, William, 10, 11, 12
Snyder, Susan, 32, 42
Sontag, Susan, 96
Soowthern, K., 12
Sousa, Geraldo U. de, 17
Southall, Raymond, 249
Southampton, earl of (Henry Wriothesley), 95, 120
Southwell, Anne, 120
Southwell, Robert, 9, 13, 18, 65
Sowerby, Robin, 28, 55
Spearing, A. C., 27
Speght, Thomas, 265
Spenser, Edmund, 7, 9, 11–13, 15, 18–24, 26, 29, 32, 34–39, 45–48, 54–56, 61, 62, 70, 86, 88–90, 93, 100, 106–08, 112, 115, 117, 120, 129–31, 143, 154, 157–58, 168, 173, 180, 190, 191, 194, 199, 208, 215, 226–38, 245–57, 264–65
Spevack, Marvin, 21
Spiller, Michael R. G., 33
Squarzafico, Hieronimo, 85
Stallybrass, Peter, 23, 45, 54, 55, 56, 167, 198, 239
Stampa, Gaspara, 228
Stanford, Henry, 140
Stanley, Thomas, 264
Stapleton, M. L., 29, 47
Staub, Susan C., 21
Steane, J. B., 47, 48
Steele, Oliver, 5, 6
Stein, Arnold, 34
Stein, Gertrude, 237
Steinberg, Theodore L., 46
Stern, Virginia F., 20
Sternhold, Thomas, 256
Stevens, Wallace, 31
Stewart, Susan, 258
Stillinger, Jack, 45
Stillman, Robert E., 44, 45
Stimpson, Catharine R., 53
Stone, Lawrence, 27
Stow, John, 14
Striar, Brian Jay, 47
Strier, Richard, 24
Stringer, Gary, 139
Strong, Roy, 165, 202
Stubbs, John, 14

Stump, Donald V., 17, 41, 56
Suckling, John, 264
Sullivan, Ernest W., 140
Sullivan, Maxine, 113
Surrey, earl of. *See* Howard, Henry
Suster, Gerald, 38
Suzuki, Mihoko, 30, 44, 56
Sylvester, Richard S., 9, 10, 11, 87, 103

Taffin, Jean, 212
Tempo, Antonio da, 85, 167
Theocritus, 14, 34
Thomas, Keith, 38, 266
Thompson, Charlotte, 43, 229
Tichborne, Chidiock, 10, 13
Tillyard, E. M. W., 28
Tofte, Robert, 10
Tolliver, Harold, 31
Trager, H. L., 79
Traub, Valerie, 178
Travitsky, Betty S., 13
Trill, Suzanne, 19
Tromly, Fred, 47
Tufte, Virginia J., 35, 229, 237
Turbervile, George, 13, 259, 265
Turner, Myron, 49
Tusser, Thomas, 13
Tuve, Rosemond, 37
Tyler, Margaret, 126
Tyndale, William, 211, 257
Tyrwhit, Elizabeth, 134

Ule, Louis, 20
Urry, William, 20

Valois, François Hercule de, 207
van de Passe, Simon, 133
van der Noot, Jan, 86
van Dorsten, Jan, 46
Vance, Eugene, 33
Vaughan, Stephen, 211
Vega, Garcilaso de la, 86
Vellutello, Alessandro, 85
Venafro, Sylvano da, 85
Vendler, Helen, 8, 110, 239
Vergil, 14, 28, 32, 34, 95, 190
Vernon, Elizabeth, 120
Vickers, Brian, 21, 38, 57
Vickers, Nancy J., 24, 53, 95, 103, 174, 181
Vives, Juan Luis, 121
Vivian, Percival, 216

Waddington, Raymond B., 22
Walker, D. P., 38
Wall, Wendy, 96, 156, 159, 198
Wallace, Malcolm William, 20
Waller, Edmund, 264

INDEX OF NAMES 331

Waller, Gary F., 16, 19, 27, 28, 46, 55, 124, 126, 134
Walsh, William P., 49
Walsingham, Catherine, 165
Walsingham, Thomas, 72
Walton, Izaak, 223
Warkentin, Germaine, 33, 45, 46, 228
Warner, J. Christopher, 43
Warnke, Frank J., 203
Watkins, W. B. C., 23, 237
Watson, Elizabeth Porges, 6, 7
Watson, Thomas, 10, 88, 124
Webster, John, 63
Weever, John, 95, 97
Weiner, Andrew D., 45
Wells, Stanley, 18, 21, 53
Wells, William, 19
Welsh, Andrew, 31
Whetstone, George, 247
Whigham, Frank, 37
White, Micheline, 138
White, Paul Whitfield, 50
Whitman, Charles Huntington, 19
Whitney, Geoffrey, 64
Whitney, Isabella, 11, 12, 13, 33, 115, 121, 123
Whitworth, Charles, 21
Wickert, Max A., 229
Wilbur, Richard, 8
Willaert, Adrian, 86
Willen, Gerald, 54
Williams, John, 3, 13, 52

Williams, Raymond, 260
Wilson, John, 109
Wilson, Thomas, 13, 249
Wiltenburg, Robert, 21
Wimsatt, W. K., 76, 77
Wind, Edgar, 29
Wine, M. L., 234
Winters, Yvor, 23, 24, 258
Wolley, John, 13
Wood, Allen G., 36
Woodbridge, Linda, 18
Woods, Susanne, 22, 62, 77, 213
Woodward, Daniel H., 234
Wordsworth, William, 237
Woudhuysen, H. R., 9, 11, 12, 16, 45, 55, 56, 87, 140, 156, 257, 265
Wraight, A. D., 20
Wroth, Mary, 12, 13, 33, 62, 110, 115, 138
Wyatt, Thomas, 8, 9, 10, 12–14, 18, 21, 29, 30, 81–84, 86, 87, 110, 129, 131, 134, 139, 147, 163, 175, 199, 204, 210, 216, 227, 249, 256, 258, 263–64

Yates, Frances A., 38
Yeats, William Butler, 237

Zagorin, Perez, 27
Ziegler, Georgianna, 18
Zim, Rivkah, 46, 136, 137
Zitner, Sheldon, 24
Zunder, William, 19, 47

Modern Language Association of America

Approaches to Teaching World Literature

Joseph Gibaldi, series editor

Achebe's Things Fall Apart. Ed. Bernth Lindfors. 1991.

Arthurian Tradition. Ed. Maureen Fries and Jeanie Watson. 1992.

Atwood's The Handmaid's Tale *and Other Works*. Ed. Sharon R. Wilson, Thomas B. Friedman, and Shannon Hengen. 1996.

Austen's Pride and Prejudice. Ed. Marcia McClintock Folsom. 1993.

Baudelaire's Flowers of Evil. Ed. Laurence M. Porter. 2000.

Beckett's Waiting for Godot. Ed. June Schlueter and Enoch Brater. 1991.

Beowulf. Ed. Jess B. Bessinger, Jr., and Robert F. Yeager. 1984.

Blake's Songs of Innocence and of Experience. Ed. Robert F. Gleckner and Mark L. Greenberg. 1989.

British Women Poets of the Romantic Period. Ed. Stephen C. Behrendt and Harriet Kramer Linkin. 1997.

Brontë's Jane Eyre. Ed. Diane Long Hoeveler and Beth Lau. 1993.

Byron's Poetry. Ed. Frederick W. Shilstone. 1991.

Camus's The Plague. Ed. Steven G. Kellman. 1985.

Cather's My Ántonia. Ed. Susan J. Rosowski. 1989.

Cervantes' Don Quixote. Ed. Richard Bjornson. 1984.

Chaucer's Canterbury Tales. Ed. Joseph Gibaldi. 1980.

Chopin's The Awakening. Ed. Bernard Koloski. 1988.

Coleridge's Poetry and Prose. Ed. Richard E. Matlak. 1991.

Dante's Divine Comedy. Ed. Carole Slade. 1982.

Dickens' David Copperfield. Ed. Richard J. Dunn. 1984.

Dickinson's Poetry. Ed. Robin Riley Fast and Christine Mack Gordon. 1989.

Narrative of the Life of Frederick Douglass. Ed. James C. Hall. 1999.

Eliot's Middlemarch. Ed. Kathleen Blake. 1990.

Eliot's Poetry and Plays. Ed. Jewel Spears Brooker. 1988.

Ellison's Invisible Man. Ed. Susan Resneck Parr and Pancho Savery. 1989.

Faulkner's The Sound and the Fury. Ed. Stephen Hahn and Arthur F. Kinney. 1996.

Flaubert's Madame Bovary. Ed. Laurence M. Porter and Eugene F. Gray. 1995.

García Márquez's One Hundred Years of Solitude. Ed. María Elena de Valdés and Mario J. Valdés. 1990.

Goethe's Faust. Ed. Douglas J. McMillan. 1987.

Hebrew Bible as Literature in Translation. Ed. Barry N. Olshen and Yael S. Feldman. 1989.

Homer's Iliad *and* Odyssey. Ed. Kostas Myrsiades. 1987.

Ibsen's A Doll House. Ed. Yvonne Shafer. 1985.

Works of Samuel Johnson. Ed. David R. Anderson and Gwin J. Kolb. 1993.

Joyce's Ulysses. Ed. Kathleen McCormick and Erwin R. Steinberg. 1993.

Kafka's Short Fiction. Ed. Richard T. Gray. 1995.

Keats's Poetry. Ed. Walter H. Evert and Jack W. Rhodes. 1991.

Kingston's The Woman Warrior. Ed. Shirley Geok-lin Lim. 1991.

Lafayette's The Princess of Clèves. Ed. Faith E. Beasley and Katharine Ann
Jensen. 1998.
Lessing's The Golden Notebook. Ed. Carey Kaplan and Ellen Cronan Rose. 1989.
Mann's Death in Venice *and Other Short Fiction*. Ed. Jeffrey B. Berlin. 1992.
Medieval English Drama. Ed. Richard K. Emmerson. 1990.
Melville's Moby-Dick. Ed. Martin Bickman. 1985.
Metaphysical Poets. Ed. Sidney Gottlieb. 1990.
Miller's Death of a Salesman. Ed. Matthew C. Roudané. 1995.
Milton's Paradise Lost. Ed. Galbraith M. Crump. 1986.
Molière's Tartuffe *and Other Plays*. Ed. James F. Gaines and
Michael S. Koppisch. 1995.
Momaday's The Way to Rainy Mountain. Ed. Kenneth M. Roemer. 1988.
Montaigne's Essays. Ed. Patrick Henry. 1994.
Novels of Toni Morrison. Ed. Nellie Y. McKay and Kathryn Earle. 1997.
Murasaki Shikibu's The Tale of Genji. Ed. Edward Kamens. 1993.
Pope's Poetry. Ed. Wallace Jackson and R. Paul Yoder. 1993.
Shakespeare's King Lear. Ed. Robert H. Ray. 1986.
Shakespeare's The Tempest *and Other Late Romances*. Ed. Maurice Hunt. 1992.
Shelley's Frankenstein. Ed. Stephen C. Behrendt. 1990.
Shelley's Poetry. Ed. Spencer Hall. 1990.
Shorter Elizabethan Poetry. Ed. Patrick Cheney and Anne Lake Prescott. 2000.
Sir Gawain and the Green Knight. Ed. Miriam Youngerman Miller and
Jane Chance. 1986.
Spenser's Faerie Queene. Ed. David Lee Miller and Alexander Dunlop. 1994.
Stendhal's The Red and the Black. Ed. Dean de la Motte and Stirling Haig. 1999.
Sterne's Tristram Shandy. Ed. Melvyn New. 1989.
Stowe's Uncle Tom's Cabin. Ed. Elizabeth Ammons and Susan Belasco. 2000.
Swift's Gulliver's Travels. Ed. Edward J. Rielly. 1988.
Thoreau's Walden *and Other Works*. Ed. Richard J. Schneider. 1996.
Voltaire's Candide. Ed. Renée Waldinger. 1987.
Whitman's Leaves of Grass. Ed. Donald D. Kummings. 1990.
Wordsworth's Poetry. Ed. Spencer Hall, with Jonathan Ramsey. 1986.
Wright's Native Son. Ed. James A. Miller. 1997.